Mary Francis Cusack

The nun of Kenmare

An autobiography

Mary Francis Cusack

The nun of Kenmare
An autobiography

ISBN/EAN: 9783742835710

Manufactured in Europe, USA, Canada, Australia, Japa

Cover: Foto ©Lupo / pixelio.de

Manufactured and distributed by brebook publishing software (www.brebook.com)

Mary Francis Cusack

The nun of Kenmare

Sister M. Francis Clare Cusack
late Mother General of the
Sisters of Peace

THE NUN OF KENMARE

AN AUTOBIOGRAPHY

London:
HODDER AND STOUGHTON,
27, PATERNOSTER ROW.

MDCCCLXXXIX.

[All rights reserved.]

TO HIS HOLINESS POPE LEO XIII.

HOLY FATHER: — It is with great grief and regret that I address this letter to your Holiness. I am obliged to resign into your hands the Office to which you were pleased to appoint me, and to leave to others the work of the Order of Peace which your Holiness has authorized me to establish.

I have not taken this step without long and careful consideration, for I see every day more and more the necessity of such work as this for Working Girls. They have been indeed the great support of the Roman Catholic Church, and they deserve all that can be done for their comfort and encouragement.

But I have found such opposition to this work, which I so dearly love, from certain bishops whose influence is so powerful that other bishops do not like to support what they disapprove, even though it has the sanction of your Holiness, that I am obliged to retire from it. My health, always delicate, has completely given way under the pressure and pain of this discouragement. I have in vain pointed out to these ecclesiastics that the fact of your Holiness having permitted me to establish a New Order should have satisfied them that I was, as the document sent from Propaganda to the Right Rev. Bishop Bagshawe said, "worthy of confidence and trust." This document says, "I may assure your lordship that due notice, acknowledgment, and consideration has been taken of whatever has been written or sent to Propaganda, and nothing was found to prevent the Cardinal Prefect from recommending her (Sister M. Francis Clare) to the Holy Father, not only to dispense her from belonging to the Poor Clares, but to give her that dispensation to establish and direct a new congregation under your lordship. That very fact is an evident testimony of the judgment passed in Propaganda that she is worthy of your lordship's confidence and trust, and that of any one who may put herself under her guidance."

Notwithstanding the above, reports are circulated both by ecclesiastics and in the public press under the control of ecclesiastics, making false charges against me ever since I came to this country, which are most defamatory to me as a religious; and what is far more disedifying, these charges against me reflect on the wisdom and prudence of your Holiness in appointing me to such an Office, and on the judgment of the Sacred College of Propaganda, as they are circulating, both in public and in private, the very charges against me which Propaganda has declared, after a careful judicial inquiry, to be false.

I am now publishing in a volume an account of my life. The facts and documents which I shall print will show how groundless are the charges which have been made against me by these influential ecclesiastics, and will show that I was not unworthy of the honorable position to which your Holiness appointed me. If in this publication certain bishops shall be seen to have thrown obstacles in the way of the work which your Holiness committed to me, by speaking of me as if I were an unworthy sister, your Holiness will be pleased to remember that before publishing these documents I gave them many opportunities of clearing me, publicly or privately, of their false charges, and even in such a manner that it might not appear that they were the authors of them. It will be seen, indeed, that I have treated them with every consideration and patience.

I have now, Holy Father, to express to you my highest respect and my deepest gratitude. The memory of your kindness will remain with me to my dying hour.

With regard to the sisters who have been associated with me in this work, I am certain that no ecclesiastic can say anything but good of them. Holy Father, take these good sisters, whom I have so long loved and cherished and trained for this work, to your heart. Be assured that I will altogether keep from them, and shall not give a pretext to any ecclesiastic for any opposition to them on my account. They certainly cannot be held responsible for my supposed faults, and I will be as one who does not exist, as far as they are concerned. God alone knows what this sacrifice will cost me, but I make it willingly, as I see that it is the only way to secure permanence and prosperity to this work.

As during the thirty years which I have served the church as a sister I have always acted in strict obedience to canonical rule and observance, I have sent in my resignation to the Right Rev. Bishop Bagshawe and the Right Rev. Bishop Wigger. The former, in his reply to me, expresses his deep regret that my state of health obliges him to accept my resignation, and his sense of the great value of the work done by the Sisters of Peace in his diocese.

I beg to subscribe myself, with the highest respect, your Holiness's most grateful,

SISTER M. FRANCIS CLARE CUSACK.
Late Mother General of the Sisters of Peace.

FROM THE
APOLOGIA PRO VITA SUA.

By Cardinal Newman.

"For twenty years or more I have borne an imputation, of which I am at least as sensitive, who am the object of it, as they can be who are only the judges. I have not set myself to remove it, first, because I never have had an opening to speak, and, next, because I never saw in them the disposition to hear. I have wished to appeal from Philip drunk to Philip sober. When shall I pronounce him to be himself again?

"Whatever judgment my readers may eventually form of me from these pages, I am confident that they will believe me in what I shall say in the course of them. I have no misgiving at all that they will be ungenerous or harsh towards a man who has been so long before the eyes of the world; who has so many to speak of him from personal knowledge; whose natural impulse it has ever been to speak out; who has ever spoken too much rather than too little; who would have saved himself many a scrape if he had been wise enough to hold his tongue; who has ever been fair to the doctrines and arguments of his opponents; who has never slurred over facts and reasonings which told against himself; who has never given his name or authority to proofs which he thought unsound, or to testimony which he did not think at least plausible; who has never shrunk from confessing a fault when he felt that he had committed one; who has ever consulted for others more than for himself; who has given up much that he loved and prized, and could have retained, but that he loved honesty better than name, and truth better than dear friends.

"Moreover, I mean to be simply personal and historical: I am not expounding Catholic doctrine; I am doing no more than explaining myself and my opinions and actions. I wish, as far as I am able, simply to state facts, whether they are ultimately determined to be for me or against me. Of course there will be room enough for contrariety of judgment among my readers, as to the necessity, or appositeness, or value, or good taste, or religious prudence, of the details which I shall introduce. I may be accused of laying stress on little things, of being beside the mark, of going into impertinent or ridiculous details, of sounding my own praise, of giving scandal; but this is a case above all others in which I am bound to follow my own lights and to speak out my own heart. It is not at all pleasant for me to be egotistical; nor to be criticised for being so. It is not pleasant to reveal to high and low, young and old, what has gone on within me from my early years. It is not pleasant to be giving to every shallow or flippant disputant the advantage over me of knowing my most private thoughts, I might even say the intercourse between myself and my Maker. But I do not like to be called to my face a liar and a knave; nor should I be doing my duty to my faith or to my name if I were to suffer it. I know I have done nothing to deserve such an insult, and if I prove this, as I hope to do, I must not care for such incidental annoyances as are involved in the process."

CONTENTS.

CHAPTER I.
WHY THIS BOOK WAS WRITTEN.

The Immediate Cause of my Giving up the Work which the Holy Father Authorized me to do — Constant and Irritating Interference on the Part of Archbishop Corrigan — I am Required to Apologize for what I did not do, and when my Apology is Offered, it is not Accepted 1

CHAPTER II.
MY RECEPTION INTO THE ROMAN CATHOLIC CHURCH.

First Leanings towards Catholicism — Acquaintance with Dr. Pusey — Entering the Anglican Sisterhood — Miss Langston — The Crimean War — Confirmation by Cardinal Wiseman — He Requests me to Devote my Life to Literature — Rev. Father Whitty, Miss Whitty, and the Sisters of Mercy — The Sisters' Call — Opposition of the Archbishop 11

CHAPTER III.
LIFE AT NEWRY.

Desire to Work for the Poor — Cardinal Newman's *Apologia* — The Bishop and Cardinal Antonelli — The French Governess — Journey to Newry — Miss O'Hagan — Her Character and History — Entrance to the Convent — Life at Newry — Taking the Habit — My Health — History of the Poor Clares — Trials of Religious Houses — Estrangement from Relatives — Literary Work — Trouble over my Publications — A Jealous Priest and a Dedication — My Book "Pirated" by a New York Priest — Building Operations and Money Troubles — The Bishop Interferes. — A Momentous Visit is Paid us 25

CHAPTER IV.
GOING TO KENMARE.

Archdeacon O'Sullivan Desires a Foundation at Kenmare — His Noble Character — The Kenmare Sisters — Miss O'Hagan Undertakes the Foundation — Dr. Moriarty, the New Bishop — Lord and Lady Kenmare — The Bishop's Mistake — Status of Priests in Ireland — Exposed to Social and Political Seductions — Bishop Moriarty Won Over — Life at Kenmare — Choir and Lay Sisters — Unfortunate Selection of New Sisters — My Literary Work Continues 49

CHAPTER V.
MY LITERARY WORK AT KENMARE.

Success of my Books — Blamed for Writing Them — Illiberal Criticisms — Causes of Trouble in the Church — Unjust Interference of the Archbishop of Dublin — Letter from Bishop Moriarty — His Approval of my Literary Work 64

CHAPTER VI.
THE FAMINE YEAR IN IRELAND.

Chronic Distress in Ireland — Favor of the Holy See for England — Attacked for my Historical Writings — State of the Irish people — Relations between Irish and English Catholics — the Catholics the Oppressors of Ireland — Dr. McCarthy, His Character — Lord Lansdowne's Attitude — Attacked by Rev. Mr. Angus — Appeal to Cardinal Manning — Letter from Archdeacon O'Sullivan — Two Archdeacons O'Sullivan — A Curious Episode — Mr. Angus continues his Attacks — He is Silenced by Legal Proceedings — The *Morning Post* Apologizes — My Labors in the Famine Year — Distress of the Poor — Indian Meal for a Family of Five — Letter from W. J. Sullivan to the *Freeman's Journal* 70

CHAPTER VII.
THE NUN OF KENMARE'S DISTRESS FUND.

The Nun of Kenmare's Distress Fund — Object of the Fund — Methods of Relief — Letters from Mr. O'Connell, Rev. C. O'Sullivan, from

Protestant Clergymen, and Others — Appeals and Thanks from Convents — A Threatening Letter — Appeal to Chief Secretary Foster — His Reply — Indignation Meeting at Kenmare — Remarks of Ven. Archdeacon O'Sullivan, Rev. J. Molineux, Mr. Fitzgerald, Mr. Harrington, and Others 91

CHAPTER VIII.
MONEY MATTERS.

Money Left at Kenmare — I Send for it from Knock — It is Refused — Bishop Higgins Interferes — Illegal Claims of the Kenmare Sisters — Bishop Higgins Afraid of the Secular Courts — His Opinion of "Heretical Laws" — An Unfair Decision — Letters and Comments on the Case 128

CHAPTER IX.
BISHOP HIGGINS'S TREATMENT OF SISTERS AND PRIESTS.

Changes at Kenmare — Death of Father John — Of Miss O'Hagan — Interference of Father Higgins — Ill-treatment by the Sisters — Bishop Higgins's Arbitrary Management — I am Boycotted by Him — Loss of Money — Other Sisters Oppressed by Bishop Higgins — The Saurin Case — A New York Case — A Sane Sister Sent to Blackwell's Island — Her Rescue 138

CHAPTER X.
LEAVING KENMARE.

I Leave Kenmare — Rev. M. Neligan Accompanies me on my Way to Knock — Accused of Going Without Leave — The Presentation Sisters at Killarney — Presentation Convent, Portarlington — Claremorris — Rev. Canon Bourke — My Journey Continued — Wretched Conveyances — I am Seriously Ill 177

CHAPTER XI.
VISIT TO KNOCK.

Arrival at Knock — Welcomed by Archdeacon Cavanagh — Prayer on the Scene of the Apparition — A Miraculous Restoration — Requested to Found a Convent at Knock — Letters from Dr. McEvilly, Archbishop of Tuam, and Father Cavanagh — Care in Getting Permissions — Visit to Tuam — Reception by the Archbishop — He Writes a letter of Approval — Comments on the Archbishop's Letter — Letter to Bishop Higgins — His Reply — Change of Ground by the Archbishop — His Inexplicable Anger — Injustice of Catholic Methods of Discipline — Opinion of the Late Bishop of Cavan — The Harold's Cross Convent — Its History and Peculiarities — Cordial Reception at Newry — Bishop Leahy's Letter — Return to Dublin — Astonishing Reception at Harold's Cross — Forbidden Shelter by Cardinal McCabe — Turned into the Winter Streets by his Order — Popular Hatred of Cardinal McCabe — Why was I so Treated — A Dark Mystery — Remarkable Letter from Bishop Higgins 185

CHAPTER XII.
WAITING FOR PERMISSION TO RETURN TO TUAM.

Abandoned by my Friends — Miss O'Hagan's Relatives Desert me — A Gleam of Sunshine — I Seek Refuge — A Grateful Cabman — A Serious Difficulty — I Write to the Archbishop of Tuam — A Forged Despatch — Duplicity of the Kenmare Sisters — Bishop Higgins's Vacillations — Contrasted Extracts from his Letters 217

CHAPTER XIII.
DEPRIVED OF THE SACRAMENTS WITHOUT CAUSE.

Permitted to Return to Knock — Unjust Treatment by Archbishop McEvilly — Ingratitude of a Sister — Commissioned to Hunt me Down — A Hard Winter — A Sad Christmas — Forbidden the Sacraments — Archdeacon Cavanagh Dares not Confess me — I Appeal to Bishop Leahy — His Response — Archbishop McEvilly Consents "For Once," and Sends me to Claremorris — A Little Consolation . . 226

CHAPTER XIV.
CLAREMORRIS.

I Move to Claremorris — Plans for the Endowment at Knock — Girls to be Taught Household Industries — State of Ireland — Absence of Industrial Employment — Theoretical Training Useless — Methods of the Training Houses — Houses to be Self-Supporting — Cordial

Letter from John Kelly — Industries Practised — The Kindergarten — Archbishop McEvilly's Requirements — Father Cavanagh Afraid of the Archbishop — Different Orders of the Church — Idea of a New Order 237

CHAPTER XV.

CLAREMORRIS CONTINUED.

Correspondence and Labors — Letter from Rev. Dr. Croke, Archbishop of Cashel — Fresh Attacks from Mr. Angus and an Anonymous "Bishop" — Bishop Higgins Compelled to tell the Truth — Father Cavanagh Begins to Change — Advised by Archbishop Croke to Publish my Letters and Documents — The Anonymous Bishop Continues — I Write to the *Weekly Register* — Letters from Archbishop Cavanagh and Bishop McCormack 256

CHAPTER XVI.

KNOCK.

I Go to Knock — Sister M. — Her Peculiarities — Living in a Stable — Neither Food nor Bedding — A Serious Illness — A Nurse who wanted Rich Patients — I Receive Permission to Build — The Ground Selected — Leased from Lord Dillon — Mr. Hague Chosen as the Architect — We Rent a House — Trouble with our Landlord — Improper Behavior by his Family — The Work Interfered with — Workmen Enticed to Drink — I Send for my Solicitor — Father J. — A Quarrelsome Curate — His Abusive Conduct — Interference of Sister M. — Her Complaints — I Ask for a Visitation — Refused by the Archbishop 268

CHAPTER XVII.

MORE DIFFICULTIES AT KNOCK.

Archbishop McEvilly's Contradictions — Canon Bourke — I Stop the Works — Father Cavanagh Claims my Funds — Visit from Rev. Dr. Lynch, Archbishop of Toronto — His Approval — His Letter to his Coadjutor Bishop — Appeals to Continue the Work — Obstinacy of Archdeacon Cavanagh — A Pretended Miracle — The Deaf and Dumb Impostor — Letter from Canon Bourke — Dr. McEvilly's Excuse — Sister M—— makes Trouble . . 285

CHAPTER XVIII.
KNOCK CONTINUED.

A Pilgrim's House Needed — Miserable Condition of the Place — A Retreat from Rev. Father Gaffney, S. J. — His Distress — I Ask Leave to go to Rome — Am Refused — I go to Dublin — Father Gaffney Brings a Document from the Archbishop — An Extraordinary Demand — To be Signed Unread — My Refusal — My Health Failing — I Ask Leave to go to England to see Cardinal Manning — Leave Granted 298

CHAPTER XIX.
I GO TO ENGLAND.

I Reach London — Visit to Cardinal Manning — His Cordial Reception — Call on Rt. Rev. Dr. Bagshawe — Transferred by the Archbishop of Tuam — Father Cavanagh's Dislike to my Work — Nature of my schools — An Incapable Teacher — Knock Schools — A Letter — Petition to the Archbishop — Letters from Michael M. Waldron, Canon Bourke, James Rogers, and others 313

CHAPTER XX.
GOING TO ROME.

The New Order Approved by Cardinal Manning and Bishop Bagshawe — Character of the Order — Sent on a New Mission — An Undesirable Priest — Preparations for Rome — I Stay at Lourdes — Another "Knock" — A Broken-Hearted Priest — The Shrine of the Sacred Heart — Paray-le-Monial — Kind Reception in Rome — A Visit from Cardinal Howard — In Charge of Mgr. Gualdi — Absurd Espionage — Favors in Rome — I see Mgr. Macchi — Public and Private Audience with the Holy Father — His Holiness Recognizes the Life of O'Connell — He Approves my Plan and my Writing — Letter from Father Gaffney, S. J. 354

CHAPTER XXI.
GOING TO AMERICA.

America Proposed — Bishop Bagshawe — His Character — Intrigues of English Catholics — Wealth of the American Catholic Church — Arch-

Bishop Corrigan Calls for $400.000 — My Plans Approved — The Journey Ordered — Canon Monaghan Accompanies Me — Cardinal Manning's Friendship — Parting from my Sisters — Mother Mary Evangelista 377

CHAPTER XXII.

ARRIVAL IN NEW YORK.

Refused an Interview by Cardinal McClosky and Bishop Corrigan — Inexcusable Discourtesy — Comment of Mgr. Capel — Word of Avoidance Passed Around — Opposed by Mgr. Quinn — Letter to Cardinal McClosky — Circular in Aid of Immigrants — Miss Charlotte O'Brien — The Bishop of Cloyne — His Interest — Forbidden to Work at Castle Garden — Father Riordan's Mission there 388

CHAPTER XXIII.

GOOD WORKS THAT HAVE NOT BEEN ACCOMPLISHED.

Mission of the Church — Sisterhoods Often Opposed — Catholic Persecution of her own Saints — Oppressed when Living — Canonized when Dead — La Salle an Example — The Church Afraid to let the Truth be Known — The Poor Neglected — Priests Suppressed — Established in Jersey City — Rude Treatment in Philadelphia — Project for Blind Asylum Abandoned 404

CHAPTER XXIV.

WHO IS ACCOUNTABLE?

A Sorrowful Record — Dependence of the Roman Catholic Church upon the Liquor Interest — Received Kindly by Cardinal Gibbons at First — Father Didier's Home for Girls — Invited to take the Management of it — Plan Defeated by the Interference of Some Priest — Offered a Summer Home Near Baltimore — The Priest Very Anxious that I should Accept It. — Cardinal Gibbons Forbids it Under the Influence of Other Ecclesiastics — Invited to Visit Mother

D——'s Convent for my Health — Archbishop Corrigan Sends a Lady to Her to Express His Strong Feeling Against Me, and to Desire Me to Leave — Asked to Found a Home in Cleveland O. — Forbidden by the Archbishop — Asked to make Foundations in Tacoma W. T. — Suddenly Forbidden, after all Arrangements had been Made — Offered a Home for Girls in St. Pauls, Minn. — Urgent Need for this Work there, but Father Shanly Forbids it, and makes a Gross Attack on Me in the Public Press — Without any Expression of Disapprobation from his Bishop 426

CHAPTER XXV.

MY ONLY INTERVIEW WITH ARCHBISHOP CORRIGAN.

Discourtesy of Archbishop Corrigan — He Wishes to see Me — His Charges Against Me — A Not Forthcoming Letter — Priestly Differences — A Poor Compliment to the Holy Father 463

CHAPTER XXVI.

CONCLUDING SCENES.

The End of All — Other Sisters Deprived — Case of Miss K. — The Girls' Home in Baltimore — Visit to the South — Incivility of a Southern Bishop — Application to Archbishop Keane — Contrasted Letter from Archbishop Bagshawe and Archbishop Keane 472

CHAPTER XXVII.

THE END.

A Weary Task — No Justice to be Had — Church Regulations — An Easily Offended Priest — A New Libel Manufactured — An Adventuress and a Thief — Father C——n as Protector — Other Misrepresentations 483

APPENDIX.

LETTERS AND DOCUMENTS.

PART I.
Papal approbations and briefs 497

PART II.
Letters of Archbishop Croke and others endorsing Sister Mary Francis Clare's conduct, and advising publication of the letters showing that she had the usual canonical authorizations for her removal from Kenmare 501

PART III.
Bishop Wigger's letters of approval 506

PART IV.
Copies of letters addressed by Sister M. Francis Clare to Archbishop Corrigan, asking him to investigate the charges which some of his priests were constantly making against her . . . 507

PART V.
General letters. Copy of letter addressed by the sisters to Bishop Keane, now the Rector of the new Roman Catholic University at Washington. Specimens of attacks made on Sister M. Francis Clare by priests 514

PART VI.
The troubled life of the foundress of the Sisters of Notre Dame . . 531

PART VII.
Extracts from letters from the sisters to Sister M. Francis Clare . 536

PART VIII.
List of Works 548

"Publish a short account of your departure from Kenmare, showing you had full leave." — *Letter from Most Rev. Dr. Croke, Archbishop of Cashel.*

"The American people are anxious to know why you left Knock. Tell the truth — that would bring about the necessity of giving you and your spiritual children that convent back, which Americans and others have founded." — *Letter from Very Rev. Canon Ulick Burke, P. P., Claremorris, Ireland.*

"Publish a sober statement of your case. Keep quiet until you can say all." — *Letter from Very Rev. Father Porter, S. J., of London, England; now Right Rev. Archbishop Porter.*

THE NUN OF KENMARE.

CHAPTER I.

WHY THIS BOOK WAS WRITTEN.

The Immediate Cause of my Giving up the Work which the Holy Father Authorized me to do — Constant and Irritating Interference on the Part of Archbishop Corrigan — I am Required to Apologize for what I did not do, and when my Apology is Offered, it is not Accepted.

THE writing of this book has been a subject of long and serious consideration. I am not ignorant of the very grave issues which it involves; they are serious to myself, and they are serious to men of very high position, whose actions are herein detailed.

Though the recent circumstances which have led me to a final decision belong properly to a later part of the present narrative, I think it will simplify matters if I state them here briefly.

I have written this work, because I know that I owe an explanation to the many thousands who have contributed, not out of their wealth, but out of their poverty, to the good work which I tried to establish in Kenmare, in Knock, and in America.

Further, when I was advised by my ecclesiastical superior, Bishop Bagshawe, to go to Rome, I was obliged to make a public appeal for the pecuniary help which was necessary to enable me to make the journey; because when I left Knock with the sisters who accompanied me to England, I had no money, except a few thousand dollars which were invested for the support of the sisters, and which could not be used for any other purpose; though even this was claimed by Archdeacon Cavanagh for himself, as his letters given later will show. All the money which I had collected for the Knock Convent and Industrial Training School was expended, and I have the receipts of the builders and architect to show how it was spent.

I received a most generous response to my appeal for my expenses to Rome, and for those of the sister who accompanied me. These expenses were necessarily considerable, as I had to remain in Rome for four months while my case was under consideration.

I shall never forget the affection shown to me by many of the contributors, who begged me to write to them for more, if I needed it, and not to spare expense when it would save me fatigue, or procure any alleviation of the sufferings which such a journey must cause to one in my weak state of health.

I feel it is right that those who contributed to the Knock Industrial School and to my expenses to Rome, should know why, and how, their benevolent desires have been defeated, and their sacrifices rendered of no avail. My letter to the Holy Father at the beginning of this book explains why I have kept silence so long, and why I took blame to myself to screen others. Those who so unselfishly gave of their little all, when they found I did not return to Ireland after my visit to Rome, and that Knock was still allowed to remain a ruin, were greatly surprised, and not without reason.

I shall only say here that Archdeacon Cavanagh would not allow me to return, and preferred to let the convent remain a ruin and to see the work for his people abandoned. On this point the evidence of Bishop Bagshawe will be found in this volume, and also that of many others who have expostulated in vain with the archdeacon on this subject.

Yet, although Archdeacon Cavanagh would not allow the work to be continued even after it had been approved by the Pope, he, or others for him, made it appear that I was the person in fault. I have only too good reason to know how widely this false report was circulated. It certainly produced the effect which was intended. Still I hoped that patience and silence would win the day, and that those who were accusing me falsely would tire of their unworthy task, or, perhaps, be touched by my silence; and that they would not always allow me to remain under the burden of false accusations. It seemed to me that respect for the Holy Father would have obliged the bishops to contradict reports which they well knew were false; but this book will show how vain my hopes were.

Four years have now elapsed since I came to America, by the desire of my bishop, and with a heart full of hope for the extension of my work for Irish emigrant and working girls. Before I left Queenstown, I was told by a priest that my mission in America would be a failure, and the reason; and yet even then, with all the experience which I had had, I could not believe there could be so much selfishness amongst those who made such high professions of religion. The two discouraging circumstances which were told me, I hoped would prove only a temporary hindrance. America is a large place, and here, at least, there should be room enough for all.

I found that a succession of priests had been for some time going to America from Queenstown to collect for the unfinished spires of the Roman Catholic Cathedral, at Queenstown, which were to cost a fabulous sum; and whatever other virtues Roman Catholic prelates may have, counting the cost of buildings which their successors must finish is not one of them. The priests thus sent out would naturally look with an unfavorable eye on any one going on a mission of charity; they would especially dislike mine, because they knew the people would be favorable to it, as I was well known to have worked so long for Ireland.

Then there was another obstacle; a priest had opened an immigrant's home in New York, and I was told he was especially opposed to me, supposing that my plans might interfere with his, though nothing was further from my thoughts. He knew that people would naturally say, as indeed they did, why should not Father Riordan and the Nun of Kenmare work together? and when it was found that Father Riordan or his ecclesiastical superiors, or both, would not allow this, I, for one, am not surprised that the reports which were carefully, actively, and widely spread to my disadvantage were accepted as the reason for a course which seemed so inexplicable. It was obvious to any unprejudiced mind that a work for immigrants was a woman's work.

I found later there was yet another object in view. The priests who came from Queenstown to collect, made a somewhat sentimental appeal, saying that it would help to preserve the faith of emigrants to see these marvellous spires as their last sight of Irish land. Father Riordan, not to be behindhand, said that he would build a church in connection with his immigrant home, so that the immigrants should be greeted on their arrival by the sight of a church. For myself it was very well known that my ideas were of a practical character, and while quite respecting and appreciating the idea of a church, I thought good practical training in housework, for which Irish girls have so little opportunity in their own country, would also contribute to their religious good in its own way. I knew from many years' correspondence with girls who had emigrated to America, how much a good practical training in housework would have benefited them. But as I shall explain the method and object of my work fully elsewhere, I will say no more here on this point.

It is evident that as the work which I proposed to do could not be found fault with, the only resource left for those who were determined to prevent its success was to discredit *me*. How this object was accomplished, the present work will show.

It only now remains for me to show briefly here the immediate cause of my writing this letter to the Holy Father, and why I decided to retire finally from all attempts to continue the work which he was pleased to approve.

The reader will find later an account of the very serious illness from which I suffered in the fall of 1887, and the cause of it. The sisters became so anxious about my health that they asked and obtained leave from Bishop Wigger for me to spend the winter in the South, as the doctors said it was absolutely necessary I should do so. This leave was kindly granted, and I agreed to the wishes of the sisters all the more readily because I hoped that my absence might bring kinder feelings towards me on the part of those who were causing me so much suffering. On the 5th of November, just before I set out on my painful journey, I received a letter from Bishop Wigger with the usual complaints against me from Archbishop Corrigan. That these complaints were always found to be groundless did not seem to matter to those who made them. To me they were a constant source of worry and distress, and most injurious in my state of health. "The archbishop again complains," wrote Bishop Wigger, but as the history of this complaint, and of the only interview which Archbishop Corrigan allowed me to have with him, is given in full in the latter part of this book, I will only say here that the accusation was as groundless as usual, and, I might say, as absurd.

While I was in the South, and seriously ill after

a severe attack of rheumatic fever, another charge was brought against me. In the fall of 1887 I wrote a book called *Anti-Poverty and Progress*, which was published by Belford, Clarke, & Co. In February following I received a letter from Bishop Wigger, in which there was another accusation. He said, "You make in your book an unwarranted, unjust, and scandalous attack on Archbishop Corrigan, his vicar-general, Mgr. Preston, and on the members of the diocesan council. I hereby require you to make a public apology to these gentlemen." I replied that nothing was further from my thoughts than to do what I was accused of, and begged to know what I had said wrong; but this I was not to be told. The practice of the Inquisition still holds in the Roman church, as I have found again and again, and as this book will show. You are condemned unheard. In this case, as in so many others where I was concerned, history repeats itself; I thought well and carefully over the matter; I knew if I refused to apologize, all sorts of tales would be circulated. It would be said I had "quarrelled with my bishop"; the true facts of the case would be carefully concealed; moreover, Bishop Wigger had been very kind to me. Still, it was hard to apologize for something I had not done, and of which I was not even to be told the particulars. However, I thought I would have peace at any price. I did not reflect that I had to do with those who were determined upon war.

I therefore wrote and sent the following apology to Bishop Wigger : —

"March 19, 1888.

"MY DEAR LORD, — I am very much distressed to learn from your lordship's letter that you consider I 'have made an unwarranted, unjust, and scandalous attack on Archbishop Corrigan and his council, in a pamphlet published by Belford, Clarke, & Co.,' and in compliance with your lordship's desire I hereby apologize.

"Your obedient child in Christ,
"SISTER M. FRANCIS CLARE."

I hoped this would be the end of all my troubles, and I returned home as soon as possible. In my weak state of health, I was obliged to travel very slowly. As I did not receive a reply from the bishop I supposed he was satisfied, and that there would be peace until Archbishop Corrigan made some new complaint; but I also determined if more causeless trouble came that I would give up my office, for it was becoming quite plain to me that a longer struggle must have the same result in the end, my health was quite broken down by this incessant persecution, and I was threatened with serious heart trouble.

On my return from the South, I sent a sister to Bishop Wigger to ask for the usual leave for the profession of a novice. To her great surprise, he would scarcely speak to her, and seemed very angry, and positively refused the permission. She thought it more prudent to withdraw. After a week I sent her again, but she met again the same reception ; as far as she could ascertain, he was not satisfied with my apology ; she begged him to say what he did want, but he would not. As I knew that I had kept back matters which would have been very damaging to Archbishop Corrigan if they had been published, and Bishop Wigger knew this also, and as I felt that the silence which I had kept under every species of provocation only exposed me to worse treatment, I at last decided to withdraw from a work which it was quite evident I should not be allowed to accomplish under any circumstances.

CHAPTER II.

MY RECEPTION INTO THE ROMAN CATHOLIC CHURCH.

First Leanings towards Catholicism — Acquaintance with Dr. Pusey — Entering the Anglican Sisterhood — Miss Langston — The Crimean War — Confirmation by Cardinal Wiseman — He Requests me to Devote my Life to Literature — Rev. Father Whitty, Miss Whitty, and the Sisters of Mercy — The Sisters' Call — Opposition of the Archbishop.

I WAS received into the Roman Catholic church on the 2d of July, 1858.

The change of opinion which led me from the Anglican into the Roman Catholic church occurred at a period when I was suffering from a long illness. At the time of my reception into the Roman Catholic church I read a great many religious books. As I could not bear to see visitors, this was my only pleasure, and Keble's "Christian Year," together with Manning's and Newman's sermons, became my constant companion. Gradually, through this reading, I began to grasp the idea of a visible church, and to long for certainty of belief.

At this time I became acquainted with a Lord and Lady F——, whose friendship had a great effect on my life. Dr. Pusey was a personal friend of the family, and he visited their house on the different occasions when he came to that part of England to meet his penitents. At that time the practice of confession had begun in the Anglican church, but, as it was sternly repressed by the authorities, the practice was carried on as far as possible in secret. Indeed, both priest and penitent had every reason for silence. I shall not go further into this subject than to say that I became acquainted with Dr. Pusey. His writings had long been familiar to me, and I found in him all that I had longed for, and even more.

I have rarely met with a man so intensely sympathetic and capable of entering into the feelings of others, and the little apparently unimportant circumstances which add so much pain to heavier sorrows.

By his advice I decided to enter a sisterhood which had then been opened in London, and which was under the guidance of an excellent and very superior woman. This lady, Miss Langston, was a person of considerable mental culture, but entirely unfitted for the life of a sister in other ways. From the first I loved her, and I always found her a sympathetic friend; but the other sisters did not get on with her, and the constant friction which was daily inevitable made the sisters' lives anything but happy and comfortable.

If in the Roman Catholic Church, with the experience of centuries, such institutions are very far from being a paradise of charity, how could they succeed better when they were a new experiment!

I believe the trouble in some Anglican sisterhoods at that time arose from one cause, a cause which has done grievous harm to all similar institutions; it is the rock on which not only Anglican sisters, but many in the Roman Catholic church, have made shipwreck.

In the present work I wish to confine myself to my own history. If I were to enter into a religious controversy, I could not do justice to the reader or myself; I only, therefore, touch on subjects just so far as they touch on my life. The name of St. Francis de Sales is as well known as that of Fénelon and St. Thomas à Kempis to the general reader. This good theologian and shrewd man of the world expressed himself in very plain language in a work which he wrote for the use of the sisterhood which he founded. He warned young ladies who desired to enter convents that the life was not all sunshine or all piety, and that if they merely entered a convent because they wished to escape from the troubles of home, they might find worse troubles even there.

Now, if such troubles arose and such difficulties

existed in sisterhoods founded by a saint and presided over by a saint, are we more likely to escape them to-day?

Leaving aside altogether the question of the value of the sisterhoods of the church, whether Roman or Anglican, it is safe to say that the same troubles arise now as occurred in the time of St. Francis de Sales.

The question of injustice in the government of such institutions by local superiors or bishops is quite another matter. In many cases Roman Catholic priests and superiors put obedience to themselves in the place of obedience to God, and, though they do not and dare not teach a theory of personal infallibility, they act as if it were an article of faith, and make it a sin if obedience is not rendered to commands which are often wrong, because they are contrary to the true spirit of Christian charity. We have lately had an instance of this in the case of a Roman Catholic priest who, without any pretence to a fair trial, was driven out of his home with but a few hours' notice, under circumstances of heartlessness and injustice which startled every thinking man. We know of a great many cases in which sisters have been treated with equal injustice and without any assigned cause.

Such proceedings dare not be attempted by

secular courts, and why should ecclesiastics be supported in practising what seculars dare not attempt?

And then follow the deepest evils of all. If any priest or layman ventures to express an opinion he as at once denounced as disloyal to his church, as if the action of a bishop or priest should be protected from criticism more than the action of a layman.

The outcome of this is too often not merely a miserable demand for silence on the part of those who look on these evils with a sorrow which they dare not express; but often an expression of approbation of what they condemn is required. An expression of confidence in the conduct of the ecclesiastical judge must be got at any cost. And the priest knows what he must suffer if he dares to refuse his signature to a declaration which he abhors, and the consequences of refusal are such that few men dare to risk it.

I must pass briefly over this period of my life, or my autobiography would be far too long for the patience of my reader. The Crimean war broke out, with all its attendant miseries, while I was in the London sisterhood. The Anglican sisters were as prompt to obey the call as the Roman Catholic sisters, and there was a holy emulation as to which should do the most for God and for the suffering. Miss Langston and several of our sisters offered themselves for the work. For myself, how my heart longed for it no words could say, but my health was such that I would not have been accepted. To have gone to the Crimea, and to have died in the service of our brave men, would have been too happy an ending of my life.

Once again I was thrown amongst strangers, and in very painful circumstances. The London sisterhood to which I belonged passed under the control of a lady of whom I shall only say that she knew very little of the true spirit of the religious life. I had seen the dear mother of the Clewer sisterhood, since dead; indeed, she came to London especially to see me, as she was a relative of my mother's family, and when our home in London was placed under new management I often regretted I had not gone to her.

I had by this time acquired a very thorough knowledge of the London poor and their surroundings, and how often since have I pictured to myself the scenes I then witnessed! No wonder the Chartist and the socialist have sway, when the rich care so little for the poor, and leave them to suffer unheeded.

I can scarcely tell when I entertained the first idea of entering the Roman Catholic church; my principal reason was the strong assurance which that church gives that it has always taught and always will teach the same doctrine. But I have lived to see a stupendous change, which I know of my own knowledge has shocked the moral sense if it has not offended the conscience even of many bishops.

When I first was received into the Roman Catholic church I was taught, as all Catholics were taught then, that the church was infallible; that when the Apostles said, "It seems good to the Holy Ghost and to us," they spoke collectively, as the church did then; and that the Roman Catholic church and the early Catholic church could also say, "It seems good to the Holy Ghost and to *us.*"

What a change from this dogma to the present teaching of the same church! No longer do you hear, "It seems good to the Holy Ghost and to us," but the cry is, "It seems good to the Holy Ghost and to *me.*" The voice of the church is practically lost in the voice of a single man.

There was yet another subject which was the immediate cause of my change of religious opinion. Dr. Pusey, and those who thought with him, taught a doctrine on the subject of Holy Communion, which, as it seemed to me, nearly approached that taught by the Roman Catholic church. I embraced his teaching to the full, and on one occasion, when I saw great though unintentional irreverence offered to the Blessed Sacrament, I decided not to receive the Holy Communion in the Anglican Church any more. I went soon after to a priest in the Roman Catholic Church. He also was a convert, and expressed himself as greatly shocked at what I told him. Alas, he did not tell me that I should find, as I eventually did, far more irreverence amongst those who are far less excusable. I soon came to know that there are many things which experience alone can teach us, and that those who make the highest professions of belief are not always the most perfect in their actions.

I was received into the Catholic Church in London, and confirmed by his Eminence the late Cardinal Wiseman. After my confirmation I was asked to breakfast at his house, and was introduced to a number of the leading converts and Catholics whom I had not previously known. Several Sisters of Mercy breakfasted with the party, which I found was not unusual on such occasions.

I was introduced to the reverend mother with a view to the probability of my entrance into that order. A few days later I was invited to a private interview with Cardinal Wiseman, when his Eminence warmly congratulated me on my conversion, and told me that his especial object in seeing me alone was to obtain a promise from me that I would devote the rest of my life to Catholic literature. Though I was then quite young, I had already begun my career as an author. I willingly gave the required promise, and, though I never saw Cardinal Wiseman again, he corresponded with me continually, encouraged my literary work, and wrote to me almost the last letter he ever penned.

I made at this time also another friend, the Rev. Father Whitty, who afterward joined the Jesuit fathers, and who now holds a high position in that order. He was then, I think, vicar-general of the Westminster archdiocese. It had happened that he knew some of my relatives, and, though all were Protestants, he held them in very high esteem; a curious circumstance had increased this intimacy, and given him a more than ordinary interest in my conversion. His sister, Miss Whitty, was the superioress of a well-known convent in Dublin. The order of Sisters of Mercy, to which she belonged, had been founded by a Miss McAuley. That lady was a convert to the Catholic faith, and had the zeal and earnestness of converts. In her efforts to help to save poor girls, she met with the usual opposition from selfish and self-interested ecclesiastics, but she eventually succeeded. For some reason the order (Sisters of Mercy) has not increased much out of Ireland. There are apparently few convents of Sisters of Mercy in America, but in Ireland there is one in nearly every village. Miss McAuley was persecuted by one of her Protestant relatives, and on one occasion she was driven out on the streets of Dublin late at night. She fled for refuge to an uncle of mine, who, though he was a Protestant, did not fail to sympathize with her, and did all he could to console and protect her. Father Whitty was, of course, well aware of all these circumstances, and consequently felt additional interest in my affairs. He was also, I was told, very much impressed with the circumstances of my conversion, thinking I had shown much moral courage in coming alone to London while so young, and facing the brave ordeal of such a change of belief without one friend to help me. For myself, I may truly say I never gave a thought to the consequences of what I was doing; I believed it was right to become a Catholic; what it might cost me spiritually or temporally never weighed with me in making a decision.

Perhaps one of the most eventful circumstances in my eventful life was the coincidence between the kind and considerate treatment which my Protestant relative showed to this converted Catholic lady, and the way in which the Catholic archbishop and cardinal of Dublin afterwards treated me. In the very same place and in the same street where this Catholic convert lady, who like myself was the foundress of a new religious order, was received and sheltered by my Protestant relatives, I was driven out by the then Roman Catholic archbishop, without one thought of pity or justice, or one word of consideration, without even a charge of any kind being made against me.*

As I am writing facts, and as I believe that a great deal of the evil and injustice of life is caused by the silence of those who are either afraid or ashamed to speak out, I will add here a few words. During the famine of 1879, I had, as will be shown later, very large sums of money placed at my disposal. I need not say that I tried to be careful and conscientious in the distribution of these funds. I believed then, and I believe still, that I disposed of them in the best way, by giving a large proportion to the Sisters of Mercy; for, as I have said above, they have convents in nearly every village in Ireland, and are well acquainted with the needs of the poor.

* A full account of this will be given further on. The account of how my relative, Surgeon Cusack, received and protected Miss McAuley can be found in the life of that lady, written by one of the American Sisters of Mercy, and published in this country.

When I came to America, I thought the Sisters of Mercy here would be pleased to see me, and help in any way they could one who had been so practically devoted to their order. I suppose the word had been sent them by ecclesiastical authority that I was to be "boycotted"; however it may have been, when I called on the sisters in New York, I was received with freezing coldness. In the month of July, 1886, two Sisters of Mercy came to New York from Big Rapids, where they had a convent, but had found it "too poor" a place to live in. These sisters did not go to their own sisters in New York, they came to our poor sisters in Jersey City. Indeed, our hospitality has often been asked by sisters, and has never been refused. While I was in charge of the order, I tried to do all that I could for those who, like ourselves, were trying to do their best in their own way for God and the poor.

As a matter touching on the difficulties of sisters and their difficulties in dealing with ecclesiastical authorities, I may give the following incident.

The sisters of the order of the G——S——, belonging to the A——y diocese, came to our convent in Jersey City and earnestly begged for a few weeks' hospitality. The sisters said they were going to collect in New York, and it was not convenient for them to remain with the sisters of their own order there. I readily consented, having first asked if they had all the necessary episcopal permissions. The sisters replied "yes." They came to us in a few days and remained some weeks, during which time they spent their entire days collecting in New York and Brooklyn.

I learned later that the sisters had no permission to collect in either New York or Brooklyn; whether they had permission from their own bishop to do this I do not know. The reason they came to me was simply that if they had gone to a convent of their own order in New York, they must have been seen by some of the priests there, who would have recognized them as strangers, and they might have been forbidden to collect.

There is an amusing incident of this collecting under difficulties, the circumstances of which are also known to me. Two sisters came from Australia wishing to collect some thirty or forty thousand dollars for an institution there, which had suffered from some local cause. I understood that the priest who sent these poor sisters over the world, for they had even been in Africa, was a man of great wealth. I hope this was not true, but I heard the report from good authority.

They came to New York full of hope, as the

priest who had sent them was nearly related to an influential politician, and it was supposed that the archbishop would not venture to refuse his requests. This politican called on the archbishop with the two sisters, and was refused for some inscrutable reason. It mattered little, however, to the sisters; their friend was determined not to be baffled so easily. If his Grace gave the desired permission, well and good; if he refused, his refusal was of no moment to a gentleman whose political influence was too important for any delinquences to be visited with episcopal displeasure. So, after expressing his feelings in choice language, he left the palace and took the sisters himself on the round of collecting, the result being, as I heard, some $25,000 in a few days. The sisters called on me afterwards, accompanied by one of Dr. McGlynn's most devoted followers, who was also assisting them in every way in her power. She being, of course, as independent of the archbishop's displeasure as the politician. And so as the money was got, the sisters were perfectly indifferent how it was obtained, having such powerful protection against the archbishop's interference.

CHAPTER III.

LIFE AT NEWRY.

*Desire to Work for the Poor — Cardinal Newman's *Apologia* — The Bishop and Cardinal Antonelli — The French Governess — Journey to Newry — Miss O'Hagan — Her Character and History — Entrance to the Convent — Life at Newry — Taking the Habit — My Health — History of the Poor Clares — Trials of Religious Houses — Estrangement from Relatives — Literary Work — Trouble over my Publications — A Jealous Priest and a Dedication — My Book "Pirated" by a New York Priest — Building Operations and Money Troubles — The Bishop Interferes. — A Momentous Visit is Paid us.*

I HAVE said that I do not intend to enter on controversial subjects, but there are two points on which I think I should say a few words. I have indicated briefly how the idea of a divinely appointed church, and of a divine authority to teach, came to my mind at this time; a time when men's minds were sorely tried on matters of faith. The claims of the Roman Catholic church began to receive grave consideration. Men who were very much in earnest about religion, grasped at the idea of certainty when there was so much confusion of religious thought.

I remember my two great difficulties in accepting the teachings of the Roman Catholic church were the fact that I knew the claim which the

Greek church had to valid orders, and that this was acknowledged by the Roman Catholic church. I asked, then, why might not the claim of the Anglican church be equally valid? And I knew that this was admitted even by some Roman Catholic divines, and that some Anglican converts who had become Roman Catholics would not accept reordination, and remained simply laymen. I was also doubtful and distressed about some of the forms of worship which were paid to the Blessed Virgin.

My experience of Anglican sisterhoods after I left the Home in London had been exceedingly painful, but all this did not lessen my desire to live the life of a sister, to give my life entirely to God, and to work for His poor. This seemed to me the only object worth existing for. It did not occur to me to look into the history of the Roman Catholic church. It never occurred to me that there could be any real evils in the communion which I had entered, because I believed it was so perfect.

I certainly was not wilfully deceived by any one. I was ignorant by accident rather than from deception. I may say also that I know there are a considerable number of converts, and I know there are thousands of Roman Catholics, who have not even the least idea of the evils which unhappily I know too well. My knowledge of these things has come from no seeking of mine, but through the course of a very remarkable Providence. There is a passage in Cardinal Newman's *Apologia*, (page 271,) where he touches on the subject of the "Character of Priests," and he asks why they should live so self-sacrificing a life if they were not sincere in doing so.

Now, there can be no doubt about Cardinal Newman's sincerity; but the question is, whether he was likely to have had full opportunities of information. In weighing the value of an opinion, there must always be a consideration of the source from whence it is derived, and the opportunities of knowledge which the individual has possessed.

It is well known that Cardinal Newman lived in a very restricted circle; and it is also well known that Bishop Ullathorne, in whose diocese he lived, was extremely strict with his priests. I myself heard one of the very fathers who belonged to Cardinal Newman's order speaking of him in a most disrespectful manner, but of course such disrespect would never reach Cardinal Newman.

I knew a bishop who was living in Rome, in the Vatican, and on the most intimate terms with the late Cardinal Antonelli when the latter was living a sinful life; and I believe this bishop when he told me that he knew nothing of what was going on until long after he left Rome, and that even then he could scarcely credit it. This bishop was at that time a priest and convert, a man of large property and great influence also, and anything like scandal would consequently have been carefully hidden from him.

The first faint breath of suspicion that anything could be wrong in those who were devoted to the service of God came to me at this time, but I put it from me with the consoling reflection that scandals must come. Later I had to learn, to my infinite grief, that scandals of a most serious kind exist, and exist unreproved, which is the real evil.

A French lady, who was governess in the family of a friend, spoke of the priest of our mission in a way which I considered most disrespectful, and for which she maintained that she had cause. She gave a history of her experiences with priests very freely, and in a way which was not calculated to make them respected as a body, if her statements were true. She was soon after removed from the place, to the very great relief of many of us.

The next case was that of a priest and a Jesuit father, and I heard from his own lips bitter complaints of the conduct of some of his superiors; and he was not a convert but belonged to an old English Catholic family.

My journey to Newry was made on the 2d of

July, 1859. There had been a railway accident some little time before, and a large bridge near Drogheda was so seriously injured that the trains could not pass over it. Passengers were expected to walk, and it was a rough and difficult undertaking. I felt indeed sad and lonely; every one else seemed to have friends and companions to help them; I had no one. I was going to strange people and to a strange place, and on an errand which was to influence my whole future life. I was to all appearances a free agent; and I was still young, I had full liberty of choice; yet I felt then in some strange way, as I have often felt since, that I had no choice; that I was led or moved or influenced by some exterior power.

I was received by the reverend mother, who kept up the grand title of "Abbess" by which superiors were distinguished when the order was in its original state. The office was then held by Miss O'Hagan. She was a remarkable woman. Her family were persons of humble origin, Mr. O'Hagan having lived and died, master of a small boat and later, I believe, owner of a little liquor store in Belfast. Yet such is the force of native talent that, although she had entered the convent with very little education, she became the superior of this institution, and her brother, who had an extraordinary gift of native eloquence, rose from the position of reporter on a local paper to a high place in the Irish bar, and later was given a peerage for services done to the Gladstone government.

Miss O'Hagan, though not well educated, had refined taste, an attractive manner, and a very excellent judgment. She had joined the sisters very young, and was one of the truest and best religious I have ever known. From the first moment of our meeting we formed a mutual attachment, which never ceased until death divided us.

A few hours decided my future. I resolved to enter this convent, and I returned the next day to Dublin to arrange some affairs. As I had no one to consult, and was entirely my own mistress, I came back to Newry in, I think, five or six days from the date of my first visit.

On the whole, the life there was peaceful and useful. There were large schools, where we taught during certain hours in the day. The instruction was thorough and careful, and much good was done also by Sunday classes of girls, young women, and even of much older persons. We were spared one great trial of the American sisterhoods; there was no begging. Every young lady who entered the community was obliged to bring a sum of money with her to be invested on good security, the interest of which would be sufficient to provide her with food and clothing. This money belonged to the community as a body, and could not be claimed or used by any individual, except in the case of removal to another convent. Of course in a community long established, and where this rule was strictly observed, as sisters died, their money remained, and considerable property was accumulated.

I was not long an inmate of the convent before I discovered that life there was very much like life anywhere else. It had its sorrows and its joys. Differences of temper often broke out and made unpleasantnesses. Miss O'Hagan was a comparatively young superioress and had her own troubles with some of the older sisters. They were themselves entirely unfit for office, but were none the less jealous of her.

I was urgently pressed to receive the religious habit on the 12th of August, just one month after I joined the community. The usual period of waiting was six months and often more. I remember well the very place in the convent garden where Miss O'Hagan, the "Abbess," told me that all had been arranged. I objected strongly, and even positively refused. I said I desired more time to consider, but I at last yielded to persuasion and affection. I saw that she was very much vexed and that she considered me very ungrateful. I could not bear to be thought ungrateful, and I knew she was granting me a very special favor. I loved her so sincerely I could not bear to pain her, and I saw she would be greatly pained by my refusal. I consented, but it is only justice to all concerned, to say that I believe I should have made the same decision if the usual time had elapsed, or even if I had been given a longer time for reflection.

My health had always been delicate, and every consideration was shown to me. I had always been accustomed to English food and comforts, and felt the loss of them keenly, but this never caused me to shrink for a moment from my vocation.

If I had been of a more robust frame, I should have entered an order where I could have worked in a hospital or amongst the poor, that having been the desire of my life from my childhood, and long years before I ever thought of joining the Roman church. I was at this time comparatively ignorant of the customs of the different religious orders, and naturally it did not occur to the Poor Clares to explain to me that the Irish branch of the order had altogether departed from their original rule, and that their vow of inclosure is merely episcopal. Their rule is verbally almost the same as that of the Sisters of Mercy and the Presentation Order. When the Irish Poor Clares were established at the beginning of this century, they were dispensed by the Holy See from all the fasts and abstinences of the Poor Clare rule. They were dispensed from saying the Divine Office ; in fact, every observance of the original rule of the Poor Clares was dispensed, in order to enable the sisters to teach. The vows of the Irish Poor Clares are also simple vows, and though the vow of inclosure forbids the sisters to go outside of the convent grounds without the permission of their Bishop, they have no grating in the parlor ; and seculars, and even gentlemen, can go and do go through the convent, especially in Kenmare, where the sisters go into the public church, and into the grounds belonging to the public church, which adjoins the convent. Those who know of Poor Clares only as a strictly inclosed and contemplative order have expressed surprise how I found so much time for active work, supposing I was in a contemplative order ; but as explained, the work of the Poor Clares in Ireland is not contemplative.

I soon found that Miss O'Hagan was very anxious that I should continue my literary work. I think she would have made any sacrifice to enable me to do so ; but no sacrifice was needed, as my literary work became a source of considerable pecuniary gain to the sisters, a fact of which they very gladly availed themselves.

A convert to the Catholic faith is led to enter that church, not merely by the belief and hope that it is the one true church, but also by the very natural conclusion that it is the one holy church. I believe the cause of some of the trouble in convent life is a mistaken view of human nature. Those who enter a religious house, young, and full of hope and zeal, and with such sublime ideas of perfection, still take with them poor humanity. To believe that putting on a religious garb will at once alter the dispositions, tempers, or personal peculiarities, is a sad delusion. It is true that we may, by generous efforts, change in some respects, but nature is slow, and habit is strong. We come into the convent full of imperfections, perhaps of grave faults, and we expect to find every one there perfect; but they, like ourselves, are human.

No doubt (and indeed I know this from personal experience) there is far more peace and happiness in some religious houses than in others, and much depends upon the superiors in effecting this difference. But the wisest and most capable superior has immense difficulties, never for one moment suspected by those outside, who little know the interior trials and troubles of even those who are nearest and dearest to them.

When visitors come to a religious house, they come, as St. Francis de Sales has said, "to be consoled," they do not come to sympathize with troubles which they never suspect.

In consequence of my having been much separated from my relatives during my early life, I was known to them only by name or by a rare interview. To this cause I attribute some of my troubles. This unintentional estrangement was greatly increased and intensified by my becoming a Catholic, and by their very strong anti-Catholic feelings. I was in Ireland now, certainly, and within easy reach, but I never should have thought of asking my relatives to visit me in the convent. Hence, I was singularly and painfully alone in the world. I had also, by becoming a Catholic, severed myself from very dear friends in Devonshire, a family with which I once expected to be closely united. Their protection too, if available, would have been invaluable, and indeed their affection has never ceased. But distance, and by degrees the interests and duties of my new life made a complete separation unavoidable.

A young priest assisted at my reception at Newry who promised to be an ornament to the Church. His sister, who had not been long professed, came with us later on the Kenmare foundation, and I attribute at least some of the suffering which she there caused me to the trouble which she was in from the conduct of her brother, who unhappily abandoned his vocation and gave himself up to a life of intemperance.

My time was principally employed in writing. The only occupation of the sisters was teaching the poor children, and, as there was quite a number of well-educated sisters in Newry, my services in that department were not needed. In connection with my literary work I first came to know that ecclesiastics were not the perfect beings I had supposed. One of the works which I wrote in Newry Convent was a life of St. Francis of Assisi, the great founder of the Franciscan Order. This book had cost me a great deal of labor and research. It was published by subscription as the best means to realize money from the publication for the sisters. They wished me to dedicate the volume to Miss O'Hagan, our "Mother Abbess," and I was very willing to do so. But an obstacle arose from an unexpected quarter.

A priest, an English convert, who happened to be then officiating in Dublin, and had recommended me to visit, and subsequently to enter Newry Convent, had written a short preface to the work. This preface was quite unnecessary, but the sisters thought that he expected the compliment to be paid to him of asking him to write it. He heard of my intention to dedicate the book to Miss O'Hagan, and his anger was the first painful intimation I had that priests were, after all, human. Still, with all possible allowance for poor humanity, I certainly have met in some priests, instances of almost childish intolerance and readiness to take offence, such as are far less common among men of the world. A large measure of allowance must be made for their education and their very peculiar circumstances, yet, on the other hand, one might fairly expect that the stupendous graces of their ordination and their mode of life would help to make them as truly fathers in heart as they are in name.

I can, however, only relate facts as they happened. This good priest had acquired a small literary reputation for writing little sketches of the lives of the saints; his classical education which, as he was a convert, was, necessarily, far above that of the ordinary run of priests, gave him special knowledge, and he used it well. He had an idea that he could in some way claim the authorship, or at least the credit and chief share in my work, and he thought if I dedicated it to any one, his claim of authorship would be lessened. As obviously, it was the author's right to dedicate her works, and as I was the author and the sisters the publishers, the latter had their way. I did not interfere, but I was never forgiven, though I was not the guilty party. I fear I must say so, that I have found, and I only hope I am more unfortunate than others, that priests are the very last persons who will forgive either a wilful or an imaginary offence.

My next clerical experience in connection with this work was equally unpleasant. A Franciscan priest in New York managed to get an advance copy of the book. He republished it without the slightest reference to me, or the slightest acknowledgment, and never even condescended to reply to my expostulations. With this solitary exception I met with universal consideration on the part of American publishers, and have been very liberally repaid when my works were reproduced.

At my profession the usual time was also shortened, but in this case I made no objection. I wished most earnestly to dedicate my life to God, in this way, and my experience so far had not been altogether an unhappy one.

The little domestic jars which I witnessed while at Newry, were only such as might occur in any family, and there were some most excellent and edifying religious in the community. I believe had I remained there, my life would have been one of comparative peace and happiness.

I may give here another of many instances of the troubles I was made to suffer by Roman Catholic priests in connection with my literary work. They are of course, with rare exceptions, protected by the bishops, no matter what they do, as this work will show by evidence past dispute. The Roman Catholic bishop exacts the most abject submission to himself from the priest; but in return he puts the shield of his protection, in a way which no Catholic dare dispute, over the actions of the priest, a fact which will explain many matters which are not easily understood by those who have not had experience.

While in Kenmare I wrote a life of St. Patrick, the great saint of the Irish people. The complimentary Apostolic letter which I received for this from Pope Pius IX. is too long to insert here in full, but it will be found in the appendix. I give a brief extract from it here,—

[EXTRACT FROM THE APOSTOLIC LETTER OF POPE PIUS IX., TO SISTER M. FRANCIS CLARE.]

"*To Our Beloved Daughter in Christ*, MARY FRANCIS CLARE, *of the Sisters of Saint Clare*, PIUS P. P. IX.: —

"BELOVED DAUGHTER IN CHRIST, — Health and Apostolic Benediction. We congratulate you, beloved daughter in Christ, on having completed a long and difficult work which seemed to be above woman's strength, with a success that has justly earned the applause of the pious and the learned. We rejoice, not only because you have promoted by this learned and eloquent volume the glory of the illustrious Apostle of Ireland, St. Patrick, but also because you have deserved well of the whole Church ; for in recording the actions of so great a man, you have placed before the eyes of the world the benefits received through the Catholic religion so clearly, that they can no longer be questioned. We certainly augur this successful issue from your labor ; and at the same time we impart to you and to your sisters, most lovingly, the Apostolic Benediction, as an earnest of God's favor and a pledge of our good-will.

"Given at Rome, at St. Peter's, the 6th October, 1870, the twenty-fifth year of our Pontificate.

"Pius P. P. IX."

An English, or Irish, or Canadian priest (for he claimed various nationalities), did not agree with the pope, and thought he could write a much better work himself ; of course as he was a priest, he could easily run mine out of the market. He also had very wealthy and influential relatives, who, it was whispered, were anxious to procure his advancement in the church. They were people of humble origin who had made their money in

Ireland and could afford to spend it in England for the benefit of their relative. I need scarcely say that I knew this priest had a right to publish a book in opposition to mine, if he thought he could advance his interests by doing so; but certainly I had a right to expect he would acknowledge his obligations to mine, but this he carefully avoided doing. I think I may say for my Life of St. Patrick, that it was the first life of that Saint which could lay claim to be the result of original research; all previous lives had been made up from each other without any reference to valuable documents which were not generally accessible, and moreover were written in very ancient Celtic, which could not even be read, except by a few Celtic scholars, who had studied it for philological research.

Most of these scholars were German, but there was one eminent Irish Celtic scholar who translated a very important document for me which I published in this work; and which probably would never have been published if I had not brought it out. A fact which was very well known and appreciated by many literary men. I had protected my copyright, but of course this made no difference when a priest was concerned; I was indeed unfortunate every way with this book, for a large edition of it was sent for sale to Mr. P. Donahoe, of Boston and was burned in the great fire at Boston, in 1872.

The work of this priest which was taken almost literally from mine, without the least acknowledgment, has of course superseded mine. In this case I felt the loss to the charity for which the profits of my literary labors was devoted, much more than the injustice to my literary reputation. I must say also, that loving the Roman Catholic church, to which I have given such practical proofs of my devotion, it has always been a grievous pain to me to see any falling from the high ideal which it professes and of the practice of which I have seen so little. As soon as Father Morris's Life of St. Patrick was published, I wrote to the press showing how he had compiled it from mine, and that he had not done me even the literary courtesy of an acknowledgment; but as usual the priest was protected by ecclesiastical authority and I was silenced.

In 1878, I published the lives of two other famous Irish saints, Saint Columba and Saint Bridget, and received the following approbation of my work.

"IRISH COLLEGE, ROME, May 29, 1878.

"MY DEAR SISTER, — I am happy to state that Mgr. Kirby presented to-day, in my name, your life of St. Patrick, St. Bridget, and St. Columba, to

His Holiness, who, in return, sends you his thanks and his best blessing. His Holiness wishes you every success in your literary labors, hoping that they may be useful to religion, and contribute to the salvation of souls.

" His Holiness was greatly pleased with the way in which the life of St. Patrick was brought out.

" Wishing you and all your pious community every blessing, I remain,

" Yours faithfully,

"Paul, Cardinal Cullen."

To Sister Mary Francis Clare, Convent of Poor Clares, Kenmare, Co. Kerry, Ireland.

Cardinal Cullen always encouraged my work, he was a man of some education and very conscientious. His successor, Cardinal McCabe, was a very different character.

But I soon found that these approbations were not any advantage to me; on the contrary they only intensified dislike to myself, and created jealousy. It was long before I could realize that the Holy Father's approbation was practically of no value, unless it suited the plans and purposes of the Roman Catholic bishops. Every one knows how the Jesuits were approved or disapproved just as it suited the powerful bishops of their times. Even in our own day and in this very year, we have had evidence in the case of Rosmini, and

Lassere, how influence can be brought on the pope, to make him change the most strongly expressed approvals. And all the past history of the Holy See goes to prove the same thing, though it is sometimes found convenient to forget it.

During my novitiate I had one very unpleasant experience; I brought a good deal of money with me into the convent, and certain buildings and alterations were going on which embarrassed the superioress (Miss O'Hagan) considerably. She was a very nervous and delicate woman, of a very highly strung organization, and felt dissension and trouble keenly. I was greatly attached to her, and was always very careless about money, so when a little pressure was brought to bear on me, I very readily offered to give what I could to relieve her embarrassment. The sister who was mistress of novices, however, took a different view of the case. She told me that she considered the expenditure unwise, that no novice should be asked for, or even allowed to give any money under such circumstances, and that she herself had been greatly distressed and annoyed by appeals made to her own friends on this head.

Although long years have passed, I remember every word and every incident as if it had happened only yesterday. It was my first experience of real dissension and trouble in a convent.

I believe this sister must have spoken to the bishop, who was also our confessor. The immediate result was that the bishop gave peremptory orders to stop the buildings and alterations, and told me that he positively forbade my giving or advancing any money. As usual, I was a victim in an affair in which I had never interfered in one way or the other, — save only to help as far as I could.

The sister who, as remarked before, had so much trouble with her brother, had formed a passionate attachment to Miss O'Hagan, and was her chief favorite now, turned on me as if I had been the cause of stopping the work. Her language and her passion I shall never forget, and I believe she never forgave me for what she chose to imagine I had done. It was useless to reason with her then or at a later period. When in Kenmare she caused me much trouble by the same overbearing temperament. I learned later on, that affection for the superior is often the cause of dissension in convents, and leads to jealousy and bitterness which, for obvious reasons, are more likely to be kept up in such places than in the outer world. This sister thought that I had told the bishop about the money, and so brought the trouble upon Miss O'Hagan, but I never mentioned the subject to him; he heard it from others and then spoke of it to me.

It is commonly supposed that those who devote themselves to God in a religious house are freer from temptations and trials than persons who live in the world. This is far from being the case ; no doubt every state of life has its own special trials and temptations, but there is a difference both in degree and in kind.

Nor is there any attempt to deceive sisters on this subject. A good mistress of novices will make it her first duty to point out the difficulties and temptations of this kind of life and to prepare those under her charge for them. And in the many books written during centuries of the church's history which treat of the religious life, whether for men or women, these special trials are always noted.

The day before my profession, I made, as was usual, a deed of renunciation of all my worldly property. I cannot now remember the exact amount. I know that I did just whatever I was asked to do, and I should not allude to the subject except that it has an important bearing on a grave act of injustice, which the Kenmare sisters and the Bishop of Kerry tried to accomplish at a later period.

A certain sum of money, according to the usual custom, was placed in the bank with the other moneys belonging to the convent, the interest of which was to serve for my support. This was right and usual. It was suggested to me also to leave a certain sum, the interest of which was to be used for having masses for my intention. This point should be noted as I shall have to return to it again. A further sum was placed in the bank, the interest of which was to be used for the support of some sister who might be considered a desirable addition to the community, but who might not have the money necessary to be received. What remained, was spent on the building, and on the church attached to the convent, for which I procured stained-glass windows and many other ornaments.

All this was done by deed of gift, so as to leave me no power of altering the agreement. I think in this matter I was not treated quite fairly, as I had no idea of the stringently binding nature of the documents. I concerned myself but little, except to try and fulfil my religious obligations to the best of my power, and to please those who then at least promised to be true and faithful friends for life. I could not then believe that either priests or sisters could act unjustly. Was not the church to which they belonged, the church of saints? Was it not the holy Catholic church? Had I not a right to expect that even if there were imperfections and stains such as must be in all human undertakings, that there they should at least be few?

If I dreamed a happy dream and came to a sorrowful awakening had I not some foundation for the dream and some right to expect its realization? Perhaps I was singularly unfortunate in my personal experience of sisters and bishops, yet I know the life histories of others which have not been altogether dissimilar from my own.

In the month of October of the following year, a visit was received at the convent at Newry, which resulted in a complete change of my life and plans, a change which I could not have anticipated when I made my vows.

CHAPTER IV.

GOING TO KENMARE.

Archdeacon O'Sullivan Desires a Foundation at Kenmare — His Noble Character — The Kenmare Sisters — Miss O'Hagan Undertakes the Foundation — Dr. Moriarty, the New Bishop — Lord and Lady Kenmare — The Bishop's Mistake — Status of Priests in Ireland — Exposed to Social and Political Seductions — Bishop Moriarty Won Over — Life at Kenmare — Choir and Lay Sisters — Unfortunate Selection of New Sisters — My Literary Work Continues.

IN the early part of the month of October, Archdeacon O'Sullivan, the parish priest of Kenmare County, Kerry, came to Newry Convent to ask if some of the sisters would make a foundation in his parish. The archdeacon was, indeed, a noble specimen of an Irish priest. The good of his people and the advancement of his church were his only objects.

He had saved money, and had been left some more, by a deceased bishop, for the purpose of building a church and convent, and all his energies were bent on this one object. He was a man who esteemed education very highly. He was an excellent Latin scholar, and though he had not the advantage of a cultivated English style, he had made a translation of Bellarmine's well-known

"Commentary on the Psalms," and won approval by his rugged exactness and force of diction.

His memory will be forever held in benediction. For myself I can only say I lost in him the kindest of friends and the best of fathers. But I anticipate; yet, I may be forgiven, for his memory brings back the few happy recollections of my religious life.

Some sisters had preceded us in Kenmare. They belonged to an Irish order founded about the same time as the Sisters of Mercy. But these sisters (the Presentation Nuns, as they were called) did not spread as rapidly or as widely as the Sisters of Mercy. They are an inclosed, but not a contemplative order, and hence were in some sort an anomaly, like the Irish Poor Clares to whom I belonged. Strangely enough, the Irish Presentation Sisters kept a far stricter inclosure, at least in Ireland, than the Poor Clares.

These sisters for several reasons did not suit Archdeacon O'Sullivan's views. He was very anxious about the education of his people, and I think their teaching was not considered up to the mark, and our schools in Newry had a very high name. Besides this, Father John, as Archdeacon O'Sullivan was always called, had a weakness, who has not? He saw that Miss O'Hagan's brother was a rising man, and rising rapidly.* He was not then a "Lord," but he was on a fair way to become one. It was the policy of the English government to advance a few men like Mr. O'Hagan, who had just enough nationality to be popular to a certain extent with the Irish people, and who had quite sufficient care for their own advancement to make their nationality subservient to their personal interests. Miss O'Hagan was then just the person to suit the good archdeacon's views in every way, and as he was a man of business and quick action, he decided to come himself and secure his object.

There were many difficulties raised on the part of the sisters. Their nominal inclosure was no obstacle to new foundations, yet it seemed to them as if the world must come to an end, as far as they were concerned, if changes were made. Miss O'Hagan was superioress, but her health was so bad she seldom left her room, except for a few hours in the day, and though her younger sisters were much attached to her, she was no favorite with the older ones, for many reasons.

* The English government is always anxious, for political purposes, to encourage Roman Catholics by bestowing titles on men who have shown sufficient qualified patriotism to make them acceptable to the Irish people, no matter how humble their origin may be, and who are henceforward bound to be loyal by their acceptance of rank or office.

At last all was settled. For myself, my wish would have been to remain in Newry Convent. The sister who had been my mistress of novices was a truly good religious. She was made superioress in Miss O'Hagan's place, and was better liked by some of the older sisters. I believe Miss O'Hagan was sincerely and honestly attached to me. She certainly was most anxious that I should make the Kenmare foundation with her. Some of the Newry sisters were equally anxious that I should remain there, so that I was strongly pressed on both sides. My love for Miss O'Hagan, and her entreaties, prevailed, and I decided to go with her.

I concerned myself very little about money matters, but Miss O'Hagan took care to take sisters who had money, and to secure all she could of what I had brought into the convent at Newry. I speak of this also, only because it throws a light on future events.

Amongst other moneys which I had given, she got the money invested for masses; as she said, that, of course, the masses should be said for me where I was going. For myself, I should have been quite as well content to have had them said in Newry as in Kenmare, and I am quite sure the obligation would have been fulfilled there with scrupulous exactness. It will be seen later how

I was treated in this matter by the Kenmare sisters.

We left Newry, I think, on the 20th of October, 1861. I know we arrived in Kenmare on the 24th. That day being one of special devotion in the Catholic church, it was impressed on my memory. As far as I was myself concerned, I had no particular regrets in leaving Newry. I had not been there long enough to have formed any strong attachment either to the place or to any person. Several other sisters came with us. One returned to Newry in a few months, not finding the sisters' life at Kenmare at all like what she had left. Another sister who, like myself, became a special object of dislike and persecution by our ecclesiastical superior, and by the young sisters who had joined us after we came to Kenmare, returned to Newry Convent also. This occurred not long before I left Kenmare, but as these ladies had wealthy and influential Catholic relatives, neither ecclesiastics nor sisters could venture to criticise their conduct unfavorably.

On our way to Kenmare we stopped a day and a night at the convent of the Irish Poor Clares, in Dublin. Newry Convent had been founded from it years before. We then travelled to Killarney, where we were received in the bishop's palace, a magnificent building, in strange contrast to the misery, dirt, and wretchedness around. And here I had my first real introduction to Irish poverty. Having spent my early life in England, and amongst those whose prejudices were as anti-Irish as they were anti-Catholic, I had much to learn as to the state of Ireland, and being keenly observant I learned quickly.

My experience of Catholic bishops and priests had been, on the whole, favorable. Certainly, I wanted nothing from them, and I was able to do a great deal for them. As a convert I was very warmly welcomed into the church, as I have already said, and most of those ecclesiastics whom I met were gentlemen by birth and education, and had been trained in the Episcopal church.

I found in our new bishop, Dr. Moriarty, a man who was their equal in culture and refinement, if not in birth. I do not think it would have been possible for him to have done an act of injustice to a sister, or indeed to any one. Unfortunately, his real merits and goodness were overshadowed, as far as the Irish people were concerned, by political considerations. He certainly leaned to the cause of the rich and the great, and he made one unfortunate speech, which I always believed was taken in a sense different from what he had actually intended. But, all the same, the evil was done.

Most assuredly, there can be no greater danger

to the cause of religion than when the poor suspect those who, from their profession, should be especially their friends, of caring more for the rich than for them. Appearances may be false, but the poor naturally judge by them, and perhaps not without reason. It so happened that Lord Kenmare's family were Catholics, and that they owned a considerable portion of the land around Killarney. The family certainly spent very little time or money in Ireland, and did very little for their tenants; but at this time the land agitation had not begun, and there were not the same causes of bitterness that now exist. Bishop Moriarty was a man of very courtly presence, a splendid conversationalist, social, and with that tone of dignity which well became his ecclesiastical character. He would have been an acquisition in any society; and Lady Kenmare, who was fastidious and English, was only too glad to have him for a frequent guest at her dinner table. Whether her English visitors were Catholic or Protestant, she could introduce them with satisfaction to the courtly favorite. Naturally, the bishop gravitated to the wealthy and influential classes; naturally, too, his sympathies were with them. God help our poor human nature, and God help those who are easily influenced in their judgment by exterior circumstances. The state of Ireland should be known personally to be understood; the hard feelings which existed, the internal bitterness which the people feel when any ecclesiastic takes the part of the landlord class, or in any way even appears to sympathize with it.

But Bishop Moriarty did more than this. On one public occasion he denounced the Fenian rising in scathing language, and amongst other words used an expression which has become historical, "Hell," he cried out, "is not hot enough or eternity long enough to punish their crimes."

I believe that when the bishop used this expression he alluded to the class of informers who have been the curse of Ireland. Men, who as has been fully proved in state trials, deliberately profaned the Sacrament for the vile purpose of betraying their fellow-creatures and fellow-countrymen. Indeed, men were hung more than once on the perjured evidence of those wretches, and enthusiastic boys were led into the meshes of the law to afford subjects for the vile greed of their temptors.

The bishop's expression, however meant, was certainly taken as denouncing any attempt to free Ireland or to oppose English rule. And the result was a terrible blow to religion. I know, because I have heard it on evidence that I cannot doubt, that men who had once been devoted Catholics not only ceased to frequent the sacraments, but they even cursed their bishop as he passed.

I believe the spirit which has resulted in making Kerry remarkable for outrages even now was fostered, if it was not caused, by the bishop's supposed or real indifference to the sufferings of his people. This is a fact which can be easily explained. For long centuries the people and the priests were hunted and oppressed alike. The priest ministered to the people. He gave them all he could of spiritual help and comfort, the only consolation they had. For them he made every sacrifice; but then he was also one of themselves.

The rich or higher classes of Catholics who had been landowners changed their religion with very little hesitation, when they found that by so doing they secured their estates, while they hated, despised, and feared the poor. The poor, for whom they in turn had no love, in their turn looked upon them as apostates. For long years, on the other hand, priests and people had one common status in society; they were equally despised and equally persecuted. But a time came when to be Catholic and to be rebel were no longer convertible terms. Then came the divergence, — the divergence which nearly became a fatal division. Within recent memory the people were still oppressed, but the priests were no longer persecuted. On the contrary, it became the policy of the English rulers of Ireland to court the priest in public and in private; to pay him the compliment of an invitation to dinner; to give a liberal donation to his church or his schools. In fact, the priest, and above all the bishop, was no longer an object of persecution; he was a power on whom a great deal depended, and he was treated accordingly.

It is marvellous, and it is an overwhelming proof of the intensity of Irish faith and nationality, that so few priests yielded to these advances. But the bishop was the great object of attention. He "held the fort," and those who needed his services knew his value and his power.

And Bishop Moriarty was won over very readily. His very nature was one likely to yield easily to such influences, and to enjoy the society which he certainly graced. His ideas of law and order were the ideas of the English government, and of their representatives in Ireland; but he was not a man to hoard up money, or to turn his face from the sufferings of the poor, except where political influences blinded his perceptions.*

By the earnest desire of Miss O'Hagan, who

---

* I may mention here, as an instance of his peculiarly kind disposition, that on one occasion, when one of the Sisters of Mercy in Killarney was moved to another convent for change of air, he took pains to see that a pet dog which amused her in her illness should be sent after her.

still continued superioress, I devoted myself to writing, as I had done in Newry.

Several young girls joined our sisters at this time, but they were of an entirely different class from those received in Newry Convent, — where only ladies were admitted, except as lay sisters, — and the result was anything but desirable. They were girls who had all the vanity of ignorance, and a little education, which they thought was very great.

Kenmare is a lovely village, three hours' drive from Killarney, which, with all the beauty of its scenery, is itself little better than a village. The very few gentlemen's families who lived in or near Kenmare were Protestants, so that we were obliged, if we wished to increase our numbers, to take poor girls from the schools. On this subject I must say a few words of explanation, as it had a serious effect on my future troubles and life.

The customs of the religious life in Ireland and England are naturally different from those which obtain in America. There are two classes of sisters in every Irish convent, and the distinction between the two is very broadly marked. These two classes of sisters are called *choir sisters* and *lay sisters*. The distinction is also observed in some American convents, and it seems to me strangely out of place in a country which boasts of its equality as well as of its liberty. It must, however, be understood that this is a mere matter of opinion on my part, though it is an opinion founded on considerable experience.

The distinction between lay and choir sisters is one fully approved by the Roman Church, and has the sanction of long custom. The original idea no doubt was that those who were sufficiently educated to recite the long Latin offices of the Church, as is still the custom with sisters who belong to contemplative orders, should be spared the fatigue of household duties. Also, it afforded to devout and uneducated girls, and to those who had no money, an opportunity of dedicating themselves to the service of the Church in a special manner.

I must admit for myself a strong leaning to the custom of apostolic times, where all things were in common, and when no distinction was between servant and master. It has always seemed to me that in the religious life, where a community of goods is practised, that it should be complete, and that no distinction should be made between the wealthy sister and the poor one.

Distinctions which are right and necessary in the world are certainly not necessary in a convent, where everything is planned on entirely different principles.*

As a matter of experience I found the plan of having lay sisters, as they are called, very useless and very injurious. On going to Kenmare, we decided not to have lay sisters, but if help should be necessary, to have servants in preference. Certainly, this plan worked very much better. But I think it is better still to receive all on an equality, and to divide the duties and employments of the convent, according to the capacity of each; so that all, like sisters, work together for the common good and for the good of the poor.

Unfortunately for the peace of the Kenmare Convent, some girls who had been monitresses in the public schools were received by us. They were entirely ignorant of the world, had never travelled beyond their native village, and had all the ignorant ideas and pride, almost inseparable from the kind of education which they had received.

The education given to the poor, and especially to the Irish, in national (public) schools is deplor-

* In some religious orders, as for example the "Sisters of Mercy," the lay sisters wear a different dress, and even in the choir have to wear a white apron as a badge of servitude. Lay sisters are not allowed to have any voice in the affairs of the convent, and consequently can hardly be expected to take the interest of those who have.

able. It is undoubtedly the cause of much of the trouble which is felt in America, arising from want of proper training for domestic service. As I shall enter fully into this subject, when I explain my reasons for founding a new religious order, I allude to it here only so far as it is necessary to explain my position and difficulties in Kenmare Convent.

Two of the girls who asked to enter our convent were, as I have said, monitresses in the national school, of which we were now to take charge. They had been made a good deal of by the sisters who had preceded us, and indeed, had been very useful to them. As these girls had been educated from childhood in the public schools, they knew the system thoroughly, and were quite equal to the mechanical labor of teaching well.

There had been a warm feeling in the parish against our coming, which was concealed from us until we came, and our position was a difficult one. Father John, however, was a master of strategy, and he determined to secure the very leaders of the revolt to our interests, and the ringleaders were these two girls. He himself brought the girls to us, and believing that both had vocations for the religious life, he induced them to enter our convent. This removed some difficulties and was a great help for the time, but the result was not so fortunate for the future peace of the convent.

The daily events of a convent life leave but little to record, and matters of great interest to the sisters, such as professions and school festivals, are of little importance to those outside.

At this period, and indeed during the entire time of my stay in Kenmare, I was occupied exclusively in literary work, to the very great pecuniary benefit of the sisters. None of them were able to lighten my labor in any way in this matter, but there was a way in which I could have been spared a great deal of labor, and of unnecessary labor, which was positively refused. Of this I shall say no more.

CHAPTER V.

MY LITERARY WORK AT KÈNMARE.

Success of my Books — Blamed for Writing Them — Illiberal Criticisms — Causes of Trouble in the Church — Unjust Interference of the Archbishop of Dublin — Letter from Bishop Moriarty — His Approval of my Literary Work.

I DO not care to enumerate all the works I wrote in Kenmare, but as I know some account of this subject will interest many readers, I cannot altogether pass it over. My position was an exceptional one, but it had the cordial approval of my superiors. Some trouble indeed was given by priests and bishops belonging to other dioceses of England and Ireland, who were anxious to alter my mode of life according to their own particular views.

When I was at Knock, in Ireland, I published some devotions and prayers written by St. Alphonsus Liguori, who is not merely a canonized saint, but is also a doctor of the Roman Church. The devotions were at once attacked, and their theological correctness was most severely criticised by a priest in the public press. The good priest thought I was the author. I replied in the same paper by simply referring him to the works of St.

Alphonsus, from which the devotions which he so severely criticised were taken, word for word.

Another priest who blamed me for writing and for the large circulation of my books, which he said brought me too much before the public, accused me openly of heresy. I had written a Life of the Blessed Virgin, which promised to have a very large circulation, and in this I said, "Did not He (our Divine Lord) know that He was God?" The context showed plainly that I knew he did know, and that this made it more wonderful that he should have endured the sufferings of Gethsemane. It was, however, in vain that I explained my obvious meaning and pointed to similar passages even in other Roman Catholic writers. I was put to a heavy expense and loss by being obliged to cancel this page, and the injury to my literary character was serious; for this matter, trifling as it was, was written about and discussed with a large margin of exaggeration, and yet all the trouble was caused by priests who had no right whatever to interfere in my affairs.

One cause of trouble in the Roman Catholic church, both to priests and sisters, is a custom which is tolerated if it is not encouraged by Roman Catholic Bishops. If a person is in any way annoyed or supposes himself injured by priests or sisters, he at once takes his revenge by "writing to their bishop." The amount of petty annoyances to which a person can thus be subjected can be easily understood. These complaints are received by the bishop as a sort of compliment to his position and authority, and reference to him is received by him much as the Pope receives the requests of kings and emperors to arbitrate in their affairs. These things cause many serious heartburnings which are never known outside, because the least display of resentment is put down at once, and "called disloyalty to the church."

During this period I was publishing my books myself, and devoting the profits to our convent. At first I gave employment to Roman Catholic printers only, but I soon found it was quite hopeless to get them to do business steadily. There are, no doubt, some quite respectable men of this class, but I was unable to find them. One Roman Catholic printer came down to Kenmare from Dublin without my knowing his intention until he arrived. He implored me to give him employment, which I was most unwilling to do from past experience, but I yielded at last to his entreaties.

Before the work was half finished, he got into financial difficulties, and as I refused to pay him until his order was completed, he went to the then Archbishop of Dublin, and told him I had refused to pay him. This archbishop had no right to interfere with my affairs, as I did not belong to his diocese, but he did so all the same, and wrote a very angry letter to me, without waiting to inquire into my side of the question. I was very angry, too, which I suppose I ought not to have been, and replied by telling his grace what I thought of his uncalled-for interference, and how this man had forced me to employ him and then broken his own agreement. For years afterwards, and for all I know, to this day, this incident was reported all over Ireland and England, and was given as another proof of my disposition to disagree with ecclesiastical authority.

The Right Rev. Dr. Moriarty was my bishop and ecclesiastical superior for many years, and he wrote the following letter to me in consequence of the annoying interferences and criticisms, blaming me for occupying myself in literary work because I was a sister : —

"THE PALACE, KILLARNEY, Oct. 24, 1876.

" MY DEAR SISTER IN CHRIST, — I learn that you are issuing some new works, and some new editions of those already published. Your literary labors reflect honor on your convent, on your order, and on your diocese.

" But I rejoice much more in this, that you are contributing to supply some of our greatest needs — a Catholic Literature. I know, too, that the funds realized by the sale of your works are exclusively devoted to the service of religion.

"Praying God to bless you, and to preserve your health and strength, yours sincerely in Christ,

"† D. MORIARTY.

"To SISTER M. FRANCIS CLARE, Convent of Poor Clares, Kenmare, County Kerry"

I remember the occasion of this letter. I had been very much annoyed by attacks made on me for writing, and absurd as it may seem, the large circulation of my books was made a special ground of censure. Our good bishop used to visit Kenmare frequently, and on this occasion I spoke to him about my trouble. He opened a desk which lay on the table near him, and after writing the letter given above, he handed it to me for publication.

I knew of course, very well, that Bishop Moriarty very highly approved of my literary work; but in the difficulties which I had had to encounter, his written approbation, and one so plain and explicit, was a great consolation to me.

It is quite evident that if every sister occupied her time in writing it would not be consistent with the object of a sister's life, but every rule has its exception, and a bishop even reproached me once with occupying myself in any way except writing. He said, "You get your gift from God, you cannot hand it down to your children. You are bound to use it to the utmost."

Nor is this occupation out of harmony with the religious life. On the contrary, it was one of the chief occupations of some of the most saintly religious. Montalembert, in his "Monks of the West," gives examples of sisters who excelled in every branch of literature, as linguists, as writers, as historians, as scientists, and as in the case of St. Catharine of Siena, as political writers.

I may add here another amusing story of my ecclesiastical critics. When I was in Rome, the superioress of a convent there told me, that one of the many charges made against me, (all of which were examined into and disproved), was that I wrote novels.

CHAPTER VI.

THE FAMINE YEAR IN IRELAND.

Chronic Distress in Ireland — Favor of the Holy See for England — Attacked for my Historical Writings — State of the Irish people — Relations between Irish and English Catholics — the Catholics the Oppressors of Ireland — Dr. McCarthy, His Character — Lord Landsdowne's Attitude — Attacked by Rev. Mr. Angus — Appeal to Cardinal Manning — Letter from Archdeacon O'Sullivan — Two Archdeacons O'Sullivan — A Curious Episode — Mr. Angus continues his Attacks — He is Silenced by Legal Proceedings — The *Morning Post* Apologizes — My Labors in the Famine Year — Distress of the Poor — Indian Meal for a Family of Five — Letter from W. J. Sullivan to the *Freeman's Journal*.

WHO needs to be told that Ireland is in a chronic state of famine and distress? Who needs to be told that since Pope Adrian handed Ireland over to the English by papal bull and by his infallible authority, in return for a payment of Peter's pence, Ireland has been in a state of constant misery? Unhappy Ireland! and yet the Irish people all over the world are the best support, both temporally and spiritually, of the Pope.

Truly, they are a marvellous people.

One thing is historically certain: the Holy See has always thrown its strongest support on the side of England, and England is well aware of this, and necessarily makes it an important element in her political calculation.

But there is another view of this subject, not so well known to the general public in America. It is this: English Roman Catholics and the upper class of Irish Catholics, or those who like to be considered such, have always been the sternest opponents of Irish nationality, and the harshest in their dealings with the Irish people.

I do not doubt that if Ireland were left exclusively to the government of English Protestants it would to-day be prosperous; but it would also be Protestant. In the past of Ireland, its religious history and its political history cannot be separated, and it is one of the most curious of national records.

Neither time nor space will admit of my going into this matter here, but a list of my published works, or at least some of them, will be found in the *appendix*,* and in several of these, full reports and explanation on the subject can be obtained.

I must also say that when I entered the Roman Catholic Church, I was entirely ignorant of Irish history and of the disputes between English and Irish Catholics. I was soon to receive full and very painful enlightenment.

I did not occupy myself with historical writings until after I went to Kenmare, when I wrote the first of my many histories of Ireland. I was by no

* See Appendix.

means prepared for the storm of indignation with which the work was received by some English Catholics. Say what they will, they were English first and Catholics after.

The secret of their treatment of Ireland is a simple one. Before the act of emancipation (for which English Catholics, whether of distinguished or of humble parentage, have to thank Ireland and O'Connell) they lived as a body apart, they rarely if ever associated with their Protestant neighbors, and, like all exclusive bodies of men, became intensely selfish and intensely proud. They were under the impression that they alone constituted the church; and if they did not say so in so many words, they certainly acted at least as if they thought so. They considered that they had paid the church a very high honor by remaining members of it under so many centuries of persecution, and certainly English Roman Catholics were at one time as much persecuted as the Irish. But then English Catholics were very little thankful for emancipation; I believe because emancipation gave the Irish political liberty, and they only expressed gratitude when they found the additional social advantages it obtained for themselves.

The Irish people, when they were placed under the feet of the English by the bull of Pope Adrian, were despised by the English as a conquered nation. Those who are guilty of injustice, with rare exceptions, despise their victims. To the English Catholics it was galling to be related even in faith to this despised people. They would have disowned them altogether, but, as this was impossible, all they could do was to show their contempt for them, even more plainly than their fellow-countrymen. The whole proceeding was simple and natural, and the situation can easily be understood.

But there was yet another element in this peculiar case. A number of English Catholics, after Catholic emancipation had been obtained for them by the blood and sufferings of the Irish race, began to occupy positions of trust and honor, and as Irish Catholics rose also in the social scale, some intermarriages took place. This was by no means to the advantage of the Irish people. English Catholics need money to support their position as much as their Protestant neighbors, and where could money be got more easily than from an Irish estate, where "rent" can always be raised and mortgages effected.

Some English Catholics also purchased land in Ireland when property was selling under the Encumbered Estates Act. Hence quite a number of English Catholics became Irish landlords, and they showed their love and loyalty to the Pope by calling on him frequently to make their hapless tenants pay their rent and to silence their complaints. It mattered little to them where the rents were to come from ; the tenants may starve at home, or their children may work in America to get it, but if it is not paid, their religious feelings are deeply hurt, and they exclaim in horror at the wickedness of a race who still persist in not doing what both God and man have rendered it impossible for them to do.

To write a fair history of Ireland was bad enough, but it came to the famine of 1879, and all the English Roman Catholic landlords were quite as angry as Protestants, and more so.

Indeed, the Irish question may be fairly described as a money question, and the landlords in a chronic state of wanting their rents (for rents are money), and the Irish people in a chronic state of refusing to pay them, because bad seasons and the failure of crops, which were their only pecuniary resource, had left them without the money which was so fiercely demanded.

If some safer means of making lands productive could be found than the hapless pig and the everfailing potato, there would be an immense saving of misery and police force.

It has always been to me perfectly incomprehensible why Irish landlords, whether Roman

Catholic or Protestant, and the English government, whether liberal or conservative, could not see that if one half of the money spent on coercion, special commissions, and famine funds, were expended in opening up industrial resources for the people, which would enable them to earn the money to pay their rents, there would be some ground to hope for the peaceful conclusion of the Irish question.

I must admit, however, that my own failures in this matter were palpable and discouraging; the history of them will be found when I relate what I attempted to do in County Mayo.

The Right Rev. Dr. McCarthy was bishop of Kerry in 1879. He was for many years President of Maynooth College, and otherwise associated with it. He told me more than once that such was the misery and distress in our diocese, that he would have resigned his see if I had not come to his assistance, by procuring food for the people.

He was a man of great learning, of great piety, and of a very tender heart; he was also intensely national.

It did not answer, of course, for these English Catholics to denounce me for helping the poor, that would not have looked well; so they took another course, they denounced me for interfering in politics. Never was there a more absurd accusation, but it answered the purpose all the same. It mattered nothing to me who was in or who was out of office, or who was member for Dublin or for Kerry; but it did matter to me a great deal in view of our common humanity, and in view of my love of the poor, that I should do all I could for those whom He had loved so well; and from special circumstances I had the power to do a great deal.

It was my misfortune, or my fate, to live near the property of two gentlemen not remarkable for their humanity to their tenants. One was the Marquis of Landsdowne and the other was the Earl of Kenmare; one Protestant, the other Catholic. Both of these gentlemen lived principally in England, and rarely ever visited Ireland; they came only to economize or to get their rents from their tenants, which rents they spent in England or on the Continent. Now, if all the money which is got in any place is taken from that place and expended elsewhere, how is that place to prosper?

If saying this was interfering in politics, then I must plead guilty of having interfered in politics. It seems to me, however, it was not a question of politics, it was a question of humanity.

Lord Landsdowne's brother, Lord Fitz Maurice, took up the dispute on his brother's behalf, but being a gentleman, he wrote as a gentleman.

A Scotch priest, the Rev. Mr. Angus, took up the quarrel for the English Catholics; and whether they selected him, or he selected them for this office I do not know. This poor priest had neither property nor friends in Ireland, and his only qualification for his interference in other people's affairs, was presumably his ignorance of the country, and a natural inclination to pose as an important person.

As I was a woman and a nun, I was an easy prey. It would be necessary for me to write a volume if I gave a complete history of his impertinent interference in my private affairs, and he is not worth it. But he did all the harm which persons of his class can generally do.

His attacks on me in the English Catholic papers were so gross that Archbishop Croke at last interfered, and so far silenced him that they were obliged to refuse him space in their columns for his calumnies. These papers, at least one of them, were very dependent on Irish support, and though it did not matter to have a sister attacked for taking the part of the poor, it was quite another matter when a Catholic archbishop interfered.*

The storm was quieted for a time, and the meddlesome priest silenced, but it was only for a time.

* See Appendix, pages 501-506, where Archbishop Croke's and other letters will be found on this subject.

The following amusing letter will show that he needed occupation, and I most sincerely wish he could have found it in some other way besides interfering with me.

"DEAR SISTER MARY FRANCIS, — "It may be consoling for you to learn that Father Angus, your last defamer in the *Weekly Register*, is merely an amateur West London priest.

"He was formerly an Anglican parson, and what works of mercy or missionary duty he did as such, I am not aware ; but as a Catholic priest I know that, if you reckon in Ireland among the works of mercy a chaplaincy to an old lady, with the additional 'missionary duty' of having to air her pug dog every evening in Kensington garden, he will obtain a high place among the saints of heaven. "Believe me, yours faithfully,
"PHILIP P. PURCELL, Priest.
"P. S. You are at liberty to use this letter.
"Lincoln's Inn Fields, London, W. C., December 12, 1881."

This priest next commenced a series of attacks in the London *Morning Journal*; the editor, little supposing that a priest would make upon a sister an attack which was false from end to end, allowed him space. This poor priest was at that time in Cardinal Manning's diocese. Every one knows that Cardinal Manning is the very soul of honor and uprightness, and indeed, he also has suffered a good deal, especially from English Catholics, for taking up the cause of the Irish.

I appealed to Cardinal Manning for protection from this man, and my appeal was received with his usual kindness, but it was useless. Mr. Angus was one of those people who are always anxious to interfere in the affairs of others, and to play the *rôle* of director, but who would not submit to his own superiors.

Cardinal Manning's secretary wrote to me saying that Mr. Angus had again promised to discontinue his libels. But I seemed to have an irresistible attraction for him.

A letter of Archdeacon O'Sullivan, who was then and is now the parish priest of Kenmare, will show what was thought of his conduct by those who had a right to advise me. I give his letter here, —

"HOLY CROSS, KENMARE, May 13, 1882.

"MY DEAR SR. M. F. CLARE, — "I have waited till I finished my stations, to answer your welcome letter. I am glad to hear that you are succeeding in your noble undertaking, notwithstanding the many obstacles *Old Nick* is putting in your way.

"I was greatly annoyed at the attack made on you by the Scotch or English priest, Father Angus. Did this man imagine he was called to do the work of Irish bishops and priests who ought naturally look after and correct Irish nuns, if they were going astray.

"I sincerely sympathize with you in the many heavy trials you had to endure since you left Kenmare.

"You may remember I was opposed to your leaving; however, I knew if you were convinced that you were called to found a convent at Knock, nothing could deter you.

"Horrible business, the murder of Lord Cavendish and Burke. A feeling of sickness comes over me when I think of it. Will Ireland ever outlive the villany of her own sons?

"Accept the inclosed five pounds as a small token of my sincere regard for you, and the noble work you are engaged in. I truly regret my means don't permit me to make the offering a hundred times greater.

"With warmest wishes for your happiness here and hereafter, believe me, my dear Sister M. F. Clare, ever sincerely yours,

"M. O'SULLIVAN, P. P."

I should explain that there were two Archdeacon O'Sullivans in Kenmare at different times. The first Archdeacon O'Sullivan was the "Father John" who brought us to Kenmare, and whose death was such a grievous loss to me. I have seldom met any one with such sublime ideas of

God. He used to speak out very plainly about some Roman Catholic devotions which he did not approve, and I often heard him criticise the lessons in the breviary, which all priests are obliged to recite daily, in a way which would have very much astonished the authorities in Rome if they had heard him. He was a great reader of the Bible, and often told me how much he wished it was more read by Roman Catholics. It is certainly no injustice to his memory to say he decidedly discouraged those devotions to the saints which are so popular with priests. Still when some ladies tried to proselytize some of his flock, by sending a Bible reader amongst them, he took very summary measures to stop them.

I may say here that I found Father John was by no means singular in his views on these subjects. I was visiting the Jesuit Fathers in New York last year on business, and as I was going up the steps to the college, I met a lady who appeared to be a stranger, and who asked me if she could see one of the fathers. I told her I was going to ask for one of the fathers whom I knew, and if he could arrange her business for her I could wait. She then told me she was a Southern lady, and was remaining only a few days in New York; that she had been requested by a near relative to procure a picture of the Holy Face for her, and so long as she obtained what she wanted, it did not matter whom she saw. I asked for the father with whom I had business, and thought he would be just the person to arrange this matter. When he came into the parlor, I offered to leave the room, but the lady requested me to remain, as she did not desire to have any private conversation with the father.

She then told him what she wanted, and I shall never forget his exclamation of, I may say, indignation. "The Holy Face!" he exclaimed, "why by and by we shall not want Almighty God any more." It would take too long to relate the whole conversation, and I could only listen in utter amazement; as for the lady, she was too surprised to speak, and she withdrew without saying one word, except that she thought that this devotion was approved by the Roman Catholic church, which it certainly is.

But I must return from this episode of my many curious experiences, to the second Archdeacon O'Sullivan, whose letters to me will speak for his goodness of heart and mind, and his regard for me, which has never failed. This good priest succeeded the present bishop of Kerry, Dr. Higgins, who was a parish priest of Kenmare for a short term before he was made bishop. He had nearly as many votes for elevation to the episcopate as the present bishop, but he had not the same powerful influence at Rome through the landlord class, who have a strong voice in such affairs.

I wrote to Cardinal Manning several times about the annoyance Father Angus was giving me, and his eminence each time tried to stop him. The following letter will show how he evaded the requests of his eminence, and how little idea he had of submission to ecclesiastical authority.

It will be seen from the letter given below that I was at last obliged to place this matter in the hands of my solicitors.

After this, Father Angus ceased his public attacks on me over his own signature, but he continued them anonymously all the same, and over his own signature in private.

"22 FINSBURY CIRCUS, E. C.
"24 November, 1883.

"To MESSRS FRY & SONS, SOLICITORS, DUBLIN:

"GENTLEMEN: The cardinal has given me your letter, and in reply thereto I beg to say that I have seen Father Angus on several occasions, and spoken most seriously about his communications to the newspapers. He, on each occasion promised me they should cease. By this post, at the request of his eminence, I am communicating with him, and I trust this will have the desired effect, and prove satisfactory to Sister Mary Francis Clare and yourselves.

"I am, gentlemen,
"Yours very truly,
(Signed) "DANIEL (CANON) GILBERT,
"*Vicar-General.*"

It would seem indeed, that Mr. Angus was free in promising obedience to his superiors, but somehow the temptation to speak evil of me was too much for him. In October, 1882 I was obliged to take legal proceedings to silence him.

The editor of the *Morning Post* was shocked when he found how he had been deceived; he at once apologized to me very fully in his paper, and inserted a contradiction of Father Angus's libels.

Mr. Angus was now silenced, as far as public attacks were concerned. For some time previous he had occupied himself in sending me anonymous letters, and extracts from papers containing abusive and insulting paragraphs about myself. As I could not bear the worry and annoyance of these things, I returned many of his letters unopened. But this only excited his indignation still more. It seemed, unless he was sure that I knew of his attacks on me, that they could not give him any satisfaction.

In England, happily, there is a law to protect character, and if you are libelled in the public press, you can obtain the name of your libeller and take an action for damages against him, or against the paper that has published the libel, or both.

I regret now that I did not take an action against Mr. Angus, as doing so would probably have silenced him in private, also, and perhaps saved much of what has happened since; but as he was a priest, I forebore.

Later it will be seen that I had also to obtain the name of a priest who had libelled me in the press in connection with the Knock schools, and to my great grief, I found that this priest was no other than Archdeacon Cavanagh. Indeed if I had not seen the libel in his own handwriting, I could not possibly have believed that he was the author of it.

One of the absurd accusations which Mr. Angus brought against me was that I belonged to the " Ladies' Land League." It so happened, that I never had anything to do with that body. I believe that an American bishop is under the same impression at present, probably having obtained his information from the same untrustworthy source.

It will be right for me here to give some account of what I did in the "Famine Year" of 1879-80, and I will let others speak of it rather than myself.

When the distressed state of the country was known, funds poured in from all parts of the world, and as I had a very large correspondence, and was well known through my writings in Australia and India, as well as in America, it was natural that money should be sent to me for distribution. Some people doubted public committees and other mediums of distribution, and they thought I would know best when and where to expend their charity for them.

After Mayo and the West, Kerry is the poorest part of Ireland. But I did not do more for it than I did for other places, although I lived in it. Unless a place was specified, as often happened, by the donors, where they wanted the money spent which they sent me, I distributed it as fairly as possible wherever I knew it was most needed. I felt it to be a most sacred trust, and tried to fulfil it as sacredly and carefully as possible.

One of my objects was, while helping for the present, to provide for the future. The potato, being the staple food of the Irish people, had degenerated, and new seed was most urgently needed. Indeed the principal cause of the distress was the failure of the potato crop, and the inferior quality of the seed.

A clergyman of the Episcopal church sent me

a dozen potatoes from a parish near Cork, in a letter; they were about the size of marbles, and these, he said, were all the people had to live on. The Catholic priest and he acted together most harmoniously and he joined with this clergyman in an appeal to me to send them seed potatoes. A similar appeal was made to me from Achil by the Episcopal clergyman and the priest.

A gentleman writing to the *Bolton Guardian*, England, said, —

"It is not long since an important letter appeared in a London contemporary under the heading 'Distress in Ireland.' It was from the pen of Miss Cusack, the well-known nun, Sister Mary Francis Clare, of the convent Kenmare, County Kerry. I cannot introduce my present subject better than by citing one or two sentences from that letter. Miss Cusack says she knows, at this moment, families of comparative respectability who live on dry bread and tea. As to meat of any kind, it is an unknown luxury. As for the poor laborers, Indian meal is their sole subsistence. Few of us in England know what Indian meal is; it may be described as a coarse and watery apology for food which was introduced into Ireland at the time of the famine, and which has lingered in the markets ever since as a sort of **alternative against starvation.** No millowner in

Bolton would consider it good enough for his horses.*

"Miss Cusack gives the case of a poor woman who came to the convent to her the other day and confided her circumstances to her. The poor woman's husband had just recovered from fever, his head was swollen, and he was not able to work. She had three children who were receiving education in the free school of the convent, and the poor mother begged, for the love of God, 'we would give her a stone of Indian meal a week.'

"'A stone of Indian meal a week,' exclaims Miss Cusack, 'and nothing else, for a family of five.' If this is not poverty, I know not what poverty is. Fourteen pounds of Indian meal a week, and nothing else for a family of five. Two pounds of Indian meal a day for five persons, of whom one is recovering from fever, and where there are three growing children. Six ounces of Indian meal a day and water! no milk, no bread, no tea, for each member of an Irish home! This is the fact which Miss Cusack gives to the people of England as a sample of Irish distress. The object of this excellent lady is to raise contribu-

* My American readers will be surprised to hear "Indian Meal" spoken of so disrespectfully, but I must explain that the sweet, delicious "Indian corn" of the American dinner-table is not even known in England or Ireland. If Americans could see or taste the compound, I fear of sawdust and bad flour, called Indian meal or "yallow male" which is doled out in famine and other times to the poor Irish, they would not wonder that it is considered not good enough for horses, and hardly fit for pigs.

tions to relieve the distress. I can only wish her godspeed. I thank her for the fact and for the beautiful spirit manifested in her letter."

The following is an extract from a letter written by Mr. J. Sullivan, Kenmare, to the editor of the Dublin *Freeman's Journal:*

"Distress in its very worst form is sapping the lives of our ablest bodied peasants, and making them, in appearance, animated skeletons. I have ventured to send you an account of a scene I was a most unwilling witness of in this town to-day. About midday there were assembled some five hundred to six hundred men and women, of all ages, whose faces denoted want and misery; starvation being too plainly imprinted on visages which, in more prosperous times, would have bloomed with the ruddy hue of health. This mass of starving humanity rushed in evident frenzy to the several provision stores, to get the dole meted out to each individual by the gentlemen who form the committee for distributing relief; and wobegone, indeed, was the expression of the face of him or her who was kept too long waiting for what seemed to be a long-expected meal. Such a scene the writer never witnessed before, although he has passed through several towns where relief was being distributed. Distress seemed to have reached its culminating point here, and hard, indeed, must be the hearts of landlords and agents who can say no great distress exists, or who have made no efforts to save the people, when such cases are daily enacted in their presence, as they are here.

"Now, I find on inquiry that the fund which purchases food for this starving population has been obtained solely by that most estimable lady, 'The Nun of Kenmare.' The landlords or agents, with one or two exceptions, have not done anything to aid her in her noble efforts. The poor, starving people have to depend almost entirely on the funds obtained by that lady for relief. She has disbursed within a very short period, very little short of $10,000, to the poor of this district, and it might be truly said, if there was no 'Nun of Kenmare' many a cold grave would be filled through starvation ere this. Such a benefactress is worth a legion of speechmakers; for while they are talking she is working. Work such as hers should not be allowed to pass unrecorded, and her noble donors will, no doubt, learn with delight they have opened their purses to one both capable and willing to apply the funds at her disposal to the object for which she has appealed, and possibly, supplement her store, and give her ample means of carrying out her heaven-born ideas of saving a wretched, starving people from disease and death."

CHAPTER VII.

The Nun of Kenmare's Distress Fund — Object of the Fund — Methods of Relief — Letters from Mr. O'Connell, Rev. C. O'Sullivan, from Protestant Clergymen, and Others — Appeals and Thanks from Convents — A Threatening Letter — Appeal to Chief Secretary Foster — His Reply — Indignation Meeting at Kenmare — Remarks of Ven. Archdeacon O'Sullivan, Rev. J. Molineux, Mr. Fitzgerald, Mr. Harrington, and Others.

THE object of my fund was, first, to supplement, as far as possible the relief, often wholly inadequate, given by the public funds. Second, to enable clergymen of all denominations, and sisters, to exercise a most necessary discretion in assisting their destitute people, and to enable them to give such help in cases of severe sickness or weakness, as would not be allowed to be given from the public funds.*

One priest, in by no means the worst parish in Ireland, wrote to me: "I got thirteen shillings yesterday for Masses, but I gave it all away in five minutes after. I am keeping part of what you

* Nothing was allowed to be given except "Indian meal"; not even to the sick, the dying, or little children. The horrible suggestion was made by London newspapers that even this was to be made as distasteful as possible. The reader should know also that this meal had often to be eaten uncooked; there had been a failure of fuel (turf) as well as of the potato.

sent ($250) in hand, for the priests must have something to give, the people expect it from us. When I say, 'Where would I get it from?' They answer, with their beautiful and pure faith, 'Oh, from God.' How then can the priest shake the faith of the people, that faith which has been their stay for ages?" And the priest who writes me this adds, "when they say this I am shut up at once. I take what you have sent 'from God.'"

It was important to have a fund to help the convents in the distressed districts; besides which there was the additional advantage of bringing the children to school, by giving them food and clothing. Thousands of children were unable to attend school for want of food and clothing.

I could fill a volume if I gave extracts from the letters I received from priests and nuns in every part of Ireland. I will only add a few letters received by me within the space of a few weeks from Protestant clergymen, Catholic gentlemen, Protestant ladies, and Catholic priests, all unknown to each other, and living in districts hundreds of miles apart; proofs that the distress was increasing; that it would continue for many months; that the amount given to each place by all the public funds, *even where all gave to one place*, was far short of supplying anything like the amount necessary even for existence.

Mr. O'Connell of Derrynane, to whom I sent large help, both in food and seed potatoes, wrote:

"I hope you will be able to send us more aid; we want it badly, as the pittances we get from the Duchess of Marlborough's fund and the Mansion House funds only go a very little way in this large district."

In another letter he says, —

"MY DEAR SISTER FRANCIS CLARE, — You have done a wonderful work in and about Kenmare, in relieving the poor, and in other parts of this diocese. For your munificent gift of $500 for seed potatoes to this district, I and my poor neighbors can never be sufficiently grateful. As for Kenmare itself, from all I know and hear, I believe you, and you only, have prevented a famine there. I can only hope and pray, that you may be enabled to carry on your good work to the end, and to support the poor for the next few months, the most trying time of all. That you will have your reward hereafter, I am sure; the prayers of God's poor cannot fail to be heard for you."

In a third letter he says, —

"I wish you could give us some more help for food soon. We have seven hundred families to provide for. There are two other districts in Iveragh which sorely want aid. Glenbeigh, where the distress is terrible, no relief works of any kind, and no one save the priest to do anything. Father Magin will, I know, be grateful if you can help him.

"The other district is the two parishes of Prior and Killmalage, both very poor, and very little being done in the way of drainage, etc. If you can send help for them, you may rely on its being properly expended and accounted for. I shall of course keep an account of the distribution of your potatoes. I can do it without any expense."

I sent over $1000 to this district in one month, and yet another urgent appeal came.

It is well known that Mr. O'Connell is one of the best landlords in Ireland, devoted to his people, and no absentee. I received from other gentlemen, some of them Protestant landlords, similar appeals, all saying that no matter how they economized, or what help they have got, starvation and nakedness were felt on every side.

The Rev. C. O'Sullivan, P. P., The Mines, writes, —

"A thousand thanks for your magnificent donation of $500, and a thousand blessings. There are fresh applicants every day. It is now the distress is only setting in; and I am afraid that no assistance, no matter how large, will be able to cope with the poverty and misery of this district (South Kerry) in the months of April, May, June, and July next."

He then cites a number of cases, and one family whose sole help for the support of seven people was sixpence a day, earned by a little girl in the mines. Five hundred dollars seems a very large sum of money, and those who have not the experience of priests and nuns imagine it ought to feed thousands for months to come. But when there are perhaps four thousand, sometimes six thousand, in one parish, all having no food whatever, or any way of getting food, it is easy to calculate how far this sum will go in food of the coarsest kind, and to see that nothing will be left for clothing.

The parish priest of Achill, and the Protestant rector, to whom I sent help, wrote that at the best of times the population were on the verge of starvation. What must it be now? They said an English lady had written to them about providing clothing; but unless an immense quantity were sent it would be useless, as there were from five thousand to six thousand people almost naked. In many parishes there were hundreds of children who could not go to school because they had not sufficient clothing for common decency. Some of the teachers told me, with tears in their eyes, they had to send the children home, because they could not, especially in the mixed schools, allow the poor children to come so destitute even of decent covering.

The Protestant rector of Achill sent me a vote of thanks for the relief I sent to him and the Catholic priest. I must say that I had no little consolation in this matter. Again and again I received warm-hearted thanks from Protestant clergymen for the help that I had sent to the Catholic priest, as well as for the help I had been able to give them; and not the least warm thanks were given by the Protestant rector of Kenmare, and of the two neighboring parishes.*

The Protestant clergyman of Achill wrote me, —

"The committee wish to convey to the good Nun of Kenmare their heartfelt thanks for her generous and large-hearted donation. They have a strong reason to enlist the charitable sympathy, as well as the influence and powerful voice, of Sister M. Francis Clare for Achill, and they wish to make known to her the dire and terrible distress prevailing at present in this immense parish. Out of one thousand one hundred families, six thousand five hundred souls, nine hundred and sixty families are in urgent need of weekly relief from the committee, and seventy more families are in equal need, but cannot be relieved for want of funds.
(Signed) "*Protestant rector*, J. B. GREER, Clk.
"*Catholic priest*, R. BIGINS, C. C."

* This portion of the present work consists principally of documents which may perhaps be useful to future historians, and it will at least give a good idea of the state of Ireland from private and contemporary sources.

A Protestant lady wrote to me to ask if she could use part of the help I had the happiness of sending her for clothing. I knew she could manage to make a little money go further than any one else in her district, where there were no nuns, and the help had been sent for food. She said, —

"I cannot find words to thank you from myself, and on behalf of the many poor creatures whose hearts your generous gift will comfort and make glad. But I would ask you kindly to allow me to expend one half of the amount of check in clothing. You can form no idea of how miserably naked many poor creatures are. I saw some girls doing some spring labor in my husband's fields a few days ago with nothing on them but a threadbare flannel petticoat and the tattered shreds of an old shawl tied across their shoulders. I am doubtful if they had any under garments; they felt shy at even my having seen them. I never seemed to notice, but I did feel in my heart for them, and will now, God helping me, exert myself in every way to get them a little clothing. Don't I wish we had Father N—— here for a few weeks, left to his own resources, and he would feel as well as see what Irish distress means." *

The Protestant rector of Inchiguila wrote, —

"We (the parish priest and himself, who are

* Father N—— was an English priest who expressed doubts as to the distress, which prevented help from coming there.

working most happily and unitedly) are much obliged for the discretionary powers you have given us in dealing with your very large donation. O, that we had even a few such! we would then be enabled to bring gladness to many a home, now wretched homes, and joy and hope to many a sad heart. We have not received from all quarters anything like an equivalent to the demand. We yesterday relieved on our own responsibility, doing so in faith and hope, 249 families, comprising 1,379 individuals. In this work of faith and hope, we were greatly cheered by your kind letter and contents. Our great and pressing want is seed; but we dare not, with the means at our disposal, venture on the providing it. Why it is we do not get a share of the Castle Fund we do not know. I think that were the distribution more general, and evenly dealt out to all in distress, the contributions would be large and continuous. We cannot call it an institution for the relief of distress in Ireland that overlooks and passes by on the other side a section of the destitute of Ireland."

Here are some brief extracts from appeals or thanks for help from convents.

Sister M. P——, Convent of Mercy, C——, wrote, —

"You have no idea of the pain it gives us not to be able to help our poor school children.

There is an opposition school called the Church School. I had an encounter yesterday with a poor widow who came to take her child away from us to the parson or any one who would feed and clothe her. The poor child was actually starving. The one hundred dollars you sent will save many a soul."

The Rev. Mother, Convent, B——:

"Your two hundred and fifty dollars was indeed a welcome gift to a convent in such a poverty-stricken district; there are hundreds of human beings crying for relief, and we have no means to help them."

The Rev. Mother, Cl——:

"May God bless you for your charity, so pure, universal, and disinterested. The number in terrible need of clothing and food would puzzle one. All asking for work, and no work for them. Your one hundred dollars will do great good."

Mother A——, Convent, B——:

"We have got no help, except ten dollars, since you sent the last two hundred and fifty dollars, and we have had fever, many cases of which we are attending as they cannot be moved to hospital. We got spillars (fishing lines) out of the last money you sent, so this will be a permanent relief, and seed potatoes, which Father —— is distributing."

Sister M. P., Convent of St. —— :

"Your two hundred and fifty dollars will indeed relieve hundreds who are truly in a pitiable condition."

It is useless to occupy space with further details. I have taken these extracts without selection from a pile of similar letters.

The Rev. J. O'Sullivan, Port Magee, —

"There are thousands here on the verge of ruin. In one house, yesterday, I saw seven children crying with hunger."

I sent two hundred and fifty dollars at once, though we had not half that sum left, but God be praised, more than that came next morning, and was sent to other places and other priests, equally destitute.

Canon Bresnan, P. P., Caherciveen, writes, —

"There are upwards of 800 destitute families here. How we are to struggle through the next five or six months, I know not; as for clothing, $4,000 would not supply the barely necessary want, whilst some 500 children are unfit to appear in school through this want. Dear sisters, do all you can to help me in this great work of need and charity. Praying God to send you more and more, " I am, yours most truly,

"J. CANON BRESNAN."

In November, 1881, I received a threatening letter from London, which caused a great deal of feeling in Ireland, and all the more so because some of the National Party were accused of having sent letters to obnoxious landlords. I took the matter for what it was probably worth, a mere bravado. If I had been assassinated, to have died for the cause of charity would have been a happy end to my troubled life. The matter was communicated to Mr. Forster, then chief secretary for Ireland, and I received the following letter in consequence. The threatening letter which I received was posted in London, and was apparently written by an educated person. I append here a copy of the letter received from Mr. Forster in consequence of communication made to him on the subject.

CHIEF SECRETARY'S LODGE, PHŒNIX PARK,
DUBLIN, November 15, 1881.

"MADAM, — Mr. Forster desires me to acknowledge the receipt of your letter of the 8th inst., and is sorry to hear you have received so insulting and atrocious a letter.

"Mr. Forster can only add that atrocious and insulting letters appear to be often written in Ireland, and the nature of the offence is one which makes it very difficult for the law to deal with.

"I am, madam, your obedient servant,

HORACE WEST, *Sec.*

"TO SISTER M. FRANCIS CLARE."

A public meeting was held in Kenmare, to denounce the writer of this letter, on the tenth of December, and I give a few extracts from the report as published in the *Kerry Sentinel.* As is usual in Ireland, the meeting was held on Sunday. I may perhaps say that I have never received even the least expression of sympathy or interest from the Kenmare people since I left Kerry, which shows how little their expressions of gratitude and excitement were worth.

THREATENING THE NUN OF KENMARE — GREAT INDIGNATION MEETING AT KENMARE.

(From the *Kerry Sentinel.**)

KENMARE, *Sunday evening.*

The answer which South Kerry has this day given to the insult offered to the gifted nun, who has made Kenmare famous the world over, was both dignified and defiant. The promoters of the meeting rightly interpreted the threatening letters to Sister Mary Francis as an expression of anger on the part of the landlords or their partisans at the testimony which she has given in her writings and in her interviews, to the sad condition of the people of the district, and hence the meeting received the character of a monster land demonstration as well as indignation meeting. The town

* An equally full report of this meeting was published in the Cork and Dublin papers.

was filled long before twelve o'clock Mass. Large crowds came in from the different parishes surrounding Kenmare, headed by their priests. The Killarney brass band brought from Kilgarvan direction the largest contingent. They were met outside of the town by a splendid body of Kenmare men, marshalled by stewards wearing green rosettes. They carried a splendid banner, with the device "Kenmare resents the insult offered to Sister Mary Francis. Behold her bodyguard." There were between six thousand and eight thousand persons present at the meeting. Green favors were worn by the great majority of those present, and by the ladies, who mustered in very large force at the meeting. The proceedings commenced shortly after two o'clock. The meeting was held in the inclosure attached to the magnificent church, where a platform was erected.

On the motion of the Rev. M. Sheehan, P. P., seconded by Rev. J. Molyneux, the chair was taken by Ven. Archdeacon O'Sullivan,* P.P.,V.G.

The venerable chairman, who was received with loud cheers, then* addressed the meeting. He said, — I thank you, my friends, for the honor conferred on me in asking me to preside at this great meeting. I beg to assure you it is with feelings of the deepest pain I refer to the occasion which has called you all together to-day. I need not

* The Archdeacon O'Sullivan who presided at the meeting was the second of the name, as stated at page 80.

anticipate the expression of your detestation of the dastardly conduct of that vile specimen of humanity who dared by his threatening letters to insult the gifted and noble-hearted lady who has shed a lustre, not only on the holy community of which she is such an ornament, but on the country at large. She has made the name of this little town known, wherever the English language is spoken, and where literary labors of the highest excellence are appreciated. O'Connell never conferred on his native Kerry more honor or more glory than has the Nun of Kenmare on this hitherto unknown and remote locality. To enumerate to you the numberless productions of her pen, which have graced the various walks of literature, would be beside the purpose and object of this great meeting. The thousands of pounds she collected and distributed amongst the starving inhabitants, not only of Glanerough and Dunkerron, but of every parish in and out of Kerry from which the cry of distress reached her ears, prove to you, if proof were necessary, that the spirit of her holy founder, St. Francis of Assisi, pervades her soul, and that she is anxious to realize in her own conduct the great love that he manifested for the poor of Christ. And because in the exercise of her free will and judgment, she dared to give her views on the burning question of the day, which engrosses the attention of statesmen of all parties, and thoughtful men of all classes, a cowardly person has sent from London an anonymous letter, threatening her with the fate that Rory of the Hills has in reserve for the victims of his displeasure.

A VOICE. — Let them come and try it.

The CHAIRMAN. — In the annals of human depravity, nothing more detestable or base could be found, and I need not ask you, my friends, what you think of such conduct and how it ought to be dealt with, when in a nation of gallant men, of men of honor and of cavaliers, ten thousand swords would have leaped from their scabbards to avenge the insult offered to this illustrious lady. The London miscreant who penned it seemed to forget that Ireland is still Catholic, and that nuns and the monks cannot here be maltreated with the same impunity as in England. He seems to forget that the foul anti-Catholic spirit which is now manifesting itself in Germany, France, and Italy, has no home in Ireland, and with God's blessing never shall have. The infidel in England and the infidel revolutionist of the Continent may think it safe amusement to assail and insult the members of religious orders, but should they avow their purpose in Ireland something worse than the threats of vengeance uttered by " Rory of the Hills " might befall them. Do not we live under the Constitution? Is not every subject born under this much vaunted palladium of liberty entitled to give his views freely and fearlessly on public men and public measures, on Irish landlords and Irish agents, and on English home and foreign policy. And why should this right be denied to Sister Mary Francis Clare?

The Rev. M. Nelligan, who acted as secretary to the meeting, read the following letters of apology which he had received : —

"ADRIGOLE, Dec. 3, 1880.

"DEAR AND REV. SIR, — I deeply regret that it will be quite impossible for me to be present at the great indignation meeting in Kenmare on Sunday. Need I assure the Dunkerron and Glenerough men, assembled in their thousands to sympathize with the noble-hearted Sister M. F. Clare for the insult offered her, that I am with them in spirit. The indefatigable and successful exertions of the gifted Nun of Kenmare, on behalf of her famine-stricken fellow-beings has drawn on her devoted head the ire of some enemy of the Irish race. That she did not confine her labors and charities to Kenmare alone, where she did wonders to avert famine, is notorious. She has been the generous benefactress of many places, her charity being as unbounded as distress was deep and widespread. In this afflicted barony of Bere no parish was left unaided. When want and sickness raged from end to end of my own Clenlaurence, her fifty-pound checks came regularly, and in time to save hundreds from the horrors of starvation. Knowing where and when to give, she fed the hungry; scores of ragged and naked children were clothed at her expense; for those who had not a potato to put in the ground, she sent seed to crop the land. For this poor district, and others like it, she has, alone and unaided, done more to relieve distress than the largest and best-disposed of the charitable committees. In return, she has what to her is dearer than the treasures of earth — the good wishes of the poor.

"JAMES NELIGAN, P. P."

"EXTON PARK, OAKHAM, ENGLAND, Dec. 8, 1880.

"DEAR SISTER, — I have just seen the announcement in the papers that you have received some threatening letters, and feel impelled to write and say how deeply I feel the disgrace that any one who has labored as you have done for the good of common humanity could have been made the object of such petty spite. . . . I only hope it may be so, and that in any case God may long preserve you to work for our poor, persecuted race, as you have hitherto done.

"Wishing you every blessing for the coming season, I remain, sincerely yours,

"HENRY BELLINGHAM, M. P."

"THE PALACE, KILLARNEY, Dec. 1, 1880.

"MY DEAR FATHER NELIGAN, — I am sorry I cannot attend your meeting on Sunday, to join my voice with the many thousands which will be raised to condemn the unmeaning, ungentlemanly outrage that has been offered to the good Nun of

Kenmare. Wishing the meeting the success it deserves, I remain very sincerely yours,

"M. M'CARTHY, C. C."

"SNEEM, Dec. 3, 1880.

"DEAR REV. FATHER, — I can well understand why that the people of Kenmare and its surroundings cannot help being indignant at the mean, gross, and cowardly insult offered to Sister M. F. Clare. Though I should wish very much to be present at the meeting on Sunday next, to raise my voice in condemnation of so wanton an outrage, yet the duties of the day will render it impossible. "Yours faithfully,

"T. DAVIS, P. P."

"THE PALACE, KILLARNEY, Dec. 2.

"MY DEAR FATHER NELIGAN, — In reply to your kind note of invitation to the indignation meeting in Kenmare on Sunday next, I beg to express my regret that parochial duties will render it impossible for me to attend. Sympathizing heartily with the object of the meeting, and wishing it every success, believe me, yours very sincerely, "M. A. DILLON, C. C."

"FARRANFORE, Dec. 2.

"MY DEAR FATHER NELIGAN, — I regret that the obligation of Sunday duty here will not allow me to join in your expressions of indignation at the conduct of those who have offered insult to the good Nun of Kenmare, otherwise I would gladly do so; and whatever shall be said at your meeting in defence and vindication of that brave, learned, and true-hearted woman, shall command my entire sympathy and approval. Her charitable and able pen has been more nobly employed in soliciting and distributing alms to thousands of God's poor than that of the English lordling in vindictively maligning the good Nun of Kenmare.

"I remain, yours very faithfully,
"P. O'CONNOR, P. P."

"SNEEM, Dec. 3.

"MY DEAR FATHER NELIGAN,—I am very sorry that Sunday's duty will render it impossible for me to be present at your proposed meeting. I am very sorry for this, as of course the object of the meeting commands my sincerest sympathy. Hoping that your public protest against such cowardly outrages as your meeting is summoned to denounce, may prove a complete success.

"I remain, yours very sincerely,
"MAHONY LEYNE, C. C."

"THE PRESBYTERY, BALLYBUNNION, Dec. 7, 1880.

"MY DEAR FATHER NELIGAN,—I owe you a thousand apologies for not writing sooner. The fact of the matter is, that I have been so occupied for some time past that I could not read many of the letters I received. To give you an idea, as late as Friday last I had twenty persons, teachers and pupils, transcribing certain statistics I was

preparing for the Land League and Land Commission. Rest assured that no one attended your meeting, who more heartily condemns than I do, those dastardly attacks on that noble and benevolent woman, who has done so much for our suffering country, and I will add, in particular, for the people of this parish. Yours very sincerely,
"M. O'CONNOR, P. P."

The Rev. J. Molyneux supported the resolution. He said they had all come there at great inconvenience, and many of them from long distances; but he was sure that every man of them would come double the distance, and suffer ten times the inconvenience, in order to attend that meeting. That gifted lady, the Nun of Kenmare, had done more within the past year to save the lives of the people than all the landlords and agents in Kerry had ever done. If the Nun from her convent cell could see that magnificent meeting, she would see that they were a people worth laboring for, and worth fighting for. Last summer an American with whom he travelled said to him, — he was a Protestant and a gentleman of position in the United States, — "There is no living Irishman or Irishwoman better known or more respected in the United States than Sister Mary Francis Clare," and he added the extraordinary statement, "She is better known and more respected than even the Pope himself." They would all, he was sure, pray God might grant her strength and long life to work for the people of Kenmare and for Ireland. I myself have seen many a poor man trudge through yonder streets with the look of death upon his face, with the pinches of starvation on his forehead, and without a penny in his pocket, begging of the Kenmare merchants to give him as much provisions as would support himself and his little family for the ensuing week. But in most cases the merchant's books were closed, the poor man's credit was gone, and he went home like a waif, — a wandering waif, — dispirited and brokenhearted. But during the time there was a star arising, not in the firmament, but in that convent hard by, destined to brighten the night of that poor man's despondence, and to bring home peace, plenty, and comfort to the bosom of his poverty-stricken family. Yes, fellow-countrymen, that star has arisen, and the people call it Mary Francis Clare, and, like the star of Bethlehem, which guided the Magi of the Eastern nations to Jerusalem, so did Sister Clare guide and direct the charity of a world towards the support and regeneration of that unfortunate and famine-stricken land. From her lonely cell by the banks of that purling little Finnehe her voice rang over the Rocky Mountains of America; it was heard by the waters of the Pacific, and along the shores of San Francisco, and many the generous purse flew open at that call, and many, many the exiled Irish heart, blest that angelic voice which they ever heard raised in behalf of the poor, and holy Ireland.

A VOICE. — May God bless her.

MR. FITZGERALD. — Fellow-countrymen, you all heard of the spectral ghost which invaded the land in '46, '47, '48, and many among you to-day remember it. Yes, my friends, you remember your fellow-creatures being taken in boxes to the grave by the dozen, and a cat would not call it a grave. It was a huge yawning sepulchre, which swallowed up the manhood of this valley. It was an unlettered cairn where the bones of the poor lie mixed and mouldering to the present day. Now we had last winter a visit from the very same spectre, which, like a winged fury from the infernal regions, spread a terror and a gloom over this land. Thank God, he was scared away from this valley. But by whom? Was it by that government, that sent us buckshot? Was it by the landlords, that sent us writs? Was it by the guardians, that intimated emigration and transportation? No, my friends, he was scared away by the charity of foreign nations accumulated in Kenmare by Sister Clare. God bless her — may her shadow never grow less; and here to-day I proclaim from the platform that we want no hirelings to protect her. For did she require it, we'd form a rampart of our bodies around her, and our best hearts' blood would, for her sake, stain again the fields of old Ireland. That dastardly English coward, whoever he be, never made a greater mistake in his life than if he thought by his threats to intimidate our Nun from raising her voice on behalf of the poor and oppressed tenants of this country. He little knew the fire and patriotism that animated that noble heart. He little knew the love of fatherland which she infused into some of the young blood of Ireland. Through many a foreign country there are men to-day who, when boys, eagerly drank up the patriotism which flowed from the lectures of Sister Clare, and some would tell you to-day that they shall never forget her, for she taught them how to be Irishmen. Then, my friends, let us, too, profit by her teachings, be pure, be virtuous, be kind to your neighbors, and true to your country.

Mr. J. D. Sullivan, P.L.G., who was warmly received, proposed this resolution : —

"*Resolved.* — That, as the cause and root of the distress amongst all classes of the community, which this devoted child of St. Clare so largely relieved, still remain unremoved, we call upon the government and legislature of the country to pass such a land bill as will root the Irish farmer in the land of his birth, and save him and the laborers who coöperate with him in the tilling of the soil, from the periodic returns of famine and starvation."

He said: "Now, fellow-countrymen, what is the cause of this great distress amongst you? It is certainly owing to no fault of your own; it is owing to the pernicious land laws of the country, and until that same system has been removed, you may expect those peroidical famines. As long as your landlords have the power of life and death over you, as long as your landlords, let them be good or let them be bad, have the power to screw out of you the fruits and benefit of your hard toil and labor, so long you are sure to have those awful famines, which many amongst you have felt for the third time during your lives, and which has given our fertile, but unhappy country, the shameful name of a perpetual beggar. All of you tenant farmers recollect that about ten or twelve years since, you had a few years of comparative prosperity. You were then able to meet your demands — to rear and support your families in fair decency. But, my friends, you know what your landlords then said to you; they said, "You are now full of money from the produce of our lands, and you must pay us from twenty to thirty per cent increase on your rents." They said to you, "let us hear no grumbling, you must do it," and you had, my friends, to submit, and the few pounds you should have put into your pockets and laid up for an evil day, were forcibly robbed from you. But when the hour of distress came, what did your landlords do for you?

A Voice. — They did nothing.

Mr. Sullivan. — I will tell you; they allowed your cries of misery and distress to reach that good nun of that convent, to tax the energies of her fertile brain, and with its industry appeal to the charitable world for help for you,. which appeal was most generously responded to, and which help was by her so liberally distributed that even the landlords, for their own interest, were most anxious that their tenants would not be forgotten.

A Voice. — She was the means of paying the rent to many of them.

Mr. Sullivan. — You are now here, fellow-countrymen, protesting against that land-law, and demanding, with the farmers of all Ireland, that the government and the law makers of this kingdom should pass such a land bill, and enact such a law as will root you in the land of your birth, where the sweat of your brows, and the manhood of your youth have been buried, and that that sweat and that manhood should never again be confiscated. You demand at least fixity of tenure at fair rents, settled once and for ever, and a power of free sale, not that power that your landlord could say to you, "I will allow you sell to your interest, but the purchaser must pay me five shillings to the pound increase of rent," which power of sale is only an inducement to landlords that you should sell.

A Voice. — That's the Ulster custom in Kerry.

Mr. Sullivan. — "Now, my friends, you will excuse me when I say that you should lay a great share of blame at your own doors, on account of the mad competition for land which many amongst you have practised these years past, and which practice has ruined yourselves and injured the country at large. But, my friends, perhaps you ought to be excused also, for you were not then enlightened; but now you are, thanks to whom? to that great Irishman, Mr. Parnell. Fellow-countrymen, pledge yourselves this day, before that sacred temple near which you stand, and which has been the tomb and the shroud of that great Archdeacon, its builder, who was and will be long remembered as the great and the good Father John, who during life was the terror of tyrants, and who in his honored grave is the friend of the poor — not to take or not to purchase any farm, the rent of which has been increased, and by no means and on no account take any farm from which your neighbor has been evicted. These are peaceable but strong weapons in your hands, and weapons that will prove effective. You should also pledge yourselves not to commit crime, nor allow it to be committed, if you can; because at the present time, crime at your hands is the strongest and most powerful weapon your enemies and oppressors could wear or wield. The smallest crime is magnified, and from it, as it were, a small matter is made as big as Mangerton mountain yonder. You know a lying Tory press, and a landlord conspiracy are watching you. Now, my friends, having demanded an honest and a good land bill, you also say that no bill will be satisfactory which does not provide for the farm laborer, and improve his condition; you cannot say it is happiness to have the farmers prosperous and contented, and the laborer miserable and dejected; the laborer ought to be fairly housed, fairly clad, and well fed. The laborer is as useful and as essential to the farm and the farmer, as the key of the door is to the lock; because without the laborer the soil cannot be opened, just as the lock cannot without the key; the prosperity of the farmer and the laborer should go hand in hand. But, countrymen, should the government of England (in whom, I think, we ought to place confidence, though they made a great mistake in their prosecutions), fail to pass the land bill we require, what then will be the consequence? A continuation of famines, and, in all probability, you may not have another Sister Francis Clare to come to your rescue; or, even if you have, what will the nations of the world say to her.

MR. T. HARRINGTON, Editor, *Kerry, Sentinel.* — There are millions of our fellow-countrymen, the world over, to whom the name of the good and gifted Nun of Kenmare is more than a household word, and who would give the greater part of their earthly possessions for the proud privilege of standing here "to avenge even a look that would threaten her with insult." Far as the fame of Sister Mary Francis has extended — and who will deny that it has reached every land where the scattered Clan na Gael have found a home? — equally widespread and equally universal will be the feeling of indignation which this outrage shall call forth, and the exiled son of Ireland, in his log hut by the Susquehanna, or his home beneath the Southern Cross, will fiercely re-echo the cry of indignation which arises to-day from you, men of Glanerough and Dunkerron. Why has this gentle follower of St. Francis been assailed?

Simply because in the fulness of her womanly compassion for the miseries of the people, she has not only kept them from actual starvation, but has dared to point to the system in which these miseries have their origin. She has dared to give offence to landlordism by stating that there was distress in and around Kenmare last winter, and by appealing to the sympathy of the Christian world for the relief of the suffering victims.

Her urgent, incessant, and touching appeals reached every clime, and were respected by every grade of society, and in a short time she had collected no less than £15,000 for the relief of the people. Many amongst you, who retain a vivid recollection of the appalling famine of '47, can best appreciate the result of this herculean effort. You who saw the famished victims die in thousands by the roadside at that time, who witnessed the awful sufferings of a people to whom death would have been a mercy; who looked upon the sliding coffin and the inhuman form of burial which consigned, some say, even the living to an unconsecrated grave —

A VOICE. — Some were buried alive.

MR. HARRINGTON. — You who witnessed these things can say how much Kenmare is indebted to her, who, under Providence, was the means of preventing a recurrence of those dread scenes last winter. "If I could go on a platform," said a Kenmare lady to me, during the past week, "I could tell them what Sister Clare has done. I could tell them that last year would be as bad as '47 and '48 only for her, and I remember that time well. I remember the people dying by dozens by the roadside every day and buried without coffins, and though the whole place almost was turned into a poorhouse, yet there was more influence used at that time to get a pauper admitted than there is now for the appointment of a master or a matron. Mr. Stuart Trench, whose memory, no doubt, is still fresh amongst you, who, by the way, must have assisted in tying the matrimonial knot for some of you here, for, in addition to the qualities of land agent, he united, it seems, those of a couple-beggar — tells the tale of that period in the following words, —

"At least five thousand people must have died of starvation within the union of Kenmare. They died on the roads, and they died in the fields; they died on the mountains, and they died in the glens; they died at the relief works, and they died in their houses. So that whole streets or villages were left almost without an inhabitant, and at last some few, despairing of help from the country, crawled into the town and died at the doors of the residents and outside the union walls." *

A VOICE. — He says nothing about the Lansdowne ward.

MR. HARRINGTON. — This is but a picture of the misery which the good Nun of Kenmare prevented last winter. The landlords, perhaps, would have thanked her more had she allowed the people to starve, and then joined Mr. Townsend Trench in his scheme of emigration. His father writing of the scheme which he set on foot in '48 says, —

"In little more than a year, three thousand five hundred paupers had left Kenmare for America, all free emigrants, without any ejectment having to be brought against them to enforce it, or the slightest pressure put upon them to go. Matters now began to right themselves. Only some fifty or sixty paupers remained in the house, chargeable to the property of which I had the care, and Lord

---

* This is an extract from a book on Ireland, written by Mr. Trench in which, strangely enough, he makes many statements, very damaging to landlords. The title of the book is *Realities of Irish Life*.

Lansdowne's estates at length breathed freely." Yes, "breathed freely," when the people were banished, and Lord Lansdowne's rental was not taxed to any extent for their support. There is no sigh for the brave hearts and manly arms that are lost to Mother Ireland, no moan over the graves of the famine victims, no sympathy for the many hearts forever broken by sad separation, no word of anxiety for the future of those who were banished — all other considerations are lost in the gloomy satisfaction of having got rid of the people.

Mr. Trench's spirit did not die. His son inherits the same philanthropic intentions. He too devised another scheme of emigration this year, though I myself heard him state, that he never knew a year in which the poor were better off than last winter. But I think the day is fast approaching, when our people will refuse to go into exile at the whim of any taskmaster. The day is approaching when they will insist upon their right to live in the land of their birth, and when they will turn to the exterminating hypocrite and say, "If you think Ireland overpopulated, then go you into exile and you will confer a lasting benefit on your country." A great flood of light has recently been let in on the dark deeds perpetrated here, in the name of landlordism. *Hinc illæ lachrymæ.*

Give to the insult which has been offered to Sister Clare, that reply which shall most glad her patriotic heart, the resolve to struggle with might and main against oppressive rack rents and unjust eviction, until you see the whole island free from the iniquitous system. Tell the miscreant who has offered her insult that, to use the words on that banner before me, you are her bodyguard, and that more of Ireland's true and trusted sons would volunteer in her service to-day than all the gold of Irish landlordism, aye, or all the wealth at the command of Britain's Queen, could purchase, in an ignoble cause.

The following reports of relief committees are taken from the *Freeman's Journal* (Dublin). They refer to the period preceding the indignation meeting when I was distributing relief so largely. At that time I think at least seventy-five thousand dollars must have passed through my hands. The principal part of this money was sent to me from America, and from persons whom I had not known previously. Bishop Higgins was the parish priest of Kenmare, but was succeeded immediately after by Archdeacon O'Sullivan.

A VOTE OF THANKS PASSED TO SISTER M. FRANCIS CLARE BY THREE RELIEF COMMITTEES OF THE PARISHES OF KENMARE, SNEEM, AND KILGARVAN.

" *To the Editor of the 'Freeman's Journal'* : —

"SIR, — As secretary of the Kenmare Relief Committee, I am only required to furnish the press with a summary of their proceedings in your advertising columns ; but, sir, I feel I would be wanting in my duty if I did not place on record the noble exertions of the Nun of Kenmare. Were it not for her we would have no committee, because they would have no funds to distribute, having only received, up to the present, £50 from the Mansion House Fund and £28 from the Duchess of Marlborough's. I intend giving your readers a very brief idea of what this one member of the Order of Poor Clares in this remote district has done. Landlords of Kerry, it will shame your apathy and indifference to the sufferings of the poor. Look carefully at our advertisement, and see what the exertions of one noble woman from the seclusion of her lonely cell on the banks of the Finnehe has done to cheer their miserable homes, and to fill the empty stomachs of our starving people.. Am I not right, then, in stating that were it not for that heaven-sent guardian of the poor, many a poor Glenorough man and woman would to-day have fixity of tenure in the lonely graveyard ? — I remain, dear sir, yours faithfully,

"MICHAEL CRONIN,
"*Hon. Sec. Kenmare Relief Committee.*"

Kenmare Relief Committee.

At a meeting of the Kenmare Relief Committee, held on the tenth inst., the following resolutions were adopted unanimously, the members of committee present being, —

Chairman — Archdeacon Higgins, P. P., V. G.; *Treasurer* — Daniel O'Brien Corkery, J. P.; *Secretary* — Daniel Mahony, P. L. G.; *Assistant Secretary* — Michael Cronin. Rev. Maurice Neligan, C. C.; J. D. Sullivan, P. L. G.; G. M. Maybury, J. P.; Charles John Maybury.

Proposed by G. M. Maybury, J. P; seconded by Charles John Maybury, —

"That this committee return their heartfelt thanks to Sister M. F. Clare for the generous assistance which she has given in relieving the poor of this district, they having received through her £100 for meal, together with one hundred and fifty sacks of meal for distribution, seventy blankets, and also £380 for the purchase of seed potatoes. They also return their grateful thanks to the superioress and sisters of the convent for their exertions in clothing and feeding so many of the poor during the present severe distress."

(Signed), Archdeacon HIGGINS, P. P., V. G.

Proposed by D. O'B. Corkery, J. P; seconded by J. D. Sullivan, P. L. G., —

"That this committee implore of Sister M. F. Clare to continue her hitherto herculean exertions to procure food and seed potatoes for the poor of this district, as every effort will be needed to save the people from starvation, and prevent a repetition of the dreadful scenes of the famine year again occurring in our midst."

(Signed), "Archdeacon HIGGINS, P. P., V. G.,
"*Chairman*."

In addition to what has been given to the Relief Committee here, the Nun of Kenmare has expended the following sums from collections entrusted to her care, —

Clothing poor children in Kenmare, £100; clothing to the poor of the school of Kenmare, Templenoe, and Cahir, £150; bales of clothing supplied to the poor, £200; for meal and other food, £154 6s. 6d; weekly assistance to poor families, £50; distributions during Christmas week to 125 poor families, £87 16s; employment given, £78.

Cash sent by the Nun of Kenmare to districts outside this parish, £464, —

Valentia	£30	Tuosist	£10
Cahirciveen	20	Kilgarvan	60
Port Magee	10	Bonane	20
Cahirdaniel	20	Galway	55
Ferriter	20	Meath	25
Waterville	20	Cavan	5
Ardigole	60	Cork	9
Sneem	20	Dublin	5
Castletown Bere	80		

Kilgarvan (Co. Kerry) Relief Committee.

It was proposed by the Rev. W. B. Smith, Prottestant Episcopal rector, and seconded by Mr. Joseph Aldworth, P. L. G, —

" Resolved : That the committee return their most sincere and deeply grateful thanks to Sister M. F. Clare for her generous donation of £60 to alleviate the suffering of our famine-stricken people, who, in this remote and desolate part of Kerry, have few friends to aid or help them to struggle through this terrible season of distress and depression. Were it not for the gigantic efforts and incessant appeals made by Sister M. F. Clare to all parts of the world in behalf of our poor people, the majority of them would be to-day either in their narrow graves, or obliged to seek a shelter in the workhouse, the last refuge of the pauper. We, therefore, cannot say less here to-day than that this true lover of God's poor ones has by her exertions saved this whole district from famine, as she has nobly and generously responded to the cry for help made to her from various quarters, both by priests and people."

(Signed), "MICHAEL SHEEHAN, P. P.,
"Chairman."

This resolution to be published in the daily and weekly papers.

The distress in this parish is most severe, and

there is no employment of any kind for the people. Donations are urgently requested, which may be sent to any of the committee, or to Sister Mary Francis Clare, Kenmare. Help to purchase seed is specially needed.

Sneem (Co. Kerry) Relief Committee.

At a meeting of the Sneem Relief Committee, held in the court-house on the twelfth inst., to consider the claims of about five hundred applicants for relief, on the motion of the Rev. M. A. Horgan, C. C., the following vote of thanks to Sister M. F. Clare was proposed by the Rev. Mr. Tynan, Protestant Episcopal Rector, and seconded by Thomas H. Fuller, Esq., —

"Resolved: That the special thanks of the members of this committee are due to the distinguished authoress, Sister Mary Francis Clare, Kenmare, for her generous donation of £20 towards the relief of our suffering people, and that the secretary be requested to convey to her our sense of gratitude, inclosing at the same time a copy of this resolution, and that it shall be published in the daily and weekly papers."

(Signed), "REV. T. DAVIS, P. P., *Chairman.*"

CHAPTER VIII.

MONEY MATTERS.

Money Left at Kenmare — I Send for it from Knock — It is Refused — Bishop Higgins Interferes — Illegal Claims of the Kenmare Sisters — Bishop Higgins Afraid of the Secular Courts — His Opinion of "Heretical Laws" — An Unfair Decision — Letters and Comments on the Case —

It will be remembered that when I was leaving Kenmare, I asked Miss L——y, who was then superioress, to keep the money which should have been given to me on leaving, until it was settled whether I should remain in Knock or go to Newry, and she readily consented. In fact, she knew very well that the Kenmare convent was likely to be in very serious difficulties after I went, and later events showed that she had determined to keep this money if possible. I have heard since that Bishop Higgins was left an immense sum of money after I left Newry, so perhaps he shared with those who did his bidding so well in my case.

The arrangements about money in our convents were very simple. When a sister went to another convent, whatever money she had brought with her was returned with her, and no superior would dare to refuse to do this. In my case all was different, every one seemed to do just what he or she pleased, and if I said a word I was at once accused of being "disobedient to ecclesiastical authority" and "making trouble."

As soon as I was settled at Knock and my ecclesiastical position was settled there beyond all dispute, I wrote to Miss L——y, the superioress at Kenmare, and asked her to send the money to me. To my surprise, she positively refused to give it to me. I certainly did not expect this, well accustomed as I was to injustice of all kinds. She said she would send it to Newry but not to me. The absurdity of this did not seem to occur to any one concerned. It would be useless and uninteresting to record all the annoyances which followed. Even after I left Kenmare, I had sent money to the sisters, and I have a letter of thanks from Miss L——y for this. When I left Kenmare, I was ready to forgive the sisters freely for all the trouble which they had given me; but I soon found they were determined to keep up the same spirit as before.

In this letter Miss L——y admits my having given $2,500 to the fund for the poor children, and my sending five hundred more to add to it. When writing to her I had said that, considering all I had done and collected for the Kenmare convent, I thought it would be only just if she and the sisters would give me a small addition to the money which I had a right to claim; I did not know myself, and I do not think any of those concerned really knew what the canon law on the subject was. But under the circumstances there should not have been any question of the strict rights of the case, when I came to leave the sisters so much after doing so much for them in so many ways; if they had one spark of good feeling they should have even stretched a point to do anything I asked. If I had asked even for half of all I had earned for the convent by my writings, or that had been left to me by legacy, they might have objected. But they refused even to give me what had been given to every sister who had left the convent before. Even the money which was left for masses they would not give. This was a positive outrage, as they should have been even more particular about this than the other sums, for sisters are supposed to be very particular in religious matters; Miss O'Hagan had taken good care to bring this money with her when we came to Kenmare, saying that it was only right that the masses should be said wherever I was. If she had been living, and if her long period of ill health had not so completely demoralized the sisters, I think some, at least, of this evil might have been saved. But ideas of right and wrong used to get curiously mixed when my affairs were in question.

Bishop Higgins now took up the matter and wrote quite a number of indignant letters, taking it for granted, as usual, that no one knew anything about canon law but himself. I believe his mind was thoroughly confused by the sisters. He had no other way of knowing anything about the affairs of the convent, except what they told him, and as they laid themselves out to please him in every way no doubt he was easily satisfied, and it must be said that a sister who could forge a despatch merely for the purpose of giving pain to one who had never given her any cause of annoyance, was not likely to lose a safe and easy opportunity of doing her an injury if she had a purpose to gain. I saw a letter which was written by this sister to a bishop, whom she hoped to prejudice against me, which contained the most absurd accusations, and at last I came to realize the source of many, if not of all, the scandalous stories that had been circulated about me. How could people suppose that those for whom I had labored so long could turn against me in this way! As I was quite in the dark myself, how could I suspect the actual originators of the report? Miss L———y told this bishop that I wanted to claim *all* the money which I had made by the sale of my books.

This was not true, and she knew it was not true, but she did not tell this bishop that she had refused to pay what she was lawfully obliged to do.

The whole question of property, where the rights of authorship is concerned, is very little known even to the most learned theologians. It depends on the nature of the vows; that is, whether they are what is called simple or solemn. The vows of the Irish Poor Clares are simple vows. As far as I could learn, the Kenmare sisters had a right to the money I earned by my writings while I was in Kenmare, but they had no right or claim on my writings after I left. It was very remarkable how anxious they were about the strict observance of canon law and how very unhappy they were about me, and how scandalized if they thought the law could be in any way construed against them. Miss L——y indeed wrote a letter in which she laments with much pious grief over my supposed grievous sin in asking her to do her plain duty. Bishop Higgins, as usual, was quite sure he, and he alone, was the only bishop in Ireland who was capable of deciding his own case correctly. In a letter to a much perplexed bishop, now before me, he utters sad lamentations over my supposed wickedness in thinking of appealing to the "secular courts" though I never had any idea of doing anything of the kind. To appeal to "the secular courts" would be a "crying scandal." It is remarkable how much some bishops are afraid of public opinion or investigation. In the conclusion of this remarkable letter, which was sent to me by the bishop to whom it was addressed, he says, —

"As the case seems to arise in the province of Munster, Dr. Croke is the proper judge. Let her bring her case before him. Let him not arbitrate (sic) pronounce the law upon it, and if I see no clear reason to question his official judgment, I shall submit. But to submit such a question to a tribunal ruled by heretical laws is a treason I shall not be guilty of."

And though this bishop was so determined not to submit "to the heretical laws" of the English government, where he was concerned himself, he refused the rites of Christian burial to a poor boy, because without any intention whatever of violating these laws, of which Bishop Higgins had such a pious horror, he had happened to be killed accidentally near the place where some moonlight outrage was being perpetrated. To obey the law was a "sacrilege" when there was any fear that it might cause justice to be done to a sister. But even to appear to disobey it, when a poor man was in question, was a crime to be visited with the severest penalties of the church.

Further, it should be remarked that Bishop Higgins expresses his willingness to submit to the archbishop's decision, if he finds that this decision is in his favor. If it is not, he will have none of it.

The case was decided as usual where I was concerned. I had to take what I could get, and be thankful. I got the money for masses, at last, which had been kept from me so long. It was another of many evidences from which I have seen the difference between Roman Catholic teaching, and Roman Catholic practice. I had to allow the sisters to take what they pleased; I had to pay them a thousand dollars to be allowed the sale of my own books. But I would have borne more than this for peace. The circumstances of my case were, of course, unusual, and therefore, according to secular law, I should have had the benefit of any doubt. But it is not so with ecclesiastical law; the bishop gets, or, which is practically the same, takes the benefit of any and everything.

I do not profess to know much about canon law, but I made inquiries of several very eminent canonists, and they were all unanimous in my favor. Of course, I knew well that it would have been quite useless to offer their opinions to Bishop Higgins as he had said plainly that he would not accept any opinion unless it was in his own favor (see his letter, quoted above), even though that opinion should be given by his own ecclesiastical superior.

In the first place, I had a right to whatever advantage the fact of my having made only simple vows gave me. A Jesuit father told me when one of their fathers, who was an author, was sent from one house of their order to another, that the income from the sale of his books went with him. Bishop Higgins got to hear this, and he wrote a very angry letter to this father in consequence, which the father sent to me.

In the second place, and I believe this was a very important point in canon law, I had been for years the publisher of my books; they were published in my name, M. F. Cusack, and the copyrights were in my name, and this had been done with the full knowledge and consent of the community. The law of the land was on my side, as Bishop Higgins well knew, and this was why he had such a dread of any appeal to it. It did not follow, however, that canon law and civil law should agree, but I have heard canonists say that in a doubtful case, civil law should have weight, in an ecclesiastical decision; that is, if the bishop allows it.

I saw also a letter from Miss L——y to a bishop, in which she tried, with more ingenuity than honesty, to make out that the sale of my books was not of so much advantage to the convent after all. But if this was true, it only showed still more their animus against me, in trying to deprive me of them. The way in which she made out her case was amusing; I had often been much annoyed by the great, but, to a certain extent, excusable ignorance of the sisters on business matters. They knew that I had to pay out very large sums of money to printers and others, and, with almost childish ignorance, they thought that all this was so much money taken from the convent. They were too ignorant to understand that if this outlay had not been made, there could not have been a return of profit for themselves. And this brings me to the last, and not the least important point of this case. For years, with the consent of Bishop Moriarty, I had kept an account in the Kenmare Bank in my own name for the books. The money received from sales was placed by me in my name, M. F. Cusack, and I drew checks in my own name to pay the bills, so the money connected with the sales of my books was a separate and personal account of my own; and, I must say, that the sisters were very inconsiderate of my convenience. Often when they wanted money to pay a bill, for convent expenses, they would come to me and insist on getting it, though I might want it myself urgently to pay my own bills. It mattered not what suffering and inconvenience I had to endure, so that I often had great care on my mind. I always wished to pay all the printing accounts first, and then let them have what was clear profit, but I was always overruled in everything.

After Bishop Moriarty's death, and while Bishop Higgins was parish priest of Kenmare, he said it was quite wrong for me to have this private account. It was in vain that I said it had been arranged by Bishop Moriarty. Bishop Higgins was always sure he was a better authority than any one else, and, as he insisted, I gave up my account, and signed a check to the credit of the superior, and all the money I had in hand went into the convent fund. To myself, personally, this made no difference, as even if I had wished it, I could not have used any of this money for myself in any way. I told this to Bishop McCarthy when he became bishop, and he told me Father Higgins was quite wrong, and that he had no right to interfere in the matter, as he was not our bishop, then. He said if I wished I could go back to the old arrangement, but I did not care to change again.

CHAPTER IX.

BISHOP HIGGINS'S TREATMENT OF SISTERS AND PRIESTS.

Changes at Kenmare — Death of Father John — Of Miss O'Hagan — Interference of Father Higgins — Ill-treatment by the Sisters — Bishop Higgins's Arbitrary Management — I am Boycotted by Him — Loss of Money — Other Sisters Oppressed by Bishop Higgins — The Saurin Case — A New York Case — A Sane Sister Sent to Blackwell's Island — Her Rescue.

I must now return to my own history, from which I have digressed in order to give the account of my work in the famine year consecutively. It will be seen that I had exceptional sources of information as to the condition of Ireland, and as to the cause of the chronic discontent of the Irish people.

I knew well that there were thousands of honorable and honest Englishmen who would gladly do justice to the Irish people if they only knew what could be done, but every one suggested a different remedy until the case seemed hopeless.

And yet to me it seemed so simple: the landlords wanted their rents, and the people could not pay them while they had not even money to purchase food. In many cases the landlords were harsh and exacting, and in some cases the people took advantage of the disorganized state of affairs to refuse rents which they could have paid. But whoever was to blame, it certainly was a miserable state of affairs, and it has often surprised me that the English people have borne it so long. The state of Ireland is not creditable to nineteenth century civilization.

The obvious cause of this inability to pay rent was the failure of the potato crop. It seemed to me that one of two courses should have been adopted; either to find another crop on which the people could subsist, or to find some source of remunerative employment for the people. The climatic conditions of the country are such that it would be very difficult to find a substitute for the potato. But at least the potato crop should not have been allowed to degenerate. I have already quoted from a letter on this subject written to me by the Protestant rector of one of the largest parishes in the county Cork, and I received many other communications to the same effect. I therefore made it a special point to protect the people against future famine by getting a supply of good seed potatoes from Scotland; but the little I could do was but a drop in the ocean. When the people were crying out for food to save them from starvation, there could not be a question of providing for the future. Still, where I was able to give seed, and to secure that it should be planted and not eaten, I have found the good results were lasting, even to the present day. The other plan of providing some employment for the people did not seem to me altogether impracticable; I began to do this in a modest way at Knock, and I think the history of my failure is as instructive as it is sad. The Irish are themselves one of the great obstacles to their own prosperity. But in judging them we must always consider their peculiar circumstances. For centuries they have been deliberately forbidden all commercial industries by the English people, and when an attempt like that which I began so successfully at Knock, is put down by the priest, what can the people do?

But I must return to my life at Kenmare. The sisters having a lace industry there, I knew it would be useless for me to suggest anything else. It was a good show for visitors, and as a great deal of the lace which was sold to tourists was made by the sisters, it really was of very little practical use to those who were supposed to get the benefit of it. Of course it was an indirect benefit to them, but I am considering now the very important question of a work which should be of future benefit to the people. I think few who have not lived in Ireland can realize all the difficulties which come, and are put in the way of, any effort to do common-sense practical work for the Irish people.

I often saw this lace sold to tourists by the sisters as the work of the girls; they had no idea of being deceitful, and no doubt thought the benefit to the institution justified them.

But, as already explained, the work was a very useless one for poor girls. In the first place, it entirely unfitted them for any other kind of work. The sisters and the girls who did this exquisite lace could not touch any other kind of work; their hands had to be kept as soft and smooth as the hands of a lady of fashion. If a regular set of girls could have been employed in this work, and in no other way, it might have been a benefit to them, but this was impossible. Only a very few girls could have made a living by it even under the most favorable circumstances. What, then, was to become of the rest?

It was certain that ninety-five per cent of these girls would have to make their living by very hard work, and for this they were entirely unprepared. I saw the evil, I saw the remedy, but I was powerless to apply it. Irish sisters are somewhat easygoing, like the rest of their country people, and are inclined to "let well enough alone," and their idea of what is well enough, is apt to be "what has been." It was "good enough" for those who went before them, it was a sort of religious treason to suggest change, and woe to the hapless being who ventured to do so. I was simply a unit; what could I do?

Shortly before the famine, Father John's health quite broke down. It was very sad, for we all loved him dearly. If he had been in his full health and vigor at this time, and seen how easily a great work could have been done for his people, I am sure he would have helped me in every way to carry it out. But his life work was done, and for some time before his death his mind quite gave way, and the noble tree withered from the top.

Father John's death was a great shock to Miss O'Hagan. She never was quite the same afterwards; all the circumstances of his death were made more painful by the restrictions of our rule of inclosure, which were such that we could not attend him on his deathbed. This troubled Miss O'Hagan very much for many reasons; but I have often thought that it was a blessing both for him and her, for she was what I can only describe as fussy and excitable in a sickroom; she would have done herself harm, and have been no real comfort to him. Our vow of inclosure was certainly anomalous. When Father John was dying we could not go to him; when he was living he could go into any part of the convent and bring strangers of either sex with him. We were shut in to a certain extent, but strangers were not shut out. Visitors were naturally curious to see the rooms occupied by the sisters; and, above all, to see the more private apartments of the sisters, such as the "cells," as the rooms are called where the sisters sleep. These were always shown to visitors at Kenmare, and no doubt it removed some prejudice in regard to sisters when it was seen that cells were not such very dreadful places, though it seemed to me that to bring strangers through them was contrary to the spirit of our rule.

Father John went to his eternal reward in November, 1874. His end was peace. I believe he was quite unconscious for some days previous; I was told that he asked especially for me, and that at one time, not seeing the sisters round him and not being able to realize the unavoidable cause of their absence, he felt much depressed. Whether it was a fancy of sickness, or that a good Providence allowed it for his consolation, I know not; but I was told that he said to those who were watching near him, in a moment after, quite joyfully, "There is Francis Clare," as he always called me; "I knew she would not leave me."

As I have said, Miss O'Hagan's health was always very delicate, and she was almost reckless with regard to it. I was the only one who had any influence with her, or could dissuade her from doing the most imprudent things. The position of a superior in a religious house is something very different from what those outside imagine it to be, even amongst Roman Catholics. She has not an easy task, she has to keep peace with the sisters and amongst the sisters. She has to be responsible to the ecclesiastical superior not only for what she does herself, but for what others do. She must set the first example in everything. Whether she is able or not she is expected to attend every duty and every call. No wonder that so many superiors of religious houses break down completely in health after a few years. A superior who is sensitive to public opinion is sure to do so. Her absence from any duty is remarked upon and criticised, when the absence of others is passed by unnoticed. If any care is taken of her health, no matter how necessary it may be, it becomes a subject of remark, and is attributed to anything but the right cause. I do not say that this is always so, but I know that it is often so.

Not long before I took the step which has necessitated the publication of this book, I received a letter which is an evidence of this. A sister wrote to me from one of our convents in England:—

"I find that Father —— is talking just the same way about dear Sister M. B—— as Father John did about you at Knock; you know how delicate she is, and how sensitive she is, I do believe it will kill her. He says she could get up to mass every day, if she liked. But you know she cannot, and how valuable her life is to us all. He says the sisters will be disedified if she does not."

I replied very decidedly that I did not care whether the sisters were disedified or not, or the priests either; even if her life was not so valuable to us all, I should insist upon any sister under my charge doing everything that was necessary for her health and ordinary comfort. But I knew all the same how hard it is for a sister in charge of others as she was, to do anything different from others. Miss O'Hagan certainly had no cause to fear any remarks that might be made on her by either priest or sisters, her brother's position was a sufficient protection for her; but from some sensitiveness, or pride, or peculiarity of disposition, she felt very keenly any remark that might be made about her. I have often seen her going about the convent almost in a state of collapse, when she ought to have been resting, and she often distressed others by this so much, as to do away with much good she might otherwise have done.

Father Higgins came to be parish priest of Kenmare the Christmas after Father John's death.

At first he showed me every kindness, and I hoped I had found in him another good friend, if not another Father John. He devoted himself to Miss O'Hagan in every way possible, from the first moment of his arrival. Father Higgins was a special favorite of Bishop Moriarty, and who was still living; he took the same views of political affairs, and was decidedly, to all intents and purposes, a "landlord priest"; he, too, naturally gravitated to persons of Lord O'Hagan's position and influence. Even then he was looking to the much-coveted mitre, as Bishop Moriarty made it no secret that he had sent in an urgent petition to Rome that Father Higgins might be appointed his coadjutor. Bishop Moriarty died soon after, and it seemed as if all my best friends would be taken from me. During the long illness which preceded Miss O'Hagan's death, I was confined to my room by severe illness, and indeed I scarcely cared to leave it. There was practically no head to the convent, and very great evils resulted, which I neither anticipated nor could have imagined possible, and I found afterwards that when I never even suspected it, Father Higgins's mind was being prejudiced against me in my absence. I do not suppose it would have made the least difference, even if I had been warned in time; those who had an object to gain were always on the spot to carry out their plans. I was always suffering alone, and knew very little of what passed in the community, and, unfortunately for myself I was very unsuspicious, so those who had an end to gain had it all their own way.

The sister of whom I have spoken before as having been so absorbed in grief on account of her brother's conduct, which was now known far and wide, was acting in Miss O'Hagan's place as superior, and was singularly unfit for the office. She was full of prejudice, had very little education, and naturally was led and guided by the young sisters who taught in the schools, and on whose services she was so entirely dependent that she was obliged to let them treat every one in the house as they pleased, so long as they kept up the schools. It need scarcely be said that this was not the way to promote the general good of a religious house; but it was the only way she knew. Many a time during Miss O'Hagan's long illness, sisters came to me to complain of the way these sisters acted towards the other sisters who were not in their good graces, but I was powerless to help; in fact, I needed protection from them myself. There were other sisters in the schools better educated than they were, and of better families, and these poor sisters often came to me in tears to complain of the way they were treated before the children ; since I came to America I have met many of the girls who have been educated in the Kenmare schools who told me how often they had seen the way in which some of the gentlest and best sisters in the schools were insulted before all the children at this time. Even when Miss O'Hagan had her ordinary health and, vigor, she had trouble enough in these matters.

Somewhat to the surprise of a great many people, Dr. McCarthy, who had been president of Maynooth College for many years, was appointed Bishop of Kerry in Bishop Moriarty's place. Why Father Higgins did not get the mitre then, I do not know. I really feel unwilling to write many things here which are a necessary explanation of my position and difficulties, but they have been made so public by the parties themselves that I have not the same delicacy about the matter which I should have under other circumstances.

It should be said that at this time Father Higgins and his friends were confident that he would be made bishop. I received a letter from a person in New York, who was very intimate with many priests, and who asked me if I remembered one occasion in Kenmare, about this time, when Father H———n breakfasted at the convent with Father

Higgins. Miss O'Hagan was living then, and she I were both present. Dr. McCarthy's nomination had not then been made public. Some of us spoke of Father Higgins's possible success ; he certainly gave us all reason to think he had got the appointment, but he would not say so definitely. " Father H——n," said my correspondent, " saw him look at you in a way that did not promise well for your future happiness, as he thought you preferred Dr. McCarthy, which certainly you could not be blamed for doing, as he had been such a devoted friend of yours for so many years."

I must say I tried to give no cause of offence, and to be very careful in giving any opinions. In fact, I found myself so perpetually misrepresented by the sisters that I kept silence on all subjects, and, as I have said, on the rare occasions when I was able to come to the recreation, I was not allowed to speak, as the sisters would not reply to any remark I made, so that I preferred to remain in my own room. It may be said, how could sisters be guilty of such inhumanity and injustice ? It may as well be asked how there comes to be so much evil in the world ? I may also say, when the superior of a religious house was capable of forging a despatch for the purpose of giving me pain, was it likely that she would hesitate to do any other act of injustice ? I may also add that I heard from a priest lately, who knew all the circumstances of the case, that he knew from one of the principal parties concerned, that the sisters were constantly telling Father Higgins that I said and did things I never even dreamed of saying or doing. I was slow to suspect them; certainly, even during all this miserable time, I never refused to help the sisters and their friends, on whose wants I expended many hundreds of dollars — I might say thousands. I did often feel it was hard that they should come to me only when they were in trouble, or wanted something for themselves or their friends, but I never refused them. In one case I paid all the expenses of the near relatives of a sister to Australia, and also procured an excellent situation in Dublin for a brother, which he still holds, and yet the sister for whose family I did all this was one of the most unkind to me, and I never received one word of thanks from her or those for whom I provided. I have no doubt that Father Higgins was deceived by the sisters to an extent he never suspected, and probably would not believe. No man likes to admit, even to himself, that he has been the victim in such a case.

During the long period of Miss O'Hagan's illness, there was naturally considerable discussion as to her successor. Those who are least fitted for the office of a superior are generally most anxious to get it. For many reasons I thought Miss L——, who had been acting with more or less incapacity during this time, was the most suitable person to succeed her. It is true she was always lamenting over her poor brother, but I hoped the responsibility of the office would bring her to a happier frame of mind; besides, I had seen so much evil arise from having such an office in the hands of a person in delicate health, like Miss O'Hagan, that her robust health also made her advisable for the position. It seemed to me, however, very unbecoming to have the subject discussed while poor Miss O'Hagan was living, even though her recovery was quite despaired of; but I was never allowed to express an opinion on any subject, so I kept my thoughts to myself. I was not a little surprised when I was asked to go to the parlor one day to see a sister of one of the sisters. This person was a widow, and very poor; her late husband had belonged to a very respectable Protestant family in the neighborhood, and though they took very little notice of her in her husband's lifetime, as they were naturally angry at the marriage he had made, which they considered quite beneath him, yet after his death they befriended the poor woman a good deal, by giving her clothing for her children, and paying for their schooling. The woman took what she got with very little thanks to her benefactors. Family pride ran high in Kenmare, as it does so often in Ireland, and this woman considered herself and her family quite as good as the family of her late husband. Hence considerable recriminations, and a great deal of thanklessness for benefits. To my surprise, Mrs. M—— did not want me, as usual, to do something for herself or her family ; she had come on a very different mission. Being a roughly spoken and uneducated person, she came out plain and straight with her object. It was to tell me that Father Higgins had been at her father's house to say Mass that morning, and that he had quite decided that her sister, Sister M—— J——, was the proper person to succeed Miss O'Hagan. I certainly was very much displeased at the want of common decency in disposing of poor Miss O'Hagan's office before she was dead, and at this piece of impertinent interference on the part of those who had no right whatever to interfere in a matter of such grave importance. In the choice of a superior in most religious orders the person is voted for by the sisters only, and by a strictly private ballot.

Indeed, all the regulations of the Roman Church are as nearly perfect as possible in these matters. But human frailty, which made even Paradise a desolation, comes in everywhere, and blights if it cannot destroy. As it happened, there could scarcely have been a worse choice than this one, or one on which the sisters were less likely to agree. Sister J——'s temper was notorious, her manner anything but refined or ladylike, and though she was clever and capable as a teacher in the schools, where very little ability was required beyond the thorough knowledge of the simplest grammar and arithmetic, which she and girls of her class naturally thought something wonderful, as they had never had any opportunity of knowing more. I gave this woman to understand very plainly that I considered neither she nor Father Higgins had any right to discuss such a subject; above all, while poor Miss O'Hagan was still living. After all, it was an affair in which even Father Higgins had no right to interfere, I have no doubt that she reported the matter to Father Higgins, with her own comments and in her own way, and I had another cause of enmity laid up against me.

I did not blame the poor woman for wishing to see her sister in what she considered the grand position of superior, but it was the way in which the matter was discussed that displeased me. I doubted, too, if Father Higgins had talked in this way, as he certainly knew the rules of convent life, though he did not always care to observe them.

When this woman saw that I was displeased, like all persons of her class, she thought I was looking for the office myself, and said, rudely, "You know you cannot be made superior yourself, your health is so delicate;" I replied, quietly, that "I was aware of that." It would have been useless to have told her that I would not have accepted the office, even if my health had been as strong as her sister's, nor that I had already arranged to leave Kenmare Convent.

Many changes occurred, during a few years, in Kenmare. Father John, the good old priest who had brought us there was dead; Miss O'Hagan died soon after; and almost her last words to me were, "I give you not one, but fifty thousand blessings." Several of the sisters had died, and several had returned to Newry because they were dissatisfied with many things which they were powerless to alter. One of these things was the constant presence of the parish priest at the convent; he also required the personal attendance of the sisters when he came in from working on his farm, on which he occupied a good deal of his time; and where certainly he did a good farm hand's work, and did more hacking and hewing on himself than on the hedges and ditches which he was cutting down and digging out.

It would be necessary to understand the peculiarities of convent life to know how the recreations of the sisters could be made a source of misery instead of pleasure, by the presence of a person who was not a member of the community; though an occasional visit from an ecclesiastical superior could be a source of pleasure to them at times. During the day, the sisters have a certain time to converse freely together, and if there is any person present who necessarily absorbs conversation, who expects special deference to his opinions, it is no longer a free time.

There are many people who are quite as ignorant of the history of their own times as they are of the history of the past. When they hear something startling which has not reached their ears before, they at once come to the not very wise conclusion that it cannot be true because they have not heard it; this is not very wise, neither is it wise to accept statements merely because they are new. I know many persons, and quite as many Roman Catholics as Protestants, who will be surprised by statements in this book. But very little is known of either the joys or the sorrows of convent life by those outside. Even at the risk of making a digression, I may say a few words on this subject here.

Sisters are not all unhappy, nor are they always treated unjustly by their ecclesiastical superiors.

But there is a great deal of unhappiness in convents which ought not to be and especially in America. I was perplexed and shocked, very soon after I came to this country, at the number of sisters who had been in convents who came to me asking to be received into our order. All these sisters had been professed for some years in the convents which they had been put out of with little ceremony, and little care for their future. I heard and inquired into the case of many of these sisters, and found that they had often been treated with great injustice. I shall mention some of these cases later. I think I was asked to help some fifty or more sisters who had been thus treated.

But I wish to remove the impression which prevailed at one time in England that there would be any benefit to sisters in convent inspection. At one time there was a regular rage on the subject in England. It was supposed that there were a number of sisters detained against their will in convents, who would be thankful for release. Statements of this kind may be made for sensational purposes, but they are not true in the sense in which they are believed. A sister is as free to leave a convent as she was to enter it, from one point of view. She is bound in another and a very painful way, but no convent inspection could help her. I am saying this because I firmly believe that there will be a reaction against the Roman church in America unless there is a reform in that church which its past history does not lead us to hope for. A church which claims infallibility in all its doings as well as for all its doctrines will neither listen to a cry for needed reforms nor avert calamity. And it will not even learn from history. Already there are signs of the beginning of the end, if only those who could avert evil by reading them aright would read them.

The peace, happiness, and well-being of a convent depends first on the local superior. I have explained why this protection failed me. Next it depends on the bishop, whose sacred duty it is to see that every sister is treated with impartial justice ; and lastly, the parish priest, or pastor as he is called in this country, has almost unlimited power. He is the local pope and he knows it, and takes care that every one else shall know it also. Let it be supposed that such a power is constantly present in an institution, and that all the inmates have a great deal to gain by propitiating him, the consequences to any one who is under his ban may be imagined, and in proof that this is no imaginary or infrequent case, I refer the reader to the lives of the saints and to some notes on the subject at the end of this volume.

When Bishop McCarthy came to Kenmare I

told him all my trouble, and he arranged at once for me to have another confessor, and seemed surprised that I should have confessed so long to Father Higgins when he was acting so strangely towards me. But this made little difference; Father Higgins was the power at hand, and the bishop was the power at a distance, and the sisters knew it. Beside, the sisters never liked Bishop McCarthy; I think because he was much attached to me, and had paid me the very unusual compliment of quoting from one of my books in a treatise which he had written for theological students.

Even in sickness I was made to suffer, but I wish to say as little as possible on this painful subject, and I would not have said anything had it not been necessary for me to say something about why I left Kenmare, in consequence of the false reports spread by the sisters and their relatives.

Even some of the sisters were indifferent to my work for the poor in the famine year, though their own families benefited by it largely.

After the death of Bishop Moriarty, I think Father Higgins had great hope of being elected. He was passed over, however, but only for a time; Dr. McCarthy, president of Maynooth College succeeded, but, to my very great sorrow and grief, he died after a short time. He was fully aware, as I have said, of my condition in the Kenmare convent, but he was powerless to interfere.

All the sisters, with two or three noble exceptions, were against me; and the new superior was still more so.

After the death of Bishop McCarthy, Father Higgins obtained the long-sought-for mitre, and I knew the Kenmare convent could no longer be my home. The sisters thought it would be a discredit to them to have it said that I had left Kenmare when my name was so closely connected with it. Yet they made no change in their daily conduct, except to be still more unkind, and to show even publicly their triumph in the election of Bishop Higgins, though they knew that it would be the signal for my departure.

Perhaps if I relate the circumstances connected with this matter, they will give a better idea of the state of affairs in the Kenmare convent, and of my many difficulties and trials. I should have said that I had been able to do a great deal for the Kenmare convent and church out of the profit from the sale of my publications and other sources. I do not remember everything I did, even if I cared to recall it. I did it for God, and never doubting that Kenmare would be the home of my old age, as it might have been. For if the sisters had been indeed such in fact, as well as in name, I might have returned there even after I had founded other convents, and left them well established and in good hands. I built a considerable part of a new addition to the convent, and the sisters are at present enjoying an income from money left to me by several friends who never could have supposed that I should have had no benefit from it in my later years. Even since I left Kenmare, the sisters managed to get possession of some money that was left to me for charitable purposes, and were helped to do this clever trick by a near relative of one of the persons in Kenmare whom I had helped most generously in the famine. The sisters have besides, a good deal of the money which I earned by my writings. Of course they claimed the rights of "canon law" in this matter, for like a good many people of their class they are strong on the rights of the church, when these rights are in their own favor. As for me I was supposed to have no rights. Still I did not complain, and if I am left destitute in my old age I would rather it should be so than to have been unjust to others.

I was able to do something for the church also. The confessionals were very old and very uncomfortable for the priests; I got new ones and other costly and useful things. I had played the organ in the church for a great number of years. It was a splendid instrument, with three benches of keys, feet and side pedals, and, as the sisters who came to us first, scarcely knew anything of music, I had to take the whole burden and to teach them also. This organ was placed in a very inconvenient position for the sisters, as it was at the end of the church. The sisters had to go out through the public yard to get to it, no matter how severe the weather might be, or else they had to pass up the long aisle of the church before all the people. It was a choice of discomforts. I determined that the sisters who took up the work when I was no longer able to do it should not suffer this inconvenience any more. I forget now what moving the organ cost; I know it was a considerable sum of money, and, besides this, a new gallery had to be built for it. All this was done, and now the sisters could go by a covered way from the convent to the church.

At the time of which I speak, Father Higgins had been made Dean of Tralee; Father O'Sullivan, always my fast friend, was parish priest of Kenmare, and archdeacon, and we expected every day to hear that either one or the other had been appointed Bishop of Kerry. As I have said, Archdeacon O'Sullivan had nearly as many votes as Father Higgins. He was far more popular with the priests and the people, but not with the English government or the Archbishop of Dublin, who had an important voice in the matter.

The sisters knew well what I should feel when the announcement of Bishop Higgins's promotion should be made. One Sunday they heard a vague report that he had been appointed, and the sisters, with a singular want of respectful feeling towards Archdeacon O'Sullivan, as well as to myself, had the *Te Deum* sung after mass, and to make their ill-feeling more flagrant, it happened that Archdeacon O'Sullivan was at mass. The only excuse for them was their want of education or refinement, which made them incapable of understanding the feelings of others. One of these sisters was English, but of a class which does not possess the ordinary refinement of educated people, still, she had been brought up in a convent, and should have been taught there, at least, the ordinary duty of Christian charity. This sister was very ignorant and rude in her ways, but she had a strong voice, which was very useful in the large church, and the most extraordinary physical strength I ever met in any woman.

The triumph of the sisters after this was unbounded. It certainly was a poor specimen of the value of Father Higgins's teaching when it made them forget common courtesy to an excellent priest like Archdeacon O'Sullivan, to say nothing of myself. The next day when I had to go to the general room, where the sisters met for recreation, for a few moments on some business, I was attacked by this sister in the most violent way, and without any cause whatever. In fact the sisters nearly all lost their heads, and sisters will sometimes be as silly as children. I told her quietly that I would not enter into any discussions with her, or any of the sisters; that I only wanted peace and quiet, but she again began to pour out a torrent of angry and ignorant abuse, in which she was upheld by several other sisters who happened to be present. I had been treated this way several times before, but I was determined this would be the last time I would subject myself to it. I therefore said, as quietly as I could, "Sister M—— C—— you have treated me often in this way before, and I am sorry to say you have made me very angry. I will not submit to it any more. If your affection for Father Higgins obliges you to treat a sister in this way, I am sorry for you and for him; but if you continue speaking to me so rudely, I will leave this room, but remember, I will never enter it again." She still continued, so I quietly rose from my seat and left the room, and I kept my word, for I never went into it again, and left the convent as soon as possible after.

I am sure I had put up with so much that the

sisters thought it mattered little what they said or did as far as I was considered, and, as they had Father Higgins's example before their eyes, perhaps they were not so much to blame.

I now determined to leave Kenmare as soon as possible. I had made arrangements with Archdeacon Cavanagh to see what could be done about a convent at Knock, and I had decided to go back to Newry if this arrangement could not be concluded in a satisfactory manner. Indeed, the superior there had written many times very strongly to the sisters in Kenmare concerning their treatment of me, as she had heard a good deal about it from others than myself.

Nothing could have been simpler, or more in accordance with the regulations of the Roman Catholic Church, than the arrangements which I had made. Before I left Kenmare, I got all the necessary permissions, and yet later on it was made to appear by Bishop Higgins, who gave the permissions, as if they had not been given, the facts and the letters to the contrary, notwithstanding.

Bishop Higgins has indeed been very unfortunate in his dealing with his people, his priests, and his sisters. The reports in the public press show that those who are under his pastoral charge are a most disaffected and disloyal people. In Ireland, his diocese Kerry, has obtained most unfavorable notoriety for crime, murder, moonlighting, boycotting. This state of things is a most unhappy contrast to the peace and quiet which reigns in the next diocese, where Archbishop Croke rules.

As for his priests, I have personal knowledge that they are by no means well affected to his arbitrary rule. While I was in Kenmare, one of his curates who lived in his house, was sent to "Coventry" for six months, as Bishop Higgins, who was then parish priest, never opened his lips to speak to him during all that time. They met at dinner, at supper, at the altar, and at the sick bed, and still this somewhat peculiar ecclesiastic never spoke to him; though on these occasions he conversed quite freely with his other curate, who was a personal favorite.

I myself was subjected to just such treatment from him for nearly a year before I left Kenmare. Father Higgins never opened his lips to me, and what made it far worse was, that the majority of the sisters were weak minded enough to follow his example, either from a desire to please him or from their own free will. Ill and suffering as I was, the trial was a terrible one, and I often wonder that my mind did not give way under it. In consequence of my ill health, I was seldom able to leave my room; but whenever I did leave it and joined the sisters at the time of recreation, Father Higgins was generally there, as he spent most of his time at the convent. If I attempted to join in the general conversation, his example was all powerful, so that at last, I remained in my room entirely.

In justice to myself, I must add that I asked Bishop Higgins, who was then the parish priest and confessor, what was the cause of this extraordinary boycotting, but he always refused to tell me. I told him twice that if I had done anything to offend him or displease him, if he would only tell me what it was, I would make an apology or any reparation in my power, but it was the usual story; I was condemned unheard. Since then, and indeed quite lately, I met a priest who knew all the circumstances well, and he told me that stories carried by the sisters to the bishop were the cause of all the trouble. Again, I must say, why did not he take the trouble to inquire from myself whether all their stories were true or false? Although Bishop Higgins's family were persons of very humble origin, he was not without some cultivated tastes, and he took great interest, at first, in my literary work, so that the change was all the more remarkable.

I was made to suffer also from unkindness on

many occasions when I was seriously ill. Once when I was trying to rest after suffering very painful medical treatment, a sister insisted on moving some furniture in the room underneath mine, so that I was greatly disturbed, although several sisters begged of her not to do so. The same sister, I may say, was the final cause of my leaving Kenmare.

I am very reluctant to relate these circumstances. I know how trifling they may seem when reading about them, but they were not trifling when suffered, and I believe I may save others from suffering by recalling such cases. We cannot expect perfection at this side of Paradise. Every institution, no matter how good may be its object and aim, is human, and those who carry out its teachings are human also.

I should say here that on the death of Father John, whom I have previously mentioned, both the principal and interest of a very large sum of money was lost, which had been invested by him for the benefit of the poor. How necessary it was for them can only be known by those who have witnessed their poverty as I did, and it will be a matter of surprise to numbers to know that many of the sisters were perfectly indifferent on the subject.

I managed to collect about $2500 to replace

this money, and hoped by degrees to replace it all, but I had little sympathy from the sisters in my efforts, though it was of very much importance to the poor of that poor district, because the interest of the money was used to feed and clothe the destitute children attending the convent school. On one occasion one of the sisters said to me, "Oh, it matters very little about the poor; they can always get on, somehow; but I am very sorry for Lady F——," mentioning the name of the wife of a millionaire landlord who had suffered some reduction of rent.

I was not the only sister who fell under Father Higgins's displeasure or dislike; I really do not know which to term it. The sisters who had these troubles with Bishop Higgins had influential and wealthy friends and relatives, which fact was a protection to them, that I sorely needed. In their case, of course, it was not safe to work in an arbitrary or capricious manner. When they determined to return to the convent from which we all came, there were few difficulties made, and they were allowed to take with them, as they had a perfect right to do, the money which they had brought with them to Kenmare.

One of these sisters returned to Newry, soon after we came to Kenmare; and another sister left Kenmare about a year before I did, and returned to Newry also; she was subject to the same annoyance at recreation as I was, but as she was young and in vigorous health, she was better able to bear it. There is no doubt if I had had any influential Catholic friends and relatives, or if the priests had thought there was any danger of my appealing to my Protestant relatives, I should have been treated very differently.

I have said that Bishop Higgins has been unfortunate in his dealings with his people, his priests, and his sisters. As regards the people, the evidence is before the public in the press. As regards the priests, there are a good many who will read this and know what I say is true. As regards the sisters, a very sad case has just been published in the Dublin papers.

A sister in the convent of Castletown had frequently appealed to Bishop Higgins to be removed to another convent of her order, as she considered she was being treated harshly and unjustly by her superiors, but the bishop refused her reasonable request. At last the sister could no longer bear her agony of mind, and, such things are not altogether impossible in convents, human nature gave way; she fled from the house one day, and it would seem as if she knew not where she was going, but a great public scandal was the result. She was by some means induced to return, and I do not know whether she remains there still or not. But those who know anything of sisters will know what she must have suffered before she went to such extremes.

Some years ago, the Saurin case was brought before the public, with all the petty and miserable details of similar circumstances. Wherever there is a sensible and intellectual superior, and a bishop who is not incapable of doing justice to all, there may be no happier life than the life of sisters; but where these most important officials are incapable, or given to petty jealousy, few places can be more intolerable to those who desire peace.

It may be well that I should say something of the famous Saurin case here. Some fifteen years since, there was great excitement in England about what was called the "Saurin case." Miss Saurin was a young lady of very good family and a Roman Catholic. She entered a convent of the Sisters of Mercy, I think, in Dublin, and went from there to found a convent at a place called Hull, in England. Her friends were very devout Roman Catholics, and very well known in Roman Catholic circles. Her brother, Father Saurin, was a Jesuit, and got into considerable trouble by taking his sister's part in the quarrel. An uncle of this lady's was parish priest in Drogheda, Ireland, and he also got into trouble with the authorities, I forget on what subject. I know, however, he went to Rome, like myself, won his case and came back to Ireland, only to find, as usual, that the Pope's writ does not run unless the bishop concerned is willing it should, and in the end, to wish either, that he had never been born, or that he had never gone to Rome, as the injustice from which he was made to suffer before he appealed to Rome, was a trifle to what he had to endure after he came back. As to the respect shown by some bishops to the Pope's authority, when it does not suit their views, I give the following story as it was told me. A certain priest in the New York diocese was made a monseigneur by the Holy Father, and rejoiced thereat greatly, as this admits of dressing very much like a bishop, which, as far as I can understand, is about all the advantage gained thereby; but according to ecclesiastical etiquette it was necessary for this compliment to pass through the hands of the bishop of the diocese, and the bishop of the diocese, not admiring the independent ways of the priest in question, refused to give it.

I cannot now remember the exact details of Miss Saurin's case, except that it was not very creditable to any of those concerned in it. It was tried for days in the public law courts in London, and as it proved that there was nothing worse than an amount of continual petty meanness in the life of the sisters, of which any decent family would have been ashamed, the Catholic party were triumphant, as they said no serious scandal came out. At worst it was a history of petty jealousy and very ridiculous assumptions of authority on the part of the superior, and the conduct of the sisters showed, just as might be expected, that they took the side of authority without the slightest consideration as to whether it was right or wrong, and inflicted all kinds of petty slights and stings on the unfortunate sister. It is human nature after all to hunt down one who is down, above all, when such a course will please a powerful party; and such wrong is done sometimes, let us hope, without a full realization of its injustice.

A case within my own knowledge has happened recently in the New York diocese. About two years since, a gentleman came to me in great trouble and told me that his sister who had been professed, for, I think, about seven years previously, in the New York diocese had been sent to Blackwell's Island as a lunatic. I was beyond measure shocked, and could scarcely think that such things could happen in this nineteenth century, though I have had a good deal of experience of what can be done when injustice is determined upon.

He said his sister was not insane, but that she had expressed some indignation at what she thought wrong in the convent. I cannot answer for her state of mind then, but I know she was not insane later, neither was she when she came to me; and she now holds a respectable position in a store in New York, with credit to herself and her friends.

According to her statement to me, she was carried off to Bellevue Hospital suddenly, and without warning from the sisters, and she assured me that neither the priest nor doctor were brought to see her before this strange proceeding. She told me, and her brother confirmed her statement, that he was not sent for, nor did he know anything of what had happened, until she reached Bellevue Hospital, whence she contrived in some way to get a message to him.

Her history of the case is a most pathetic one. She told me how she prayed to God in her agony to save her from her terrible fate. Of course the excited state she was in, induced by this injustice, only confirmed the idea of her insanity. I shall not easily forget her brother's indignation. I have a copy of a letter which she gave me after she had despatched the original to the superioress of the convent whence she had been sent to Bellevue Hospital. It was written in somewhat strong and plain language. I asked her brother why he did not make the case public, and so prevent worse or similar evils. He told me it was his first impulse to do so, but that on reflection, he knew that he dared not, as his business would be ruined if he said one word.

As there has been so much confusion and perplexity made in a very simple case by Bishop Higgins's ignorance of canon law, which led him to interfere in an affair in which he had no concern, the whole case must look so perplexing to the general reader that I think it may be as well to give a short, clear statement of my position when I left Kenmare, as far as the canon law of the Roman church is concerned. No theologian can dispute the truth of my statement. The facts are also past dispute, as documentary proof of them is given in the next chapter.

When I left Kenmare my position was this. At my own request and with all the necessary forms required by the Roman church, I had been transferred to the diocese of Dromore, as the diocese is called, in which the town of Newry is situated. From the hour in which I left Kenmare Convent, the Bishop of Kerry, Bishop Higgins, had no more right to interfere with me or my affairs, no matter what I did, than he had to interfere with a sister in New York. Further, the

Kenmare sisters had no right to interfere with my actions, or to criticise them, or to employ persons to watch me, or to send despatches to find out where I was, or what I was doing. The only bishop to whom I was accountable was the Bishop of Dromore, of whom I have spoken before, and he was perfectly satisfied, as his letters show.

All this trouble arose from Bishop Higgins's ignorance of canon law, at least this is the most charitable view to take of it, as ignorance alone can save him from the charge of worse motives. For the conduct of the Kenmare sisters there is no excuse. Before I left Kenmare, I obtained permission to visit Knock, and in fact I went direct to Knock from Kenmare, as the reader has seen. My object in going there was also arranged with all canonical permission; I could not be sure whether I could found the proposed convent there or not, for many reasons, until I saw the Archbishop of Tuam and Father Cavanagh. When leaving Kenmare I arranged with Miss Lowry, the superioress of the Kenmare Convent, who had succeeded Miss O'Hagan, to keep the small sum of money which the sisters let me have until this matter was decided, which she agreed to do; and, indeed she kept it so well, that it was not without great difficulty I got it from her at last. So there was no mistake or misunderstanding in the whole proceeding, as far I was concerned, and the rules of the Roman Catholic church were strictly observed by me. If I decided to remain in Knock it was the business of the Archbishop of Tuam to make the necessary arrangements with the Bishop of Dromore, and for me to write explaining my wishes, which I did. If I went to Cork or Dublin or to America, Bishop Higgins had no right to say one word. Nor do I think he would have made all the serious mistakes he did if he had not let his mind be confused by the busy tongues of sisters, who had their own reasons for what they did and for "hunting me down." I now proceed to give the facts of the case, which I hope will be better understood after this explanation.

CHAPTER X.

LEAVING KENMARE.

I Leave Kenmare — Rev. M. Neligan Accompanies me on my Way to Knock — Accused of Going Without Leave — The Presentation Sisters at Killarney — Presentation Convent, Portarlington — Claremorris — Rev. Canon Bourke — My Journey Continued — Wretched Conveyances — I am Seriously Ill.

I LEFT Kenmare on the sixteenth of November, 1881, — a day long to be remembered by me for many reasons. I was accompanied by my confessor, the Rev. Maurice Neligan, C. C., and by my faithful and devoted friend and secretary, Miss Downing.

After the events related in the last chapter, I did not wish to see any of the sisters, except the reverend mother and one dear sister, whom I shall always remember with tender affection. As for the other sisters, I knew their feelings too well from years of unkindness and injustice, to suppose they would care to see me before I left Kenmare. Some of them I knew were keenly alive to the pecuniary loss my leaving would cause them, but what I have already said will show even *that* was a minor consideration to their miserable desire to gain favor with a certain ecclesiastic,

After all, they had excuses. The power of an ecclesiastic is very great, and human nature is very strong and very self-deceptive. I was no one in comparison with a superior whose smiles or favor could at once raise or lower each sister in the estimation of the others. It would be impossible to describe in words such a subtle influence. I can only say that it existed.

And I have found since I left Kenmare that such cases are not altogether uncommon. At a convent where I stopped, on my way to Knock, I heard from the reverend mother an account which resembled my own in many respects. There was only this difference, and what a difference it was! The reverend mother told me that a priest, who was necessarily very much mixed up in their affairs, had taken an unaccountable dislike to one of the sisters. He left no means unused to make her feel it, and as she was obliged to hold a prominent position in the schools, it was most painful to her. But she had a help and a comfort altogether denied to me. The reverend mother was a woman of noble character and true piety. As she said to me herself, her first duty was to the sisters, and she would rather have seen the convent broken up, and have begged her bread from door to door, than to allow any injustice to be shown to one whom she was bound to protect.

I could not but feel how different my lot had been; but the ways of Providence are mysterious, and the evil that is done us may but be the cause of a good which otherwise would not have existed.

The sisters were well aware that the people of Kenmare would be indignant if they knew that I was leaving, and that probably some measures would have been used to detain me by force. They were determined, at all events, to prevent any expression of interest or sympathy with me, and as I was on this point quite of their opinion, and desired to leave quietly, matters were easily arranged.

I passed out silently and unseen through the church; but before I left that place where I had offered so many tears and prayers, and for which I had done my share of labor, I knelt at the tomb of the dear Father John for a few minutes. I cannot now remember what prayers I prayed, or what words I said, but his dear memory was ever with me, and I felt if he could have known my grief, he would have been my dearest helper and comforter. The sisters took care to have a close carriage waiting for me at the outside door, in which my confessor, Rev. M. Neligan, and my secretary had already taken their places. And yet these same sisters who saw me leave thus, contrived to have a report circulated that I had left Kenmare as an "escaped nun" without "the knowledge or leave of any superior." By my own wish I left as early as I could manage to rise from my sick bed. It was a long and weary drive to Killarney, and I could not but think of the day, so many years before, when I had passed over the same mountains under such different circumstances. I knew at that time but little of the true state of the Irish poor. I gave up my life to work for the Irish people because they were poor, and because I pitied them with all the warm enthusiasm of my nature. I then believed also that their poverty was due principally to their fidelity to their faith. The experience of years of careful inquiry and anxious thought had proved to me that the Irish were poorer than I had ever imagined them to be, but that there were worse kinds of poverty; and I learned by these years of experience, also, that their poverty was not entirely caused by their adherence to their faith.

The letters which I received after I left Kenmare from the Rev. M. Neligan, which will be found later in this volume, will show that I was not without comfort and sympathy in his companionship. I could not have had a kinder or more considerate friend on that weary journey. It is very painful to me to revert to subjects which treat on the ingratitude and injustice of those with whom I spent the greater part of my life, and for whose benefit all the labors of my best years were expended, and who are now living on what I earned at so much cost, but the truth must be told.

We arrived in Killarney late in the afternoon, and were very kindly received by the Presentation Sisters there, who could also prove, if it were necessary, how I travelled. As they were special favorites with Bishop Higgins, I should have had some doubts of my reception, not from any idea that the sisters would be unwilling to receive me, but from knowing too well how fear and inclination clash on such occasions. The Rev. M. Neligan, however, had a niece in the convent, a professed sister, and that I suppose, had its influence on the other side.

On the next day, I went on another stage of my painful journey. I had to lie down all the time in the railway carriage, and was almost lifted in and out at each station. Our stay this night was at another Presentation Convent in Portarlington, Queens County. Here also, I met with a very kind reception, and in both convents the dear sisters brought me a pile of my own books, and especially showed me one, "The Spouse of Christ," which they said was read daily by the sisters.

My next journey was to Claremorris, where I had to rest the last night before going to Knock.

The little village of Claremorris is about five miles from Knock, and I met with a most affectionate reception there. The convent, which was one of the Sisters of Mercy's, is beautifully situated and surrounded by very extensive grounds. I found all the sisters warm believers in the apparition at Knock. The parish priest was well known through the Catholic Church as a very learned and distinguished Celtic scholar, and the writer of many historical works. He was the intimate and devoted friend of the late Archbishop of Tuam, who was immortalized by O'Connell as "The Lion of the Tribe of Judah."

The very Rev. Canon Bourke had been a correspondent of mine for many years, and I looked forward to meeting him with no ordinary pleasure. All such intentions, however, were subservient to the one great desire of visiting the shrine of Knock.

During the year 1879, my confessor had visited Knock and said Mass there, for the intentions of those who had helped the fund with which I had been charged, for the famine-stricken Irish. I may say here that I have considered such matters a very sacred obligation, and I have never, I think, broken even the least promise of a spiritual character, or, indeed, of any kind, made to others. Circumstances over which I have had no control have, indeed, happened which have given me grievous pain, chiefly because they prevented me from carrying out what I had promised; but, I believe that, as God will not hold us accountable for what we are prevented, by moral or physical force, from doing, so those who have done me the honor to trust me with their money for good and holy ends, will not blame me because these ends are not carried out, through no fault of mine. Rather do I hope for their prayers and sympathy; all that I can blame myself for is, that I have so long withheld the facts of the case; but I think my motives for doing this will be understood and respected now that they are fully explained.

I was known in this convent also, not only by my writings, which they possessed, but by the help which I had been enabled to send them in the famine year, so lately passed away; if indeed, famine can ever be said to pass from Ireland. The sisters, too, took a loving pleasure in recalling to me how my Protestant relative had been the friend and protector of the foundress of their order many years ago.

The Rev. M. Neligan found kind hospitality with Canon Bourke for the night, and as I have said, he knew the way to Knock, having visited there before at my request and expense, in order to fulfil my promise to my American friends.

He was anxious to say Mass that day at Knock, so we left the convent as early as I could manage to travel, and here I found for the first time that there was a very decided ecclesiastical opposition to the pilgrimage to Knock. Several of the sisters were very anxious to go with me, but the archbishop had positively forbidden them to visit there. No doubt the position was a very difficult one for ecclesiastical authority, but of that I shall speak later.

Only those who have travelled in Ireland can have any idea of the wretched conveyances in country places. We had to travel over a rough hill-road, a succession of hills and valleys, and in such a conveyance! Father Neligan got out of the car and preferred walking a great part of the way; as for myself, I became so seriously ill, that it was a question whether I could reach Knock alive.

CHAPTER XI.

VISIT TO KNOCK.

Arrival at Knock — Welcomed by Archdeacon Cavanagh — Prayer on the Scene of the Apparition — A Miraculous Restoration — Requested to Found a Convent at Knock — Letters from Dr. McEvilly, Archbishop of Tuam, and Father Cavanagh — Care in Getting Permissions — Visit to Tuam — Reception by the Archbishop — He Writes a letter of Approval — Comments on the Archbishop's Letter — Letter to Bishop Higgins — His Reply — Change of Ground by the Archbishop — His Inexplicable Anger — Injustice of Catholic Methods of Discipline — Opinion of the Late Bishop of Cavan — The Harold's Cross Convent — Its History and Peculiarities — Cordial Reception at Newry — Bishop Leahy's Letter — Return to Dublin — Astonishing Reception at Harold's Cross — Forbidden Shelter by Cardinal McCabe — Turned into the Winter Streets by his Order — Popular Hatred of Cardinal McCabe — Why was I so Treated — A Dark Mystery — Remarkable Letter from Bishop Higgins.

WITH what anxious love and desire we who had not yet visited this shrine watched for the first glimpse of the favored place, and how eagerly the first glimpse was pointed out to us by the "boy" who drove us! It was a clear winter day, beautifully bright for that part of Ireland. And what did we see from the eminence of the first hill which overlooked the valley where the church of Knock is situated? A plain, poor church, a few rude cottages, a desolate, uncultivated country. But it was Knock — in the eyes of faith, the only site in Ireland believed to have been favored with the miraculous presence of the Mother of Jesus.

Archdeacon Cavanagh was expecting us, and waiting for us. The car drove up to the church, and there we found him. His loving welcome to myself I can never forget, though we may never meet again in this world. He took both my hands, clasped them warmly in his own, and exclaimed, "A hundred thousand welcomes. We have got you now, and we will never let you go," — yet in a few months this good but easily-led priest was deceived by people whose only interest was their own selfish ends, and a glorious undertaking for Ireland and for religion was blighted forever.

I turned from Father Cavanagh to offer a prayer on the very spot where the apparition had taken place. Let it be remembered how delicate my health was, and that for four years I had been unable to kneel, even for a moment. I know not how, but I found myself on my knees in an instant, and, I know not how, I found myself completely cured; it was certainly a cure of a very remarkable kind. I came to Knock that morning, or rather a few moments before, a helpless invalid, and in a moment I felt health and life and vigor.

Father Neligan was, as I have said, waiting to say Mass, and as I did not wish to detain him a moment longer than was necessary, I turned to him and Father Cavanagh, saying, briefly, "I am cured," and hastened into the church. I found myself able to kneel without pain during the whole Mass.

I do not intend to enter into what I may call the spiritual part of my life at Knock or elsewhere. My present work concerns only the circumstances which have obliged me to abandon my work for Ireland, and I may say the work for religion, which I had begun and hoped to carry out there, and the work which I was authorized to do by the present pope.

By Father Cavanagh's advice, I arranged to stop in Knock until I received a letter from Archbishop McEvilly. My restoration to health made Father Cavanagh still more anxious that I should found a convent here. But in all such cases the rules of the Catholic church very properly require that the consent of the bishop should be obtained, as well as the consent of the parish priest. There was no delay in this, however, for I received the next day the following letter from the Archbishop of Tuam : —

"TUAM, Nov. 13, 1881.

"MY DEAR MOTHER CLARE, — I intended leaving here next week, but as you promise to favor us with a visit, I shall remain here on Monday and Tuesday to see you, and I shall promise you the hospitality of the good nuns here during your stay.

"The idea you have in your mind, and wish to carry out, is admirable, and worthy of a religious soul, and I am sure it is one that must commend itself to every one that has the salvation of souls at heart. If it had the effect of encouraging emigration, I could not for a moment have anything to say to it. There is plenty of room and to spare for all our people at home, if things were well managed. No people feel more keenly than do our Irish Catholics, the force of the Psalmist's words, 'Better is a little to the just than great riches to the wicked' (Ps. xxxv. 16). Nor is there any part of what I conceive to be a good bill, taken all in all — a bill which, in my mind, is entitled to a fair trial (the late tenant bill) so objectionable as that portion of it that has reference to emigration. Still, regarded from your point of view, considering that people will emigrate, I think your scheme entitled to every consideration, and practicable encouragement. It has for its object to mitigate a necessary evil, and save souls that might otherwise have been lost forever. As such, I cannot but encourage it.

"Very faithfully yours,
† "JOHN MCEVILLY, *Archbishop of Tuam.*"

I also had the following letter from Father Cavanagh :—

"Knock, Nov. 16, 1881.

"Dear Sister Mary Francis Clare, — It is my highest ambition and most ardent desire to see a convent established at Knock, as I am convinced that it would prove productive of incalculable good, and the source of numberless blessings to the people, not only of the locality, but to the many pious pilgrims who resort here from America, and so many other countries.

"I trust that you will, in the merciful designs of God, become the founder of the religious community so earnestly longed for, as I am satisfied that under your benign care the good work would prosper and succeed.

"I trust that nothing will deter you from complying with my request.

"I remain, dear Sister Clare,
"Yours faithfully in Jesus Christ,
"B. Cavanagh, P. P., *Archdeacon*."

I was, in fact, if possible, over-cautious in taking care that I should have the usual episcopal, not only permission, but even approbation, for what I did. If I had foreseen my future troubles I could scarcely have acted more judiciously; but I was to learn, all too soon, that neither prudence nor justice nor the most exact observance of religious discipline would avail, where ecclesiastics, who should have been the first to protect a woman and a sister, were determined to ruin her as far as they could do so.

I need scarcely say that Father Cavanagh was greatly rejoiced when he saw the archbishop's letter. It seemed to be all that he could desire or hope for, and my cure, which was so complete, removed every other difficulty. By his advice I determined on going without a day's delay to Tuam, as the archbishop had so kindly invited me. There was no line of railway available from Knock to Tuam, so I was obliged to drive a distance of forty miles. If there was anything to show how complete my recovery was, the fact that I was able to make this journey was sufficient.

I was most anxious that my confessor, the Rev. M. Neligan, should accompany me to Tuam, but he could not do so. I know that he was anxious to return to Kenmare, where he had very laborious parish duties, and I felt I could not press him unduly.

Now as all the charges which have been made against me, both in England and America, are founded on the false statements circulated first by Cardinal McCabe, and instigated by the Kenmare Sisters and Bishop Higgins, I ask careful attention to the following points, though they are a repetition of what has already been said.

It will be remembered that I had arranged to return to Newry Convent from Kenmare; that I had obtained permission to visit Knock on my way; that it was known to my superiors why I wished to go there, (1) out of devotion to the place, (2) to see if I should found a convent there for the special purpose which had been so long in my mind, and which I knew could only be carried out in an institution for the purpose.

I had all the canonical permission necessary, and I acted throughout in accordance with the rules of the church to which I belonged.

I could not induce Father Neligan to go with me to Tuam, nor was there really the least occasion for him to do so, and I believe if he had done so, the result would not have been different, as far as I am concerned.

It will be observed that the archbishop highly approved of my plans, and as I have already said, it was no new, sudden idea, it was a design long cherished, but which was quite hopeless to attempt, in consequence of the opposition of the sisters, while I remained in Kenmare.

I was very kindly received in the Presentation Convent at Tuam, and had an interview with the archbishop the next morning. He asked me to remain with them for the present, and they cordially seconded his wish. My first desire was to get the written permission of the archbishop for the foundation at Knock. Dr. McEvilly assured me many times that "his word" was quite sufficient, and seemed to think it unreasonable that I should ask a written authorization, and I know not why I was so persistent.

I think I arrived in Tuam on Monday. On Tuesday, this interview took place; the archbishop said he would give the leave in writing, later on; I replied, I would willingly wait a fortnight, if he wished it, but that he must remember the peculiar position I was in, and see how necessary it was for me to have such a document.

The next day, Wednesday, Nov. 23, the archbishop told me, that he sat down to his desk to write letters, that some impulse for which he could not account, came over him, and he wrote the document subjoined here. This document he left on his desk in an envelope directed to me, intending to bring it to me himself. To his surprise, he found the letter gone, and on asking the servant about it, the man told him he had posted it. The archbishop told me the man had never acted in this way before, and said to me next day, I must have thought it stiff and formal to have sent it by post, as the archbishop's house and the convent were just opposite each other.

"TUAM, Nov. 23, 1881.

"DEAR MOTHER MARY CLARE, — It gives us great pleasure to accede to your request to be permitted to build a convent of your order at Knock, in this diocese of Tuam. This permission is merely conditional at present. We grant it on condition, that before the foundation of the projected convent is laid, ample funds are provided for bringing the building to a successful conclusion, and security given for ample pre-existing funds for the permanent support of the sisters who may be located there to do the work of God. We would, moreover, have it distinctly understood, that in thus acceding to your pious request, it is by no means to be inferred that we sanction or approve of the alleged apparitions or miracles said to have occurred at Knock. As at present disposed, we neither approve nor disapprove of such, we reserve our judgment until the time comes, if ever, for canonically and judicially investigating the whole matter. But at present we neither admit nor reject the alleged occurrences. So that we are in a position to approach the consideration of the subject with a perfectly unbiased mind.

Commending your pious undertaking to the mercy of God, to the favor of His ever-glorious and Immaculate Mother, and her chaste spouse, St. Joseph, the Foster Father of the Son of God, and patron of the Universal church,

"Very faithfully yours,
"JOHN, *Archbishop of Tuam.*"

Several things should be noticed in this document. First: The archbishop required that sufficient funds should be obtained before the convent was commenced. Second : he takes the opportunity of disassociating the work altogether from any connection with the alleged miracles at Knock. In this connection the archbishop uses an expression which I found was a favorite one, and one which was as unpleasant to those in whose regard it was used, as it was convenient to himself. He says, "*as at present disposed*, we neither approve or disapprove of such." In time to come, I had many weary hours in consequence of this bishop's curious style of not deciding either for or against anything. In such a case as that of deciding for or against a miraculous shrine there may have been need of this non-committal policy, but when this happened in ordinary cases, which required a decision for or against a certain course of action, it caused very serious trouble.

I learned, later on, from many of the archbishop's own priests, that this was his favorite answer. So far, all seemed well to my ignorance and inexperience. Father Cavanagh came to me at Tuam, and was greatly rejoiced at the archbishop's approval of our plans. I am convinced that there was not an ecclesiastic in Ireland, who would have taken a greater interest in my work for the poor, or would have encouraged it more heartily, than the Archbishop of Tuam, but circumstances were against him as well as against myself.

Full of hope and joy, I at once sent out appeals for help, and found encouragement on every side. The dear and good reverend mother of the Presentation Convent, handed me $25.00, a large gift from their poverty, so that she might have the honor of giving the first donation for the work at Knock.

I wrote at once, both to Newry and Kenmare, and received encouraging replies from both places, and this should be noted in view of subsequent events.

I wrote to Bishop Higgins, also, but it cost me a great deal to do so; still, it seemed the right thing to do, yet doing right, in my case at least, has not always brought its own reward. I wrote, also, at once to Bishop Leahy of Dromore (Newry) diocese.

Bishop Higgins, as will be seen from his letter, was then vicar-capitular, which I may explain, for the benefit of the uninitiated, is the title held by the priest appointed to administer the affairs of a diocese after the death of a bishop, and until his successor assumes the reins of government.

But Bishop Higgins at this time was, I think, appointed bishop; I heard later that as vicar-capitular, he had no power to grant me permission to remove from Kenmare to any other convent. I give no opinion on this subject, however, nor would I note it, except that he has made so many criticisms on the actions of other bishops. As far as I was concerned, I was not trained to know canon law, and if it was violated in my case I was not the one to blame.

One thing is certain, Bishop Higgins is responsible for all the scandal that has been caused, and for the ruin of a work which would have been of the greatest utility to our unhappy country.

That he was urged to act as he did, by others, I have no doubt; but the acts were none the less his own. I have heard from priests on whose word I could entirely rely, that the Kenmare sisters were greatly disconcerted when they found that I had met such a warm welcome in Tuam, and that I was about to undertake such an important work, and naturally, they wished to discourage it.

I give here a copy of one of Bishop Higgins's letters, the original of which I hold, and which will show that I had due permission for leaving Kenmare though I was accused, through his interference, of having gone without leave.

"TRALEE, CO. KERRY, Dec. 8, 1881.

"DEAR SISTER,— As you are aware, I gave the due canonical sanction to your requisition to become a member of the Newry convent of your

Order. Mother Abbess of Kenmare gave her sanction to the same request; the Right Rev. Leahy and the community at Newry formally accepted the transfer, and duly intimated their acceptance to you and Mother Teresa. In pursuance of this arrangement, you left this diocese for Newry.

"Things being so, you have passed from my jurisdiction, and have become subject to that of the Most Rev., the Ordinary of Dromore, and I have no authority whatever to direct or control your action; that authority, I repeat, rests in the hands of Dr. Leahy.

"At the same time, I am quite willing to aid your view of abiding in the diocese of Tuam, provided you suggest a way in which I can act without seeming intrusive to their lordships of Tuam and Dromore. I am not a bishop, you know, and I am much younger, and in every way beneath them.

"Yours faithfully,
"A. Higgins,
"*Vicar-Capitular.*"

Now it should be noted here that Bishop Higgius states clearly (1) I had his permission to leave Kenmare; (2) that he had no jurisdiction over me after I left it; and (3) that he did not object to my making the foundation at Knock. This letter, it will be observed, was written on the eighth of December.

I had also written to Newry to Bishop Leahy. In fact, I had done all that was necessary, and more than was necessary, and Bishop Higgins's letter, with its protestations of non-interference and professions of kindness, so completely deceived me that I did not suppose it possible, whatever his feelings against me might be, that he was actually then destroying my happiness for life, and bringing on me unmerited reproach and suffering, from which nothing now can ever relieve me.

As I was anxious to return to Knock for a few days, I obtained leave from Archbishop McEvilly to do so, and he very willingly granted me the permission. On my return to Tuam, the storm burst. On, I think the thirteenth of December, Archbishop McEvilly sent for me to see him in the convent parlor. The reverend mother of the Presentation Convent told me he was very angry and excited about something, she knew not what. I went, wondering what could be the trouble, and I was soon told. The archbishop held an open letter in his hand, and said he had very unpleasant news, that he feared I had done something wrong, he would not even tell me what; in fact he was greatly excited and greatly vexed, and I am not surprised that he should have been so, when I learned later the underhanded effort which was made by Bishop Higgins to injure me and destroy my happy relations with him.

I could only reply that as his grace would not tell me what I was accused of, nor who were my accusers, I could say nothing. Certainly nothing could have been more unjust; and it is precisely this unfortunate policy of condemning people without allowing them any chance of being heard, or of knowing who are their accusers, which brings such discredit on the Roman church.

I said to myself, "it cannot be Bishop Higgins or the Kenmare sisters, as I had a letter a few days ago (on the eighth of December) from the former"; in fact, it will be easily seen I was terribly perplexed. I knew of course some secret enemy had done this, but Bishop Higgins's letter, and an apparently friendly letter which I had received from the superioress in Kenmare, had prevented me from suspecting them as otherwise I should have done. This was the cause of all my future trouble. If I had been more suspicious, all might have been well.

I said at once, "Well, your grace, you have been very kind to me, I will not embarrass you further; I can go to Newry convent. I know how glad they would be to have me there." To Kenmare I had determined never to go again. I know now they hoped to drive me back there by depriving me of a home elsewhere; but I knew if they had made me suffer so much before I left, how much more suffering would they not have inflicted on me if I came back defeated in all my hopes. It is very painful to me to be obliged to write of sisters and priests as I have done, but I believe that it is my duty to tell the truth. Those who expose the injuries and injustices which are done in public institutions, receive the support of all honest men, though they certainly are not commended by those whom they expose. In the Roman church, evil is concealed and exposure prevented under the most severe penalties. The man who dares to speak is put under a ban, and is condemned for "attacking the church." A man might as justly be condemned for attacking the government because he denounced violations of law. Yet if the evil done in the church is shielded and concealed, so much the worse for the church; but if the evil is a blot on the church, why does the church condemn those who denounce it? But, if faults are condemned, those who do the evil should be condemned also, and if the church allowed this, she must denounce some of her most exalted children.

I must here relate an incident of convent life of which I was a witness and helpless to interfere. I have said that Miss O'Hagan, who was superioress in Newry convent, and subsequently in Kenmare, was in very delicate health. She went to Dublin from Kenmare, as several of the other sisters did also, for medical advice. She was accompanied by a young sister, and here I may say that I was the only one of the sisters in Kenmare in really delicate health who never left it for change, or for the attendance of skilled physicians; though my case was far more serious than theirs, and skilled medical attendance would have saved me from much suffering.

While Miss O'Hagan was in Dublin, some great trouble arose between herself and the sisters with whom she was staying, of which this young sister was cognizant. I do not believe that Miss O'Hagan was guilty of the charges which were made against her by this sister and the sisters with whom she was staying, but I know that this young sister thought that she was guilty. I spoke to our bishop, then Dr. Moriarty, about the matter afterwards, and saw that he, too, believed the accusation, but Miss O'Hagan's relatives were too influential to allow of any public scandal being made, whether the grounds for doing so were just or unjust.

The matter was quietly hushed up, and only a very few knew of it, and certainly Miss O'Hagan was never allowed to suffer for it in any way. The poor young sister, justly or unjustly, was made the victim, though she never spoke of the subject to any one except the bishop. I shall never forget the inhumanity with which she was treated. She was even more friendless than I was; and what could she do but bear the indignities which were heaped upon her? She was degraded publicly before all the sisters. Her black veil was taken from her, and she was obliged to remain in her own room. Her special and vindictive persecutor was Miss L——y the sister who had turned on me with such violent language in Newry Convent, because she thought that I had spoken to the bishop about the unwisdom of running into debt. To obtain peace, this poor sister was obliged to sign a document denying all that she had previously stated, and whether she believed it to be false or not, she had no other course. The bishop told me afterwards that it was not at all uncommon for some sisters with more zeal than brains, to make the most ridiculous charges against the superior.

But, to return to my own troubles, Archbishop McEvilly was very decided; he said, "I will not let you go, but you had better go to Newry, see Bishop Leahy, and get from him a written transfer to my diocese, and, when you come back with it, I will receive you with open arms."

It was fearful winter weather, heavy snow and

frost, and I had spent many years in Kenmare, where I had never been in any way exposed to severe cold, and to travel now was at the risk of my life.

I had already received a very kind telegram from Bishop Leahy, who was quite satisfied with all the arrangements, and this should have been sufficient for Dr. McEvilly. I asked Archbishop McEvilly could I not write to him for this document. "No," he said, "you must go and get it." Then I offered him three times to give up the Knock foundation; could I have done more? I am glad I did so, for however I have been made to suffer, my conscience at least has been clear.

The archbishop said he could not decide positively that day, but the next day he came to the convent very early and gave me just an hour's notice to take the steam cars for Dublin. Shall I ever forget that terrible day and that weary journey? It is a miracle that I lived through it all; let it be remembered that I had suffered for years from acute rheumatism and a very serious internal complaint, besides general delicacy of constitution, and that I had not for years been exposed to the weather; so the risk I ran could hardly be overestimated.

I must say here, as I am writing everything, — and an autobiography, to be truthful, should contain all important matters, — that some of the archbishop's priests told me he wanted to get rid of me quietly, and that this whole matter was pre-arranged with the Archbishop of Dublin and Bishop Higgins, certainly Miss L——y, then superioress in Kenmare, knew all that was done and every move I made. I do not like to make any charges which I cannot prove; I can only say that the priests who told me this were in the way of knowing his mind; but his actions, as will be seen in the next few pages, show that if he had not then determined to get rid of me in this way, he did so a few days later.

A very dear friend, the late Bishop of Cavan, to whom I told all my troubles later on, laughed at all this business, and said a verbal permission for a sister coming from one convent to another was all that was needed, and was all he gave in such cases.

I went directly to Dublin, and to the convent of Poor Clares in Harold's Cross, accompanied by my faithful friend and secretary, Miss D——, who never left me.

This convent was founded in the early part of the present century by some two or three ladies who had belonged to a Poor Clare convent which was broken up by the English government during the time of the Penal laws.

The sisters at that time were real Poor Clares, and kept the fasts, the strict inclosure, and all the rules of this ancient order, but they were dispersed, and for a time, at least, lived as secular ladies in a small house in Dublin. They resolutely determined to live together again, and as at that time there were no Sisters of Mercy, nor any teaching order, the archbishop of Dublin urged that they should do so, but on conditions which practically caused them to cease to be Poor Clares. Certainly, they still bear the name, but every single rule and observance of the order was abandoned.

They were no longer to observe any fasts except those of the church, though the rule of the Poor Clares required perpetual fasting and abstinence. They were to say a short office, and the rule of the ancient order of Poor Clares required them to say the divine office in choir; they were to receive orphans, to have only a nominal inclosure, though the original rule of the Poor Clares required that they should observe the strictest inclosure. The Holy See, however, on the representation of the archbishop, and considering the urgent necessity of the case, granted all the dispensations, and the sisters assumed a plain black dress, though the ancient Poor Clares' habit was brown.

All was certainly permitted by Rome, but it seemed to many that to have founded a new order, or to have taken up the elastic rule of St. Francis, would have been better. The troubled times and circumstances, no doubt, prevented such an idea from entering the mind of the archbishop, and he was only too thankful to use the material he had in hand, as it enabled him to carry out his plans quietly and quickly.

After a time the convent in Newry, where I was professed, was founded from this Poor Clare convent in Harold's Cross, and kept the observances of the sisters of the convent from whence they came. Though each convent of the order was entirely separate from the other, we certainly looked on Harold's Cross as a sort of "Mother House," it being the first founded.

Each convent also was under the exclusive control of the bishop of the diocese in which it was situated, but as sickness or any other necessity obliged us to visit Dublin from time to time, we always stopped with and received the kindest hospitality from the sisters at Harold's Cross. It will be remembered that I had stopped there with the other sisters, on our way from Newry to Kenmare, and that different sisters had gone there from Kenmare for medical advice, or in passing on their way from other places.

I need not say that the dear sisters gave me a warm welcome, and that they sympathized with my troubles. They wished me to remain with them for some time, but I was far too anxious to have my affairs settled to delay even an hour that was not necessary.

As I was greatly fatigued, I decided not to go to Newry the next day, but to rest with them, and I took the opportunity of seeing two very eminent surgeons regarding my case. I also telegraphed to Cork to the doctor who attended me in Kenmare for the internal trouble from which I suffered so long, and which was believed to be incurable. I was anxious that he should see me, as no one could give better evidence of my cure. He had attended me at Kenmare, — although he was not brought there for me by the sisters, as they would not have allowed any such expenditure for me, though the doctor there was so incapable as to be unable to do what was absolutely necessary for me.

Dr. —— telegraphed to me that he would come up on Sunday, though to do so he should travel all night. I therefore decided to go the next day, Friday, Dec. 16, to Newry; by taking a fast train and starting early in the morning, I knew that I could return to Harold's Cross the same day, and I proposed to rest on Saturday, and on Monday to return to Tuam with the document for which Dr. McEvilly had sent me.

I was received with the greatest affection by the sisters at Newry, after my many years of absence there were many changes, but there was no change in their love for me. They were very anxious that I should remain some days with them, and I was equally anxious to do so myself, but still I felt that duty called me to my work elsewhere, and I resisted all their kind entreaties.

The dear reverend mother had been my mistress of novices, and she knew from others' beside myself, the treatment which I had to bear in Kenmare, and she had written more than one indignant letter on the subject to the reverend mother and sisters there.

My object was, to see the bishop who had professed me there, the Right Rev. Dr. Leahy, and to obtain from him personally, the document of transfer to the Tuam Diocese, for which Archbishop McEvilly had sent me.

Bishop Leahy received me with the greatest kindness, fully approved what I wished to do, and gave me the subjoined document, than which nothing could be more explicit.

"CONVENT OF SAINT CLARE, NEWRY, Dec. 16, 1881.

"MY DEAR LORD BISHOP, — I release Sister M. Francis Clare, Cusack, from whatever canonical obedience she owes to me as Bishop of Dromore, and I hereby transfer that obedience to your Grace. With sincere esteem,

"Your Grace's obedient servant in Christ,
"BROTHER JOHN PIUS LEAHY, O. P.
"*Bishop of Dromore.*

"To MOST REV. DR. MCEVILLY, *Lord Bishop of Tuam.*"

All this writing, however, was quite unnecessary, as I had received a despatch to this effect and shown it to Dr. McEvilly before I left Tuam. But he had to express dissatisfaction, to get me out of his diocese, when he hoped to keep me out.

So rejoiced was I, that had there been any way of going to Tuam across Ireland, even by travelling by day and night, without going through Dublin, I think I should have gone. All was settled now, and it seemed as if nothing more was needed to begin the great work for poor Irish girls, on which my heart had been so long set.

I returned to Dublin by the next train, though as I have said, I should have liked to remain even a day with those who were so justly dear to me. I arrived in Dublin late at night, and hastened to Harold's Cross Convent. I saw that the sisters were greatly disturbed and distressed, but I could not imagine the cause; in fact they knew not how to break the terrible news to me. At last I was told everything. Cardinal McCabe, who had not been in the convent I think for four years, had called there early with his chaplain, and given orders that I was to be put out in the streets of Dublin.

The sisters were greatly distressed and asked what I had done to receive such treatment. His eminence refused any information, but to relieve them, he sent his chaplain to the nearest telegraph office, with orders to send a telegram after me, to forbid my entering his diocese again. This telegram I never received, and what is still more remarkable I could never get any trace of it from the post-office authorities. I therefore returned, as I have said, to the convent. One dear sister, so far kept her presence of mind and allowed her charity to overcome her fear of ecclesiastical censure, as to implore the cardinal on her knees, to allow me that one night's shelter, as they knew I could not return till late, and it was a bitter night. His eminence granted her request, but only on one condition, that I should be put out on the streets of Dublin at daybreak next morning. I had nowhere to go, and the sisters did not fail to remind his eminence of this. All my relations and friends are Protestants. If I had gone to any of them they would indeed have received me kindly, but I knew not how I could bring myself to tell them that I had been put out of a convent of my own order, on the streets of Dublin, without a word of explanation. The sisters wrote to me a year after, to say how they had wondered at my calmness, or that I could have borne the blow as patiently as I did, but I said, "Well, it is a great trial, but I can return to Tuam to-morrow," and I thought how much pleased the archbishop would be to receive such a document. He had sent me for it, he had declared he would receive me "with open arms" when I came back; all would be well, and God would enable me to bear the great fatigue and excitement. How could I for a moment, imagine that he had sent me for a document which he did not intend to accept.

But a short time only had passed when I was handed a despatch (telegram) from Archbishop McEvilly, which is now before me as I write.

[*From the Archbishop of Tuam.*]

"*To* SISTER MARY FRANCIS CLARE CUSACK, Harold's Cross, Dublin, —

"Don't come to the diocese till consent is given by me in writing, and I judge first if the letter be satisfactory."

I soon saw that all had been carefully pre-arranged; for shortly after, I received a despatch from the Reverend Mother of the Presentation Convent in Tuam, saying the archbishop had "commanded" her not to receive me into her convent again.

I could not help thinking that if I had been accused of committing a theft or a murder, I should have been better treated. At least, I should have had a fair trial; I should have been told what were the charges against me. I was, indeed, in a difficult position, and had not one to advise with except the faithful companion who stood by me in all my troubles. I had, at least, the night for reflection, thanks to the humanity of the dear sister who pleaded with my inexorable judge. I am sure the Kenmare Sisters thought I would be driven back to them for refuge, but even had I wished to go to them, another set of canonical proceedings must have been set going to release me from Tuam diocese.

And yet only one short week before this terrible day, Archbishop McEvilly had written to me that the work which I hoped to do for poor girls was "admirable." "The idea," he said, "you have in your mind and wish to carry out, is admirable and worthy of a religious soul, and I am sure it is one that must commend itself to every one that has the salvation of souls at heart."

Houseless, homeless, and desolate, I went out on the streets of Dublin, the very town where I was born, on that Saturday morning. It is true, as I have said, I had many Protestant relatives, but if I went to them, I felt I dared not meet the just indignation with which they would denounce the treatment I had met, and I knew not but my faith might fail me; even their affection would have been a temptation to me, because of my need of it.

I had no Catholic friends except the very poor, and one family who I was sure, and the event proved right, had been embittered against me by false impressions from Kenmare.

It was a time of great excitement in Dublin, and, indeed, in all Ireland. The people were exasperated by the famine, which they thought might have been prevented by a more paternal system of government. They were brooding over dark deeds which had culminated in the awful murders in the Phœnix Park, Dublin, a few months before. The archbishop had so exasperated the people by his opposition to the popular movement, that his door had been several times hung with crape and disfigured with the emblems of death.

I knew that if news of the way the cardinal had conducted himself towards me became known in Dublin at such a time, the result would probably have been personal violence, or an attack on his pastoral residence; and even if I had wished to speak, the dread of such possible consequences would have deterred me.

I made one last attempt to obtain a hearing. I sent for the chaplain of the convent before leaving Harold's Cross next morning, and implored him to go for me to Cardinal McCabe to show him Archbishop McEvilly's telegram, which proved that I was in Dublin by his desire and the object for which I was there, and to show him also Bishop Leahy's canonical transfer to the diocese of Tuam, which proved that I belonged to that diocese; but the priest, though courteous to myself, told me he dare not go to the cardinal; no one he said dared offer even the least opposition to his word, or ask for any explanation when he had once spoken.

I was still quite in the dark as to this mystery; but I knew there must be some cause for it. I was stunned and stupefied by the blow, but I wondered how Cardinal McCabe knew where I was. Later I knew he must have got the information from the Kenmare Sisters or from Tuam, the former as I soon learned and, as the reader will see, employed some one to watch all my movements and to report them.

A few months later, in April, 1882, the mystery was solved. I received a letter, now before me, from Bishop Higgins in which he told the facts of the case. What induced him to do this I do not know, but the date of his letter caused a good deal of amusement in Rome.

"THE PALACE, KILLARNEY, April 1, 1882.

"MY DEAR SISTER,— The Archbishop of Tuam fell into a great oversight in receiving you into his diocese without a formal transfer of your obedience, made by Dr. Leahy and accepted, all in writing, by him; or, if you were to be transferred directly to Knock, the transfer was to be effected by a similar written agreement between him and me. Hence your whole position in Knock was a false one, and the longer you continued there the more false your position would become; every act and every arrangement would be invalid, and the *denouement* would be terrible to you, and would give every one who wished to be troublesome to you, a handle of a formidable character. I was compromised seriously in the matter. If I said nothing, I was sure to come in for blame with all concerned when the real state of things came to be known; and most justly you might say, the archbishop might say, what conduct was this for one in your position; by a single word you might have saved me from a most unpleasant position, attended with great danger of a serious scandal, and for weeks and months, you would not say that one word. Hence I was very uneasy. I pondered and pondered over what I should do; I could not write to you, as you will easily understand. If I wrote to the Archbishop of Tuam, all the chances were that your staying in his diocese would be impossible; so I wrote to Doctor, now Cardinal

McCabe, and to Dr. Leahy. The former was a prudent, reticent man, and kind-hearted. I urged him to break this matter to the Archbishop of Tuam, at the same time urging him to advise Tuam (*sic*) to settle the matter quietly with Dr. Leahy, and to receive you. I said that you would be sure to make the collection for building and founding Knock a real success. You know the rest. I am, dear sister, faithfully yours,

"† A. HIGGINS."

As to the "all in writing" business, Bishop Higgins himself did not do any writing when I was transferred to Newry diocese, so his zeal on that point reflects on himself.

Now, although I shall return to this letter in the next chapter, as it is so important a document for me, I shall say a word here :—

First. Bishop Higgins talks of an oversight. There was no oversight except what he made himself. I wrote *at once* to the Bishop of Dromore (Newry) when the Archbishop of Tuam arranged for me to make the Knock foundation, and all was arranged with him, according to the strictest requirements of canon law, in three weeks.

Second. Probably, Bishop Higgins did not know this, but whether I did this or not, or whether he knew it or not, he had no right to interfere, and if he had practised the humility he expressed (page 224), all this trouble would have been saved.

CHAPTER XII.

WAITING FOR PERMISSION TO RETURN TO TUAM.

Abandoned by my Friends — Miss O'Hagan's Relatives Desert me — A Gleam of Sunshine — I Seek Refuge — A Grateful Cabman — A Serious Difficulty — I Write to the Archbishop of Tuam — A Forged Despatch — Duplicity of the Kenmare Sisters — Bishop Higgins's Vacillations — Contrasted Extracts from his Letters.

THERE was one circumstance which added greatly to the trouble of mind which I suffered in Dublin when Cardinal McCabe put me out on the streets. The peculiar circumstances of my case, it will be remembered, left me in a very friendless condition; no immigrant landed alone on a foreign shore was ever more desolate and helpless. The few who would have befriended me did not know my trouble; others who ought to have helped me were too much afraid to do so. But there were relatives of Miss O'Hagan then in Dublin who could have helped me, if they had chosen, without the least fear of consequences to themselves, and they would not do it. They knew well all I had done for her, and if they had had one spark of good feeling they should have come to the rescue now. I do not like to say all I could about what I was able to do for the Kenmare convent and sisters; I know that those who do the most for God are but instruments whom he chooses to do his work; but since he does so choose us, we may not deny his choice, or the good done by His permission. In Kenmare, there were no large funds belonging to the convent which could be used as there were in Newry for any purpose. In Newry there were some quite wealthy merchants who were always ready to help the sisters generously.

In Kenmare there was no one. There every thing had to be done for the people; we could not have a fair, for there was no one to come to it. We might have sold a few lottery tickets, but that was all. If, then, I had not been able to help, and to help very largely, by the money earned by the sale of my books, poor Miss O'Hagan would have found herself in very great difficulties, and could have hardly supported the convent or done anything for the poor. Besides, the Kenmare convent would have been unknown except to tourists, who might have bought a few yards of lace. But the extraordinarily large circulation of my books made the name of Kenmare known all over the world, as the reviews at the end of this book will show. Hence my writings benefited the convent in more ways than one, as they were the means of bringing very large donations and even legacies to me. Miss O'Hagan's friends knew this well; they knew well how many an anxious hour I had saved her. Lord O'Hagan was poor; he had no private property, and needed all he got as a government official to support his family.

Still he had great influence and moved in the highest circles of Dublin society, and his daughter, who lived there, was well known to Cardinal McCabe, who dared not have refused her an interview had she asked one; she not only refused to help me in any way, but she actually spoke of my leaving Kenmare as if it had been a crime, and helped to excite feeling against me amongst her friends in Dublin. I knew her mind had been poisoned against me, and by whom. But her conduct in so readily believing evil of me was not the least of my many trials.

I had one little gleam of sunshine in this dark hour. As soon as it was daylight, I started to obey the orders of Cardinal McCabe and leave Harold's Cross Convent.

I had spent the night thinking where I could go safely and quietly, and decided to take temporary shelter with a Mr. M——n at whose house I knew sisters often stopped when passing through Dublin, and whom I had employed for some years as an agent for the sale of my books.

He was astonished at my arrival, but so fearful

was I of public scandal, or of exciting feeling against Cardinal McCabe, that I did not tell even him why I had come to his house. He received me most kindly and proceeded at once to do all that he could for me.

When I went to pay the driver who brought me to his house, he asked me was I "the Nun of Kenmare, the good sister who had saved so many people from famine?" I replied sadly enough that I was. "And do you think I would be mane enough to take money from you that kept the life in the Irish people and children?" And he drove off in all haste, to show his determination not to be paid.

I now had to consider carefully what I should do. I knew that, according to the canonical law of the Roman Catholic church, all the bishops concerned had made very grave mistakes. I belonged canonically to the Tuam diocese by the archbishop's own request. Still I made another effort to set myself right quietly, and wrote to a priest in Dublin, a near relative of the late Bishop McCarthy, who had been my great friend, asking him to go to the cardinal and beg that he would even look at my authorization, but he, also, dared not interfere. I wrote also to the Archbishop of Tuam, reminding him that he had sent me for a certain document, that I had got the document and sent him a copy of it. I received an evasive reply, and found myself still in the same position. I knew that if I forced myself on him when he was so prejudiced against me, from whatever cause, my doom was sealed. Yet what was I to do unless I gave up the religious life altogether! I had then no resource but to compel the archbishop to do me justice. I wrote to him in reply, that as I belonged by his own act, and of his free will to his diocese, I could not go elsewhere, that there was but one course for me, to go to Rome and ask there what I was to do. This brought a reply from him to say he "supposed that I could go to Knock." Later, when I showed this letter to some priests, they were greatly amused at it, but it certainly was very sad to me.

I now began to get some light as to the source of this persecution. During the few days that I stayed at Mr. M——n's, a despatch was handed to me by the servant, which was addressed to him. The girl said "I suppose this is for you;" without mentioning the name. I opened it without noticing the address, supposing it was for myself, and read the contents. It was from Mrs. D——, the mother of the young lady who was with me, and who as I have said, has been for many years my private secretary and dear friend.

The object was to try and induce her to leave

me, and to make Mr. M———n mistrust me. The more I reflected on the matter the more strange it seemed to me. Mrs. D——— had always wished her daughter to be with me. The answer, it was said, was to be sent to the Convent Kenmare, and this perplexed me also. I thought it very unlikely that Mrs. D——— would have sent such a despatch, and it was still more unlikely that she should have asked to have the reply addressed to the convent instead of her own house, for neither she nor her family had been in favor with the sisters.

I began to suspect what I found soon after was the truth. Mrs. D——— knew nothing of the telegram. She had not authorized its despatch, either directly or indirectly, and was indignant when she heard the use that was made of her name by the sisters. It was to this despatch that I alluded, when I said I had reason to know that the Kenmare sisters kept a close watch on all my movements.

All kinds of wild rumors now began to fly around. I heard from both friends and foes what things were said, and where they had originated. It was said that I had gone to a public hotel in Dublin, that I had gone to an obscure and low hotel, that I had gone out of my mind, that I had quarrelled with the Archbishop of Tuam, and I know not what else; and a paragraph was put in one of the Dublin newspapers that Bishop Higgins asked me to sign a paper saying that I would give up all political writing; the fact being that Bishop Higgins had never even suggested such a thing. But plainly the whole trouble was caused by him, as his own letters show, and it is difficult to understand what motive he could have had, or why he should have made such contradictory statements.

The whole matter was a mystery to me, as well as Bishop Higgins's talk about all this "pondering," and why he should have written to me of his "pondering" occupying "weeks and months," when it was actually only a few days, or declared his inability to write to me at the very time when he did write to me and that more than once.

If I have dwelt at some length on this point, I have done so only from the necessity of the case, because all the trouble which I have had, dates from the interference of Bishop Higgins, and the result, that I was put out on the streets of Dublin on a false charge by Cardinal McCabe, through his uncanonical and uncalled for interference in what was no affair of his, in whatever light my case is considered. During this fortnight between the third and thirteenth of December, Bishop Higgin's mind must have been in a very disturbed state. The following extracts will show this.

December 8, 1881, he wrote to me, —

"You have passed from my jurisdiction, and I have no authority to direct or control your action."

In his letter to me of April 1, 1882, he says, —

"I pondered and pondered over what I should do — so I wrote to Dublin to Doctor, now Cardinal, McCabe; I urged him to break this matter to the Archbishop of Tuam."

In a letter, dated December 15, 1881, he says again, —

"You have passed from my jurisdiction — I have no desire to obtrude advice on you — you would not have me of my own accord to obtrude my views upon two such people as Archbishop McEvilly and Dr. Leahy."

In a letter of April 1, 1882, he says, —

"I urged him (Cardinal McCabe) to advise Tuam (*sic*) to settle the matter quietly with Dr. Leahy, and to receive you."

Now there was nothing to settle except poor Bishop Higgins's own mind, and why Archbishop McEvilly should have been advised by any one to "receive me" when he had received me, or to settle matters quietly when all was settled, until Bishop Higgins himself set to work to unsettle it, is a mystery which Bishop Higgins alone can solve.

On the 1st of October, 1882, I received a letter from Archbishop Croke, in which he says, —

"I think it would do no harm to publish a short account of your departure from Kenmare Convent, showing clearly, as you can do by documentary evidence, that you had full leave and license to leave Kenmare and go to Knock, and thence to Newry, and finally to settle in Knock, with a view to the erection there of a convent of your order. Dr. McCabe had been told that you had no leave to quit Kenmare; this I know. Hence, I suppose, the eviction."

Who told this to Cardinal McCabe. Bishop Higgins says in his 1st of April letter, that he wrote to him, and if he did not say what he knew to be false, he must have gone within measurable distance of doing it.

A number of letters will be found in the appendix to this work which will show that I was not without the sympathy of some good priests in this trouble; but very many of the charges which Bishop Higgins made against me to Cardinal McCabe have been wilfully credited by many bishops to this day.

CHAPTER XIII.

DEPRIVED OF THE SACRAMENTS WITHOUT CAUSE.

Permitted to Return to Knock — Unjust Treatment by Archbishop McEvilly — Ingratitude of a Sister — Commissioned to Hunt me Down — A Hard Winter — A Sad Christmas — Forbidden the Sacraments — Archdeacon Cavanagh Dares not Confess me — I Appeal to Bishop Leahy — His Response — Archbishop McEvilly Consents "For Once," and Sends me to Claremorris — A Little Consolation.

I RETURNED to Knock the day after I received Archbishop McEvilly's permission to do so. I would have gone the same day if I could. But I was indeed in a most painful position. Any priest will know that I belonged lawfully and with all due canonical form to the diocese of Tuam, and if Archbishop McEvilly had the courage of his opinions he should have allowed me to return at once to Tuam Convent until arrangements could have been made for beginning the work which he had authorized me to do. Such a proceeding would have been simple and honorable, and would have even saved himself a world of trouble. But Archbishop McEvilly knew the feeling which Cardinal McCabe had against me.

From that hour until I left the diocese of Tuam, I was treated by Archbishop McEvilly exactly as if I had done the evil of which I was so falsely accused, and as if I had "left my convent," instead of being put out of it with such injustice.

Rumors were circulated everywhere, and believed, though they were of the most absurd character.

The sister of one of the Kenmare sisters, whom I had helped for years, even clothing and feeding her children, wrote me a most unchristian letter, which I still have, which, little as she thought it, gave me a clue to the source of my trouble. She said she "had been commissioned to hunt me down." But there was another expression in her letter which later on I understood better. It was this : "You are a wicked fool, and have left your sainted order." I thought but little of these words at the time, because the poor woman was as violent as she was illiterate, but she kept her word.

Shortly after I left Kenmare I received a letter from one of her brothers, imploring me to lend him some money, as he was in great distress; and he said he, "did not fear to ask me, as I had been for so many years the generous benefactor of his family and relatives."

I returned to Knock just before Christmas in 1881. It was very severe weather, such as rarely happens in Ireland; and in that country, as the people are unaccustomed to extreme cold, there is no preparation to meet it, and the suffering it causes is all the more intense.

We arrived in Ballyhaunis, the nearest station to the village of Knock, late in the evening. The windows of the railway carriage had been thick with ice, and we had been well-nigh frozen to our seats on the way from Dublin. At Ballyhaunis, matters were far worse. The only conveyance we could get, was a wretched "inside car," the cushions of which were saturated with icy water. Nor was there any more comfort at Knock. The only place of shelter I could find, was in a poor thatched cottage, where as a great luxury I got a little bare closet, which just held a bed and a chair, and was lighted by a window only a foot square.

I shall never forget that Christmas. Archdeacon Cavanagh seemed very glad to see me, and I had a very warm welcome from all the people, who were full of hope as to what I might do for them. They were all at the Christmas merry-making and rejoicing, as the poor people will do in Ireland, but for me there was not even spiritual consolation.

After all I had suffered, I looked to have the one comfort of receiving the sacraments of the church, but even this was denied to me. When I asked Archdeacon Cavanagh to hear my confession, he refused, and said it would not be prudent for him to do so until I had obtained permission from Archbishop McEvilly.

I must explain here a rule of the Catholic church, which is not generally known even amongst Catholics. The bishop of every diocese is required to appoint certain priests as the confessors of the nuns or sisters,* and no other priest can hear their confessions, nor can they lawfully confess to any other priest. Besides this, a second priest is appointed, who comes four times in each year to hear the confessions of the sisters, and he is called the extraordinary confessor. But when sisters are travelling they can go to any priest, and any priest can give them absolution.

In my case it was obvious that either rule might apply, and Archdeacon Cavanagh knew that he could have admitted me to the sacraments without any special permission from the archbishop. But he had an object in view and a wise one. He said as there had been so many disputes, the more clearly my position in the diocese was defined the better, and that I must write and ask the

* The word nun is more generally used in Ireland. In America those who dedicate themselves to the religious life are called sisters. There is, however, a technical difference. The term nun is properly applied to those who make a vow of strict religious inclosure.

archbishop for faculties for him to hear my confession.

The burden, as usual, was put on me, but it was the archdeacon's duty to have asked for these faculties for himself. And so at a time when I most needed the consolations of religion, I was deprived of them. It was a curious experience. If the teaching of the Catholic church was true, and if those who held the keys of the kingdom of heaven believed in their own powers, surely mine was a special case for the exercise of grace.

Christmas passed; the Feast of the Circumcision passed; the Epiphany passed, and still I was refused the sacraments without cause. No reason was assigned, but some of Archbishop McEvilly's own priests, told me that he hoped to make me leave his diocese of my own accord, so that another charge could be brought against me, and I could be got rid of this way, as the Dublin plan had failed, without its appearing to have been done by him. The truth was, that none of the bishops concerned could find any excuse, or even fault by which they would have been justified before the public in sending me adrift on the world. There was only one resource left, and that was to drive me to despair in order that I might commit some deed for which they might condemn me. But by a wonderful mercy of God I was kept from at least this form of desperation.

The archbishop wrote an evasive reply in the style which was so useful to him, and so trying when one needed an explicit answer. It was penned in the style of his decision about Knock, that "as at present advised," he neither believed nor disbelieved that I belonged to his diocese, and he "doubted" if he could give the faculties to any priest to hear my confession. In fact he doubted everything, when it was inconvenient to be decided.

I wrote to Bishop Leahy, always my true friend, telling him my trouble and that Bishop McEvilly had refused me the sacraments. And here I may say, that I have often wondered how it was, that knowing as they did, that I was a convert to the Roman Catholic faith, they were not afraid of driving me in disgust or despair to return to the religion of my happier days. No doubt injustices are practised by members of Protestant churches, but they who suffer have at least, the protection of the strong arm of the law, and of public opinion. If I had not been a Roman Catholic sister I could have taken an action for defamation of character or libel against any of my accusers. As a Roman Catholic sister I could not do this, no matter of what I might be accused. Surely when the higher ecclesiastical powers are protected on every side from their subjects, they should use no ordinary justice, not to say mercy, in the exercise of their irresponsible power.*

Bishop Leahy's reply is before me now. He seemed perplexed, as well he might be. He reminds me that he had already transferred me canonically to the diocese of Tuam, and asks, "What more does Archbishop McEvilly want?" Adding with infinite goodness, that "if the archbishop would draw up any paper which he considered more binding or regular, he would at once sign it."

I sent a copy of that letter to Archbishop McEvilly and received a reply, in which he said that he had granted faculties to Archdeacon Cavanagh to hear my confession for once, and *for once only*, — (the italics are the archbishop's). That I was giving great scandal by remaining at Knock, (it

---

* If Roman Catholics are denounced or excommunicated for making an appeal to the secular power for justice, the church should form a court of appeal, the judges of which should be, above all, free from suspicion of partiality. But in the Roman Catholic church the bishop is judge, jury, and executioner, and the unhappy being who refuses submission to an injustice, may be very sure of scant shrift at a second appeal. An appeal in the case of a priest is sometimes allowed to the archbishop's council, but such an appeal is a mere farce. The council are men who must either agree with the bishop or take the consequence. They generally agree with him.

will be remembered that he had sent me there himself, and that I went in obedience to his orders), that I could go either to Claremorris Convent or to Swinford, and that my staying in Knock was much talked of in Dublin, and would not tend to make people think more of the Knock devotion.

The convent at Claremorris was the one at which I had rested on my way to Knock, when I went there first with my confessor and my secretary. It was in Archbishop McEvilly's diocese. The convent at Swinford was not in the archbishop's diocese, and I could not understand how Archbishop McEvilly could have asked me to go to a convent not in his diocese, at the very time when he was so troubled about my canonical position. Like Bishop Higgins, I "pondered and pondered," and the more I pondered the less I knew. The extraordinary confusion which existed in Bishop Higgins's mind appeared infectious.

I asked Archdeacon Cavanagh and several of Archbishop McEvilly's own priests what they thought of this offer, and they unanimously advised me to go to Claremorris. I myself saw at once, that if I went to Swinford a new set of complications would arise, and the priests seemed to think that such a consummation was desired.

Certainly, everything was done from the hour I left Kenmare until I passed out of the reach of these bishops to make me commit myself to some act that could be condemned; and as it was found impossible to do this, the only means left was to spread calumnies about me in every direction.

I went to Claremorris with my companion as quickly as possible, and arranged to pay the sisters there for their hospitality. Here I had the great consolation of the friendship and affection of the Very Rev. Canon Bourke, so well known as a historical writer and a Celtic scholar. He was the parish priest of Claremorris, and had been one of my correspondents for years. I fear, however, his friendship for me was a source of many troubles for him. Yet he was far too just and too generous to consider his own interests when he could defend or comfort me.

On the sad Christmas day when I was deprived of the spiritual graces which were granted to even the most wretched prisoners or criminals, Canon Bourke drove over to Knock to see and cheer me.

Later I received the following letter from my confessor, the Rev. M. Neligan, C. C., of Kenmare, who travelled with myself and my secretary, Miss Downing.

THE PRESBYTERY, KENMARE, March, 9, 1882.

"MY VERY DEAR SISTER F. CLARE, — Your letter of this morning simply astounds me. The calumny that you left Kenmare without the proper permission from your superiors is too absurd. Don't mind; patience and resignation will right things.

"I accompanied you at the request of the mother abbess here, and with the sanction of the bishop, then *vicar-cap*.

"When we arrived at Knock, Archdeacon Cavanagh was so enthusiastic about your foundation there, that I thought it quite unnecessary to remain longer than the few days I did.

"As well as I remember, the Archbishop of Tuam expressed himself similarly by letter to you. You wrote to me afterwards, saying his grace's interview at Tuam tended to the same result. Hence, things being so, I am simply bewildered at its being even mooted that you left Kenmare without the necessary permission. I *repeat again*, you had the fullest sanction, and *that* from your superiors, to leave.

"You have now thrown yourself into the good cause at Knock, and that, together with your many years of most valuable service here, and particularly your splendid and successful efforts during the late famine years, will soon put an end to these false reports.

"Sincerely wishing you health and success in the cause of God and our country, in which you have always labored so hard and unselfishly,

"My very dear Sister F. C.,

"Yours as ever,

"M. NELIGAN, C. C."

CHAPTER XIV.

CLAREMORRIS.

I Move to Claremorris — Plans for the Endowment at Knock — Girls to be Taught Household Industries — State of Ireland — Absence of Industrial Employment — Theoretical Training Useless — Methods of the Training Houses — Houses to be Self-Supporting — Cordial Letter from John Kelly — Industries Practised — The Kindergarten — Archbishop McEvilly's Requirements — Father Cavanagh Afraid of the Archbishop — Different Orders of the Church — Idea of a New Order.

As soon as I had the archbishop's permission, I moved from Knock to Claremorris. I had many inconveniences to suffer there, though the sisters were not unkind to me. I continued active and successful, collecting the funds required by the archbishop for the building endowment of the convent of Knock.

It may be well here to say something of the plan I had in view. I had long seen that industrial employment was the great need of the Irish people. They had been living for centuries in a state of chronic starvation, principally because they depended exclusively on the potato plant for food, and the pig for rent; nor were the Irish people by any means to blame for this state of affairs. It is a matter of history that the English nation broke up every attempt at trade or manufacturing, and we all know that when manufacturies are once destroyed, it is no easy matter to restore them or revivify decayed industries. I had not the capital to commence manufactures on a large scale, but I have always believed in small beginnings; for some, at least, come to great ends. I knew that it would not be possible for me to do anything for the men, but I saw it would be quite possible to do a great deal for the women, if I could get the necessary episcopal permission (the "if" certainly was an important factor in the case). But I had every reason to hope for success, as the Archbishop of Tuam had said in his letter of authorization, that the idea I had was "admirable and was worthy of a religious soul, and I am sure it is one that must commend itself to every one that has the salvation of souls at heart."

My plans were very simple, and did not require much money to carry them out. How they were approved by the late Mr. John Kelly of New York, his letter quoted at the end of this chapter will show. He was an eminently practical man.

I wished to teach girls how to avail themselves of the great benefits, social, and, we may even say, religious, which will certainly follow the practice of practical home industry. To teach them to occupy every moment in some way that will be both useful and remunerative; to teach each what each has most aptitude for doing, whether as teacher, or lace-worker, or knitter, or domestic servant; to teach them how to make their poor homes more comfortable for their fathers and their brothers, by practising simple industries, by keeping bees, by rearing fowl, by saving their eggs properly, by making their butter so that it will command a high price, by knitting stockings in odd spare moments; to teach them to win their households — for these girls will, most of them, one day be wives and mothers — from drunkenness. For though it is said that drunkenness is the cause of poverty, I believe the reverse is rather the true state of the case, and that poverty is the cause of at least a great deal of the drunkenness.

And this is what I had actually begun to do at Knock. I tried to interest the Kenmare sisters in plans of this kind, but without success; and, as I have said, the sisters there were not of the class who take a large view of such subjects.

I well remember the indignation of a gentleman who came to Kenmare, hoping some practical industrial trade would have been established there, and who turned to me expecting that I would express my opinion in his favor; but my opinion there would only have injured his cause.

Only those who are familiar with the state of the poor in Ireland, not by a mere run through the country, but by a residence there, can have any idea of the condition of the poorer classes.

In Mayo and the west, in the summer, you see droves of men, for I cannot otherwise call them, standing at each wayside depot, with their little all of clothing in a bundle on a stick thrown over their shoulders, on their way to England to earn the rent; and earn it they certainly do in the sweat of their brow. How much of this same rent is earned in England, and how much more in America? It would be an interesting fact for the political economist if the sum total could be ascertained. It is a fact, however, that but for these sources of income, neither coercion nor persuasion could obtain this money, and there would be no way by which the tenant could procure it.

The entire absence of industrial employment for the women, with the exception of a little butter making in the south and a little flax culture in the north, is the fruitful cause of Irish poverty and Irish discontent.

The peace of the family and the prosperity of the family depend upon domestic life. Families are the units of nations. If you have peace and prosperity in the family, you have it in the nation. The subject is as vast as it is important, but I refrain from entering on it. A great deal of the political disturbance of the present day arises from the social condition of the so-called lower classes. I have no Utopian scheme for making millionaires of poor men. I have a long formed, very ardent desire to train the children of the poor for domestic life in a practical way, and I believe that if my plan was carried out carefully and extensively that it would do very much to make the houses of the poor more comfortable, and, as a necessary consequence, to make the masses of the population more contented. A great deal of the education of the present day is, I believe, an honest and generous effort in the wrong direction. There are many men of large minds and great hearts, who feel deeply for the social condition of the poor and middle classes. Naturally they suppose that the higher the education, the greater the social comfort. I respect the benevolent intentions of these gentlemen none the less because I know that their theory will not work. If you teach a girl all the known sciences, it will not necessarily teach her to earn her living or to make her home happy. Further, as the sphere of woman's work advances in the middle classes, and as she enters more and more into the duties and offices hitherto held by men, the necessity becomes greater that those who do the domestic work of the household should be specially and carefully trained for that special purpose.

Theoretical training is useless. I propose to train girls in a practical way for domestic life, so that any girls so trained will be, I hope, equally fit for domestic service and for married life. I believe the great oversight in all training for girls has been that people do not realize the fact that the girl of to-day is taught carefully everything except what will make her fit to be a good wife and a good mother.

The difference between the training which I propose, and that of other institutions where girls or young women are prepared for service is this — girls would be trained, as far as possible, to act precisely as they would in a private family, instead of being trained, as they are in public institutions.

The inmates of each training house would be divided into groups or families of ten or twelve. Each group should have their own table, their own bedrooms, and separate places for cooking in the general kitchen. The object of thus dividing the girls is obvious. Each would learn the domestic duty for which she is most suited ; one should act, for example, as cook for her group, and would thus learn how to cook, keep accounts, and provide for a small family. Another should have charge of the linen and needlework for her group ; another should have charge of the washing. Thus each girl would be carefully trained for a certain work, or for several kinds of domestic work. As all this would be carried out under an experienced supervisor, who should have charge of the group or family, the girls' training would prepare them practically for the occupations they are likely to have in their future life, whether in the service of others or in their own homes. Every girl in each group would be taught in turn to purchase the food or clothing necessary for the little family group to which she belonged. Thus a great object would be attained. It is well known that girls who have been trained in large institutions are often useless when they return to their own humble homes, or when they are engaged as servants in private families. The cause of this is obvious; everything has been provided for them, everything has been arranged for them; they have had no personal responsibility, and when they are brought face to face with this responsibility they do not know how to act.

Girls who are trained in large institutions find everything ready to their hands, and are, as a rule, all employed in one kind of labor; they are rarely occupied or taught the various minor details of household duty, which are so necessary to be practised by a good servant, and which are equally important for the peace and comfort of families where they are employed. Hence the necessity of having what may be called family training. Those girls who were to be trained for nurses would have special opportunities for learning their duties by being given the sole charge of two or three very young children. I also proposed, where such works might be desirable, and in places where they were a necessity, to have houses for friendless girls who are engaged in factories and other public works, and who are often exposed to most terrible danger. These houses may be made at least partly, if not altogether, self-supporting; as girls who had regular employment should pay a certain small fixed sum for their board and lodging. These houses should be under the charge of a trustworthy matron, engaged by the sisters, and would be constantly and closely superintended by them. Every effort should be made to make these houses cheerful and attractive for girls. Girls preparing to emigrate would also be received for particular training. This is another duty of great importance, because so many girls are placed in circumstances of serious temptation (to which too often many are found to yield), when they arrive in foreign countries without any previous training or preparation for the duties they may be required to undertake.

The following letter from the late Hon. John Kelly of New York will show how heartily he entered into my views. He was indeed the greatest benefactor I had, and his death was an irreparable loss. Had he lived, I should not have needed a protector, and his political influence would have been a power which even the Archbishop of New York must have respected.

"No. 20 Park Row, New York, June 16, 1882.

"My dear Sister, — The noble work you have undertaken in behalf of the poor people of Kerry is well known in the United States, and now that you propose to extend your labors to another locality, where poverty is equally as great, you ought to receive the encouragement of the Irish people and their descendants in this country, without regard to religious opinions.

"Your labors are not confined to sects. As I understand it, you treat all alike; it being immaterial to you what their religion may be, if they are in want.

"The Irish immigration to this country will not bear comparison as in former years with other nations, and I presume this is owing to the want of means of the peasantry to reach this country. For many years the Irish immigration predominated, but latterly the largest percentage of immigration is from Germany. In this, as well as last year, the Italians have immigrated in large numbers, and if they continue until the end of the present year as they have since the beginning, they will exceed all other nationalities.

"While it would gladden your heart to see these people endeavoring to make their way through our streets, with the intention of leaving the city as soon as they find employment elsewhere, you would pity them on account of their scanty household furniture, and the little clothing they bring with them.

"It is very unfortunate that some provision has not been made by European governments to aid these people to leave the countries where they are ekeing out a miserable existence. As a matter of political economy, the government would be benefited.

"You are pursuing the methods which will be exceedingly beneficial to those who are living in a state of ignorance, by teaching them industrial pursuits, and adding to their knowledge by presenting new ideas to them, relative to labor, which no one has undertaken before.

"For instance, the young girls have been taught trades that will be valuable to them should they immigrate. They could find ready employment in the large manufacturing establishments in our metropolitan cities.

"I fear I am tiring you with matters with which you are already acquainted.

"Permit me again to congratulate you upon the

good you have already done, and to say that you have my sympathy and prayers to enable you to continue your good work. Very truly yours,

"JOHN KELLY.

"SISTER MARY FRANCIS CLARE, Knock, Ballyhaunis, County Mayo, Ireland."

This kind of special, or if I may say, common-sense training, would I hoped have been a special advantage to Irish girls, who are not in the way of finding employment in stores or factories, and who must go into domestic service either in America or in Ireland. In either case, the training would have been equally beneficial and necessary.

There were so many little industries which Irish girls could have practised if they had only been taught and encouraged; and so much could have been done to make their poor homes more comfortable, if they could only be told what to do and how to do it.

I began at Knock by giving employment to about forty girls in knitting stockings; and a London firm very heartily entered into my plans, as indeed did every one except those who had power to prevent me. From this firm I got a supply of fine twine for netting horses' ear-caps and fly-protectors, used for the large dray horses in London during the summer months. This firm kindly paid the expense of the material and of the manufactured articles to and from London. I found some difficulty in this work, as, simple as it was, it required care, and the girls, quite untrained to any kind of employment, were not careful. This carefulness was very hard to teach; still I hoped I could teach them something. The firm was very patient with our failures. The girls were earning a trifle weekly, instead of standing about doing nothing. I tried to make them proud of their little earnings and soon they began to be so, and to try to do better in order to earn more.

I have somewhat anticipated events in this chapter, but I think it better to complete this part of the history.

I also opened a kindergarten, making it suitable to the place and circumstances. Several of the sisters were admirably fitted for this work. I arranged some special songs and rhymes for them myself. The bright, sweet babies, for some of them were little else, soon found it quite a pleasure, and were more eager to come to us than to play with the pig, or make dirt pies on the roadside. When they had not older sisters to bring them to school, I paid a boy to bring them to and from their poor homes.

I doubt not that some of the American tourists who came to see us will remember what a success this undertaking was, until it was ruthlessly broken up.

Before leaving this subject, I should say also, that I have always felt that working girls should have a religious and moral, as well as practical training for domestic service, and in this I always include domestic life. The girl who has learned to be a good servant is making the best preparation to be a good wife and a good mother. She is learning habits which can only be taught by daily exercise in religious and moral training. I also wished to teach them, and this teaching can only be given effectually while they are young, that domestic service is not a degradation, and that the woman who does her part best in life is the woman who does best all her domestic duties, whether in the family or in special employment.

It will be remembered that Archbishop McEvilly had required in the authorization for the establishment of the Knock Convent, that sufficient funds, the amount not being specified, should be obtained before it was begun. This was a perfectly fair arrangement, but the wording of his permission was sufficiently vague to excite comment, and there were many priests in the diocese who told me privately, that the sum when named, would prove very large and probably very difficult to get.

There was another subject at this time under

consideration, and this was making alterations in our rule, or founding a new religious order suitable for the work. While I was in Claremorris, Father Cavanagh was very anxious about this. On the 19th of May 1882, he wrote to me in regard to some manuscript which I had sent him: " I got the introduction to the new rules; so far, I consider they are very good and very satisfactory. I hope to have the pleasure of seeing the matter arranged on the day of His Grace's visit to Claremorris." I begged Archdeacon Cavanagh to speak personally to the archbishop when he came to hold his visitation of the clergy of the diocese on the 24th of May, same year (1882), but although he promised, he failed to do this. Archdeacon Cavanagh seemed to be always afraid of the archbishop; I believe because he thought any annoyance might prejudice him against the Knock apparition. The fate of nations has often depended upon the health of kings, but it is very sad that important matters affecting the deepest interests of religion, should depend on the temper of a bishop or his personal likes or dislikes.

Indeed on one occasion I had to make peace between the two ecclesiastics. An American priest who came to visit Knock had written an account of some vision which he had seen. The whole narrative read as if it were either a production of a lunatic or a burlesque on visions in general. All the same, Father Cavanagh gave it full credit, and it was published in the local press. The archbishop was very angry, and a bishop's anger is not generally modified by ordinary restraints. Father Cavanagh was in such a state of fright as I could hardly have supposed possible. He was always so afraid of any difficulty about Knock; but the archbishop if quickly angered was also easily placated by an abject submission, which he generally received, nor was he one to keep up anger. I wish to call attention to the fact, that Archdeacon Cavanagh fully approved the change of religious order at this time and that I have it in his own handwriting, because he said afterwards that he had always disapproved of it.

It seemed to me that there were quite a number of people who felt they had a mission to do all they could, to hinder my work. If I had, as a secular, opened a hotel at Knock, or a liquor saloon in Dublin, or a gambling house on the corner of the square where Cardinal McCabe lived, I might have gone on in the even tenor of my way. But as I wished to do a work for the benefit of humanity and the Catholic church, it changed everything.

The different religious orders of the Catholic church have each been founded to carry out some particular work. The Little Sisters of the Poor, had their origin in their desire to help the aged and friendless ; the sisters of Saint Vincent de Paul were established to care for little children ; the education of the rich seems to have been the *raison d'être* of the Ladies of the Sacred Heart.

I have said elsewhere, that there is a distinction between what are called active and contemplative orders, and when I made my vows as a Poor Clare, I was entirely ignorant of these distinctions, neither did I understand anything about the mitigations and alterations which had been made in the rules of the Poor Clares. These had been so numerous, that the sisters in making their vows, repeated continually, that this or that observation had been modified or altered by this Pope or that ; and often I have heard the sisters say, they wished the vows could be made to suit their present work once for all, and left so.

It would have been easier and simpler, if a new order had been founded when the Poor Clares were required to do active duty ; or if they had belonged to the third Order of Saint Francis, which is so elastic that almost any active work can be done under its rule, than to have made all these mitigations and alterations.

It will be remembered that Father Cavanagh had already suggested the idea of a new order in connection with Knock, and that he had approved the idea which I had, while the archbishop held a neutral position.

I was myself in considerable difficulty ; for a very long time I could not see my way clearly. Much as I prayed on the subject, no definite idea came to me at first. I believed it to be God's will that I should begin such a work, and I wanted to be sure that it was God's will before I moved in any way in the matter. Throughout the whole affair I acted in the way approved and appointed by the Catholic church. I first consulted my confessor, and he assured me that he believed my wish was entirely in accordance with the will of God.

Having always a great devotion to Saint Francis of Assisi, and the Poor Clare order being under his patronage, (although so much altered from the original rule which he established through Saint Clare) I felt very unwilling to found an order which was not directly under his patronage. My confessor's reply to this difficulty, which I have in his own handwriting, was, "Be sure that Saint Francis will never object to anything that is done for the glory of God." I may add, that every founder or foundress of a religious order in the Roman church has had difficulties and ecclesiastical opposition.

On the 11th of May, 1882, I received the letter from my confessor, from which the above extract is taken. I must also say that, with the one exception of the Kenmare sisters, the other sisters belonging to the different houses of the Poor Clare order never made the slightest objection to my change; neither they or the Kenmare sisters had any right, either directly or indirectly, to interfere with what I did, as each house was separate and independent of the other; still, knowing them all so well, I valued an expression of their good will greatly. Quite recently I saw a letter from the superioress of the Harold's Cross Convent, Dublin, to a lady in America, in which she said she was sure I would do anything I could to help her as she brought a recommendation from them, for she knew how I loved the order, although I had founded another.

In fact, I still have most affectionate correspondence with all the houses of Poor Clares in Ireland, with the one exception of Kenmare.

My first idea was, that we should belong to the third Order of Saint Francis, and the Franciscan fathers were very anxious that this should be done. They have always been interested in my work, and anxious to help me in every way possible, though they were not so well disposed to the Poor Clares for many reasons. But every effort I made in this direction seemed to be discouraged in some way or another, and eventually the idea of the

Sisters of Peace seemed to come to me as a happy inspiration.

My next duty was of course to put this matter before my bishop. Step by step I followed the regular canonical course in what I did; beginning by asking the advice of my confessor, and finishing by asking permission of the Pope, with the result of obtaining the permission of His Holiness. As to Archbishop McEvilly, he invariably gave me the same reply, he would not sanction any change "at present." In a letter dated Oct. 19, 1883, he reminds me of this, and adds these remarkable words, "and I have always underlined the words *at present.*"

I should also say that Archbishop McEvilly approved the new order so far as to authorize me to establish a confraternity to be called Saint Joseph's Confraternity of Peace.

Now if the English language has any meaning, if a person writes to you and says he will not authorize anything "at present" is it not natural to suppose that he may authorize it in the future? And when he writes to you saying, I have always underlined the words "at present," will not any ordinary mind conclude that the writer means, "though I will not do so and so at present, I may do so at some future time?"

CHAPTER XV.

CLAREMORRIS CONTINUED.

Correspondence and Labors — Letter from Rev. Dr. Croke, Archbishop of Cashel — Fresh Attacks from Mr. Angus and an Anonymous "Bishop" — Bishop Higgins Compelled to tell the Truth — Father Cavanagh Begins to Change — Advised by Archbishop Croke to Publish my Letters and Documents — The Anonymous Bishop Continues — I Write to the Weekly Register *— Letters from Archbishop Cavanagh and Bishop McCormack.*

I HAD now an immense correspondence on hand. As people were looking to the proposed work at Knock as one likely to benefit the Irish race, not only at home but abroad, and both from a spiritual and a social point of view, money was sent to me freely and generously, and the late Mr. John Kelly was not the only munificent helper of my work.

Some of the priests of the Tuam diocese seemed to sympathize with me; I say seemed, because whether they really did so or not I cannot say, as later there was a marked change, when it was found I was not in ecclesiastical favor.

I hoped now to live in peace. As far as I knew, Bishop Higgins had ceased to interfere in my affairs. I knew the Kenmare sisters kept a close watch upon my movements; indeed, my secretary, who went home to see her mother, the Mrs.

D—— whose name had been forged by the sisters to the despatch, told me that she could not imagine how they got to know so many details of what I was doing. Still I hoped it was not possible for them to injure my work further, though I knew from tourists how they spoke of me to travellers passing through Kenmare.

At this time I had nearly given up all literary work, as I had only time to attend to business. I hoped I should be allowed to go on quietly with my work.

But this was not to be. The most Rev. Dr. Croke, Archbishop of Cashel, had always taken a warm interest in my work for the poor. As I have already said, he defended me when the Rev. Mr. Angus began his attacks on me in Kenmare. Scarcely had I settled in Claremorris convent, when I received a letter from this archbishop, in which he told me that a "bishop" had written to him to say that my leaving Kenmare was "a simple escapade" accomplished without the leave or license of any superior, underlining the word "any." I at once sent Archbishop Croke, Bishop Higgins's letter which showed that I had his leave, and of course that was all that was needed. But this was quite useless. The anonymous bishop was determined to believe the libel, and my work was hindered and delayed as it has been so often. For several weeks I was wearied with letters on the subject, and the affair was only ended by Archbishop's Croke's kindness, as he brought this bishop face to face with Bishop Higgins in Dublin, and compelled Bishop Higgins to tell the truth, and to say that the charge against me was absolutely without foundation. The charge, however, is being continually renewed even to this day.

It is quite evident that those who started the calumny were anxious to propagate it and continue it without the slightest regard to its truth or falsehood.

There were only two parties who could have made the charge in such a way as to induce this anonymous bishop to be so positive that it was true. One was Bishop Higgins, the other was the Kenmare sisters. I will leave the matter between them.

It will be remembered that I left Kenmare and went to Knock with my confessor, Rev. James Nelligan. When the reports were started by this bishop, I wrote to Father Neligan, and received a letter from him which will be found in full in the appendix. In this he says, —

"The calumny that you left Kenmare without the proper permission of your superiors is too absurd. Don't mind: patience and resignation will right all things. I am simply bewildered at its being even mooted that you left Kenmare without the necessary permission. I repeat again, you had the fullest sanction from your superiors to leave."

This bishop was so positive that he was right that he said, when shown all the documents by Archbishop Croke, that I had obtained the leave, after I left Kenmare, and not before, which was also false. If any gentleman had been deceived, as this bishop had been, by false reports, he would have felt it a duty to retract publicly what he had publicly stated; but of course such an act of justice would not be considered consistent with the dignity of a Roman Catholic bishop.

The wearying anxiety of defending myself against these unceasing accusations began soon to tell upon my health.

At this time, Father Cavanagh appeared favorably disposed both to me, and to the work I wished to undertake. It was not until he came under the fatal influence of his relatives at Knock that he changed so completely.

The superioress of Claremorris Convent happened to be a great friend of Father Cavanagh, and on the 17th of June he wrote to me,—

"I am delighted to find that you have got such a kind and hearty reception at the convent; indeed, it could not be otherwise, especially as my dear friend Mother Columba is superioress; this is a very favorable circumstance, on which I must congratulate you as well as myself. Everything will go favorably now."

And perhaps everything would have gone on favorably to the end, if Father Cavanagh had not allowed himself to be influenced by persons who cared nothing but for their own selfish ends, and if persons like this unknown bishop had not occupied themselves with my affairs.

About this time, Archbishop Croke wrote me a letter, an extract from which is placed at the beginning of this work. I sent this letter to Father Cavanagh, March 4, 1882, and he replied, —

"You ought to act on Dr. Croke's advice to publish the letters of Bishop Higgins and your confessor, which prove how utterly and maliciously false this bishop's reports were, for Archbishop Croke is surely a great and sincere friend. Both from his exalted position in the church, and his great learning and ability, he is held in the greatest esteem by his countrymen all over the world. Circulate his very memorable letter to you everywhere, at home and abroad.

On the 8th of March, a few days later, Father Cavanagh wrote: —

"As to what an unknown bishop says of an 'escapade,' I do not see how he can conscientiously use such a term; I will not say a word about the utter inapplicability of such a term, but it is unjust and unmerited. It is very strange phraseology under such circumstances, and I regret that any bishop would have made use of such language."

I give another extract from a letter of Archbishop Cavanagh's, to show how interested he appeared to be in my work. Knowing from the reports of the physicians that I was threatened with heart trouble, he wrote to me on the third of February, 1882, — "You ought to take special care of your health, and be very cautious when going up or down stairs to walk slowly." At that time I was not forbidden by the doctors to go up or down stairs as I have been since. I could give many other extracts from his letters, but these will suffice. His natural kindness of heart seemed to have altogether forsaken him when brought under the evil influence of his friends at Knock.

"The documents which you have sent Archbishop Croke ought to satisfy this bishop and any unprejudiced mind, that your coming here was in perfect accordance with what the church requires. You had the approbation of your religious superior, the sanction of the acting bishop of your diocese, with the full concurrence both of His Grace the Archbishop of Tuam and myself, as both of us had written to you to Kenmare, testifying that they were well aware of your coming here, and arranging with you about establishing and founding a convent here. These facts have appeared before the world long since, and I do not see the use of saying any more about them."

On this subject I quite agreed with Archdeacon Cavanagh, but what could I do, when these charges were, and are, repeated again and again, to this very day.

The extent to which I was interfered with would scarcely be credited if I had not documentary evidence. These busy bishops, priests, sisters, and ladies, never gave one thought to the poor for whom I was so anxious to work; it seemed as if they were of no account. And yet all this time poor Ireland was in a state of seething discontent, for which I alone proposed a practical remedy, which even if it had failed could have done no harm in the trial. The poor in Dublin were in a most wretched state, and needed help sorely. The threats of the church proved perfectly useless when the sympathies of the archbishop were against the people. A gentleman, well known for his interest in the poor, wrote to me, "You need not expect help from any of us in any work for the church, since the pope has taken the part of our enemies; only for him, we would have long since obtained freedom and peace." It would be a revelation if I could publish some of the letters I received at this time. When Cardinal McCabe was not busy denouncing the Land League, and courting the English government, he occupied himself denouncing some ladies who were trying to save the poor children; who, notwithstanding all the priests and convents in Dublin, were running wild in the streets, and graduating fast for the jails or reformatories. I have often wondered how some Roman Catholic bishops can occupy themselves in denouncing evils which they never attempt to remedy. The case of these poor children was most sad. They were mostly the offspring of drunken parents, who drank half the time, because they had nothing else to do. I thought, not unnaturally, that the cardinal would be rejoiced to find some one who would care for these unhappy children, and save them from these ladies whom he was so busy denouncing. But I soon found I was mistaken; I offered to take them to Knock as soon as I could get a place for them, to train them for domestic service at my own expense; to send some to America where I knew that they would easily get good places if they were properly trained, and where they might become a credit to their church and to their country. But, though the archbishop never ceased denouncing the Protestant ladies who were trying to save those poor children, he would not hear of anything of a practical character being done for them. In fact, a priest who ventured to preach on their miserable condition was sent away from Dublin, though he did not say even one word which could have reflected in any way on ecclesiastical authority. A lady in Dublin, who would have been much better occupied in caring for these poor children, wrote me volumes of letters, dictated by a priest, with full directions what I should do to make public reparation for my scandalous conduct in "leaving my convent without permission." Father Angus continued his mission of directing my affairs with zeal and energy; as for the poor, no one thought of them. I had some curious experiences of how extremes meet; a distinguished member of the Land League was sent to Knock to discredit it as much as possible. A prominent dynamiter wrote to me over his own name to say that I must give up all attempts to establish any work for girls at Knock until the country was "settled." An evidence, if such was needed, that if I had been allowed to carry out my plans in peace by Bishop Higgins and his friends, it might not have been the least unlikely way of bringing peace to poor Ireland

and settling it, under those "heretical laws" which he was always so anxious to maintain when they did not interfere with his own ideas of justice. Another accusation against me was, that I belonged to the Ladies' Land League. I saw this stated in a letter to Canon Burke written by a bishop who was then in Rome, and who was quite favorable to my work. Between injudicious friends and hidden foes, I had a hard time. This bishop said he was sure I must succeed, as I was "president of the Ladies' Land League." Now it so happened that so far from being president, I had some reasons for not approving of this movement, and never associated myself with it in any way. But this, of course, was of no moment when a priest made the charge.

I know that my case was very much prejudiced in America by these statements. The Bishop of Cleveland, Dr. Gilmore, had trouble with some ladies of his congregation whom he denounced as "unsexed viragos," because they had joined the Ladies' Land League, I know that poor Father Angus was in active communication with him, and I have good reason to believe that the bishop was assured that I belonged to this association. Of course the bishop, being a Roman Catholic, would not consider it necessary to inquire whether this accusation was true or not before acting on it.

As it happened, I was appealed to on behalf of the wives and families of the Fenian prisoners who had confessed their share in a murder case. The Land League party, while giving money freely to those who would not make any confession, gave these people nothing, and, forsaken by every one, they were actually starving; so I should have merited the special approbation of some of these bishops. I have some letters which would throw a curious light on public affairs if I chose to publish them.

But there were two persons who would by no means leave me in peace altogether, — the anonymous bishop and "Father" Angus, or "Anguis," as some of his ecclesiastical brethren used to style him. Like the sisters in Kenmare, he felt that he "had a mission" to perform in "hunting me down." It is hard to say which did the most harm; but I fear, Father Angus did more injury to religion, as he had greater opportunities.

I have already spoken of his persistent personal attacks; I shall have to return to the subject again. While I was in Claremorris, he was occupied as usual; indeed, he seemed to have very little else to do except to give me annoyance, and I was obliged to "deal with a fool according to his folly." I wrote a reply to his attacks in the London *Weekly Register*, Jan. 6, 1882, and received the following letter from Archdeacon Cavanagh on the subject, —

"I have received your excellent, I would say admirable letter, in reply to the scurrilous articles that appeared in the *Weekly Register*. Your letter is very clear, forcible, and convincing. It will, I am sure, remove from the readers of the *Register* any erroneous impressions made by his foolish and wretched attacks. Your letter, all through, is high-toned and convincing at the same time. I look on it as a lucid vindication of your acts in what you wrote or did for the poor, without going one whit beyond the sanction given by your religious, as well as ecclesiastical superior."

I may also quote from a letter I received about this time from Bishop McCormack, who governs the next diocese to that of Tuam. After thanking me for some service which I had done to his nephew, he says: "You should not take to heart these clumsy calumnies; time is a great settler, and it will clear up these false charges to your entire satisfaction."

But these false charges are still repeated, even in America, by American bishops, and by the public press under their control, and the kindly prophecy remains unfulfilled.

CHAPTER XVI.

KNOCK.

I Go to Knock — Sister M. — Her Peculiarities — Living in a Stable — Neither Food nor Bedding — A Serious Illness — A Nurse who wanted Rich Patients — I Receive Permission to Build — The Ground Selected — Leased from Lord Dillon — Mr. Hague Chosen as the Architect — We Rent a House — Trouble with our Landlord — Improper Behavior by his Family — The Work Interfered with — Workmen Enticed to Drink — I Send for my Solicitor — Father J. — A Quarrelsome Curate — His Abusive Conduct — Interference of Sister M. — Her Complaints — I Ask for a Visitation — Refused by the Archbishop.

IN the month of August, 1882, the archbishop gave me leave to go to Knock and to open a convent there. I was indeed overjoyed at this concession, for which I had long been urgently entreating. When he gave the permission, the great difficulty was to find a house suitable for sisters. There was also a difficulty about getting a sufficient number of sisters to begin the work with. The Poor Clare convents had so few sisters, that they could not spare any, and the archbishop was very unwilling to let me receive postulants without professed sisters. All these difficulties were eventually got over, and the work fairly started, and by the archbishop's desire, I went to the convent of Poor Clares at Cavan, and while there obtained the services of a professed lay sister, who proved one of the greatest troubles of my life, and one of the causes of the breaking up of the Knock convent.

This sister was entirely uneducated, she could neither read or write, but her appearance was very much in her favor, and she was gifted with that peculiar low cunning which is very often the heritage of her class. She made a great display of love and zeal for religious observances, and was very anxious indeed to see them practised by others. But the sisters often remarked how little her practice corresponded with her precepts.

Immediately after I returned from Cavan with Sister M———, I had a serious illness at Knock, in which my life was despaired of. The persons who owned the only house there, refused to rent it to me except at an exorbitant price. I had no resource then, except to hire the stables belonging to this house, and fit them up as best I could. We were indeed living in "holy poverty." The stables were a wretched wooden structure, open to all the winds of heaven; and after the comfort, and I might almost say, the luxury, that the Kenmare sisters have, the wonder is, not that I became dangerously ill, but that I lived. This poor lay sister had at least, one good qualification, she was an excellent nurse. She had become very much attached to me, and I believe very much of the subsequent trouble arose from her jealousy, and because I could not allow her to be first in everything. If she had had a good adviser in Father Cavanagh, her life and mine would have been very different.

I can never forget the day I arrived to open the convent in Knock. When we came to the stable everything was wanting, even the beds which I had ordered had not arrived, We had no food, and neither the archdeacon or his niece had thought of providing anything for us. The suffering I endured in consequence was serious, even the man whom I had left to make some repairs to the stables in order to make them a little habitable, had neglected his work, and spent his time drinking at a bar or liquor saloon, which the people who owned the house had opened for the benefit of the pilgrims.

The illness from which I suffered was tonsilitis and diphtheria. There was an awful storm of wind and rain on the night of my arrival, the stables were literally open to the winds and rains of heaven, and it may be imagined how unsuitable a place it was for a delicate person even if well, much more for one who was dangerously ill. Later we managed to find shelter by pasting thick brown paper all over the gaping planks.

My illness soon became so serious that it was necessary to have a skilled nurse. A despatch was sent to the nursing sisters (Bon Secour). A sister came down, but only to her disappointment and mine. She was accustomed to nurse only the rich, and I was obliged to let her go in a day or two from a place where there was nothing but poverty and discomfort. I also wanted her only at night, and she could have slept all day; but she would not do this, and insisted that I should call her when I needed her; I had no bell of any kind, and the pain of speaking was so great that I preferred to arise, though I knew it was a dangerous thing to do, rather than call her. I recovered very slowly and owed much to Sister M——'s good nursing and devoted care. Several young ladies then came to join us, who were not deterred by our poor condition, and who are now professed and valuable members of our order.

I had almost despaired of getting leave of Archbishop McEvilly to begin the building of the convent at Knock. A considerable sum of money had been collected by me with his permission, and by his desire, so that there were now quite sufficient funds in hand. He could not but see that the money was coming in very quickly, and that there would be no deficiency on that point.

I now come to a very important part of this

narrative, important to others as well as myself. On the 24th of May, 1882, I got leave from the archbishop to begin to build ; and in order to save trouble for all parties I was to make the contracts with the builders and architect. This permission I got in writing, and I wish it to be specially noted. The money I received was sent principally for the purpose of helping the industrial work which I was anxious to carry out at Knock, and not on account of the apparition that took place there. I mention this particularly, because later on Archdeacon Cavanagh made a claim to these funds. In every case they were confided to myself personally, and for one particular object.

I was, of course, the person who was responsible to the builder and architect for all expenses.

I have long borne in silence all the blame of having left Knock to ruin, of having left Ireland, of being capricious, and of having been guilty of I know not how many crimes. I have kept silence a long time, probably too long, and now that I speak at last I shall speak quite plainly, as it is a case in which I must say all or nothing. Those who have been the cause of my speaking out, or who spread the false reports, must take the consequences.

When I obtained the archbishop's permission to

build the convent, the first thing necessary was to obtain ground to build on.

My own wish was to have the convent attached to the church, and built on the ground surrounding the church, so that our private chapel would look on the sanctuary. This arrangement would have been convenient both for the sisters and the priests, and it would have saved considerable expense, but Father Cavanagh so positively opposed this plan that I had to give it up.

My next object was to secure a suitable site as near the church as possible; and there were some fields just opposite which were exactly what I wanted. Father Cavanagh had rented part of these fields, but had no use for them, and was very willing to give them up. Obviously, however, it was necessary to secure a lease of the ground, which belonged to Lord Dillon; he refused to sell it, but offered a lease of ninety-nine years. The archbishop did not like this arrangement at first, but finally consented. A question then arose about the trustees of the convent. I will merely say that Archdeacon Cavanagh, having had a serious quarrel with the owner of the land (some of the particulars of which will be found in the appendix), the latter positively refused to allow his name in the lease.

It was then decided that the trustees should be

Archbishop McEvilly, Mr. Waldron of Ballyhaunnis, and myself. The lease was left in my keeping, after being duly registered in Dublin, and I have it now in this country.

It will be seen from this that Archdeacon Cavanagh had no claim on our property, either on ecclesiastical or secular grounds.

I obtained leave of writing from the Archbishop of Tuam to employ a Mr. Hague as architect and a Mr. Clarence as contractor. The archbishop specially approved of my employing Mr. Hague, whom I found to be in every way satisfactory.

I drew the plan for the institution myself, and asked the builder to have it as plain as possible, as I have always been opposed to spending money on architectural ornaments for religious houses.

As I found it impossible to remain another winter in the stables, we had no resource but to rent the house which had been used as a hotel, and which was owned by Father Cavanagh's friends.

These people were in very great distress for money, in fact, they would probably have been turned out of their house, if I had not rented it; and common gratitude should have made them act in a very different way from what they did. They charged us an enormous rent, which I paid in advance, to save them from eviction, and were encouraged to do so by Archdeacon Cavanagh, who never interested himself in the least in anything which would benefit the convent; but, on the contrary, always tried to make us pay as much money as possible to his friends for whatever was done for us.

We had scarcely settled ourselves in this house when all the arrangements I had made were set at defiance. In fact, it was generally known that plans had been made to try to drive us out of Knock by annoyances, and these annoyances were of a character which any priest should have at once put down. But when these people found they had Father Cavanagh on their side they were triumphant. No matter how they acted or what they did, they were supported by him, and I was left to battle single-handed.

The arrangements about renting the house were peculiar, but simple. Mr. K——, the landlord, as I have said, had a license for a bar, where he sold whiskey; this license he was determined not to give up, and it would have been taken from him, if his family had not occupied two rooms in his house as the license was attached to the house. This arrangement I agreed to, as I had no choice. There were two rooms in the back of the house which were only accessible by an outside staircase, and I had the door which communicated from them to our part of the house boarded up; still, any unusual noise could be heard through. I used the room next to these rooms as a chapel, and the Blessed Sacrament was kept there. Mr. K—— had promised me that no one should occupy these two rooms except his wife, and a servant. In a very short time his two sons were moved into them, and the sisters found it impossible to make their meditations or say their office with the noise which was made. The young men were constantly singing songs of a disgraceful character, shouting, swearing, and drinking; and all this while we were occupied at our devotions.

.As I could not for one moment suppose that Father Cavanagh would sanction such irreverence, and as I knew him to profess so much special respect for holy things, and for the Blessed Sacrament, I thought I had nothing to do but to tell him of the trouble, which one word from him would have stopped. I myself tried first to put an end to it, but they only laughed at me; they knew too well that Archdeacon Cavanagh would never object to anything they might choose to do, no matter how annoying it was to us.

I went to Father Cavanagh at some inconvenience, but he would not listen to one word I had to say, and only replied that, "If the sisters were minding their prayers they would not have heard what was going on in the next room." He did not seem to be at all troubled about the irreverence to the Blessed Sacrament.

My eyes were now beginning to be opened, and I realized for the first time how terrible my position was. I was utterly alone and unprotected, and at the mercy of people who would not scruple to do anything, no matter how bad, so well were they assured of protection.

I saw that my work would most likely be broken up, and my heart bled for the poor. How could I forsake them? How could I abandon them in their misery? How could I disappoint all the generous souls who had given such abundant help not only out of their wealth, but out of their poverty? I know this book will be read by many who helped, who had hoped to see a magnificent institution at Knock for the benefit of the poor of Ireland. They will see how and why my plans and their good intentions were frustrated, and that it was not my fault that the money which they so generously gave has all been thrown away. What I suffered before I gave up, God alone knows, and he will surely repay those who helped, all the same as if it had succeeded.

As I knew that it was my duty as superioress to protect the sisters from annoyance, and the Blessed Sacrament from disrespect, I asked

Canon Bourke to come over to me; I knew that he had very great influence, and, in fact, one word from any priest would have stopped the nuisance. I knew, also, that these people would be afraid to continue it if they knew that it would be spoken of generally through the country.

Canon Bourke came to me, and was shocked at what he heard; he was very unwilling to interfere in Father Cavanagh's parish, but as he knew his interference was absolutely necessary, he went to Mr. K—— and spoke out in very plain terms. The young men were then removed from the room, which, under the agreement, they had no right to occupy. Archdeacon Cavanagh was very angry with me for asking Canon Bourke to do this, and it did not improve my position at Knock.

The men who were working on the building began now to be enticed up to the bar to drink. The contractor came to me and said he must throw up the work, as it was a country place where it was impossible to get other hands. I went out to the roadside different times, and met the men coming up to drink at the bar and managed with considerable difficulty to get them to turn away; they were, however, watched by Mr. K—— and his friends, and enticed back again at once. What could I do, a woman, single-handed, and with both priest and people against me?

But I had another and very determined enemy. Father Cavanagh had insisted on a young lady joining our sisters, who had been cured at Knock. He had almost forced her to enter, but we soon found she had no vocation for the life of a sister, and she very properly determined to leave, whether he liked it or not. She was an exceptionally agreeable person, and we were all attached to her and sorry to lose her. This lady, Miss O. N——, had come from a hospital in Boston, Mass., to get a cure at Knock. She was a very great friend of a near relative of Father Cavanagh, who lived with him; this relative came up to our convent determined to remain with Miss O. N—— for many hours. I begged her not to do so, and as Miss O. N—— had determined to remain a while in the village of Knock before returning to her friends, these young ladies could have had as much of each other's society as they wished. This girl, however, being a relative of Father Cavanagh, thought she had a right to do whatever she pleased in the convent, and as she was leaving she turned at the hall door, and said she would make me "pay for my refusal yet," and she kept her word.

I now sent for my solicitor from Dublin to come to Knock and see if anything could be legally done to prevent these nuisances. This was in

September, 1882. He told me that it was useless to attempt anything so long as the people had Father Cavanagh's protection, and that the only thing I ought to do was to leave. This was easier said than done.

Another serious trouble was caused by the curate of the parish, and poor Sister M—— had a great deal to do with this also. As I have said, she expected every one to keep the rule except herself; and she managed to get herself into the good graces of the curate as well as Father Cavanagh. It was arranged that Father J—— should say Mass for us every day, and as he was well paid for it, he appeared at first to be quite satisfied. He, however, lived in a state of chronic feud with all the parish, so it was little wonder that he fell out with us also. Generally speaking, his feud with the parish was on the subject of oats for his horse, which never appeared to be delivered in sufficient quantities to satisfy his demands. I believe the people (for the Irish are ever over-generous to their priests) would have given him even more than he asked if he had shown, shall I say more courtesy, or less rudeness, in his way of asking. His sermons usually ended with the happy announcement to his congregation that they would be damned, and damned forever; and the people with ready wit gave him the appellation of "damned forever." His father had been a small, or, as the Irish call it, a "shoneen landlord," a fact on which he prided himself, and denounced the "Land League" and all its works with an acrimony born of the difficulty of collecting his small rents.

It is usual for the priest to have his breakfast after Mass in the convent parlor, and in most places the superioress, who is obliged to pay special deference to ecclesiastical authority, presides on the occasion. For myself, in common with many other reverend mothers, I thought this arrangement a terrible nuisance. It occupied valuable time in the morning, and even had it not done so, it seemed such waste of time to talk platitudes every day, when one had to think of very serious matters.

Delicate in health as I was, and slowly recovering from an attack of diphtheria, I was quite unfit to rise early to assist at Mass, much less to spend a weary hour in the parlor after.

I little knew until afterwards what offence I gave by not doing what I was physically unable to perform. Unhappily, priests rarely ever have any consideration for ill health in others, and their mode of life and early training makes many of them unconsciously selfish as well as imperious when their desires are not complied with. This priest was one of this class; everything should give way to his comfort and convenience.

I did not like to send one of the younger sisters to him, and, in fact, it never occurred to me that he would take offence until long afterwards.

Sister M―― was not slow to see her opportunity; she had determined to push her own way, and she succeeded. I found later that she used to spend a considerable part of the morning with him, and, ill in bed as I was, it was hopeless for me to interfere. She complained to him of every one and everything in the convent, and he was quite ready to listen to her, being already aggrieved on his own account.

She interfered not only with the priest, but with every one and every thing in the convent, and especially with a young sister who was a distant relative of her own, and who is now one of the most valued members of our community.

One day, finding myself a little better than usual, I went to the convent parlor to see Father J――, little anticipating the storm that was to come on my hapless head; he turned on me with the bitterest, I had almost said the fiercest, language, told me that I neglected my office, that I had remained wilfully from Mass, and that he had "other charges to make against me." His rage and violence were terrible, and, in my weak state, caused me a great deal of suffering. I called in one of the sisters who was passing by for my protection, but it was no use; before her very face he called me a "perjurer and a liar," and for what reason to this day I do not know.

I quietly took out a pocket-book and began to take down his words, and said I should report the matter to the archbishop, but he only laughed a scornful, bitter laugh, and said I need not trouble to do that; every one knew the archbishop was against me, and that he never would allow me to finish building the convent at Knock.

The archbishop, who should have been my protector, treated the whole matter with perfect indifference. Father J—— had managed to get into Father Cavanagh's good graces, and the archbishop was only too thankful to leave him there, as before he went to Knock he was obliged to move him frequently.

Such a state of things was simply abhorrent to me. I had always wished to have peace, but I was not to be allowed to have it.

I asked the archbishop again and again to hold a visitation in the convent, and to investigate the whole matter. This he refused to do, although it was one of his first duties as a bishop.

Later, I found that Archdeacon Cavanagh had been writing to him also against us, all on the reports given him by Sister M———. But the archbishop, like a good many other people, wished to keep himself out of trouble if he could. He was afraid of Father Cavanagh, who had then an immense reputation for sanctity, founded on the somewhat illogical conclusion that because his parish had been favored with an apparition of the Blessed Virgin, he himself, though he had not seen it, and had at first refused to believe it, was a saint.

At Christmas, 1883, we had a retreat given by the Rev. Father Columbian, a Passionist Father, and a personal friend of the archbishop, who assured him, both by letter and in private interview, that he had never given a retreat to sisters with more satisfaction, and that he found religious observance in the best state.

In September, 1884, we had another retreat, given by the Rev. Father Gaffney, some of whose letters will be found in the appendix; he also gave the same report as the bishop; both of these men were skilled in giving retreats, and in studying the conduct of religious houses, where they went for that purpose.

CHAPTER XVII.

MORE DIFFICULTIES AT KNOCK.

Archbishop McEvilly's Contradictions — Canon Bourke — I Stop the Works — Father Cavanagh Claims my Funds — Visit from Rev. Dr. Lynch, Archbishop of Toronto — His Approval — His Letter to his Coadjutor Bishop — Appeals to Continue the Work — Obstinacy of Archdeacon Cavanagh — A Pretended Miracle — The Deaf and Dumb Impostor — Letter from Canon Bourke — Dr. McEvilly's Excuse — Sister M—— makes Trouble.

DR. McEVILLY's contradictory way of acting made it very difficult to work under him. It is obvious that no work can be carried on with any hope of success when the workers are blamed one day for what they were authorized to do on the previous day. I shall now give another instance of this.

Archbishop McEvilly had given me permission to collect for Knock convent; in fact, he had given a donation at the time himself, and urged me to exert myself in every way to get subscriptions. Yet when Canon Bourke made a collection for us he was censured severely by the archbishop for doing it. When this fact was known, a very amusing correspondence took place in the Dublin *Freeman's Journal*, between the archbishop and the priest. The archbishop wanted Canon Bourke to deny that he (the archbishop) had given leave to have the collection made for me. The canon was in a difficulty, he could not tell an untruth, and he did not know how to act so as to satisfy the archbishop, so he wrote a rather long letter in the style in which a lawyer would speak who was compelled to apologize for calling the judge a liar, by saying, that if what he had said was true, he was sorry for it.

As I found I should not be allowed, either by the archbishop or Father Cavanagh, to carry out the work which I had been at first authorized to do, I gave notice to my architect, Mr. Hague, and to my builder, Mr. Clarence, that the works should be stopped at once. I paid Mr. Clarence and the architect for all the work done, and I hold their receipts in full and have them here in America.

I certainly was not going to complete a building which I should not be allowed to occupy, or involve myself and the sisters in difficulties which we might not be able to meet. No matter how I have been misrepresented, I have acted conscientiously in all business matters, and I could not in conscience make more appeals for money to finish the building under these painful circumstances.

I found, when all just claims were satisfied, that

there only remained a small sum to my credit in the bank, and the sum of money which had been placed in the funds for the support of the convent. This money was invested in the name of Archbishop McEvilly and Father Cavanagh, as well as my own, and I could not have supposed when this was done that the latter could have thought of claiming it for himself? In fact the principal part of this money, funded for the benefit of the sisters, was my own money or dowry, as it is called in Ireland, of which as I have said, the Kenmare sisters had made such struggles, shall I say to deprive or to defraud me.

Father Cavanagh knew this well; he knew that the money which was invested for the support of the sisters could not be used for any other purpose. Yet with that curious obtuseness of intellect which has caused so much trouble, he actually claimed the money for himself, for the purpose, as he said, of finishing the convent. It certainly was a curious idea to think that he could claim a convent for himself, which had been built for certain sisters and a certain community.

I now began to see one of the objects of the efforts which were made to drive me out of Knock. A lady who visited Knock after I left it, told me, that Father Cavanagh's friends had great trouble to quiet the people, and only did so partly, by telling them that other sisters would soon come and finish the convent.

I knew that Father Cavanagh had two nieces who had been largely dowered by him in the Sisters of Mercy, but I must say that I doubt if either one of them would have been guilty of such an injustice as to occupy a convent out of which another community had been driven.

Amongst those who visited Knock when I went there first, was the well-known Archbishop of Toronto, Canada, the Most Rev. Dr. Lynch. He was attracted to the subject of the Knock apparitions in America, and when he found that I was about to open an industrial institution, he most heartily rejoiced in the whole arrangement; his large mind and generous heart enabled him to realize the great work that could be done there for the poor, and he determined to do all that he could to help it forward. In the month of June, 1882, I had the pleasure of receiving a visit from him in the Claremorris convent, where I was then staying.

In a letter which he wrote to his coadjutor bishop in Canada, he says, —

"After dinner we took a carriage with the Very Rev. Canon Bourke, and two lay gentlemen, friends of mine, and drove to Knock, about six miles and a half distant. Alas, on the road I was saddened to death at seeing a number of cabins deserted, with the doors roughly walled up with cobble-stones. The land around appeared to be of the worst kind, and was left untilled. Nineteen poor families were recently evicted from these miserable cabins and bad land. The scene of desolation was most oppressing, and the more so when we considered the sufferings of the poor former inhabitants of these cabins. I visited a neat wooden cottage, such as you would see in America, built on a safe piece of ground for a poor evicted family, by the charity of the people through the Ladies' Land League, without whose help thousands would have perished of cold and starvation. The children were some of the most graceful and beautiful I ever saw. They were evicted from the place of their birth and childish happiness. I thought that it was a most merciful condescension on the part of our Immaculate Mother to appear in the neighborhood of such a place, and to give the patience and courage of saints and martyrs to these poor people who had to bear a cross — one of the heaviest that could be imposed on a father, mother, and children — to be driven from their homes by no fault of theirs, but because in the mysterious ways of providence, three bad harvests had deprived them of the means of paying their rents. I have been told by their parish priest that these poor people left their homes as quietly as saints, resigned to the will of God, but praying to the Holy Mother for patience and another home.

"With a heart depressed by the thought of human depravity, and consoled in turn by the thought of human virtue, and praying that these poor people might be comforted by the Almighty God in their affliction, we approached the Church of Knock.

"We returned to Claremorris the same evening, calling at the convent, near Claremorris, to see the good nuns, and Sister Mary Francis Clare, formerly the 'Nun of Kenmare,' who resides with them until she can build a convent of her order at Knock.

"Sister Mary Francis Clare is collecting funds for her new convent, and is awaiting the orders of the ecclesiastical superiors to commence the work. We have sent our little contribution towards the good work to the Archbishop of Tuam."

Archbishop Lynch had returned to Toronto when my great trouble came, but he did not forsake me; through Canon Bourke he had constant account of all that was going on, and of all difficulties.

On the 6th of February, 1884, Canon Bourke wrote to me :—

"I send you a letter written by his grace of Toronto to me. I will read it to Father Cavanagh, but what is the use; besides, on my two visits to him I impressed on the archdeacon its very motives, and the results which his grace himself forwarded for his consideration."

This letter made a most powerful appeal to Archdeacon Cavanagh to protect us from annoyances and to allow us to continue our work in Knock. He (Dr. Lynch) wrote strongly of the injustice with which I was treated, and still more strongly of the injustice to the poor in depriving them of the help which I could give them. He said, even had I been guilty of any serious fault, that I should still have been encouraged in my work; that I had already done so much for the church and for the poor, and that it was disgraceful for him to act towards me as he had done. He finished by saying that the Irish people at home and abroad, "would weep over my leaving Knock as Christ wept over Jerusalem."

But those who knew Archdeacon Cavanagh, knew that nothing would change him, and that nothing could be said by any one that would make the slightest difference to him. Even the pope's approval and commendation of my plans was not noticed by him. As to the miraculous cures alleged to have been performed at Knock, the more absurd were the stories told him, the more probable did they seem to him, and the more readily they were accepted.

This was the cause of the great difficulty which the ecclesiastics had in coming to any decision about the miraculous apparitions at Knock. I, myself, was an eyewitness of a very amusing instance of this disposition to believe what he wished. A poor woman and her son came to Knock with great expressions of piety; in fact, her piety was too prominent for me. She said that her boy had been born deaf and dumb, and declared that he had obtained both his speech and hearing at Knock; of course such a change would have been a wonderful miracle, so I quietly set to work to ascertain the facts of the case.

Certainly the boy, when urged by his mother, would say a few words in an imperfect way; but certainly, whatever miracle had occurred, he had not recovered the full power of speech.

I soon found, also, that the mother was making use of his supposed cure as an excuse for getting money from the pilgrims; her handclappings and crys about the "Mother of God" were evidently all put on for a purpose. The case was one of heartless imposture. I got proof that the boy had been at a school for deaf and dumb at Cabra, Dublin; I wrote there to make inquiries. I received a letter from one of the brothers by return mail saying that the woman was a regular impostor and had been a great nuisance to their institution; that the boy was not born deaf, but had been born partly dumb, and that they had taken him for a time to see if they could teach him to speak a little plainly, but without success, and whatever he spoke now he always spoke, no less and no more.

Yet poor Father Cavanagh, though I showed him the letter and all the facts, was very unwilling to send him away from the place, and said his mother "was a charity" and why should people not help her. I do not think he was quite pleased with my actions in this matter.

On the 31st of December I had another letter from Canon Bourke, in which he said, speaking of a personal friend, —

"He knows something of what you suffered here, your name and fame will long be defended by some of us, and after a time, by most people. Mr. —— had hoped to have realized $6,000 for you in the coming year, but now of course, he will do nothing. God help the poor, they have suffered more than you will, for where can they expect to find such a friend as you were to them."

In January he wrote to me again, —

"O, it is terrible. It is all a series of scheming by which people are lead astray. The lies told of you here will be corrected as far as some of us can do so. I have told some priests and some ladies who inquired about you here, the true version of the case. I also told the Bishop of ——, and he was very glad to hear the right story."

"I have heard a good deal more of the insults which these young gentlemen [the sons of the person from whom we rented the house] used towards you when they saw or met you on your grounds. My dear reverend mother, there is no use in fighting with silk gloves on with those who tried to trample you to the ground when they had you under their power; it is your business to get back to Knock and to finish it."

It was easy for good Canon Bourke to say this, but how was I to contend against so many powerful opposers.

I knew that one priest to whom I was greatly attached, and who was also a canon of the diocese, knelt before the altar at Knock and prayed God that he might see me back there again before he died. But alas, his prayer was not heard, and he has passed to that land of eternal peace.

According to some reports in the public press, agitation has been more active in the west and in Kerry than in any other part of Ireland. If the families of these men had been employed in industrial pursuits, a great deal of crime would have been prevented,

It must be quite evident that, in order to justify himself before the public for obliging me to leave Knock, Archdeacon Cavanagh must have had some apparently valid excuses. The excuses were all the idle tales which he obtained from Sister M——, and which he reported to the bishop.

A Protestant gentleman of high position told me that Dr. McEvilly gave as his reason for not interfering in affairs at Knock when he ought to have done so, that he could not quarrel with Archdeacon Cavanagh, and that he was bound in duty to support Father Cavanagh, but that he could not speak too highly of my capacity for work. By law, social law, moral law and equity, Archbishop McEvilly was bound to inquire into the facts so as to ascertain for himself the rights of the question and to support whoever was right.

The first idea I got of how matters were going wrong about Sister M——, was one day when Father Cavanagh suggested to me that she should be made a choir sister. I had no doubt this suggestion came originally from herself. He said she was such an excellent religious, and so on.

I at once refused to take any part in this matter. I told him that, according to the rule of the Poor Clares, which we then observed, such a change could not be made without a special brief from the Holy See, for which application should be made through the archbishop. Like many other people, Father Cavanagh was very apt to be very lax about rules when he wanted changes, and very strict about anything that he wished observed. He would not have hesitated for a moment to have made Sister M—— a choir sister without leave from any one, though the poor sister could neither read nor write, and it was strictly against the Poor Clares rule to make such a change. Her object was very plain. She thought if she was once made a choir sister that she could get to be superior, which was all she desired.

When we came to Knock first, Sister M——'s relations with Father Cavanagh were anything but friendly. She bitterly resented his want of thought in not seeing that there were not any provisions for us on our arrival, and for a long time she would scarcely speak to him. When we were going to move to the house from the stables, I could not stop her from talking of him in a most contemptuous way. She knew the immense rent which I had to pay his friends, and she knew also that he did all he could for them to increase it. And, when the affair was settled and I was obliged to make the change, no matter what it cost, she made herself as disagreeable as possible to us all, and would not assist in any way in moving our things; but spent her time in finding fault with Father Cavanagh, and comparing him with other priests whom she said would not have been so selfish.

Her change of opinion was remarkable, and Father Cavanagh knew well all about the way she had spoken of him, and all the trouble she had given me; but when she turned round to his side, she suddenly became, in his opinion, an excellent religious.

CHAPTER XVIII.

KNOCK CONTINUED.

A Pilgrim House Needed — Miserable Condition of the Place — A Retreat from Rev. Father Gaffney, S. J. — His Distress — I Ask Leave to go to Rome — Am Refused — I go to Dublin — Father Gaffney Brings a Document from the Archbishop — An Extraordinary Demand — To be Signed Unread — My Refusal — My Health Failing — I Ask Leave to go to England to see Cardinal Manning — Leave Granted.

ONE of my objects at Knock, and a very important one, was the building of a house for pilgrims who were crowding there from all parts of the world, and for whom there was no accommodation except little mud cabins of the most miserable description. But I was not prepared for the opposition which the proposal to do this most necessary work was to bring, though I showed Father Cavanagh and his friends that it would benefit them instead of being an injury.

Knock and its neighborhood is, perhaps, the very poorest part of poor Ireland. A letter of Dr. Lynch, the late Archbishop of Toronto which has been given, will show how much he was affected by the poverty of the people, and by the sad sight of so many roofless houses. For myself, I can only say that I looked at them with a feeling of insuperable sadness. A few inhabitants of the village of Knock, if village it could be called, lived in scattered huts or hovels of the very poorest kind. The pilgrims who came wanted at least a night's shelter, no matter where; and food, no matter how plain.*

It need scarcely be said that the poor people of Knock reaped a rich harvest from the apparition, and reputed sanctity of the place; fabulous prices were charged for everything, and from very necessity were paid for food or shelter. Later, when the apparition came to be known in England and America, thousands came, but only in many cases

* The writer of a government report says: " Where should the poorest place in the world be? The world is a very big place, and even vessels which steam fifteen knots an hour at the measured mile take a good many days to circumnavigate it. Yet, big as it is, the very poorest place upon its habitable area has been discovered by Captain Spaight, a Government inspector, who, without hesitation, declares it to be the Union of Swineford, County Mayo. The deplorable misery and poverty there to be found are attributed to " a succession of bad seasons," which have left the people without clothes and bedding, and with nothing but the huts in which they live. The only covering for the protection of a whole family from the chill, damp night air is in nine cases out of ten an old quilt or a few bags. " I have found," Captain Spaight adds, "the mother and children sitting on the mud floor eating the small, wet, ill-grown potatoes off the floor, with a little salt and nothing else, not a stool or a plate being in the house. The male portion of the population are away all the summer, and this year their earnings have not been as good as usual. A large portion of the district is in the hands of middlemen, there being no resident landlords or gentlemen, with one or two exceptions."

to be utterly disgusted by the extortions practised, and by the conduct of some of the people.

The want of proper accommodation, overcharges, and the gross incivility of one class of people was preventing numbers from coming. But selfishness reigned supreme, selfishness gained the day, and selfishness has ruined the poor.

I much regret I have not kept any of the great number of letters which I received on the subject. Even priests wrote to me from America to beg for the sake of common decency that I would try to have proper accommodation for pilgrims, but it was useless to contend with these people, they even threatened me openly to go to the Archbishop of Tuam, and insist that he should put a stop to my plans. When I found so much opposition, I gave up the plan of the pilgrim's house.

I have a number of letters from Canon Bourke on the subject of Father Cavanagh's treatment of myself and the sisters. In one of these, dated August 7, 1884, he tells me that Father Cavanagh had quite fallen out with him because he had tried to protect me from the outrages of his friends. A New York gentleman, who had been staying for some time in Knock, wrote to me, —

"Your solemn declaration on any subject would have no weight with Father Cavanagh in opposition to the words of Sister M——. When I spoke about Mrs. K——'s sons singing ribald songs, and that I often noticed smoking in the room beside the chapel, he coolly said, 'They were not in that room,' which I knew was false. It naturally occurred to me that now, at all events, he had vouchsafed one act of justice to you. But no, Canon Bourke of Claremorris it was who went to Mrs. K—— and got her to remove her young gentlemen from the place where they were such a nuisance. Your serenity at the impudence and insolence of these people astonished me. Months ago, Canon Bourke wrote to me that he had gone to Archdeacon Cavanagh in your interests, but the archdeacon would not listen to him. Taking all this in connection with Father John's calling you a 'liar' in presence of the community, it was time for you to fly elsewhere.

"At this time Dr. McEvilly, in whom you placed implicit confidence, showed what he really was.[*] He was offered a chance to do you justice, and allow you to remain, and he should blame only himself, unless he can blame Cardinal McCabe, if he has obliged you to leave.

"When I visited Dr. McEvilly at Lisdoonvarna, he spoke of you to priests who were in company with him, and to me, in a highly compli-

---

[*] Again and again I was reproached by my friends, and by some of his own priests, with confiding too much in Archbishop McEvilly, and assured that I would live to regret it.

mentary tone, alluding to your great faith, your great charity, and general ability in business matters. Yet in the very next month he allows you to be assailed in this way and villified."

In a letter dated December 13, 1883, the same gentleman alludes to the subject of Father John's conduct towards me. He says, "I pray God the people may succeed with the archbishop in getting rid of Father John."

On the 10th of December, 1883, I received the following letter from the same person, and in the appendix to this work two letters will be found which were addressed by him to Archbishop McEvilly and Archdeacon Cavanagh, expostulating with them for the way in which they were acting towards me. This gentleman's right to interfere was grounded on the fact that he had collected large sums of money for the institution at Knock.

If I were to give extracts from all the letters of those who visited Knock, and who were eyewitnesses of my difficulties, it would only weary the reader.

A gentleman wrote to me at this time, —

"I came back from an interview with the archdeacon, and have for the first time realized the appalling difficulties you have met, and the pleasure which your enemies take in traducing you."

A priest came to visit Knock; he said very little to me while he was there, but after his return to England he asked me to go with the sisters to his parish in England, where he would give us a "quiet and peaceful home." "There are plenty of Irish girls here," he said, "who need you, and who will soon build a convent for you." Still, however, I tried to persevere at Knock, where already the work was so far advanced, and so much money had been expended.

I may mention here that among the countless complaints which were made about me, one was that I would not remain for any length of time in any place, and was always wanting to change. Yet I remained in Kenmare for many years without moving, or wishing to move. During that time two sisters who had been many years professed left it and returned to Newry Convent, and there was not one word said against them. Four or five sisters went to Dublin on different occasions, at very great expense, for consultations for their health, though they did not suffer from any such serious illness as mine.

It is quite true that after I left Kenmare I moved frequently, but every move I made was in obedience to ecclesiastical superiors, and I have their written desire for what I did.

While in Knock it will be remembered that

I was sent by the archbishop himself to Newry Convent. In Dublin I was put out of Harold's Cross Convent by Cardinal McCabe, and obliged to move again.

Again, by desire of Archbishop McEvilly, I went to Knock. Then he ordered me from there to Claremorris; then he sent me to Cavan on business.

While I was in Knock I was obliged to go to England to give evidence in a trial, as money had been collected in my name under false pretences. This was a matter about which there was no choice, as the government compelled me to go, yet I did not do so without the archbishop's written permission.

I became so dangerously ill after my return that it was necessary for me to get skilled medical advice; I had to go to Dublin for that purpose, and I have in my possession the archbishop's directions for me to do so.

Finally, I was obliged to leave Knock and eventually, still with permission, to go to England.

After I had moved with the sisters to England, I was obliged to go to Rome; this was another move certainly, but it was made in obedience to my bishop.

A few months after my return I came to America, very much against my own will, and only at the positive desire of my bishop.

Since I have been in America I have never gone anywhere without permission from my ecclesiastical superior.

Until quite recently I have always thought that if those who opposed me saw the documents which I have, and knew how unjust their accusations were, that they would at once make some restitution for the wrongs they have done me. I know now that it is hopeless to expect any justice from a Roman Catholic bishop, with some rare exceptions.

When I went to Dublin I thought it would be an excellent opportunity to try and see Cardinal McCabe, to show him the letters of Bishop Higgins and Bishop Leahy, from which he could see that I had been treated by him very unjustly when he expelled me from Harold's Cross Convent, and that I had done nothing wrong.

I therefore wrote to Cardinal McCabe asking him would he appoint a time to see me. I received a most contemptuous and rude reply, in which he blamed me for not stopping in the convent of Harold's Cross; I suppose that he had forgotten how he had put me out of it a few months before. I wrote to him again, trying to conciliate him, and telling him my object in wishing to see him. He replied, curtly, that he would see me, but only on this condition, that I should get a letter from Archbishop McEvilly asking him to do so.

I was overjoyed at even this concession; I was always so sanguine that things would come right if these bishops would only look into them for themselves, and not judge from idle rumors. And now I thought I had nothing to do but to get the letter. I wrote at once to Archbishop McEvilly, and I sent Archbishop McEvilly's permission for me to visit Dublin to Cardinal McCabe. Happily, however, I kept a copy, as he refused to return me the original document, though I wrote for it more than once.

Instead of the letter, from which I hoped so much, I received a despatch from Archbishop McEvilly, which is before me now, in these words, —

"For best reasons, determined long since to give no person whomsoever introductory letters to personage in question; sorry to refuse."

The simple object throughout my religious career appears to have been for my accusers not to inquire themselves, nor to allow any one to inquire into the justice of their accusations. And if there was the least chance of documents or statements being brought before them which would justify me, they refused to see them.

The Holy Father was more easy of access than

any of his subjects; but even his approval has been of no avail.

I hoped that God had inspired me to found a new religious order, and the priest who had been my confessor for so many years encouraged me in the idea. In September, 1884, we had a retreat from an experienced and learned father, the Rev. Father Gaffney, S. J.; to this priest I confided all my difficulties and troubles, and, as his letters will show, he had no doubt that the plan of my new order was a divine inspiration, and he was greatly distressed at the position in which he found me placed. So deeply did he feel the whole matter, and so anxious was he to help me in my difficulties, that he told me he would go to Rome with me, himself, if the archbishop would permit it, and if his superiors sanctioned it, which he had no doubt they would do.

I begged the archbishop several times to allow me to go to Rome, but he refused. In fact, he would give no decision; if he had said, I will never allow you to found this new order, I should have given the matter up at once, but I have his letters which show his reply was always the same, that "at present" he could not allow any change. I was thus placed in a most serious difficulty. What rule was I to follow? What rule was I to teach the sisters? How was I to train the novices?

Were they to be Poor Clares, or were they to be Sisters of Peace?

I was by no means the first foundress of a new order who had to move from one diocese to another before she could find rest for herself and her community, or free and cordial protection in her work. Every one could see that my position was a false one, every one knew it, and those who wished to do so did not fail to avail themselves of the opposition from which I was suffering. I doubt if on earth there was a more broken-hearted soul than mine. One consolation I had, and that was in the love of my dear sisters, who entirely sympathized with me in all my designs. I felt now that matters had come to a crisis and that I must make some decided move myself.

I was obliged to go to Dublin to consult a physician, in the November of 1883. Dr. McEvilly was there on business at the same time, and, as Father Gaffney was there also, I begged him to see the archbishop and try to get some arrangement made to enable us to continue our work in peace. The result was that after a few hours, Father Gaffney came to me with a document which he said he had been given by the archbishop. I noticed something unusual in his manner, but though I was very ill, and lying quite prostrate on a couch, I was so full of joy hoping that some decision had been arrived at, that I was not in as much doubt as I might well have been, considering my past experience. I held out my hand for the document, but to my surprise, Father Gaffney would not give it to me. He said that the archbishop had given it into his hands with positive orders that I was not to read it myself, that he was to read it for me (I think he said once only), and that I was to sign it; but on no account was I to be allowed to read it over, or even see it; he was to witness my signature, and then take it back to Dr. McEvilly. I was so surprised that I did not know what to say. Father Gaffney began to read it for me; I listened to the end, as well as my indignation would allow me, then I asked Father Gaffney, "Do you advise me to sign this?" He replied promptly, "Certainly not, but I could not refuse to bring it to you when the archbishop asked me."

I cannot remember all the contents of this extraordinary production, but I remember well the principal points: I was to bind myself to finish the convent at my own expense; and I was to bind myself never to speak to one of the sisters, or go near them, as a mistress of novices was to be provided for them. In fact, my name was to be used to establish an institution, out of which I might be cast adrift on the world at any moment, without warning or excuse, and in which I was to be merely a visitor on sufferance. I heard afterwards that the archbishop was very angry because I refused to sign this document, and of course this was told all over Dublin and probably all over America, as another evidence of my unwillingness to submit to ecclesiastical authority. I was not without a suspicion where the idea originated; it would have suited the Kenmare sisters very well to come to Knock and have absolute authority there, and avail themselves of all the funds I might collect. I do not say this without reason.

I knew perfectly well also that the sisters who were with me would never submit to such a regulation.

I doubt if any other ecclesiastical authority on earth would have required a sister to put her signature to such a document, and above all when she had not been allowed to read it over quietly.

If the archbishop had held a visitation at the convent and inquired himself into what was supposed to be wrong, it would have been quite another matter. But he heard only one side of the question, and took everything for granted. I have copies of a number of letters which I wrote to him, begging him to hold a visitation, but he would not.

The feast of Saint Francis Xavier, the great apostle of the Indies, was fast approaching. I was now, the doctor feared, in a dying state, as his medical certificate will show. I knew not which way to turn, matters seemed more unsettled than ever.

I now wrote the archbishop a respectful letter, asking him again would he not allow me to go to England to see Cardinal Manning, as I could neither satisfy him nor the archdeacon, nor could I remain longer at the mercy of so many people who were trying to prevent the completion of the building at Knock.* My condition was indeed unhappy, except for the affectionate and encouraging letters of the sisters, which I received daily.

I prayed again to Saint Francis Xavier, and told him if he would obtain for me permission to go to England, I would call the first convent I founded there, the convent of Saint Francis. To my amazement, within five minutes after I had made this prayer, I received a letter from Archbishop McEvilly written certainly in the most ungracious terms, but still giving me the permission to go.

I sent at once for Father Gaffney, S. J., and for the doctor; they both advised me to go as soon as

* A priest who had given us a retreat a few weeks before, was an eyewitness to the annoyances we received from Mr. K——. whom he saw several times outside our windows in such a state, that he advised me to send for the police.

possible, as the doctor said my health was in such a state that even if I should die, it was better for me to die going to England than to die as I was, and that, perhaps, some settlement or peace of mind would help my recovery more than anything else.

CHAPTER XIX.

I GO TO ENGLAND.

I Reach London — Visit to Cardinal Manning — His Cordial Reception — Call on Rt. Rev. Dr. Bagshawe — Transferred by the Archbishop of Tuam — Father Cavanagh's Dislike to my Work — Nature of my schools — An Incapable Teacher — Knock Schools — A Letter — Petition to the Archbishop — Letters from Michael M. Waldron, Canon Bourke, James Rogers, and others.

I ARRIVED in London in the middle of December, and was received with the utmost kindness and most affectionate charity by the Sisters of Mercy, who, being under His Eminence Cardinal Manning, and knowing his interest in my work, received me very cordially.

I went to Cardinal Manning as soon as I had rested for a few days, and told him all my trouble, finding in him, what he always had been, a most sincere friend and sympathizer. I showed him the letters and documents which I had, and told him fully all my difficulties. He saw at once that it was perfectly impossible for me to try to continue my work under such opposition. He said, "that it would be better for myself and the sisters to come to England where," he added, "you will find plenty of work to do for the poor Irish; you

are, perhaps, more needed here than in Ireland."
I need scarcely say that a bishop of his prudence
and experience would not have encouraged me,
if he had not thought that I deserved encouragement, and if he had not known that I had done
nothing which could have merited ecclesiastical
censure.

Cardinal Manning then advised me to go direct
to the Right Rev. Dr. Bagshawe, Bishop of Nottingham, who had been a distinguished member of the London Oratory, a congregation of
priests belonging to an institution founded by
Saint Philip Neri, and of which the Paulist
fathers in New York are a kind of imitation. I
was received most cordially by Bishop Bagshawe,
and he most gladly accepted us at once for his
diocese.

I wrote then to Archbishop McEvilly for a
canonical transfer of myself and sisters to the
Nottingham diocese, and he promptly acceded to
my request. This document I subjoin here.

"TUAM, December 26, 1883.

"DEAR REV. MOTHER MARY FRANCIS CLARE,
— As you seem to think you can better promote
the great work you contemplate in England than
at Knock, and as the Most Rev. Dr. Bagshawe,
Bishop of Nottingham, has been pleased, as appears from his letter which you forwarded to us,

to receive you and your novices into his diocese, we, therefore, yielding to your earnest desire and entreaty, release you by these presents from all obedience due to us, to transfer to the Most Rev. Dr. Bagshawe all the jurisdiction we have over you. Wishing you and yours the abundance of all blessings, Your faithful servant in Christ,

" JOHN, *Archbishop of Tuam.*

"Given at Tuam this 26th day of December, 1883."

It will be observed that Archbishop McEvilly says in his letter of canonical transfer to the diocese of Nottingham, —

" As you seem to think you can better promote the great work you contemplate in England than at Knock, etc." Now no one knew better than Archbishop McEvilly, that I thought nothing of the kind, but the expression answered admirably to give the idea that I had left of my own free will. I left because neither Archbishop McEvilly nor Father Cavanagh would allow us to carry on the great work which he had once so much admired.

As for Father Cavanagh, he was not only indifferent to my work, but he actually disliked it.*
So long as Knock was crowded with pilgrims who paid honor to himself and to the shrine, he asked no more. As for doing anything to promote in-

* See page, 330.

dustrial occupation, or to help the poor in their struggle for life, it was quite out of his way. Their fathers before them had got on and lived and died anyhow, and had gone to heaven, and they could do the same. Certainly, his holy indifference saved him a great deal of trouble, and I wish I could have imitated it.

It must be said, in justice to him, that he was equally indifferent to his own surroundings. He lived at that time in a poor cabin, his fare was of the very plainest, and, except where the needs of his relatives were concerned, he cared very little for money.

After Knock became famous for its apparitions, when enormous sums of money were sent to him, he improved the old church a little, and built a large and very curious house for himself. He still talked, as if in a dream, about a community of priests which he intended to found, and who he expected would live there with him. But the priests, who knew him and his eccentric ways, said he would never get any one to remain with him for a month.

Although I had not been able to begin the industrial home for girls on a large scale, I had already collected a number of young girls; and I had forty in regular and permanent employment.

The house which we rented from Father Cavanagh's friends, as I said before, at such cost, was situated on a very high hill, and fully two miles distant from any school. The roads in winter were almost impassable from mud and dirt, and in summer there was no shade. The distance made it impossible for young children to attend the village school; and with Father Cavanagh's full consent, I opened a school at once, and placed it, as all Irish convent schools are placed, under the National Board. If there had not been a necessity and an urgent necessity for a school, the National Board would not have tolerated it for a day. It was a great success, beyond all my hopes, and even now I cannot think of it without tears.

I formed a kindergarten, and the dear, bright, loving little ones were precious to my heart and soul; I never expect to see such sweet children again. Even had there been a school in the village, they would have been far too young to go to it.

In addition to our babies, as I may well call them, for they were very young, there were a few older children, who for various reasons could not go to the girls' school in the village, and with the full consent of the mistress, we received them also. And then there were the boys; there was certainly a boys' school in the village, but the teacher was thoroughly inefficient and incapable of managing a school. He was so lame that he came to school on a donkey. But Father Cavanagh, with that peculiar tenacity of opinion, which some people call obstinacy, would not hear of his removal.*

In Ireland the inspectors are so much under the control of the priests, that they dare not dismiss a teacher against the wish of the priest, and the inspector pleaded in vain for his dismissal.

Archbishop McEvilly certainly recognized that the work was a good one, if he had only had the courage to help me to carry it out. But I did not suspect until after I left Knock that Father Cavanagh was not only indifferent, but that he was actually opposed to what I was doing. If I had known this sooner, I should have left Knock long before I did.

The National Board very properly requires roll books to be kept, in which the name, age, and date of entrance of every pupil is entered, and it is the duty of the inspector to see that this is carefully and regularly attended to. Therefore, even had I wished to do so, I could not have taken children from other schools into ours. Yet this is precisely what Father Cavanagh accused us of,

* It was the same tenacity which made him keep a housekeeper whose character was such that it brought a perpetual scandal on the place. It was in vain that his brother priests expostulated, and in vain that the archbishop interfered.

and he knew I took particular pains not to do this.

I know that the poor people in Knock deeply regret our departure. An urgent petition was sent to the archbishop entreating him to bring the sisters back, and to allow their work to continue. As soon as Archdeacon Cavanagh heard this he sent for the people principally concerned, and having spoken to them, ordered them out of his sight for having presumed to send in such a petition. In fact, he had got rid of us and did not want to have us back, and said so very plainly. It seemed to matter so little to him that the poor girls were left to grow up in ignorance and in need of industrial employment and training.

A lady who was driving from Claremorris to Knock told me that the boy who drove her spoke of our leaving with tears in his eyes, and said, "It was the archdeacon and Father John done it, and it was a terrible loss to the whole people." As he was speaking, an outside car drove by with a lady on it; he said, "That lady will have a fine fortune." She asked who was it, and she was answered "Miss ———," a near relative of Father Cavanagh.

The following letters will tell the rest of this painful story. Mr. M. Waldron, who keeps a large store in Ballyhaunis, is the joint trustee for the ruined convent with myself and the Archbishop of Tuam.

"KNOCK, February 13, 1884.

"*To the Editor of the 'Tuam Herald,'* —

"DEAR SIR, —My attention was called very lately to a paragraph which appeared from a correspondent in your paper, to the effect that now, as sister Mary Francis Cusack had left Knock, and was now residing in the diocese of Nottingham, that the children of this parish would be left in their normal state of ignorance. In the interests of justice and fair play, I must say that in very few parishes of Ireland are there more schools, or more ably conducted, than in this parish. These schools are a long time in full operation. The teachers are all most zealous in the performance of their duties. The children of the numerous schools (eleven) of the parish are solidly instructed in their religious duties, as was testified to by His Grace, the Most Reverend Dr. McEvilly, the illustrious and learned archbishop of this diocese, on the occasion of the confirmation held in Knock not long since.

"It was stated in your paper that of these children who frequented the convent schools, that none of them were ever before going to any other school. This, allow me to say, was untrue, as the two school inspectors, on the occasion of a visit to the convent schools, drove thirty-four pupils, boys, from that school who were decoyed away by a recruiting sergeant, to whom the Nun gave twopence for every child he could induce to go to her school.

"Thus a great wrong was done to the teachers. As the result, fees would be and were lost to the Nuns, and this in violation of an engagement entered into of not admitting their pupils.

"Yours truly,
"An Inhabitant of Knock."

When I came to know that this "Inhabitant of Knock" was no other than Archdeacon Cavanagh himself, I no longer wondered at the opposition I had met from every one in Knock.

The following reply was written by the very inspector mentioned by Archdeacon Cavanagh, and as he was present on the occasion, and Archdeacon Cavanagh was not, he had the best right to give an opinion. I must say if I had not seen this letter in Father Cavanagh's own handwriting, I could not have believed that even he could have written it. I have the original letter before me as I write. The editor of the paper sent it to me, as I positively refused to believe that Archdeacon Cavanagh could have written it, until I saw his handwriting.

As the charges which Archdeacon Cavanagh makes against me in this letter are so serious, I may be allowed to say again that the following letter was written by the government inspector.

Further, I should say that we still have the books of the Knock convent schools, and a glance at them will show at once that every one of Archdeacon Cavanaugh's charges against us were false. The books of the schools were kept by one of the sisters who had been a national teacher for many years, and even if we had wished to take children from the other schools, we could not have done so, as the inspector would have found it out at once. The "recruiting sergeant" was a poor little boy of ten whom I employed to bring the very little children to school who could not come alone. I was very careful not to take any children who had been going to any other schools. The false charges made against us by Archdeacon Cavanagh, sad as they are, show how little he cared for his poor, and how little he knew about them. The object of the compliment to the "illustrious and learned" archbishop is self-evident.

KNOCK SCHOOLS.

"*To the Editor of the 'Tuam Herald,'*—

"SIR, — The letter which appeared in your last issue over the vague pseudonym of 'An Inhabitant of Knock' is a very curious production. The animus of the writer is too plain to be concealed, but, apart from mean malice, I regret the writer did not confine himself to a plain statement of facts, and not give to the public a tissue of low lies and flagrant falsehoods. I take the statements of the writer *seriatim* only to *seriatim* contradict them, —

"As regards his first statement as to 'very few parishes in Ireland having more schools,' this contrasts markedly with the undoubted fact that when Sister Clare opened her school at Knock she had attending it between seventy and one hundred children, who were going to no other school, in this well-appointed parish, which will require a better certificate of efficiency than this nameless writer can give it.

"All the present schools are, in my opinion, overcrowded. As to their efficiency, in one instance the teacher is not particularly active, being lame and old; another is in jail! Are these evidences of efficiency and sufficiency?

"As to the statement of the teachers being zealous, I will only ask the writer to examine and contrast the returns of result fees with those of other adjoining parishes.

"As to the raid of the two school inspectors who visited the Convent School and drove thirty-four boys away, I have yet to learn upon what occasion this invasion occurred.

"I am aware that one day the present inspector, when consulted by the nun as to the advisability of having certain grown boys at her school, did turn away about a dozen of these boys, who were sent simply because they were too old for an infant school, and when they were evicted they showed visibly their signs of regret and disappointment. From this little incident your correspondent evidently reared up his stupendous superstructure of suppositions, and, in characterizing his statement, I must use your correspondent's own words, and say that 'it was untrue.'

"And notwithstanding 'the decoying' which this zealous nun was said to practise, it is, I believe, a fact that there were never a larger number 'made their days' at the ordinary schools than while the nun was there and the Convent School flourishing.

"I attribute this, sir, to the energy her bright example gave, and the contrasts brought out in her brief sojourn here.

"And still more strange is the fact that the girls' schools showed no appreciable falling off.

"Thus the statement as to the consequent wrong done to the teachers is a gross fabrication, and an unjust imputation upon a devoted religieuse who was absolutely driven from Knock by every species of persecution which ingenuity could invent and malice perpetrate. Yours truly,

"AUDI ALTERAM PARTEM."

"BALLYHAUNIS, March 22, 1884.

"MY DEAR REV. MOTHER, — Father Cavanagh, I understand, is delighted with the imagination that he can take possession, and that he will have no trouble raising the funds to finish the convent.

"I fear these ideas are 'building in the moon.' May the Lord, in his mercy, direct and assist all those who are laboring under the false delusions which are detrimental to our religion to see that such a difference as occurred at Knock could not be amended again at once, particularly when it occurred with or amongst the dignitaries of our once persecuted and downtrodden church. Our enemies again would be so delighted to have such cases as Knock to throw in our face, but God, I hope, will set all these matters right.

"I am glad you find your mission a success. I hope the business you refer to as getting settled will be Knock.

"Wishing you a safe return and a long life to labor in the interests you have at heart,

"Yours very faithfully,
"MICHAEL M. WALDRON."

"B———, 16—11, '82.

"DEAR MADAM,—I enclose you a formal intimation of ———'s consent to grant the lease. However, I explained to him that it would be the nuns that would suffer by refusal, so it is all right again. Mr. ——— says that Rev. J. Cavanagh's name is not to be connected with the lease, which, I daresay, you are not sorry for, as he appears to be very overbearing. I think I shall be in the neighborhood of Knock next week, and, if so, will run up to see you."

(Signed) ——— ———

The following letter from Archbishop Croke will show what he thought of the persecution which has caused me so much suffering. With regard to that part of his letter in which he advises the publication of my correspondence which would show that I was entirely blameless in regard to all the charges which these bishops made against me, I must say a few words. I think that those who read this autobiography will see for themselves that I have been in no haste to publish it; I so long hoped against hope that the bishops would spare me this painful necessity. But I at last learned that they are quite indifferent to anything which does not affect their own immediate interests.

When I found, after I had been a short time in America, that all the false reports which had been inquired into and disapproved before the sacred Council of Propaganda, were circulated, if they were not believed, by so many of the American bishops that the people naturally supposed that they were true, I saw that I had no other resource but to do what Archbishop Croke had advised. I hoped when the American bishops saw these documents in print, and knew their authenticity could not be questioned, that respect for the Holy See would make them silent, so I published a pamphlet in Philadelphia containing the pope's authorization of the work which I proposed to do, and what was quite as important, I published the notification from Propaganda, stating that all the reports against me had been inquired into in Propaganda, and that they had all been found false. Such a document ought not to have been necessary for any loyal son of the Roman Catholic church, as the fact of the pope's having authorized me to found a new religious order should have silenced every criticism. It is certainly a reflection on the Holy Father to circulate evil reports of one whom he honored so highly, it is at least a reflection on his judgment and wisdom in a very important matter. I soon found that the publication of these documents was not of the slightest use. The bishops were very angry with me because I published them, but they never tried to stop these reports, nor did they cease to speak falsely of me, and they allowed their priests to do the same both in public and private, without reproof.

As I followed the archbishop's advice, by publishing these letters "privately, and for the bishops only," without any good effect, the bishops cannot blame me if I now justify the Holy Father's action in my regard, as they will not do it themselves.

It would occupy considerable and unnecessary space in this volume if I gave all the correspondence I have on this subject.

The Irish Bishop who first started the report that I had left Kenmare without leave was so determined to believe it, no matter whether it was true or not, that Archbishop Croke wrote to me it was useless to send him documents or proofs.

If people wish to believe what is not true, it is their own affair; it is so with some of the bishops in this country. They had all the evidence before them, but for some reason they did not choose to believe it. But I cannot keep other people in the dark who have a right to know the truth, and who will have no motive for refusing to believe it. Archbishop Croke's advice to me to publish my justification is contained in a letter dated, —

"THE PALACE THURLES, March 2, 188 .

"MY DEAR SISTER CLARE, — All right, I am delighted, and have sent a crusher to the Hierarch in question. I think the publication of the letters from Dr. Higgins, Dr. Leahy, and Dr. McEvilly, for private circulation amongst the bishops, and nobody else, would do a deal of good. God speed and prosper you.   Your friend,
                                    "T. W. CROKE.
"THE NUN OF KENMARE."

The following is Canon Bourke's advice to the same effect, —

"CLAREMORRIS, August 7, 1884.

"MY DEAR MOTHER, M. CLARE, — I believe the American people are anxious to hear why you left Knock. I believe English people have the same feeling, and many in Ireland; but I am not in a position to offer any advice myself. Act as you deem right, and tell the truth. I think the Catholics of America and Australia demand it. That would bring about the necessity of giving you and your spiritual children that convent back, which Americans and others have founded. It was brought as a charge against me that I had a 'collection' for you. He threatened to inflict censure for that act, although you show me his letter giving you liberty to ask and receive from us.

"Yours in Christ,
"ULICK BOURKE."

I shall now give a brief extract from a letter, one of many, in which I was reproached with overconfidence in Archbishop McEvilly. It will show how far I was from being troublesome to my ecclesiastical superiors. If I had been less trustful, I might have fared better. This gentleman writes, —

"As to Archbishop McEvilly, you put your whole trust in him only to be doomed, at a critical moment, to bitter disappointment. As to the plan, or conspiracy, which drove you from Knock, had the archbishop been what you took him to be, or inclined to render a just and impartial decision, he could and would have supported you, and all annoyance would have ceased. The archbishop, no doubt, stands in momentary fright lest you should tell the whole world the history of your having to leave Knock."

In a letter to me from Archdeacon Cavanagh, dated Knock, Feb. 18, 1884, he says, —

"You have been stating that you would return to Knock if I wished you to do so; I decline to give my consent to your returning to Knock. In fact, I am resolved, for very good and solid reasons, that you and your novices, or professed nuns, will not during my lifetime return to this place.
"I remain yours very faithfully,
"BART'H CAVANAGH, P. P."

I know to my sorrow that people have thought that I had refused to return to Knock; the truth will now be seen by all. I fear that Archdeacon Cavanagh or his friends did something more than hint that it was my fault that the work at Knock was abandoned. I have borne the imputation until now, because I knew that when I spoke I should say all, and I hoped it might not be necessary for me to do so.

Nor was I the only person to whom Archdeacon

Cavanagh gave a very decided and even angry refusal to a request for our return. Both priests and people tried to move him from his resolution; for myself, knowing as I did, his character and the influences by which he was surrounded, I had not the least hope that he would change his determination. The only person who could have had any influence with him was the Archbishop of Tuam, Dr. McEvilly, and he would not interfere. A gentleman who lives near Knock wrote to me March 6, 1884, —

"I know you will travel a great deal before you will be insulted as you were at Knock; you know the devil must have some weapon to undermine good and pious works. It could hardly be expected that such good works would succeed without great obstacles."

Here again we have another of many instances by which grievous harm is done to the Roman Catholic church. Roman Catholic ecclesiastics have impressed the people with the very convenient idea that they are not to be blamed, no matter what wrong they may do; so the "devil" is made the convenient scapegoat. The claim of priests to be thus excused is a serious danger to the Roman Catholic church. Facts cannot be hidden as they were in earlier ages. People know that certain evils exist, and though they may be silent for a time, the existence of these evils is not forgotten. An open, honest admission of the evils in the church would go far to lessen them. It would, at least, save the church the awful crime of even appearing to approve evil by not condemning it.

[SISTER MARY FRANCIS CLARE AND THE VENERABLE ARCHDEACON CAVANAGH.]

"308 EAST BROADWAY, NEW YORK.
"March 31, 1884.
"*To the Editor of the* '*Tuam Herald*,'

"SIR, — I request you will have the goodness and fairness to publish the inclosed copy of a letter I sent to Archdeacon Cavanagh, P. P., Knock. It speaks for itself. Yours faithfully,
(Copy) "JAMES ROGERS."

"203 EAST BROADWAY, NEW YORK,
"March 21, 1884.

"VERY REV. AND DEAR SIR, — So mortifying to me is the deplorable treatment to which Rev. Mother M. Francis Clare has been subjected, and the provokingly false reports circulated, evidently to injure her reputation, that I feel myself obliged to communicate with you.

"First as to the assertion that 'she ran away from Knock, deserting her duties; that she robbed the convent, taking with her the contributions sent solely for Knock, to be controlled by you and not by her.' I most emphatically wish to inform you that all such moneys sent from here were sent to HER as testimony of the esteem and affection in which she is held for her efforts and services in behalf of the Irish poor and oppressed, and in the interest of religion and nationality; such moneys to be distributed by her in the relief and education of the Irish poor, or otherwise, in the interests of religion and charity as she might think fit. If testimony, by most respectable persons in America, in proof of this assertion, by you will be required, I can easily send it. It is sufficient to satisfy the public, and all concerned, except of course her persecutors and calumniators, whom nothing would satisfy except her persecution even to exile and, as it would seem at any cost, even at the cost of her life. As to the conspiracy, so determined, so scandalous, and so un-Catholic, which was planned against her, I will here avoid alluding to it in detail, merely remarking as regards its malice against the welfare of Catholicity in Ireland, but more particularly against the poor, despised, oppressed and exterminated Catholics around Knock, that it might be naturally alleged by any Irishman or Irishwoman who has preserved the faith of Saint Patrick and Saint Bridget, that its conception was indeed infernal. But I will say in conclusion that unless reparation be made both for the wrongs and the scandalously lying reports perpetrated, a full and true account shall be given to the public, indeed to the world, so that all may be in possession of the truth, and may judge for themselves as to the motives. Merciful God! How is it that by a sense of duty and justice I find myself compelled to write such a letter as this, especially to you. I could not, indeed, as a Catholic, trust to my accurate memory, nor to my reason, as regards the shocking doings at Knock while I was there last July to September, were it not that other strangers who happened to be there, including priests, partly learned of these doings also. I remain, very rev. and dear sir,

"Your most obedient servant,
"JAMES ROGERS.

"VENERABLE ARCHDEACON CAVANAGH, P.P., Knock, Ireland."

The following letter which is one of many received by me, will show the object for which money was sent to me to Knock.

"YASS, NEW SOUTH WALES, AUSTRALIA,
"February 28, 1884.

"DEAR SISTER, — Having noticed in one of our Australian journals your very zealous appeal for 'funds' to enable you to erect a 'knitting factory' for the very laudable, noble, and combined objects of rescuing from starvation numbers of the poor children of Mayo, and teaching them how to become respectable and religious members of society, by placing in their own hands the means of earning their own livelihood, I endeavored to collect a few pounds as per enclosed list, and therewith forward you a bank draft for the sum of twenty pounds for the above object.

"Your name, dear sister, has been associated during the past half century with many grand and noble objects and works to alleviate the distress and misery under which our unhappy country has labored, but your present one, I believe the noblest and grandest one of all. I trust the Almighty God may spare you to witness the results of your noble efforts, and to further indicate, — as has been your wont — the character at home and abroad of the children of our bleeding country.

"The following are the names of the contributors, and the amounts given by each. The names of all the Catholics are marked by an X.

"Soliciting your prayers at the shrine of our Immaculate Lady at Knock for all the contributors, and especially for myself, wife, and children,

"I remain, dear sister, your obedient child,

"MICHAEL COEN.

"P. S. The draft is made out in the name of 'The Nun of Kenmare.'"

It will now be seen that from the very moment in which I left Kenmare to the present hour, I have never taken one single step without the written permission of my ecclesiastical superiors.

I must now return to the sisters whom I had left at Knock. God alone knows the grief and sorrow with which they began the necessary arrangements for following me to England; and their greatest trouble, as might be expected, came from Sister M——.

I often told her when she was making so many complaints, and trying to make every one unhappy, and carrying idle stories to Father Cavanagh and his curate, that she would not stop until she had broken up the Knock foundation. Of course the poor soul was too inexperienced and too ignorant to realize the mischief she was doing until it was actually done; then, indeed, it came like a thunderclap on herself. She was sure that she could have remained and would have been allowed by Father Cavanagh to form a community of her own, and rule everything and every one as she pleased. Of course so wild an idea could only have been entertained by an ignorant and uneducated person.

Her anger and her amazement were unbounded when she found the convent was actually broken up, that we were all leaving, and that she must go back to Cavan. And bitter, indeed, were her denunciations of the priests who, she was led to expect, had such high ideas of her sanctity that they would never allow her to leave.

She had complained to me again and again of some of the sisters at Cavan, who, she said, were far too strict, because they would not let her talk at all times and in all places; and, in fact, kept her in her place, as is usually done with lay sisters. I had now to write to tell the sisters to prepare to follow me, and that she must leave.

Sister M—— at once refused to leave Knock, and it was not until she saw every one preparing to go away that she could be induced even to think of it. A letter to me from one of the sisters will explain the state of affairs, which I would gladly pass over without going into further details.

As Sister M—— could not read, I was obliged to inclose a letter for her to one of the sisters, telling her she must return to Cavan as we were all leaving Knock, and that I would, of course, pay all expenses and send some one with her to her destination.

The poor soul then realized for the first time what she had done. The sister whom I had left in charge wrote to me, Dec. 27, 1883, —

"My dearest Reverend Mother, — I received your dear letter this morning, and tried to read your inclosure for Sister M——, but she would not listen to me and ran away out of the room. My only hope is that Father Cavanagh will advise her to go quietly, but I fear he will not, after all the encouragement he has given her. It is too bad now that she will not try to calm her mind.

She had a long interview this morning with Father J——, and I know she clings to the idea that she will be kept here by herself.

"Father Cavanagh came here during the day and began to praise her to me as a good religious; she commenced all the old complaints again, saying the rule was not read. I turned to Father Cavanagh and told him the rule was read and kept by every one in the house but her; and that this was another of her many falsehoods, and she knew it. Sister M. J——, who was present also, could contain herself no longer, and turning to Father Cavanagh she exclaimed: 'Sister Martha does well to be so scrupulous when she has driven a whole community out of Knock.'"

I should say here that the poor sister dictated a letter which the Bishop of Cavan wrote for her, retracting all the charges she had made against us while she was in Knock, and that he wrote to me saying how much he regretted I should have been troubled by such a person.

I must say, however, that though I could not but feel gratified by Bishop Conaty's kindness and sympathy, I set very little value on Sister M——s retraction of her charges against the sisters and myself. Persons of her class will make charges one day, and retract them the next without any deliberate intention of being untruthful. The blame lies with those who encourage them and do not care to sift the value of evidence.

Another sister wrote to me, —

"I told Father Cavanagh that we had all copies of our rule; I also told him I would not stay in the room to hear you calumniated. I will tell you of other things she said when I see you. We all know that if the archbishop would say one word it would set it all right."

Another sister wrote, —

"We can do nothing with Sister M——, she says she will stay here until she dies, and I fear Father John has buoyed her up with the hope of being 'Mother Superior.'"

She had some really good qualities, and if left in her own place would have been a valuable sister in any religious house; but her head was not able to stand all the flattery that was shown her by consulting her and asking her opinion about matters which were no affair of hers.

At last Father Cavanagh told Sister M—— she must go back to Cavan, as even he saw that she could not remain in Knock by herself.

There was no end to the excuses and difficulties she made, and though she had found so much fault with me and with all the sisters, she was very anxious to come with us to England; an arrangement which I would not hear of for one moment, as we were only too thankful to be rid of her, and I knew if she found encouragement that she would undoubtedly have begun the same mischievous work over again. Besides this, I had received a letter from the superioress of Cavan Convent, to whom I wrote when I at last realized the harm she was doing, who told me that they always had had trouble with her from her propensity to interfere in other people's affairs.

When it was actually known that we were going from the place, it was of course written about in the papers, and it was a terrible blow to Father Cavanagh to find every one complaining of what he had done. The following article appeared in the *Tuam Herald*, —

"Sister Mary Clare has left Knock for Great Grimsby, gone from Ireland to England! Owing to circumstances which impelled the course, she was most unwillingly forced to remove the seat of her patriotic and ardent labors to a more congenial sphere. The new convent, nearly complete, is now left as it stood, and the hundred children who daily attended the schools are permitted to relapse into normal ignorance. We all here regret the departure of this good-working and noble woman who was doing so much to raise us intellectually and materially, but whose efforts are frustrated and foiled."

I had kept the difficulty between myself, the archbishop, and Father Cavanagh so quiet that, with the exception of Canon Bourke and one or two priests in the neighborhood, no one knew the real state of the case; and of course it was the interest of those who had driven us out of Knock to make it appear that we had left of our own accord and as a mere caprice. All the old stories were carefully got up again and circulated everywhere. It was said that I would not "obey my bishop," that I quarrelled with Father Cavanagh. It did not in the least matter whether these statements were true or false, they were said all the same and answered the purpose for which they were intended.

Evil, with rare exceptions, seems to triumph in this world. Those who considered themselves authorized "to hunt me down" had now a full opportunity of doing so. I had left Knock and gone to England, I was restless, I was hard to please, I was wandering about the world, I wanted change, and so on through the whole litany of absurdity and untruth. So careful had I been indeed to screen those of whom I had better have spoken openly, that a gentleman, a personal friend, when he heard of it exclaimed, "My God, why did you never say one word of all this to me, I never even suspected that you were treated so cruelly."

I must give yet another extract from the sisters' letters at this time, —

"We are so happy to get your dear letters, though they made us sad to think all you were suffering for God; but oh! dearest mother, how abundantly he will reward you for it! Think of that happiness and it will draw you to Him. Surely the cross could hardly be harder, but as you have often told us, the more we suffer in this world the more glorious will be our crown for all eternity. I wish it were in my power to comfort you. Our own dearest mother, God alone can give you the strength you so much require in this terrible affliction, and we are praying for you day and night before the tabernacle, and praying especially for the recovery of your health.

"I always doubted Father Cavanagh's protestations of friendship since the evening I heard him speak so uncharitably and disrespectfully of you. In fact, dear mother, do not be uneasy about his friendship; it is not worth having, as it is so false.

"Do keep Miss D—— as long as you can, for we know how you need her. Do not be anxious about business or letters; Sister M. J. and Sister M. E. are attending to them most carefully. We are trying to keep up regular observance."

The dear sisters knew that nothing would please me better than these last words. Whatever has happened, and whatever troubles we were under, the rules have been faithfully kept, the office regularly said in choir, the meditation made twice daily, and silence observed. We have had retreats given to us in Jersey City by several priests, amongst others by the Rev. Father Dealy, S. J., and all have had the same commendation for the sisters.

I will now give some of my correspondence in connection with this matter. I give first a few extracts from letters of Canon Bourke to me. As he lived within four miles of Knock, he was fully informed of all my troubles from personal investigation.

In one dated Feb. 6, 1884, he says, —

"MY DEAR MOTHER M. F. CLARE, — I send you a friendly letter written by His Grace of Toronto to me, in order to read for Father Cavanagh. But what use *Alea jacta est.* Besides, in my two visits to him, I impressed upon the archdeacon the very motives and results which his grace puts forward for his consideration. His grace writes to myself another long and friendly letter. He tells me that the poor immigrants to the Dominion, during the past year have in the winter suffered terribly, and but for the help rendered by the St. Vincent de Paul

Society, many of our poor Irish people would have perished from hunger and cold. These are the emigrants who left these shores for Canada during the spring and summer of 1883. There was a great banquet given lately in honor of the Governor-General, Lord Lansdowne, but his grace, though invited, did not attend, because the poor and suffering exiles were, perhaps, not a few from the Irish estates of the same noble marquis. Believe me always,   Yours very devotedly,

"U. J. CANON BOURKE."

This letter will be of interest for more reasons than one. Canon Bourke seldom signed his full signature, but I give it as it was signed to this letter. God help the poor Irish! Exiled without a thought as to what was to become of them, in the land of their exile; and the very priests who were the most energetic in denouncing the landlords who exiled them, would not allow anything to be done to keep them at home, by providing employment for them.

In another letter, dated Oct. 4, 1884, he says, —

"MY DEAR MOTHER, — There is no use in fighting with silk gloves on with those who *trampled you to the dust* (the italics are Canon Bourke's), when they had it in their power; they regarded you as a fair object for every outrage, because they saw how much you would submit to without complaint, till at last they took you to be a fool, whom they might treat as they pleased. It is your business to get Knock back, and finish it. You will succeed if your friend Dr. Bagshawe works out the matter. I told you what his eminence, the cardinal said."

In a postscript to this letter, Canon Bourke says, —

"He, (Archbishop Mc Evilly) gave you leave to collect, and threatened to censure me for giving you some help, as you will remember."

The allusion to Cardinal Manning was this: Canon Bourke had written to me some time previous, to say he had been in London and had dined with Cardinal Manning, and at the dinner table the cardinal had spoken very warmly of me and of the work I was doing. This letter I have unfortunately lost or mislaid.

In a letter dated Dec. 31, 1883, he says, —

"Your name and fame will be defended by some of us here, and after a time by most people. When the archbishop met you in Dublin did he offer any fair terms, or was his action such as I had foretold?"

I might multiply letters from priests and laymen who had personal knowledge of the way I was treated at Knock.

In a letter which I received from the Archbishop of Toronto, after I had gone to England, he writes, —

"Before you left Knock, I heard of the opposition you received, and I wrote very strong letters to Canon Bourke that he might show them to Father Cavanagh. I fear that his views are too restricted. I lately read the life of the foundress of a religious order in Belgium, who had to leave her first foundation, Amiens, and take refuge in Namur, in Belgium. However, the Bishop of Amiens afterwards recognized her goodness, and made ample apology. We have another example in St. Hyacinthe, the foundress of the Precious Blood, who was set aside by the bishop of the diocese, through an over-restricted zeal. Your case is not singular, and God will bring things to a good issue in the end. Wishing you every happiness in your new abode, and every blessing to yourself and community, I remain, dear Mother M. F. Clare,

"Faithfully yours in Christ,
"JOHN JOSEPH LYNCH,
"*Archbishop of Toronto.*"

The Very Rev. Canon Gerraghty, whose parish was next to that of Knock, wrote to me, —

"I am glad to learn that you and your sisters are happy in England I would be more pleased and happier if you were in Knock. People here do not know the real reason of your leaving

Knock. I went to Knock, and before the altar I prayed as fervently as I could that Almighty God would move the hearts of all concerned, and that, in the interests of the poor, the work might be resumed. I am sure you would work with more pleasure at Knock than anywhere else."

Mr. Richard Kelly, the editor of the *Tuam Herald* wrote to me, —

"I have heard many persons speak quite indignantly about the course adopted towards you, many lamenting the fate of the hundred little ones whom you gathered together and who must now relapse into normal ignorance. Poor Ireland, it is ever thus with her, since history first told her sad story of dissensions; more harm done to her by her own than by strangers. But there is a new and a wholesome spirit abroad that will burn out of the people that vile spirit born of slaves and bondsmen,— the spirit of deceit and jealousy, of mean-spiritedness and servility. You will yet find assistance and help from persons of all climes and creeds. As to F—— C—— I fully concur in B——'s opinion of his vanity and selfishness. But it would be a monstrous injustice to let his little game succeed, and surely you have some lien on the building to prevent it."

I need scarcely say that it was impossible for even a Roman Catholic gentleman to understand the peculiarities of ecclesiastical law as practised in the Roman Catholic church. Archbishop Lynch's letter given above should be carefully noted. The custom of persecuting any one who tries to do a good work of any kind in the Roman Catholic church is so universal, that it is looked on as something which must be. It is certainly difficult for ordinary minds to understand why it is right to persecute men or women while they are alive for doing certain things, for which they are canonized with such pomp and show when they are dead, particularly in view of the claims of the Roman Church to extraordinary sanctity and infallibility in her rulers. One would suppose that if a work is so good that the doer of it is worthy of canonization after death, it was equally worthy of commendation and support during the person's life.

A gentleman writing to me from New York, April 21, 1884, says, —

"You never told me the language Father John used to you, or how he tortured you. I know it now. It seems to me as if you had been shielding rather than accusing your persecutors, who, on their part, as I have now good reason to think, resolved at all hazards to crush and banish you."

In a letter from the same gentleman, dated December 10, 1883, he begins thus, —

"So they have done it at last! Their conduct is certainly outrageous and unpardonable. No doubt they were resolved on pursuing a desperate game, and were determined, anyhow, not to permit you to enter the new convent. I can only say that it was well you did not die, extremely fortunate for Father John, and I think the archdeacon has cause to thank God also. As to the Kelleys, from all I saw of them, they are not worth alluding to. They could not and would not have pursued the course they did to harass you, if they did not see and know that the two priests were vindictively opposed to you, and in fact determined to crush you. I suppose you can see very clearly what is, in a great measure at least, the cause and origin of all this, looking back through Cardinal McCabe, Bishop Higgins, Lord Lansdowne, and. possibly, though remotely, Vere Foster, who did not appreciate your advocacy and help in behalf of the persecuted, and your spirited and courageous, and to a great extent, successful combating with oppression."

I left Knock so quietly that no one but the sisters knew that I might never return. And may I not say that this was another proof how anxious I was to keep as quiet as I could, and to make no trouble for my ecclesiastical superiors. When, after making every effort to carry out a good work, I find determined opposition to it on the part of those who have it in their power to prevent its accomplishment, I withdraw quietly. If I am to blame, it is for not withdrawing sooner ; but it has been so difficult for me to think that this opposition would always continue, especially when it was opposition to what had the approval of the pope.

I left Knock for Dublin the first of November, 1883. I had never recovered the severe illness which had followed my move to the stables in Knock, and the constant and irritating troubles which I had to endure afterwards had added other complications. What a grief it was to me to leave Knock I cannot tell, but I had at last realized the hopelessness of persevering. Quite a number of sisters had joined me at Knock, and they too saw the hopelessness of our case, when we could not induce the archbishop to protect us, or even to make any personal inquiry into our difficulties.

On my arrival I was as usual obliged to go to a friend's house, and yet it was made a subject of reproach to me by the very archbishop who had put me out of a convent a short time before.

If I went to a convent by desire of one superior, I was driven out of it in disgrace, and if I did not go to a convent I was blamed for not going. And I had just the same difficulty to contend with in New York as will be seen later. It was not easy for me to please my superiors, I hope they did not mean to be deliberately unjust or cruel, but they certainly should not have listened to and acted upon all the unkind gossip which came from Kenmare without investigating its truth. Yet when so much of it came direct from Bishop Higgins to Cardinal McCabe, he would have had some excuse if he had not so positively refused to allow me any opportunity of explanation.

When the people of Knock saw that the sisters followed me to England, and that the works were stopped, they were in dismay and did all they could to get us back; but they had not even the courage or the spirit of the Kenmare people. They were wretchedly poor, crushed down, and miserable, and Father Cavanagh was very, very angry with them for wanting to have us back. The following letter will give some idea of the wretched state of the district. It was no wonder that Father Cavanagh's parish was a centre of Secret Societies, and the district notorious for outrages, —

"THE PRESBYTERY, CLAREMORRIS, July 2, 1883.

"MY DEAR REVEREND MOTHER, I know you are at present engaged in collecting for your own convent and lace factory at Knock; but I know also that the cry of distress was never made to you in vain. You have seen the wretched condition of the evicted tenants of Mr. Burke, and you know that in all Ireland there was not a worse landlord, even though he was a Catholic. You know how this moment they are lying out on the roadside half-starving, and you know also how thankful they would be for any employment. I do not ask for money, nor would I give it to them; but they ask for employment only, that they may be saved from starvation. I saw a letter from a priest in Kerry, who said God had sent you to our archbishop to save the people in their hour of need, as you did in Kerry, when the famine was there. I know you will not fail us now.

"I am, dear Reverend Mother,
 "Yours very sincerely in Christ,
  "JAMES CORBETT, C.C."

But there is yet a deeper depth in this misery. Dr. Burke demanded £10,000 "compensation" for his brother's murder — and it was levied off this unfortunate barony. Surely ten thousand pounds and the temporal ruin of one hundred and fifty families is a high price to ask as vengeance for one murder. And surely, fearful and awful as is the crime of murder, above all, when it comes in the premeditated form of assassination, the premeditated and merciless eviction of hundreds of helpless people is not an act of virtue.

The following letter will show the state of health I was in when I left Knock finally.

"Rutland Square, Dublin, Nov. 21, 1883.

"I certify that Mother Clare Cusack has been under my professional care for some time, with very serious symptoms of impairing health. For many years she has suffered from acute disease of the throat, which has tended to develop pulmonary irritation. Her most serious malady is —— trouble, which I am using the most prompt and urgent means to avert. Her illness has been caused by her great mental labors, and by depression of spirits, the result of wearing anxiety, a fruitful factor of —— disease. I would advise immediate relaxation from all causes which tend to depress her. John McVeigh, M.D.

"*Fellow of the Royal College of Surgeons, Dublin.*"

Dr. McVeigh considered my case so serious that he wrote to Archbishop McEvilly, to urge on him the necessity of giving me some protection from the attacks of those who were, in the opinion of this eminent physician, the cause of my illness, if not of placing my life in danger. Of this communication the archbishop took no notice, very much to the doctor's surprise and indignation.

CHAPTER XX.

GOING TO ROME.

The New Order Approved by Cardinal Manning and Bishop Bagshawe — Character of the Order — Sent on a New Mission — An Undesirable Priest — Preparations for Rome — I Stay at Lourdes — Another "Knock" — A Broken-Hearted Priest — The Shrine of the Sacred Heart — Paray-le-Monial — Kind Reception in Rome — A Visit from Cardinal Howard — In Charge of Mgr. Gualdi — Absurd Espionage — Favors in Rome — I see Mgr. Macchi — Public and Private Audience with the Holy Father — His Holiness Recognizes the Life of O'Connell — He Approves my Plan and my Writing — Letter from Father Gaffney, S. J.

His Eminence Cardinal Manning and Bishop Bagshawe both approved of the new Order which I wished to establish, and the work which I proposed to do, which seemed to commend itself to every one. There was no religious order in the Roman Catholic church devoted to this kind of work. It is true that the Sisters of Mercy, by their rule, should have devoted themselves to the care of destitute young women, but their institutions, perhaps unintentionally, have taken more the character of reformatories. My plan of individual training was not even thought of. The young women in these institutions are chiefly occupied in laundry work, and this being done necessarily on a very large scale, their training, in this respect, is of very little use when they go into domestic service or marry.

Of late years the Sisters of Mercy have occupied themselves principally with the education of young ladies, a matter which does not seem to have been contemplated in their original rule. It is obvious that sisters who are occupied in teaching cannot devote their time, care, and thought to the training of girls; a work which requires special capacity and special knowledge.

I feel as if it would seem ungracious on my part were I to speak of some of my difficulties in England where I was so kindly received by his Eminence and Bishop Bagshawe; but something must be said on this subject, if I am to make my autobiography complete.

It was with no ordinary joy that I found all the sisters around me once more. Poor Sister M—— had returned to Cavan under the care of a priest, and, to her dismay, she found that the very sister of whom she had so often complained to me as having been too strict with her, was now made her superior.

Bishop Bagshawe had several places where sisters were needed, but there was one place in particular which he was anxious that I should go to. The circumstances of the parish were very distressing, and I was sadly afraid, after my experience at Knock, of placing myself and my sisters in what might prove another painful complication.

I did not like to refuse Bishop Bagshawe, and he was very urgent about the matter. His Eminence Cardinal Manning also wished me to go there as many people had left the church, a beautiful building erected by a zealous convert, and there had not been six communions at the Christmas season. The priest was removed with some difficulty, as he was a person of influence and importance. He was, however, received at once into another diocese, notwithstanding what had occurred in the place from which he had been removed.

I was then staying with some of the sisters in Nottingham, in a private house, making final arrangements to go to our new mission. Just as I was about to leave, a priest belonging to the Nottingham diocese came to me in a very excited state, and told me he thought it his duty to tell me the character of the priest who was going in the place of the one who had just been removed.

Of all my trials, this was not one of the least. I did not like to consult with any of the sisters; in fact, there was no time to do anything, as we should leave in half an hour. I thought if I went to the bishop and refused to go, that a new story would be circulated to prove that I could not agree with my bishop; so I went, and I held my peace until the truth of what I had been told was so apparent that I felt bound in conscience to report the matter to the bishop. He was not surprised, for, of course, he knew the poor priest's failings, but what can bishops do? They must have priests, and they must often take what they can get or leave their missions unsupplied.

It had already been arranged that I should go to Rome as soon as possible. A bishop can establish a new religious order in his own diocese if he pleases, but it is not recognized by the church until the Holy See has pronounced in its favor. If Archbishop McEvilly had so pleased, he could have made this arrangement in the diocese of Tuam, and if he had allowed me to take postulants, as the superiors of more than one convent in his diocese suggested, and trained them for sisters, much trouble might have been saved. With very few exceptions, every religious order in the Roman Catholic church has been begun by a few girls or ladies who had no religious training whatever, and who often had very little education. They learn the observances of a religious life from books and experience.

In my case, as I had already made vows as a Poor Clare, it was necessary that I should have a dispensation from these vows, as well as the permission to found a new order.

I have purposely said a good deal about the Poor Clare rule and observances, and though I am well aware that some things which I have said in this book will not be of general interest, yet I have not said anything which will not be necessary for some of my readers, who will look at the matter from different points of view. With regard to my vows as a Poor Clare, there have been some grave mistatements, but I can explain their source and cause. The Poor Clare order is considered one of the most ancient of all in the Roman church, and the Kenmare sisters and their friends made it appear as if I had "fallen from grace" in leaving it. With that curious blindness, which generally characterizes those who have a motive for criticism, they forgot that when they criticised me they were also criticising the Pope and the Sacred Congregation of Propaganda. If there was wrong done, it was approved by the highest authority in the church. I have letters which show that if this report did not originate in Kenmare it was sent out from there. And it was circulated very widely in this country by those who ought to have known better.

I have shown how different the present rule of the Kenmare sisters is from the original rule of St. Clare, a fact which should have made them charitable and silent. But there is one point about their vows to which I must call attention. When they were first established in their present form, they were obliged to make a vow to devote themselves to the care of poor orphan children. This they did not do, and another of many alterations was made in their vows, and they were changed so that the vow as at present taken, stands, that they shall devote themselves to the care of poor children and especially orphans. Now the "especially orphans" is simply a dead letter in Kenmare; the sisters have no orphans there, and never had, so they actually make a vow to do what they have not the least idea of doing. The way in which this difficulty is got over is more ingenious than truthful. The sisters are told that if there happens to be any orphan child in the schools, they are to give special attention to this child. But such children are very seldom found at schools in Ireland, because they are sent to the workhouse or to an orphanage. Things being so, the Kenmare sisters or their friends should have been slow to criticise others.

It is not my purpose here to go into the details of my visit to Rome; if I recorded all I saw and heard I might fill another volume. I went provided with all the necessary credentials from my bishop and from His Eminence Cardinal Manning, and I brought with me the originals of all the documents which will be found in this volume, and of many others. I was obliged to travel very slowly on account of my health, and the rest I was obliged to take on my way afforded me a valuable opportunity of knowing something of the state of France and Italy; I talked freely to the people and in return heard a great deal from them.

I stayed some days at Lourdes, where the people seemed to me to be very good and simple, and I saw to my grief what I might call another Knock there. The priest who had been the first to make known the apparition, and to do everything for the young girl to whom the Blessed Virgin appeared, was desirous of building a church for his parishioners, and indeed it was greatly needed. The church where the apparition took place is a most costly building on the summit of a steep hill, and there is no room for any one except the pilgrims. It would have been quite impossible for the parishioners of Lourdes to hear Mass there. The good parish priest of Lourdes began his church on that costly scale which seems inevitable with those who spend other people's money. He hoped, however, that some of the enormous sums of money which were sent or given to Lourdes would come to him in its overflow, but the shrine of Lourdes was placed in the care of priests belonging to a religious order. The parish priest was completely set aside, and literally died of a broken heart in the midst of the plenty which he was the means of bringing to the place. He is buried in the ruins of the roofless church which he had begun for his people. I spoke to a priest there about their conduct in this matter, but of course it was quite useless; they are millionaires and they intend to remain so. Piety sometimes flows in capricious channels; the ruins at Knock and at Lourdes being at least existing examples.

I also remained a few days at Paray-le-Monial, the shrine of the devotion of the Sacred Heart, and to this place also I could devote more than one chapter, but as the subject is apart from my personal history, I shall only say that I saw there also, but in a different fashion, the mutability of religious belief. There were only a few sisters and a few priests to keep up the devotion of the Sacred Heart in the very shrine of its birth. It is indeed strange and perplexing; in view of the many statements that wherever the devotion is specially kept up special grace will come, and peace and piety must reign supreme. Certainly, as far as Paray-le-Monial is concerned, these statements have failed. The people have expelled the priests, and the Jesuits had a magnificent college there, which remains closed up, they themselves having been obliged to leave ; and the mass of the population are infidels.

I was received most kindly and cordially in Rome. I had not been there more than a few days when I had the honor of a visit from Cardinal Howard, then a prominent member of the Sacred College, and apparently in perfect health and vigor. I saw his eminence frequently afterwards, and he expressed his opinion very plainly as to the way I had been treated in Ireland. On one occasion he said, " It seems to me that you have been the Joan of Arc of Ireland ; you are trying to help every one. They could not burn you alive, and so they only hunted you out."

My affairs were placed in the hands of one of Minutandi in Propaganda, the late Mgr. Gualdi, a priest of great sanctity, and much thought of in Propaganda, who knew English thoroughly, having spent some years in England, and who was entrusted with English and Irish affairs.

I was surprised to find how well the characters of the different bishops were known in Rome. My business was to get a dispensation from my vows as a Poor Clare, and the permission to establish the Order of the Sisters of Peace. As I have said before, it was necessary that the Holy Father should be well assured that I was worthy of such a favor before it would be granted. All the false reports which had been circulated about me were investigated, and all the original documents published in this work were carefully looked over.

Mgr. Gualdi told me privately that piles of letters were sent in about me to Propaganda, all of which passed through his hands, and he said there was not one single charge substantiated against me. He said, "We are used to this kind of thing in Rome. Letters full of complaints, rumors, and suggestions, but not one word of fact." I heard some curious and amusing incidents of letters and statements which were sent into Propaganda about priests who were likely to be appointed bishops, from those who were opposed to them. After all, human nature is everywhere. In my case, at least, "*Roma locuta est*" has had no meaning. Rome has spoken for me in vain, to some American bishops, at least.

I may mention one incident of my stay in Rome which will show how absurd was the espionage kept on my movements, and how anxious certain persons in Ireland were to keep up the disproved charges against me.

I stayed at a private boarding-house near Propaganda, and within a few doors of Mgr. Gualdi's residence, this arrangement having been approved of by him for mutual convenience. I had a sister with me. I never left my room or joined the guests, although, while I was there, a sister was staying in the same boarding-house, and took her meals with the others, and joined them in the evening. I remained in my room with the sister who travelled with me because I preferred to do so, and partly because I knew how I was watched, and I determined to leave no cause for new reports, unless they should be manufactured as they had been before. I was not able to go out to early Mass, and I did not like the sister to go out alone in Rome, although other sisters did so. I therefore proposed to move to a convent where they took boarders, and where the sister could go to Mass with the others.

But when I mentioned this to Mgr. Gualdi he would not hear of it. He said, "This will be another removal, and one of the complaints against you is that you are constantly removing. I know that it is not true, and that you have never moved without necessity and permission, but, all the same, we must not let you be talked of in Rome, if possible."

I had many favors granted to me in Rome which I had never expected. I was cordially received in Propaganda, and was given special facilities for the preparation of a paper which I was asked to write for the Paris *Univers* on the Propaganda. It seemed to me then, as it seems to me now, a great injustice that the Italian government should have interfered with the money of Propaganda, as it was neither a national nor an Italian fund.

At the Vatican I had the pleasure of seeing Mgr. Macchi frequently, and I had the great favor of both a public and a private audience with the Holy Father. This last favor caused a great deal of annoyance in America among certain ecclesiastics, and Archbishop Corrigan showed his disapproval practically by refusing to see me until I had been nearly three years in America. If he had respected the reception given to me by the Holy Father in Rome, he would certainly have received me himself. For an inferior to refuse to show even common courtesy to one who had been received by his superior, is a strange failure of respect to the latter.

Everything has been said and written, which could be said or written, in America to do away with or to minimize the fact, but all in vain. The denial or discredit may gratify a poor feeling of jealousy, but it cannot alter facts. The official report of my audience with the Holy Father will be found in the appendix.

My audience was entirely private, as I did not require an interpreter.

Mgr. Macchi brought in the whole set of my books to his holiness, who looked at them, I think somewhat surprised at the number. Some of them were duplicated, having been translated into German, French, and Italian. He could read the title of these works, and the name of O'Connell was naturally familiar to him, as he noticed it on my "Life of O'Connell," which I brought with my other books.

His holiness specially commended the plan of my new order, and encouraged me in every way to continue writing. He gave his blessing to all the sisters present and to come, and to all those who would contribute to my work. I cannot forget his paternal and affectionate kindness, and the sympathy he expressed for the troubles I had gone through. My last audience was a public one, and at this the Holy Father noticed me specially, and spoke to those who were standing around, explaining to them in a few words that we were Sisters of Peace, and the object of our work.

I left Rome with a light heart. It never occurred to me, even for a moment, to suppose that there could be any more opposition. I was sure that those who had circulated false reports would at once cease to do so, no matter what they might feel, as Rome had spoken. I knew also how those who were interested in my work would rejoice, but my hopes were not to be realized.

Amongst my friends none was more faithful or

devoted to me than the Jesuit father whose letter of congratulation I give below.

"ST. FRANCIS XAVIER'S, UPPER GARDINER ST.,
"DUBLIN, April 5, 1884.

"DEAR REVEREND MOTHER, — Your letter of last Monday, which I received yesterday evening, has given me great pleasure, as you well understand, and I lose no time in writing to compliment you most sincerely on the great success of your visit to the eternal city. This will be a bright page in your eventful and chequered life; you will be able now to go cheerfully to work, and the great troubles you have gone through will soon be forgotten or will only serve to make you more confident in the protection of heaven. You have already achieved a good deal; the foundations are now laid, but the building is to be raised, and bear glorious fruits worthy of the happy title and name under which it appears before the world. With many others I shall watch with the deepest interest the progress of this new promising child of the church. I suppose you will visit Paray-le-Monial on your return, as you have been to Lourdes on your way to Rome.

"What happy and holy memories will be treasured up by this successful visit to Rome.

"With best wishes and most frequent prayers for your safe return and great success,

"Yours very faithfully,
"J. GAFFNEY, S. J."

Before closing this chapter, I must say a word about our work and prospects in England. I began work there under disadvantages which I did not fully realize until later. In the first place, this Scotch priest who gave me so much annoyance in Ireland still continued his interference. He had refused to obey his bishop, who as I have shown, asked him repeatedly to cease his silly persecution of my unfortunate self. And now he showed how little respect he had even for the authority of the pope, as he continued to attack me in private all the same. In public he was more cautious, as he now knew that he might be exposed to an action for libel. Bishop Bagshawe was not in favor with the other English bishops, so the very fact that he had brought me to his diocese was also against us. There is a story related of the great and God-loving St. Francis of Assisi that he went about crying out, "Poor Jesus Christ, poor Jesus Christ"; and I often thought of it in those weary days, when the last thought which any one seemed to have was for the souls of the poor and outcast. To prevent a good work seemed to be the very height of their ambition. In England, of all places, a work like ours was specially needed, but because it was begun under the auspices of a bishop who had made himself unpopular because he had taken the part of the

Irish people, and because I was the promoter, it was opposed in every possible way by the very persons who should have have had the greatest interest in helping it.

I will not give my own account of the state of the Roman Catholic poor in England, but I will let the Bishop of Salford speak; writing in the *Tablet*, the organ of English Catholic opinion, he says, —

"The question of the hour, — the question of the time, — the question that is likely to harry and trouble the mind of every Catholic who cares for the cause of God's church and his poor, for many a long year to come, is how to stop the dreadful drain which is annually robbing Catholicism of thousands of its children. In Manchester and Salford, no less than seven and thirty institutions are at work, 'converting,' not Catholic men and women, but the helpless children of the poor. In a Catholic population estimated at 100,000, there are 5,420 children, mostly very young children, 'in extreme danger of loss of faith, or practically lost to the faith': 2,341 'in great danger'; and 1,912 in 'danger'; so that there are some 10,000 children needing different degrees of special care, if we are to save them to the church and to the kingdom of heaven."

And yet this bishop would not do anything to encourage a common-sense plan to prevent the evil he so pathetically deplores. It would *seem* as if there were some people who think that writing about an evil is the same thing as *remedying* it. When speaking of my life in Kenmare I should have mentioned several circumstances which were very prejudicial to me in the views of English Catholics and of American ecclesiastics. The help which I gave to the people in the famine was one of my great offences. To give help, and above all to appeal for it, was to assert a need for help, and English Catholics, with a few honorable exceptions, were the most vehement in their denial of distress in Ireland. If the people needed food, clearly they could not be asked to pay their rents, or reproached with not doing so.

I was, therefore, especially obnoxious to this class, and I was made to feel it when I came to England. The ecclesiastical wasp who having nothing else to do was always buzzing and stinging at my heels, had succeeded, as such people often do, in hindering a good work. When I was in Kenmare, I received a letter from some lady who had arranged to present Mr. Parnell with a rug while he was in Kilmainham jail. This rug she wished to have ornamented with his monogram, and she sent money to have it done in our convent. When the letter came, I said that I thought it was not a very prudent thing to do, as I would be sure to come in for blame, and be accused of mixing in political affairs. But I was over-ruled, and an English sister, who hated Mr. Parnell as cordially as any of her country people, worked the monogram.

But it was exhibited in Dublin, as my work, and I got the credit of what I did not do, in the shape of blame from one party and praise from the other. Another matter, about which a great stir was made, and in which I was equally innocent, was this: I had published a book about Knock, and in this I had published a letter which had already appeared in the public press, written by an American tourist, the editor of a paper. In this letter, he spoke of the English government as "the most infernal" on the face of the earth; I merely published the letter to show American opinion on the state of Ireland, and did not take any note of the expression, but it was not so with my friend the busy wasp. He discovered it promptly, and great indeed was his holy grief and pious sorrow. He felt it "his duty" to call the attention of his little world to my wickedness, and to make the most of it. It was in vain that I said, what was true, that I really did not notice the word; he knew better. He wrote to the press, and to the bishops, and for all I knew, to the pope, to say what a state the Irish people were in, when even a "sister" was writing and publishing treason.

I have no doubt that he wrote to an American bishop who was of one mind with himself on such subjects, and who naturally believed all he said; and I fear from some experience, I must say, preferred to believe evil, if it fitted into his preconceived ideas. It will be understood, then, that my chances of carrying out my work in England was small. Again I must say how sad I felt to see so little care for souls and for truth amongst those whom one should suppose would, of all others, be the first to give the example of charity and justice.

The public meeting which Bishop Bagshawe called in Nottingham was of little use, as those whom it should have convinced that I had done nothing wrong, so ardently desired to believe evil of me, that the voice of an angel from heaven would not have convinced them.

There was yet another charge against me which weighed heavily with these people. Again I was blamed for what I did in obedience to my ecclesiastical superior, but this did not matter to my accusers. During the famine of 1879-80, Mr. Russell, now Sir Charles Russell, who is attracting the attention of the world in the Parnell trial, paid me a very unexpected visit in Kenmare. I was at the time ill and suffering, but I came to him, as I had known a sister of his very well, and he asked specially for me; I was often so ill that I had to ask a sister to go to visitors for me, and indeed I did not care to go to the parlor when I could avoid it. Mr. Russell told me his business promptly. He said he wanted some information from me as to the state of the country. Miss O'Hagan was then living, and had followed me to the parlor, as she and her brother's family were very intimate with Sir Charles's Russell's family. When Miss O'Hagan heard this, she stood up promptly, and said, laughing, "Then I am sure you do not want me," and left the room. I was not very much inclined to talk, for I had already trouble enough. But when I hesitated to give the information which Mr. Russell asked, he said: "You cannot refuse me; I was with your bishop yesterday, and he told me you would give all the information you could, and that you knew more about the state of the people than he did." Of course after this there was no more to be said. I told him what I knew; but, at the same time, I said, "You know I must take a good deal of my information second-hand," and I gave him the addresses of several people who knew the state of the country well, and told him to go to them. All the same, I got the blame of what I did not do as if I had done it.

Before leaving England for America, I established two convents of our order in the diocese of Nottingham; one at Great Grimsby, and the other in the city of Nottingham. Since I left England, another convent of the Sisters of Peace has been established at Hassop. But the work which I hoped to do, and for which our order was established, is not carried out as I would wish for many reasons; principally, because of ecclesiastical opposition.

It seems hopeless to expect that those bishops who utter periodical lamentations over the miserable state of the Catholic church in England, will take up the only practical means of saving these poor children. To train them properly for domestic service would be to improve the whole social condition of the Roman Catholic population of England, which at present is wretched in the extreme; a fact admitted freely when a bishop has a reason for doing so, but denied as freely when it is made a subject of reproach to the church.

It has often been made a reproach that the decisions of Rome are slow. But to this, Rome replies that they are sure. Until of late years, this sureness was not doubted. But one must ask now, is not Rome itself infected with the spirit of the age? for so many decisions which seemed so carefully and wisely made, have been reversed, that if this changefulness increases it cannot but have a marked effect on public confidence. And yet such reversing of judgment was not uncommon in earlier ages, but affairs were not as soon public property as they are at the present day.

I was told that I might have a very long time to wait before a decision was reached in my case. But though I had only to wait four months, I knew that every step was taken with the greatest care and consideration. Everything, as the document sent to Bishop Bagshawe said, was "noticed, considered, and acknowledged;" every opportunity was given to those who wished to prevent me from establishing this work for the working girl. I was told by Mgr. Gualdi, that after all had been considered, and it was proved that none of the charges against me could be established, though those who were so anxious to establish them were given every opportunity to do so; that as the last test a letter was written to the bishop who professed me, to ask his opinion as to whether it would be advisable to allow me to establish this work; and that it was only when his favorable reply was received, that the final arrangements were made. Certainly it cannot be said that there was undue haste, or lack of mature consideration. My audience with the Holy Father did not take place until all was settled. Indeed, so particular was I that I took care even to have our dress approved by the Sacred Congregation. I had a design for the scapular made ; it was submitted to the proper authority by Mgr. Gualdi. There was a dove above the cross, and it was returned to me approved, with the exception that there was to be a line drawn between the dove and the cross as an indication, if I understood it rightly, that the cross being an object of devotion, and the dove being only an emblem, they should be as it were, distinct. Indeed, I can truly say that I left nothing undone to secure the approval of the proper authorities, so little did I expect that inferior authority would condemn what was thus approved

CHAPTER XXI.

GOING TO AMERICA.

America Proposed — Bishop Bagshawe — His Character — Intrigues of English Catholics — Wealth of the American Catholic Church — Arch-Bishop Corrigan Calls for $400,000 — My Plans Approved — The Journey Ordered — Canon Monaghan Accompanies Me — Cardinal Manning's Friendship — Parting from my Sisters — Mother Mary Evangelista.

I CAME to America in November, 1884, by the express desire of my bishop, the Right Rev. Dr. Bagshawe.

His suggestion seemed to me a good one, and there was only one obstacle, my health; but long years ago I made a solemn promise to God which I have kept ever since, that I would not allow my personal interests or convenience or feelings, to interfere in any way in what I believed to be for the good of religion and especially of the religious order to which I belonged; and I think I am giving very practical proof of my sincerity now in leaving those who are so infinitely dear to me, in the hope that my absence will remove from their work the prejudices against me which have hitherto hindered it.

I must here say a word of Bishop Bagshawe, who

has long been known in England as a devoted friend of the Irish cause, and who has suffered in consequence. Those who are not familiar with the ways of the more influential English Roman Catholics, cannot form even the least idea of their absolute hatred, (there is no other word for it) of any one who shows even a passing sympathy with this hapless race. Like the Normans, who considered themselves "born rulers of men," they justify their injustice in a fashion which soothes their conscience and gives them an appearance of justice in the exercise of injustice. I have already said there are two reasons for this injustice on the part of the English Roman Catholics. They hate their Irish Catholic brethren both because they are poor and cannot pay extortionate rents, and because they are fellow members of the same church; and because they are looked down upon by some English Protestants, they consider their Irish brethren a discredit.

Since the reign of Henry II., English Roman Catholics have not ceased to use their influence as Englishmen, for oppressing their Irish brethren through the court of Rome. The history of their ceaseless and successful intrigues will form a volume of ghastly reading at the day of judgment.

If they had given an example of honest and honorable dealing towards their Roman Catholic

Irish brethren, Ireland would not be as it is to-day. But this is a subject on which I cannot trust myself to say more.

These men perhaps hardly realize their real motives, and they must have some show of justice in all this outcry against the Irish. Yet so intense is this animosity that it is not merely the Irish who are to be crushed down, but also everyone who sympathizes with them.

Even Cardinal Manning has not escaped; it is an open secret that the upper few thousands of Roman Catholics look coldly on his eminence, and long for the day when one who has already shown how he can pour contempt on the Irish people of his diocese shall ascend the pontifical throne. And yet this very prelate has been obliged to look to Irish men and Irish women for the support of the missions which he has founded for the colored people of America; and he might abandon it to-morrow if he had not found in them the sympathy and help he has looked for in vain amongst his English co-religionists of whom he is so proud.

That I was in very bad odor with this class of English Roman Catholic ecclesiastics, is a fact too well known to need further notice; but I was quite unprepared to find that this feeling against me, on the ground of my devotion to the Irish cause, extended to the Roman Catholic ecclesiastics of this free country.

One of my books, "Advice to Irish Girls in America," was in the hands of thousands, and I had proof of this in the shape of liberal payments from the publishers, and a host of letters from employers, Protestant as well as Catholic, thanking me for having written it.*

I know that any author whose works have had a large circulation must always pay the penalty in the criticisms of those who have been successful merely as critics, and I did not take much account of this kind of opposition.

But what I did not expect, and what I was not prepared for, was the opposition which I had to meet from the Archbishop of New York. In fact, I have only quite lately come to realize this in full, and to know the cause. It is the same cause which has made English Roman Catholics so bitter against Ireland. English Roman Catholics want their rents, and American Roman Catholic ecclesiastics want the dollars of the Irish girl, and cannot bear to see them go to the support of any institutions except their own. They have opposed the Land League and all its collections,

* An extract from a letter received by me from New York before I left England, will show that the feeling against me on the part of certain Roman Catholic journalists there was well known. The letter will be found in the appendix.

but this has been done privately, for obvious reasons. They need Peter's Pence, and a public denunciation of collecting for Ireland would make short work of that. Witness the trouble between the Rev. Dr. O'Reilly, the Secretary and Treasurer of the Land League, and his bishop, which was decided in favor of the former, the bishop's denunciation notwithstanding.

Ecclesiastics dare not say a word against a large body of men, and in such matters they are sharp enough to defer to public opinion. But though they cannot prevent Land League collections, they have set a very determined face against charitable collections for Ireland; and at this, one can scarcely be surprised, considering the immense number of priests who come from Ireland to America to collect, and who seldom trouble themselves to ask leave from any bishop.

Still, the wealth of the Roman Catholic Church of America is enormous. Witness the fact that the new Rector of the Roman Catholic University at Washington boasts that he has collected something like a million of money already; that he collected $75,000 in two parishes alone in Philadelphia, and yet he says that "the resources of the country" for his purposes are as yet "untouched." Yet every day new churches are being erected and the old ones are still in heavy debt; and the mass of the people are beginning to complain and ask what is done with the enormous sums collected Sunday after Sunday in the church and by fairs and picnics and by individual collections, which somehow never seem to lessen the debt.

Given this tremendous call for money, a million here and a million there, given the fact that $4,000,000, will be needed for the new university, and that Archbishop Corrigan calls for $400,000 to set up his own university in New York, and that each of the archbishops will desire to rival him and have a Washington in his own diocese, — is it a matter of surprise that outside collectors are sternly put down?

Hence one reason of which I was entirely ignorant, why my coming to America was reprobated. I believe myself that this and literary jealousy were the two simple causes which made my mission here, as far as I am concerned, a failure. I believe, however, that it will be yet an immense success, for I leave it in the hands of sisters who are capable of making it such. And I hope the interest which will be revived when the injustice with which I have been treated is known, will help to establish the sisters firmly in their great work. For myself, I only desire to pass out of sight altogether, and to offer my defeat for their success.

I fear that the Archbishop of New York knew perfectly well that the silly stories of my having left my convent without leave or my being "troublesome to bishops" were false, but it served a purpose to believe them and to circulate such reports. If the American bishops did not hear that the reports against me had been carefully investigated in Rome and found entirely groundless, it was their duty to have inquired. And certainly it was their duty for the sake of the church, to have sternly repressed calumnies which reflected upon the wisdom and judgment of the pope himself.

With regard to my plans, they were now before the world, and so also were the approbation of the Pope and of my immediate ecclesiastical superiors.

As I have said, my health was the first thought of Bishop Bagshawe. By his desire, I consulted a physician who was considered the best in Nottingham, as to the probable effects of the voyage on my constitution.

It was a supreme moment for me; I did hope the decision might be that I was entirely unfit for such an undertaking, for I shrank from the very thought of it, little as I anticipated the result. The doctor's decision was plain and straightforward. After a long and careful examination, he told me that I was entirely unfit for such a journey, but, he said, "You know your own business. If no one else can carry it out, I would not say that the voyage will shorten your life nor advise you against going."

I reported the decision to the bishop, and left the matter wholly in his hands. He wished me to go and take the risk, and, notwithstanding all the sufferings I have had, I believe he decided rightly; at all events, my course was clear when he gave me his decision.

There was one point on which I insisted strongly, and that was that I should have a priest with me; I thought the presence of a priest, besides the personal comfort to myself, would show that I had come with full ecclesiastical approbation. I never anticipated that the priest himself would be made the subject of gross discourtesy.

The bishop chose the Very Rev. Canon Monaghan, our confessor, the chaplain of our convent at Nottingham, a devoted Irishman, and a well-known advocate of the temperance cause. There was yet one other suggestion which I made to Bishop Bagshawe, with which he did not agree. I again obeyed, but the consequence of my obedience has been, I fear, the cause of a good deal of my subsequent suffering.

It will be remembered that I have had occasion to speak of Cardinal Manning's friendship to myself, and his special interest in the order which I had founded; indeed, he has preached quite lately for our institution in Nottingham, and sent me an affectionate message and blessing through Bishop Bagshawe. I was very anxious to see his eminence before leaving England to have his advice and blessing, and to ask him for an introduction to some of the American bishops whom he knew. But for reasons, which respect for Bishop Bagshawe prevent me from giving, he expressed a strong desire that I should neither go nor write to Cardinal Manning, and I obeyed. Had I brought a letter from his eminence with me, the archbishop of New York and his vicar-general might have shown Canon Monaghan and myself at least common courtesy; yet, when the Holy Father's approval of my work was not respected, perhaps nothing else would have availed.

I need scarcely say that the parting from the sisters was sad and painful; they knew too well that the journey might prove fatal to me, and we might never meet again. But I knew also with what generosity they made the sacrifice, — was it not to extend the work blessed by the head of the church, to help our poor brave Irish girls as we sisters only could help them? had they not also crossed the ocean? They support their parents at home, they keep up the church in America, they give almost their last dollar to the pastor of their church, and who helps them? When they are sick there were no homes for them; when they were weary, there was no rest for them; who was to teach them the strange ways of a strange land, or look after their temporal as well as their spiritual interest?

Oh, sad! oh, selfish! oh, fatal policy which shields itself under the cloak of religion, but knows not true religion. Avarice and greed have been the ruin of the church in many lands, and will yet, if God forbids it not, be the ruin of the church of this country.

I set out for America as full of hope as I could be, considering the disappointments of the past; but if I went weeping and sowing the good seed, I knew that the harvest is not here, I knew that the time of harvest is not yet.

My companion dear to my heart was, I need not say, Mother Mary Evangelista, on whose gentle and loving soul now falls the burden of the office which I have laid down, only because I am no longer able to carry it. For me there has been no golden jubilee, no silver jubilee, none of those honors and appreciations which are the portion of the priest and sister who has worked so long in the church's vineyard. For me there has been only the heavy burden of sorrow and age; but it cannot now be long ere I am called to the eternal rest. I have worked for a despised people, and with them I must suffer.

No doubt if I had less used the gifts which God has given me, and had kept silent when I saw oppression, and had not spoken out when I saw the sufferings of the poor, and had observed a respectable mediocrity in well-doing, I should now have applause where I receive condemnation; I should have now good will where I found only opposition. Above all, if I had devoted my life to the service of the rich, my success would certainly have been great here if not hereafter.

CHAPTER XXII.

ARRIVAL IN NEW YORK.

Refused an Interview by Cardinal McClosky and Bishop Corrigan — Inexcusable Discourtesy — Comment of Mgr. Capel — Word of Avoidance Passed Around — Opposed by Mgr. Quinn — Letter to Cardinal McClosky — Circular in Aid of Immigrants — Miss Charlotte O'Brien — The Bishop of Cloyne — His Interest — Forbidden to Work at Castle Garden — Father Riordan's Mission there.

CANON MONAGHAN had brought with him all the necessary credentials from our English ecclesiastical superior, and he waited on Cardinal McCloskey to present them in person. The canon and myself were peremptorily refused an interview, not only by the cardinal but by Archbishop Corrigan, then coadjutor bishop. For this marked discourtesy, there was no excuse, and it had the effect which was no doubt intended. The reader may imagine my grief and dismay; I had been received with marked kindness and I might say respect in Rome, but as Canon Monaghan said, "I was good enough for the Vatican, but I was not good enough for the Episcopal Palace in New York."

But there was at this time, a visitor in New York who received very different treatment. Mgr. Capel had preceded me, and was duly honored by

Archbishop Corrigan and his friends, who gave him leave to preach and lecture where he pleased. He soon heard of the very different reception which was given to me and called on me at the hotel where I was staying, with an offer of his services and many expressions of indignation for the way in which I was treated.

"Indeed," he said, with some contempt, "if they were gentlemen, at least, they would treat a lady differently." I declined his offers of services, very much to the disappointment of Canon Monaghan. If I had accepted them and arranged for a series of lectures, as he proposed, no doubt I should have realized a very large sum of money for the support of our institution. But I did not think that money obtained in this way would have any special grace, though I have no doubt, it would have obtained some favor from those who appreciate success, and honor wealth at the expense of poverty.

There were many circumstances over which I had no control connected with my coming to America which were very much to my disadvantage; at the same time, I must say that if there had been an intelligent, perhaps I should rather say a Christian interest in my work, they should not have had the least weight. They were such circumstances as would not have been considered for a moment, unless there was an object in finding fault. But they were just the circumstances which could be used to my disadvantage by those who wanted to prevent the success of this work. It is sad to say this, but it is true. When I arrived in America, I had not the least idea where I was to stay; I never thought of asking to go to a convent, and even if I had thought of it, I would probably not have asked, with my former experience. Besides, I had been long enough a sister to know how often jealousy interferes with good works. But the arrangements that were made for me were singularly unfortunate. I was so ill going from Liverpool to Queenstown that I was obliged to remain in Queenstown a week before I was able to continue my journey to New York. Canon Monaghan who travelled with us, insisted on going on to New York without me. I requested him not to do anything until I arrived, but he thought it too long to wait, and his mistaken zeal led to consequences which were not to our mutual advantage.

A place should have been taken for me in a quiet, private house, and not in a public and expensive hotel. Of all these arrangements I was totally ignorant, until I arrived, and it was too late to alter them; and, as I have said, if I had been received in a friendly spirit, all would have been well. But those who were looking for causes against me found them ready to their hand.

In addition to this, reports were given out, either to injure me, or from ignorance, that I was come to collect an immense sum of money for a cathedral in Nottingham, which report had the effect which was intended. The Irish people were more or less deliberately deceived about the circumstances under which I had left Knock, and it was not difficult to excite feeling against me.

Further, I learned later that some one in Ireland had been busy writing to the American bishops against me. Why they had preferred believing these false reports to the testimony of the Pope and Propaganda, I cannot tell.

I heard from a gentleman who had good opportunities of knowledge, that the Jesuit fathers had been specially warned against me, which was curious, considering that it was a Jesuit father who had been my great helper and encourager in all my troubles, as his letters show. However, I came to know later that there is not quite as much harmony even in the religious orders of the Roman Catholic church as those outside suppose.

I now met with a very serious accident, which compelled me to remain longer at the hotel than I wished. Again I was at the mercy of circumstances, over which I had no control, and at the mercy of people who did not concern themselves to inquire whether their denunciations of my character were justified by facts.

How far his Eminence Cardinal McCloskey was or was not able to attend to affairs at this time personally, I do not know, but his name was used by Mgr. Preston in a letter to Canon Monahan, now before me. It is no wonder that all the rumors which were carefully circulated about me were believed, when those who circulated them could say, that the archbishop had refused even to see the Nun of Kenmare; and this refusal to see me told on the public, as no doubt it was intended to do. Every one knew how cordially other sisters had been received, how priests came to New York and were often allowed to collect, whose missions certainly were not so specially and openly approved by the Holy Father and Propaganda as mine was.

I could not understand how it was every one avoided me. Later on, I learned that the word had been passed around through the priests, that I was not to be received by any one. The working men and women of New York, I have heard, were longing to see me. They knew my work for the old land, but they did not know what to do. They were expecting day after day that there would be a lecture or a meeting, or some public notice of my arrival. Reports were widely circulated against me, nothwithstanding the authorization I had brought with me from the Holy See. It was said that I had been disobedient to my bishop in Ireland, though no one seemed to know who the bishop was. It was, indeed, a time of darkness and sorrow to me, and I had not then realized the utter hopelessness of trying to carry on work to which the bishops were determinedly opposed, no matter what papal sanction I might have.

One of my principal opponents was the late Mgr. Quinn; he even went so far as to tell a Protestant lady, who was very much interested in my plans for working girls, that I was disobedient to my bishop in Ireland, and to try to prevent her from interesting herself in my work.

Canon Monahan was by no means easily discouraged; he made repeated efforts to see Mgr. Preston and to explain matters to him, but he was always put off with an evasive and not very courteous answer.

Finding that matters were becoming more and more hopeless, I thought that I had better address a letter to Cardinal McCloskey myself, knowing that if it did not reach him, it must reach his assistant, Archbishop Corrigan. I have kept a copy of the letter, which I append here.

"December 31, 1884.

"MY DEAR LORD CARDINAL,—As I find that false and very cruel reports are circulating about me amongst your eminence's clergy, I write to beg most earnestly that you will allow me an interview with you, when I can show you letters from Archbishop Croke and other Irish ecclesiastical dignitaries, any one of which will prove that I have been very cruelly and unjustly slandered.

"My Lord Cardinal, we are neither of us young, and we must both stand before the judgment seat of God shortly; if your eminence will do me an act of justice, God will repay you in that awful hour. My lord let me not plead with you in vain.

"The matter is one of great moment to me, and it is of still more moment to our holy Faith. It is very natural that the refusal of the ecclesiastical authorities in New York even to see me has occasioned a belief in these false and scandalous reports.

"The principal scandals which were circulated about me were: that I left Kenmare without leave, and that I took money from Knock which belonged to it; both of these charges were as false as they were malicious. I am no saint, but your eminence has read the lives of the saints, and you know how often and how cruelly the founders of religious orders were belied and misrepresented even by good people. Surely, the Holy Father's approval of my work should be sufficient to bring the encouragement of every bishop in the land. I remain, my Lord Cardinal,

"Your obedient servant,
"Sister Mary Francis Clare,
Mother-General of the Sisters of Peace.

To this letter I received no reply, and this was the first of many appeals which I have made unsuccessfully to the Roman Catholic bishops of America to give me a few moments of their time to see for themselves what was true and what was false. Nor could it be said that the work which I asked to do was not wanted in America. Never was such a work more needed, and this has been made evident by the large number of homes and institutions for girls which have been established within the last two years by Protestant ladies. These homes are open to Roman Catholics, and Roman Catholic girls make large use of them, finding no such help in their own community.

My first consideration in America was the work for immigrant girls. As we had large schools in Kenmare, I knew the difficulties of these girls in obtaining employment. And with strange ignorance of their own best advantage, Irish landlords are unwearied in getting rid of their tenants, and girls are sent in droves to America.

In the summer of 1881 I issued a circular,

which will be found below, and to which I desire to call special attention, in view of circumstances to be related presently.

Miss Charlotte O'Brien, a near relative of Mrs. Monsell, of the Clewer sisterhood, and who was also a relative of mine, came to me to Kenmare, on the subject of protecting emigrant girls, before she went to America for the same purpose.

I was always ready to help a good work, especially where girls were concerned; but there were many difficulties in my way. I sent this circular to all the bishops in Ireland, and had some warm letters of recommendation and encouragement, —

EMIGRANTS' AID AND PROTECTION SOCIETY.

"It is proposed to form an Emigrant's Aid and Protection Society, with the sanction of ecclesiastical authority, under the protection of Our Lady Star of the Sea and St. Raphael. The special sanction of his lordship the Bishop of Cloyne has been obtained.

"The necessity for such a society need scarcely be insisted on. Every day thousands of our people are leaving Ireland and England for America, and too often they go as little prepared spiritually as temporarily; hence so many are lost to the faith. Whatever opinion many of us may have as to the cause of emigration, of the fact there is no question. The society of Our Lady Star of the Sea will not interfere in any way for or against emigration. Its object is purely to give spiritual aid to those who will and do emigrate. But even in a temporal point of view such aid cannot fail to be beneficial.

"We cannot but hope that in saving thousands of immortal souls from danger, we shall also help them to be better citizens of their new country, and thus to benefit even the country of their birth. Miss Charlotte O'Brien, with a most commendable zeal, has called public attention to the fearful dangers through which our emigrants, and especially our female emigrants, pass. She has urged the writer of this, in words of no ordinary fervor, to undertake the promotion of a society for their protection. She says, 'Of gold and silver or merchandise, careful invoices are kept, but of the human soul no word is known.' The object of this society will be human souls, the most glorious object which we can possibly have, since it was the one object of the life of our divine Lord on earth.

The Work of This Society.

"It is proposed that this society should be placed under the protection of the most reverend, the archbishops and the bishops of the whole English-speaking world.

" 1. That the society should be under the

direction of a priest, whose exclusive work it shall be. God will provide one.

"2. That as soon as possible, a congregation of priests should be located at Queenstown, Cork, and in New York, devoted to this special work. God will inspire some of our religious orders to take up this work. We have already hopes that a congregation of missionary priests will take it up as part of their work. One of these priests, if possible, and if a sufficient staff can be had, would go out in each vessel with emigrants.

"3. Corresponding secretaries would be appointed at Queenstown and in New York, to look after the embarkation and the debarkation of emigrants, to take charge of those who are friendless until they are placed in the hands of friends, or in respectable situations, and to advise the pastors of American cities and other places of the new additions to their flocks. It is hoped that this would save thousands, if not millions, from falling away from the church, and that it would probably be the means of reclaiming multitudes who have so fallen.

"4. In order to make the working of this society as perfect as possible, it is proposed that an organization should be formed in every parish in Ireland and America, and, as far as possible, in the large English towns where there is a large Irish population, and that all Catholics should be asked to join the society as honorary or active members; the parish priest in all cases to be the president; the active members to form a small committee, with a secretary and treasurer.

"The duty of the secretary will be to ascertain the names and the addresses of the persons about to emigrate, which could be easily obtained from the emigration agents, as well as from other sources; to ascertain the destination of the emigrants, and to forward the name and particulars to the secretary in Queenstown or New York, as may be arranged. The treasurer will collect and receive donations for the general fund, which need not be large, as we know what has been done for the propagation of the faith by the pence of the poor.

"All the members, whether honorary or active, to contribute one penny per month to the general fund, and to say daily one Hail Mary for all emigrants, and the invocation, 'Our Lady, Star of the Sea, protect us until we reach the safe haven of eternity; St. Raphael, friend of wanderers, be our guide through life!'

"5. The active members will undertake to do their best to induce all emigrants to approach the sacraments before leaving Ireland, and, where it may be necessary, to bring them to a priest or nun for instruction; or, should this help not be available, to give them the necessary instruction. Even those who are most occupied during the week could find time on Sundays for this good work, and thus obtain for themselves and families a great reward from God.

"As this society is intended for all — both young and old, rich and poor — it is hoped that it may be the means of helping the spiritual life of all.

"Since we are all travellers to another country, we need, each and all, the succor of Our Lady Star of the Sea to protect us in our passage over the stormy ocean of life to the haven of rest. We need the help of dear St. Raphael for ourselves, our families, our friends, for all our little or our great adventures in life. Hence, this is a society for all — a help for all. If, indeed, hard times are coming for the church of God, we need to cling closer to each other to help and support each other with the love and fervor of the early Christians. And how many there are who are heart-broken, because some friend or brother has been swamped or shipwrecked in the treacherous sea of temptation. Do we not need the prayers of such a society to reclaim them? And then in helping others we are helping ourselves, and obtaining new strength and grace for our own journey and for its happy termination.

"6. The national schoolmasters of Ireland, who have been so faithful to their great trust, will, no doubt, help this well. If the confraternity was established in every convent school, it could be made a centre of salvation, not only for the children of the school — so many of whom will emigrate — but for all others in the parish, who could be most effectively reached in this way.

"It is hoped that, after a time, the Holy See will approve of this association, and allow it to be erected into a confraternity.

"SISTER MARY FRANCIS CLARE.
" KENMARE CO., KERRY.
"*Feast of Corpus Christi*, 1879."

Indeed I had been so long interested in the whole question of preparation for emigration, that some time before I had written a paper on the subject for the Social Science Congress in Dublin. This paper, which gave rise to a great deal of useful discussion, was read for me by Dr. Mapother, the President of the College of Surgeons, Dublin. Thus it will be seen that I was long at work on this important subject, and could not be accused of having taken it up as any new idea of interfering with Father Riordan's plans. Indeed I have heard from several persons that it was my persistent agitation of the subject which made him take it up. Be this as it may, there was a great field for us both.

Soon after, the Bishop of Cloyne, the Right Rev. Dr. McCarthy, sent a priest to me to Kenmare, to see what could be done about establishing a place in Queenstown, where a special house for emigrant girls is quite as much needed as in New York, and towards this project Miss O'Brien promised liberal help. But, as I have said, there were difficulties put in my way by the sisters.

When I was on my way to America, I saw the Bishop of Cloyne at Queenstown, and had every expectation of getting a house established there, to correspond with one in America, for emigrant girls.

I believe the opposition to this plan, which I met from ecclesiastical authority in New York, was caused partly by a very absurd idea that my arrangements might interfere with those of Father Riordan, who had opened a sort of mission for girls at Castle Garden, and who was anxious to build a church there, on the somewhat romantic idea that the girls who landed from Ireland should see a church immediately on their arrival. Certainly, if they had not learned their religion in Ireland, seeing a church when they landed in America would not teach them much. But building churches is always acceptable to certain ecclesiastics, and will always be encouraged, no matter how unnecessary they may be, or how heavy the debt incurred in consequence.

It was at once decided that I should not be allowed to establish any kind of home in Castle

Garden, or have any connection with it. Yet, to say the least, what harm could I have done there? And what could a man do in such a position? It was woman's work essentially. Poor Father Riordan is gone now,— what harm would it have done him if he had allowed me to join in his work, and to do what he could not do? In fact he really spent a very small portion of his time in Castle Garden, for I called there many times to see him, and he was almost always absent. Still, no doubt, the protection of a priest was desirable and useful.

CHAPTER XXIII.

GOOD WORKS THAT HAVE NOT BEEN ACCOMPLISHED.

Mission of the Church — Sisterhoods Often Opposed — Catholic Persecution of her own Saints — Oppressed when Living — Canonized when Dead — La Salle an Example — The Church Afraid to let the Truth be Known — The Poor Neglected — Priests Suppressed — Established in Jersey City — Rude Treatment in Philadelphia — Project for Blind Asylum Abandoned.

THERE is one express precept of Holy Scripture about which there can be no dispute, and that is the duty of charity. What we do to one of the least is counted as done to Him, who, for love of us, became the lowest and least of all men.

Again and again the rich rewards of Heaven, where only rewards are worth having, since it is only there that they will be eternal, are promised even for a cup of cold water given in his name.

The Roman Catholic church points with pride to her charitable institutions, and the world, too often taking such statements at her own valuation, looks on and applauds, and envies this magnificent organization. But how little of the truth is known. The crushing hand of ecclesiastical despotism stifles every cry of suffering or complaint. How then is the world, how is even the Roman Catholic world, to know facts as they are? There is also a certain romance, and I use the word in its best sense, about a convent life, and while there is so much hard and painful fact in this poor world of ours, we do not like to be disillusioned or have our little glimpses of Heaven taken from us. I know that Roman Catholics will cry out with indignation, and Protestants with amazement, when I say that the sisterhoods in the Roman Catholic church have often succeeded, not because of the help of the church, but in the face of its determined, and, I might say, often cruel opposition.

What a revelation there will be at the last great day, when all hidden things are made known.

I give proof of what I assert. Facts may be explained away and glossed over, but they remain facts all the same. Let the reader take up the life of the founder or foundress of any religious order and read it, and the truth of what I say will be made apparent; and let it be carefully noted that the lives of saints are not written by Protestants, nor by enemies of the Roman Catholic church. No, they are written by priests who, for the most part, would naturally be anxious to conceal all these things, and who do conceal as much as possible.

It is probable that the world would never be

allowed to know one word of this Roman Catholic persecution of her own saints, if it were not that a divine Providence has so ordered it that at least some facts must be known. In order to obtain the canonization of a saint, it is necessary to prove that he or she has practised virtue in what is called an heroic degree. Hence, it becomes necessary for the promoter of a cause for canonization to tell at least some of the sufferings which have been borne by the person to be canonized. Thus, the truth, or at least some truth, comes out.

And what a sad record these lives are. A man or a woman, priest or nun, is, according to the teaching of the Roman Catholic church, inspired by God to do the noblest work that man or woman can do. He or she gives up all life's innocent pleasures, all human natural interests, and all hope of personal advantage. They devote their existence to the poor of Jesus Christ. Might it not be supposed that words of hope and encouragement and comfort, would be given to them by the ministers of their church? Might it not be supposed that they would be at least tolerated? But no, persecution of the most unwarrantable kind follows them for the most part to the grave, and when there is no longer need of human comfort, or that spiritual comfort which is their due as children of the church, they are suddenly resuscitated for post-mortem honors and post-mortem applause. If indeed they are saints and with God, with what pity they must look down on this folly. They have their reward in the eternal sunshine of their God. They have their honors in his praise, and his praise is unchangeable. And now the infallible successors of the infallible men who made their lives a long weariness, turn round and find out they were saints, and fall down and worship them. To those dear souls, who loved God so well and his creatures for love of Him, one little word or act that would have helped them to accomplish this work for his poor would have been far dearer than the post-mortem honors that have been so lavishly heaped upon them. It was not for themselves they felt this suffering, it was only because it injured the cause for which they lived and died.

It is time for the children of the Roman Catholic church to awake from their slumbers, to see themselves as God sees them. It is time that they should take the bandage from their eyes, and deafness from their ears. If these founders and foundresses of religious order were indeed saints, what were the men who persecuted them? Is there any justification, human or divine, for the sufferings that were inflicted on them? It is useless to say that what they suffered made them saints. Does that justify those who inflicted the sufferings? As well might we justify those who persecuted our Lord. Because the results of evil are turned by God to good for those who love Him, will that justify and excuse the doing of evil? Yet in all these biographies, it is usual, or perhaps obligatory, to make excuses for the ecclesiastical persecutors, by saying that they were good men, well intentioned, and meant it for the best.

Now this argument would pass, perhaps, for fallible people, but in this case, be it noted well, we have to do with those who claim in an especial manner to be divinely inspired guides. I am not saying that individual priests or bishops claim a personal infallibility for all their acts, but this claim of infallibility has got to be so curiously elastic of late years, that it can be stretched or contracted at pleasure.

The question narrows down to one plain point. If these founders and foundresses were saints now that they are dead, they were equally saints while they were living, and how is it that these people did not find it out? It will be said, no one could be sure of their perseverance until they were dead; therefore, they should not be treated as saints while they were living. This is quite true, and very much to the purpose, but let it be observed carefully that the question is not whether their persecutors should not have honored them as saints instead of persecuting them as if they were doers of evil; the question is this: if they were saints, there must at all times have been ordinary evidence of holiness of life; and even if they were not extraordinary saints, the work which they were doing, or trying to do, was most certainly one which any good Christian should have applauded heartily and encouraged.

It is useless to say more. Those who are determined to sin, will find excuse for sinning. Men who are determined to uphold and support evil must have some excuse to do so. I do not write for such persons; it would be mere waste of time. I write for those who are capable of reasoning, and who love righteousness enough to be willing to listen to truth.

The lives of St. Alphonsus Liguori, the great doctor of the church; of St. Paul of the Cross, the great preacher of the church; of the blessed De la Salle, the great teacher of the church, are one long record of unmanly and scandalous persecutions from priests and bishops, and of the most severe trials from members of the very orders which they themselves founded.

To-day, the Archbishop of New York and the Roman Catholic press are full of praises of the Venerable De la Salle, and tell in glowing panegyrics of the good his order has done, and all honor his memory. How different was his life. He was hunted from place to place. He was suspected of heresy. He was, according to some authorities, under ecclesiastical censure when he died. He was opposed by many of his own spiritual children. He was obliged to leave them altogether at one time, being no longer able, brave as he was, to bear the constant crushing of his hopes and aspirations, or the trials from his own brethren. In all probability, if he lived to-day in New York, he would suffer precisely the same treatment from its archbishop and his council. He would be told that his work was useless and unnecessary; and the precious time which he might have given to the service of God and humanity, would be spent in sufferings which would have incapacitated him for work.

Take the lives of female saints, and you will find the same miserable and discreditable record. The Roman Catholic bishops of to-day, and the Roman Catholic press, are loud and noisy in their denunciations of the crime of those children of the church in France, Italy, and Germany, who have turned from it, and who are now driving out religious orders; but they are simply doing what Roman Catholic bishops have done before them. Why should Roman Catholic bishops complain if convents are broken up, sisters expelled, and religious forbidden to make new foundations, when they do precisely the same thing themselves, and have done it for centuries?

I know how difficult it will be for Roman Catholics to realize this fact, but it is a fact all the same. Just as difficult as it is for them to believe that there have been wicked popes, yes, and popes whose lives were so awful, so vile, that even the very worst which Roman Catholic historians can say of Henry VIII. is as purity itself compared with their record.

The disgrace of certain members of the Roman Catholic church is this: not that it has had bad popes and worldly bishops; not that it has persecuted the saints, for all human institutions are fallible, — but that all this evil is condoned, glossed over, and justified. We know what Holy Scripture says.

It is a poor religion indeed, which is afraid that its followers should know its history. It is a poor religion indeed, which fears that men should seek to know, or reason for themselves.

If I could place the life of Mother Julia, the foundress of the Sisters of Notre Dame, in the hands of every reader of this book, I would gladly do so, for that life proves the truth of every word I have written. Her work now is promoted and honored, but in her lifetime it was hindered, and she herself was the object of incessant ecclesiastical persecution.

I have said these things because they are true, and the world is never the better for hiding truth. I have said them, also, because I am now compelled to give a history of the persecution and opposition which I have experienced myself in my efforts to work for God's poor.

The history of my expulsion from Knock you are acquainted with. It is enough to make an angel weep to think of all the poor have lost. The English are denounced for their cruelty to Ireland, for their indifference, for their suppression of Irish trade and manufactures; but what is to be said of priests and bishops who do the very same thing. Even now the work which I had begun, and would have carried out to such a glorious extent for the poor of Ireland, is done in the north of Ireland by a Protestant lady for Protestant girls. Of course, no bishop or priest can hinder her work, and so it prospers.

In England I met with the same opposition, not indeed from one bishop, for the Right Rev. Bishop of Nottingham is one of the few bishops who care for the poor. But other bishops would not allow our order in their diocese, although they are crying out day after day how their Roman Catholic

children are being proselytized by Protestants.*
No wonder, when they will not allow Roman
Catholics to take care of them. I would have
carried out the work of preparing these poor
children for domestic service, caring for them on
the voyage to America; I would have had homes
for them here, to which they could have come at
any moment, if in trouble or sickness. That was
the crime I wished to commit. Well, these bishops
have succeeded in preventing this, and I trust they
may be happier for it.

It sounds so well for a bishop to write for the
press, and to publish statements, and to say how
dreadful it is that so many thousands of poor children have been lost to the church and consigned
to eternal damnation, and it looks so zealous and
devoted to the church to bewail all this in public;
but to do something practical in private, to take
up a plain, common-sense plan for their protection

---

* The Roman Catholic Bishop of Salford (Manchester, England) estimates the loss to the Catholic faith at thousands yearly. He says in the *Tablet*, the London organ of the English Roman Catholics: "In Manchester and Salford, no less than seven and thirty institutions are at work 'converting,' not Catholic men and women, but the helpless children of the poor. In a Catholic population estimated at 100,000, there are 5,420 children, mostly very young children, 'in extreme danger of loss of faith, or practically lost to the faith'; 2,341 'in great danger'; and 1,912 'in danger';" so that there are some 10,000 children needing, as the Bishop of Salford points out, "different degrees of special care, if we are to save them to the church and to the kingdom of heaven."

and welfare, that is not to be thought of, especially if the idea has not emanated from the bishop himself.

There is a Latin proverb, which I do not give in the original, because some of my readers might not understand it, but it means, that whom the gods wish to destroy they first make demented. In other words, if people do not wish to do right, God allows them to be blinded, so that they may think they are serving God when they are really helping the devil.

I have one difficulty in making this unhappy record of failure, and it is this: the few and powerful ecclesiastics who have not only kept me out of their own dioceses, but have also by their influence hindered my work in other places, are in the habit of excusing themselves by blaming me for being too zealous. Everything I did was sure to be put down to some bad motive. Would not a true spirit of charity act very differently? Supposing that I was too zealous, too anxious to work for these poor girls, can they deny that the work was a good one, and that it has had the approval of the Pope? If indeed it can ever be over-zealous to have been anxious to carry out plans approved by the Pope, then I plead guilty to the charge, and in addition, which will surely gratify these men, I will say that I will never again be guilty of this zeal; but the following pages will give proof that I have never asked to be allowed to do this work for girls in any diocese into which I was not first invited by a priest. If I am wrong, a priest was wrong, and one of my difficulties is this: if I give the names and letters of the priests who have asked me, they will assuredly be made to suffer for their zeal as I have been. Indeed I know, so severe and crushing is the tyranny (there is no other word for it) of some Roman Catholic bishops in America, that the very fact of a priest asking me to found a home for girls is quite sufficient to bring severe discipline on him from his bishop. And I ask, is it any wonder that the Roman Catholic church has so often failed to keep its hold on the mass of the people where it has had unlimited power, since such is too often its mode of governing?

The priest who finds his zeal constantly crushed and embarrassed, and who finds himself treated as a mere machine, soon lapses into utter indifference, and takes to church building as a last resource from *ennui*. That is the only occupation that is sure to meet with ecclesiastical approbation. My first experience was in the diocese of New York. A priest there, whose name I shall not give, for the reasons above stated, was very much interested in my work for girls. He told me that he had long felt that such an institution as ours was needed; that, in fact, every parish in New York should have its girls' home, as well as a place where young men could meet and enjoy each other's society. Such an institution properly managed would soon be self-supporting, as the class of girls whom this would help, would not need, except in cases of sickness, and, in fact, would not accept charity.

Several attempts have been made to carry out this work for girls since I suggested it, but they have not been very successful, principally from the want of knowledge on the part of their promoters as to what the girls really needed, and too much ecclesiastical interference. It might naturally be supposed that a religious order of sisters, founded for a certain work, were the proper ones to have charge of it, but as I was the person in question, everything was done to discourage us and help our imitators. One might as well say that the order of the Sacred Heart should be the best persons for hospital work, as to say that sisters quite untrained to the care and training of girls would be the best for this work. Nor, apparently, had the approbation of the Holy See any weight with the archbishop and his council, all of whom were my opponents.

As to the girls, who needed such help, and

wished us to have the charge of them, they were not consulted at all in the matter, and it seemed as if their wishes were not worth a moment's thought.

The priest soon found he dare not move in this affair, and I believe he was threatened with ecclesiastical penalties if he persevered. And so a work that might have done so much good for the comfort of the working girl, for the glory of God, and the good of the Roman Catholic church was prevented. Who will answer at the last day for this? Excuses may be made here, but they will not be made there, because none will dare to offer them. If the excuse was that Monseigneur Quinn told my friend, that I was "a bad religious, who had disobeyed my bishop," why did not Archbishop Corrigan see for himself whether such reports were true or false? Why did he not see me himself, or allow Cardinal McCloskey to see me? The cause is very plain, they wished to excuse and justify themselves on the plea that I was "an unworthy sister." If they had allowed me to show them the proofs that these charges were false, they could not have continued to make them. I think the priest who wished to carry out a work approved by the Holy Father was a better son of the church than an archbishop who would have none of it.

There would have been no begging or collecting for this institution either, as it was a wealthy parish, and the priest told me he could easily have obtained all the funds necessary. But, although the girls have been deprived of a home, I do not think any priest in New York is any the richer. The money that would have been given for that purpose would not be given for any other. I say this because I know that the fear that I should get money for an institution was one cause of this dislike to me. It seems to some ecclesiastics as though every cent which is given to any one else is so much taken from them. And this is Christian charity!

Several fathers belonging to a religious order spoke to me, at a later period, of having a home, and were anxious for it, believing that I had a special gift for this kind of work. But here again, ecclesiastical opposition crushed down another effort, which would not have failed to do great good.

After we had been established in Jersey City, through the kindness of Bishop Wigger, there was certainly no excuse for refusing us permission to found a convent in any diocese in America. If my credentials from Rome were doubted, and how absurd such doubt was, it was quite certain Bishop Wigger was far too prudent to accept the services of a sister who had broken her vows. I went to

Philadelphia, and other places in the South, with the written permission and blessing of Bishop Wigger. He was anxious that I should establish a Catholic home for the blind, and I had and have a number of letters from blind girls, writing from all parts of America, imploring me to undertake this work. So many letters came from those of whom I had never heard previously that it seemed more than a coincidence. Many of these girls, after having been trained in public institutions, find themselves very lonely. How ardently desired such an institution was by poor Catholic girls will be seen by the following extract from one of many letters received by me. Bishop Wigger says, in his letter authorizing me to collect for the blind institution, "To his sorrow there is no such institution." What matter? ecclesiastical authority has vindicated itself; an archbishop can put down a hapless person who is so foolish as to sorrow with the sorrows of the poor and afflicted, and prevent the establishment of a work which might have gone on happily and prosperously and made no diocese the poorer.

But it will be said, perhaps, that I failed in previous undertakings, and that bishops could not trust me or my sisters to carry out such a work. Did I fail in Kenmare? or did I fail in Knock? It is certainly not failure on your part when a work that is succeeding beyond your expectations is suddenly stopped by a power which has authority both to forbid you to try, and to crush you when you have succeeded. The note given below will show how our institutions have succeeded in England.*

The following letter, dated from Lewiston, Me., is from a blind girl. It is one of the many letters I received from blind girls.

"I hear that you are going to establish an institution for the training of the blind. I am in the deepest sympathy with you, and I think it is one of the greatest undertakings that a person could do, and I pray that God will reward you and prosper you in it. The blind enjoy living together much better than with people who have their sight. My aunt is blind, and ever since she heard of your institution, she is longing to have it completed. Besides, she says, they can listen to religious instruction a great deal more, which will

---

* "St. Barnabus Cathedral, Nottingham,
"May 17, 1886

"My dear Rev. Mother-General, — I have just heard with great sorrow that you are so seriously ill, and can only hope that by this time your health may have improved. May God grant it, and spare you long to carry on the great work you have begun. Your convents in this diocese are well and securely founded, but they could ill afford to lose you. I write to assure you of my sympathy and prayers, and, entreating God to bless you, remain
"Most truly yours,
"Edward, *Bishop of Nottingham.*"

help to cheer them so much. My aunt has been trained in an institution for the blind for five years when she was a little girl, and she has learned a great deal."

This letter goes on then to speak of other blind girls, who were anxious to come to our home, the home, that alas, has never been built for them.

It will be said, also, why did we want so many foundations and new works? and the question is a fair one. No reason or reply will satisfy men, who, like the inquisitors of old, first accused a man because they had a personal hatred of him, and then found out, or made out reasons for burning him alive. I have at last realized how hopeless it is to offer explanations to such men, but there are others who have known me by my writings, and they have a right to every explanation. There is also the great American public, to whose verdict I appeal as a defenceless woman. For these I speak, and for these I make these explanations. There are, also, a great number of charitable souls who have confided their money to my care, and it is a duty that I should tell them the hindrances I have had in carrying out the work for which they so generously subscribed.

Every one knows how poor English Roman Catholics are. The missions, as they are called in England, are kept up with the greatest difficulty.

Some years since, Rome had high hopes of converting the whole of England. When Manning came; when Newman came; when Lockhart came; and when so many others with long resounding titles came, all was supposed to be accomplished for the conversion of England. The Roman Catholic church was intoxicated with the wine of success. Roman Catholics have not only had liberty in England, but they have had license. Nothing has been refused to them. It was a triumphal march all along the line. Cardinals were courted. Bishops were flattered. Conversions became fashionable. The walks of art and society were all wide open to them. The chivalrous nature of the best people in England spent itself in doing honors to those who they felt had been wronged for so many centuries.

But what has been the result? Notwithstanding all the temporal advantages, and all the spiritual advantages, and all the literary and social advantages, it is a certain fact that conversions, after the first rush was over, suddenly ceased, and are now few and far between. The mass of the people has never been reached by this movement. All the prayers that were offered for the conversion of England, and they were fervent and multiplied, have been unanswered, and some of the best of those who had become converts have returned to the church of their baptism, or have lapsed into infidelity or indifference. Truly a sorrowful outcome of a noble beginning, and if Roman Catholics were even awake to their danger, and asked themselves anxiously why things were so, it would be less sad; but the chorus of self-praise and congratulation over the few converts of the past prevents them from realizing the poverty of the present.

Men whose pride is the rich or noble convert, blind themselves to the loss of thousands of poor Catholic people and Catholic children, and scarcely seem to have the grace to realize that the soul of the poorest child in the world is as valuable and precious to God, as the soul of the most gifted being upon earth. Hence it is, I fear, that the blind, because they are poor are left without consideration. If they were wealthy, religious orders would be founded for their instruction, and homes would be prepared for their comfort. As far as our order was concerned, we could certainly have undertaken this work — as in the place where we had Summer Homes for girls, we could always have had additional buildings for blind girls which would have entailed very little additional expense.

When I approached Archbishop Ryan of Philadelphia on the subject, and presented to him the letter from my bishop, he seemed to think that the blind of his diocese were quite as well off in Protestant institutions as in Roman Catholic, and I do not dispute his view. But surely as a Roman Catholic it was natural I should have wished for a Roman Catholic home for them.

A priest high in office in Philadelphia was asked to meet me at a friend's house, and this gentleman like many others could not understand why good works should be opposed because I was the promoter of them.

This priest, who has been named for the episcopacy, and will probably wear the mitre, was in the room smoking when I entered. He did not take the slightest notice of me, to the mortification of my friends. After a few moments he turned to me, and, without removing the cigar from his lips, he said, —

"I hope, sister, that you did not think I called to see you." The insolence of his tone and manner could not have been equalled. I was so utterly amazed, I had no answer ready. After a few moments, I left the room quietly. I should have left at once, but I wished to spare the feelings of my friends, who had acted from the kindest motives; but although they were wealthy and very influential they could not show any resentment where a priest was in question and were obliged to keep silence, whatever they felt.

Now it may be said, I know it will be said, as an excuse for the discreditable conduct of this monseigneur, that I had not any right to be in Philadelphia; that I was pressing myself on those who did not want me, and so on. To this I reply,—and beg the reply will be noted, as I shall not again justify myself, although I have to record other cases of ecclesiastical discourtesy,—even if I had acted without regular ecclesiastical permission, respect for himself should have made him hesitate before he offered an insult to a lady, even if she was a sister. And if I was over-zealous, certainly there are not many ladies over-zealous to do good to the poor. But I had come with letters from my bishop, and this fact, at least, should have protected me from insult.*

* Bishop Wigger's letter will be found in full in the appendix. He concludes it by saying,—"I warmly recommend you to the kindness of the Prelates whom you may call on, and sincerely hope you will succeed in gaining the object of your mission."

CHAPTER XXIV.

WHO IS ACCOUNTABLE?

A Sorrowful Record — Dependence of the Roman Catholic Church upon the Liquor Interest — Received Kindly by Cardinal Gibbons at First — Father Didier's Home for Girls — Invited to take the Management of it — Plan Defeated by the Interference of Some Priest — Offered a Summer Home Near Baltimore — The Priest Very Anxious that I should Accept It. — Cardinal Gibbons Forbids it Under the Influence of Other Ecclesiastics — Invited to Visit Mother D——'s Convent for my Health — Archbishop Corrigan Sends a Lady to Her to Express His Strong Feeling Against Me, and to Desire Me to Leave — Asked to Found a Home in Cleveland O. — Forbidden by the Archbishop — Asked to make Foundations in Tacoma W. T. — Suddenly Forbidden, after all Arrangements had been Made — Offered a Home for Girls in St. Pauls, Minn. — Urgent Need for this Work there, but Father Shanly Forbids it, and makes a Gross Attack on Me in the Public Press — Without any Expression of Disapprobation from his Bishop.

PERHAPS there have been few more sorrowful records than those which are related in these chapters. Let God judge. For myself there seems to be but one explanation of them, personal feeling against myself, based on wilful credit given to reports which, I fear, these ecclesiastics well knew to be false, and to this I must add there was a sad indifference to the cause of the poor, and to the needs of the poor. Any honest-hearted lover of the poor would surely have been interested, or at least would not have condemned a person, whose only desire was to help them. No doubt if the service of the Sisters of Peace had been accepted in New York for immigrant girls, a house would at once have been founded in Queenstown, which would have proved invaluable, not only to girls, but to all others wishing to emigrate, as there they could have obtained true and reliable information and disinterested advice as to their future destiny.

But this would not have suited certain ecclesiastical authority or the politicians by whom they boss, or by whom they are bossed. When it pleases a bishop to order wholesale emigration to the Northern states, so utterly unsuited to Irish people, there they must go. It matters not how many fail, so that his desires are accomplished. If it suits another ecclesiastic that the tide of emigration should be directed to the South, and suits his relatives in this way to build up their railroad lines and become millionaires, it is done.

I went to Baltimore in March, 1886, by the desire of my bishop. I had heard so much, as who has not, of His Eminence Cardinal Gibbons, of his courtesy, and of his love of justice. I was at this time very far from well. The hemorrhages had begun, which were so nearly fatal to me, and there is no doubt but they were brought on by distress of mind and anxiety.

If I had proposed in all these places, either as a secular Roman Catholic, or as a Protestant, to establish liquor saloons or houses of doubtful character, no bishop would have interfered to prevent my doing so. The liquor saloon, at least, is always useful to the Roman Catholic church, and must not be too much discouraged, though obviously it is necessary to condemn it in theory. But what matters this, when all the mandates of a Council are pointed at as an evidence of zeal, and at the same time left to lie as a dead letter.

It must be admitted, however, that no other religious body is so dependent upon the liquor saloon interest as the Roman Catholic church. In fact, it is the only religious body that looks to this interest for its support; and it is but justice to say that if the money obtained from this source, directly as well as indirectly, were withdrawn, some institutions would have a poor look-out. The liquor saloon-keeper who bosses the wards, knows how to obtain government money and subsidies for orphan and other institutions, and with the most free and generous hand these men contribute to every Roman Catholic charity.

It is none the less true, however, that it is a crying shame for the Roman Catholic church to oblige sisters to depend upon collections in such places for their support, and this in a church which can obtain millions of money for any purpose, and could save the sisters all this degradation, and waste of time and energy which should be given to the service of the poor.

I sent the sister, who travelled with me, to Cardinal Gibbons to make an appointment, as I was unable to go out, at his usual early hour in the day for receiving. He received her kindly, and received me, also, with his usual urbane manner. For a moment indeed I could have thought myself in Rome, where I received such marked courtesy from every official.

I spoke to him of the reports which had been deliberately circulated about me in New York, and offered to show his eminence the letters I had with me, which proved both their origin and the persistence with which they had been kept up; but he assured me that he had never believed them, the fact of the Holy Father having received me in Rome with such marked consideration, was sufficient. At last, I thought, all my troubles were over; here was one honorable ecclesiastic who would do me justice,—for justice was all I asked. I had again and again been reproached with the fact, a fact which I could not deny, that Archbishop Corrigan had refused even to see me, and those who knew the work I wanted to do could not understand how it was I had been refused permission to carry it on in his diocese. Again and again priests had said to me, "So long as you are not recognized in New York, the Pope's approbation is of no use to you. The Pope is in Rome, and clearly, he has done his part. He cannot be worried with incessant applications and complaints." And I felt it so. The Holy Father had indeed done all he could for me. Long as I had been in the Roman Catholic church, I had yet to learn how little the court of Rome can influence any cause or obtain even the respect due to its decisions, when the case in question is one of personal feeling or prejudice; and how easily the decisions of Rome can be altered or defeated, cotemporaneous history tells us. *

* The case of Rosmini is clearly in point. He lived and died the life of a saint, and founded a distinguished Religious Order of Charity, but his enemies even since his death have proved relentless. His writings, all of a religious and metaphysical character, were examined in Rome, and declared free from all error some few years since. His enemies were enraged, but they bided their time. Within the last few months they had these works brought to trial again and condemned, but they took good care Rosmini's representative and the head of the order which he founded, should not hear one word of this proceeding until the foregone conclusion of condemnation was announced. This he has stated publicly. In my case I have been villified and calumniated without one word of notice or excuse, and retraction has always been refused even when I have shown the falseness of these charges. Surely if the Roman Catholic religion can only be supported by condemning people without a hearing, and condemning saints without allowing their spiritual children even to know of the trial, the

A priest in Baltimore, the Reverend Father Didier, had already founded a home for Working Girls. It was an attempt in the right direction certainly, but it was not succeeding very well. Such homes require especial tact in their management. Because a girl is lonely or friendless, which one may be and yet not need any pecuniary help, it is no reason that she should have the discipline of a reformatory, or the restraints of a prison. The home should be a home, and not a place of restriction, and the more like a home such places are the better. Priests and sisters too often wish to give a monastic character to these homes. They may obtain a few inmates who are driven there by stress of circumstances, but they are not happy or contented.

Girls who need such homes have arrived at the age of reason, and it is simply an injustice to treat them as children. In saying this, I do not wish to have it supposed that I would encourage undue license. What these girls have a right to have and to ask, is perfect liberty. If a girl requires more than this, she is not fit for such an institution. If

sooner it ceases to be Roman and becomes Catholic the better. Imagine a court of law in the United States, or any states, where a prisoner could be tried and condemned in his absence, and without any knowledge of the intention to try and condemn him. This was done by the Inquisition in past ages, but it should not be continued by the Inquisition of the present day.

she is refused perfect liberty, those who refuse it are not fit to conduct such institutions.

I do not make these remarks as any criticism of Father Didier's home, because I do not know enough of its workings to give an opinion, and however I have been misrepresented, I have too much respect for myself to follow such example; but I know what girls say and how they feel about such establishments, and I know how much good is prevented even if evil is not occasioned by overzeal or unwise action.

Any necessary restraint may be exercised without its being made a burden. These dear girls find restraint and trouble enough in their weary lives, and "Homes" should bring them peace, rest, and freedom.

Cardinal Gibbons did not, I think, disapprove of my ideas. He gave me a note to Father Didier, and I had every reason to hope that my weary waiting was rewarded. Father Didier entered warmly into the plan, and he invited me to meet a committee of ladies who organized for him. They had held a private meeting previously, and asked me formally to take charge of the Home. Even the chimes were rung as a compliment. Many of the ladies, and especially a Mrs. Keane, the stepmother of the President of the Roman Catholic University at Washington, gave me the warmest welcome, and they all expressed pleasure at meeting the Nun of Kenmare, whom they had so long known by reputation and by her writings.

I must admit that when I heard Bishop Keane's name, my heart died within me. I knew how bitterly opposed he was to me, as his letter would show, though I had some claim on his gratitude, if it is possible for a Roman Catholic ecclesiastic to be grateful for anything. I had given a home and a helping hand to a poor lady whom he had sent out on the world after she had been for many years a professed sister of the Convent of the Visitation in his diocese.

I felt sure that his mother would write to him at once, telling him, no doubt, with great congratulation, that I had had the offer of this Institution, and how glad the ladies were to receive me. Whether it was his influence against me, or that of another bishop, I do not know; but as I have evidence in his own handwriting how opposed he was to me, it is not uncharitable to think that he may have interfered against me.

I was at this time stopping with some young ladies, and to my amazement, one of them came to tell me that a priest a Dr. F—— had sent for her, and spoken to her very angrily for allowing me to remain in her house. She had sufficient spirit to answer that her house was her own, and that she had a right to receive any boarders she pleased. But the anger of an influential priest is a matter that cannot be treated lightly; he has too many ways of making people suffer, if they dare to disobey him. I soon knew that my hopes were finally crushed in Baltimore. I received a note the following day from Father Didier, which I have now before me. In this he says: "There has arisen an opposition to our plan from an unexpected source," and he advises me to see the vicar-general. Alas! I knew too well the utter uselessness of seeing any one when an influential priest like Dr. F—— had determined not to allow the accomplishment of a good work.

I knew already by this time, that bishops are a close corporation, and that they do not like to acknowledge any person or work which is disliked by another bishop. The justice or injustice of this course does not matter.

Cardinal Gibbons had heard things against me. He did not believe them, — that he also admitted. But what did that matter? After all, I was only a woman doing a work for women. I had the approval of the pope, and a letter from my own bishop recommending me to the kindness of the clergy wherever I went. What matter? Perhaps even then, his eminence was occupied too much with the affairs of the Knights of Labor to be concerned with the women of Labor. He could secure unbounded applause for getting the Holy Father to see that if they were crushed, disaffection would follow, and he could show how "Peter's Pence" would be seriously decreased. To accomplish this end, he could afford to meet with disapproval from some of his episcopal brethren, but to help a poor sister would not be of any advantage to him in this world certainly.

The Vicar-General, Father Colgan, who has since died, came to see me, but he was afraid to interfere. He was old. All he could do was to give me his personal courtesy and respect. As he was going down the stairs, he turned to me and said: "God bless you for all you have done for Ireland." I shall not soon forget his words, or his manner of saying them. I replied, "Perhaps some time God will reward me, but certainly no one will in this world."

I then remembered how Bishop Duggan of Clonfert had knelt down before a number of bishops and asked, to my horror and dismay, for my blessing, for he said: "You will yet be canonized for all you have done for Ireland." And yet if I had only held my tongue when I saw injustice, and refrained from pleading with my pen, when I saw misery and starvation, how much happier my life would have been.

To add to the keenness of this trouble in Baltimore, I may say I called at the Visitation Convent, at the request of a friend who accompanied me, and there I was received with chilling coldness. My poor friend, whom I had warned beforehand of what I expected, was filled with dismay, and I may add not much edified.

A lady came to me and offered me some acres of land as a free gift, and a farmhouse near Baltimore. So that I certainly should have had a summer home for the girls there as well as the one in the city, and I need not say that the farm produce from the summer home would have been a great help. I had met a young lady while I was in Washington, who was exceedingly anxious to join our order. This lady, who belonged to a very high and influential family, went to visit friends at Baltimore, full of the idea of coming to me as soon as possible, and full of zeal for our new undertaking. On going there, she of course met different priests. In consequence of this she wrote to me: "Need I tell you that not one hour has passed since our last interview that I have not been with you in spirit. Since that time I have learned more fully the opposition you are meeting, and it is to me but the surer proof that Christ himself has called you to the work, that he has given you this bitterest of all his sorrows to share: 'Even his brethren did not believe in him.'"

Though this lady was a most fervent and devoted Roman Catholic, she appears by this letter to me, to have attended the preaching of the Rev. Father Maturin of the Episcopal church in Philadelphia, and she speaks of the great consolation which she received from his sermons. She says, —

"How happy I should be, if only I might have a part in your life; if I might be among those whom you can one day present as an offering to our heavenly Father. I feel so strongly called to your Order, I know I would be brave and faithful, if I might only fight at your side."

In another letter she says, —

"I have heard something this evening, which has induced me to write to you at once. In E—— I met the priest who has charge of it. I happened in the course of conversation to speak of you, and what was my surprise when the priest told me that you had been offered a country home, only a few miles from here. The father said, 'he thought you would make a great mistake not to take it, and that he was sure it would be a success'; that there was no institution of the kind in or near Baltimore, and even if you had not the means to support it, the means could be found, because girls who were employed in shops would be glad to board in the country. The priest seemed as enthusiastic as I was, and said that as

I knew this country so well, I really ought to write and tell you about it. I know, dear mother, that if you conclude to take the place, the greatest interest will be taken in your work."

The extracts from this letter are only a specimen of hundreds which I have received; both in regard to priests who are anxious for us to have foundations in their parishes, and from ladies who are anxious to help. Alas! it was not I who made the "great mistake," if mistake there was; it must be credited to the Cardinal, who refused me the permission to take what was so generously offered.

The hemorrhages from which I had been suffering, became now so severe that I decided to go on at once to Washington to friends, who I had reason to believe would not be afraid of any priest. I knew too well, that however brave my good friends at Baltimore might be, they were certainly not in a position to risk the anger of a priest, and I felt for their sakes the sooner I left the better. I had scarcely arrived at my friends' house in Washington, when I became so much worse that they sent at once for Dr. Murphy of the Columbia Hospital, and he kindly removed me to the hospital. I was crushed down, body and soul, ready to pray for death. Alas, death will not come for our praying, else had I more than once escaped from those who have this strange determination to hinder my work. Of one thing they may be assured, they could not be more anxious to see me in my grave, where I could no more plead for the Working Girl, than I was to relieve them of the annoyance which my existence has been to them. As I found there was no prospect of my recovering in the hospital, I removed to a friend's house, where I was attended by several physicians. My heart trouble added to the complications of the case, and the state of prostration which I was in would have moved the heart of any one but a priest.

I was quite unable to return to Jersey City, and the doctors urged me strongly to go by a night train to Orkney Springs, as dropsy had set in also. In fact I was suffering from a complication of diseases. Even during this time of suffering, I was not left in peace. Cardinal Gibbons came to Washington, and some busy priest told him that I intended to collect there. I need not say that I was utterly unable to do anything of the kind, as I could not sit up for an hour in the day. His eminence thought proper to send me a message by a man of the lowest class. This man employed another person of a still lower class, and I was most grossly insulted by him without the least consideration for the truth of the case, or the state of my health.

The fact was, the work which I proposed to do was interesting every one who heard of it. There are many Protestant ladies of great benevolence in Washington, and a great many of them had been interested in it. There was a great excitement among the priests. They were afraid that I would establish a home there. They were, also, afraid that these ladies would become interested in my work, and in myself, and that they would come to know the great injustice that had been practised on me. Besides this, if the girls learned to be independent and saving, and to look out for themselves, where would the dollars come from when the priests wanted collections? At this time they were planning the new Roman Catholic University at Washington, and I can now see that this was an important element in the affair. All the money and all the interest was wanted for that. There was only one way to crush me; to give out in an indirect way that I was not "in good standing with my church," and that was at once sufficient to discourage Protestants, who had no means of knowing the truth, and to frighten Catholics. The rumor was circulated widely and carefully. It was supposed that it was quite impossible for a man like Cardinal Gibbons to refuse permission to carry on such a work without cause. The case certainly seemed mysterious. What matter, the rumors answered the purpose for which they were intended.

A Roman Catholic lady, who had been greatly interested in my plans, and had interested many Protestant ladies, came to see me one day and said, — "I must give up all further efforts for you. Father —— has positively forbidden it. He says you are not in good standing with the church."

"Well," I said, "Mrs ——, I am in good standing with the Pope, but I see that counts for very little in America, and I am in good standing with my bishop. Here is his letter; he says, 'I warmly recommend you to the kindness of the prelates on whom you may call.' Pope Pius IX sent me a special brief, in which he said, I 'deserved well of the whole church,' and I have a document from the Propaganda, which says that I am 'worthy of all trust and confidence.'"

"Oh," she said, "I am satisfied, but of course we cannot go against the priests." The old miserable story, — the story which has been the ruin of the Roman Catholic church in so many countries in so many ages. No matter what the priest does or says, it is, "a sin against the church," if any objection or criticism is made, and so all evil is condoned. It is certainly a very easy way of securing the power to do wrong unmolested. The lady was sincerely sorry, but what could she do? "Oh," she said, "do not be troubled," for I was crying bitterly, "you know the church was always persecuted." "Pardon me," I said, "in this case, it is the church which is persecuting." She looked amazed, and replied, "Oh, I never thought of that," and went sadly home.

I was now removed to Orkney Springs, and I may say in all this time not even one priest came near me. Indeed, the Protestant doctor who attended me, said the only chance for my recovery was for me to go where the nearest priest would be sixty miles away, so indignant was he with them, for all the wanton suffering they were inflicting upon me.

At Orkney I grew rapidly worse, and decided I must go back to Jersey City, even if I died on the way. I got as far as Winchester, with great difficulty, and by slow stages, and there I became dangerously ill; at last the doctors told me, honestly and kindly, that there was no hope of my recovery, and if I wished to die at home I should go at once, as it would be impossible to remove me in a short time. I sent for a second sister, so that the sister who was with me might not be alone if I died on the way. I travelled from Winchester to Washington with great difficulty, and stopped there a night, and saw Dr. Tyler on my way; he was one of the doctors who had attended me there before. He gave me the address of Dr. H. B. Sands of New York, and begged of me most urgently to see him at once, and to him, under God, I owe my cure and my life.

In the meantime, the Mother Prioress of a Dominican Convent in the New York Diocese wrote to a sister, to beg I would go to them. The drinking water in Jersey City had disagreed with me almost fatally, and for many reasons my going there would still further endanger my life. I wrote to a sister to go to her, and tell her I feared Archbishop Corrigan would be very angry if she received me even for a day; but either the sister whom I sent to her did not explain the matter clearly, or else she had no idea that personal dislike to me could be carried so far. I need not say all my own sisters were in great distress, and looking eagerly to anything that might give me even temporary relief. For myself, I knew that if I went back to our house in Jersey City, I should certainly go there to die, and though I was quite willing to die, I could not be without feeling for the poor sisters who were so fondly attached to me, who had been with me in all my troubles in Ireland, and who knew all I had to endure, and that all includes far more than I could venture to record in this volume.

When I thought how I had left our Convent in

Jersey City so full of hope, trusting to the blessing and support of my bishop, whose last words to me were, "Good-by and good luck." I felt I could not go back to the house in my state of utter prostration and depression, and I gladly accepted Mother D——'s offer. It will be said, perhaps, why was I so anxious to extend the Order? Well, I can only say, why should I not have been anxious? According to all the teaching of Roman Catholic theology, I was bound to use all reasonable efforts to obtain success. It will be seen that I did no more than the foundresses of other religious orders. I could not be responsible for the effect to my bodily health. Why should I not wish to carry on my work and extend it, even if I did so in suffering? I suppose when God gives an inspiration to any one to do good, that he intends them to use every reasonable effort to do it. I was not only doing this, but I was doing it in the strictest obedience to the rules of the church to which I belonged. I had the permission and the especial blessing of my bishop, and now I have the great consolation of knowing that I left nothing undone, and that I never counted the cost to myself in trying to accomplish what the Holy Father authorized me to do, and as I have resigned and ceased from troubling I trust it will satisfy all who are concerned.

There was another reason why Mother D—— was anxious to show me kindness. She had sent a young lady to me, two of whose sisters are professed in her own order, one in her own convent, and the other in a convent in the Brooklyn Diocese. For some reason she had not been able to provide for this young lady, and I had received her into our Novitiate, and she is now a professed sister. Both Mother D—— and the sisters of this young lady were very grateful to me, and I have before me now some letters from them.

But poor Mother D—— was soon aroused to the enormity of the crime she had committed in offering me the hospitality of her convent. I was obliged to leave at a moment's notice. Not quite so tyrannically and unjustly as in Dublin, but the whole act was little less heartless. Mother D. came to me after I had been some days in her convent, to say that she had just received orders through a lady, a great friend of Archbishop Corrigan, who told her that he was very angry indeed because I was with her, and that she must send me away at once. "I had no idea," she said, "the archbishop had such a strong feeling against you."

I told Mother D—— I would take care she should not have any more blame on my account, for she seemed greatly frightened, and said this lady was one with whom the archbishop was very intimate, and a person of high position. And I may add here that this is yet another proof, if proof were necessary, of how thoroughly this episcopal opposition to me was circulated in every direction. I sent the sister who was with me to a place where she could drive in half an hour, to get a room for me and herself. I was beginning to recover a little from the journey, and to feel that I might get the courage tó submit to the severe operations which I had to go through soon after, and for which I had to go to a public hospital in New York. It was the talk everywhere, why did I not go to a convent? But for peace's sake I held my tongue, and never explained how I had just been expelled from one, and thus I have, over and over again, kept silence and taken blame which was entirely undeserved, and this to screen those who never ceased making false charges against me.

In the meantime, I was offered yet another foundation by a good priest, but unfortunately it was also in the New York diocese. I knew from the first that there was not the slightest chance that Archbishop Corrigan would allow me to accept it, but there were many reasons why I thought it well to ask him.

The first reason was that my bishop wished me to do so ; the next was, that I had been told so often, and knew it to be true, that, so long as Archbishop Corrigan refused even to see me, there would be little hope for the extension of my Order in America. It is not that he has any special control over any other bishop, but New York holds a sort of primacy of honor. It is the ecclesiastical port which admits to the country, and if you are pronounced a contraband article there, you need go no further. If you are boycotted by New York authorities, your case is past appeal. And I must admit that the bishops have need to protect each other. I have seen it stated, on good Roman Catholic authority, that there are at least one thousand priests in America who are "off the mission." Far the larger number are priests who have been driven to drink and despair by ecclesiastical injustice. Their condition is indeed miserable. I myself have been called on by a considerable number of such priests. Their brother priests, who are more fortunate and more submissive, rarely ever refuse them a few dollars, and so they live on, — a miserable existence. The minority, who are good-living priests, go into some secular business, where they are obliged, both for peace's sake and to avoid persecution, to conceal their identity as far as possible, while quite a number are honored and respected pastors in different religious denominations.

It is no pleasure to publish such statements, but evil concealed is evil multiplied, and the discredit to the church is not so much that such evils are too common, it is rather that they are not denounced by those who could do much to prevent them by denunciation, and who make themselves sharers in the guilt by denouncing those who expose, and by so doing endeavor to lessen such evils.

The *St. Louis Republican* of June 20, 1887, printed a letter from Bishop Hogan of the Catholic diocese of St. Joseph, Mo., which was brought out in court, and was never intended for publication; but it reveals a sad state of affairs.

The bishop appointed a German priest over an Irish congregation. This gave so great offence to some parties, that the letter in question was written in self-defence. His defence is, that the priests of his diocese were so intemperate that he was compelled to supply the parish as he did. He then gives a list by name of twenty-two priests, that were received into the diocese from 1869 to 1876, whom he was compelled to dismiss on account of immorality, especially drunkenness. Some of them are described as "constantly drunk;" one is "now going round from city to city, a drunken wreck." So disgraceful was the state of affairs, that he was compelled at last to "turn over a new leaf." He says, —

But I cannot give the rest of this letter here, although it has been widely published, it reveals so scandalous a story and on such unquestionable authority.

It is necessary for Roman Catholic bishops to stand to each other. It would be impossible to crush a good priest who was too zealous in good works, or to get rid of one who in despair had taken to drink, if the bishops did not act as one man in their likes and dislikes, and make no curious inquiries as to the rights and wrongs of cases.

The same rule holds good with regard to sisters. If a sister is sent out of a convent, and many are so sent every year, it is necessary for bishops to observe the same conditions. It does not seem to matter the least about the soul of the sister or the priest. Ecclesiastical discipline, which means an outward appearance of unanimity must be kept up before the public. Standing water is apt to become stagnant. Until the Roman Catholic church learns that her bishops are as likely to be fallible as other people in their conduct, and until it ceases to be called a sin to say so openly, there will be grievous evils and the stagnant water will remain.

What is to be the result in regard to the supply

of priests and sisters when Irish immigration is overdone, or when they cease to come from Ireland, is a matter which certainly will have its effect sooner or later.

But I must return to this last foundation. Another great good to souls was forbidden. Another help to the poor working girl unjustly denied to her. At this time, as I have said, the Rev. Father P—— was very anxious that I should establish a home for girls in his parish, where there were no sisters. He had some factory girls who needed teaching, and, as he said very properly, he could not bring them to his house for instruction in the evenings, and they could not come at any other time. Besides this, I had long been inquiring for a suitable place for a summer home for girls. The great difficulty was to find a good location, when we were forbidden to take any place in the large diocese of New York, and all the most desirable localities for the purpose are in this diocese. A very large number of such institutions have been established by Protestants, to the great comfort and help of poor Catholic girls. They are denied by their ecclesiastical superiors that help and care which they so much need, and denounced by them if they accept what Protestants offer so generously. This fatuitous policy may prosper for a while, but it will certainly have results which its promoters are too blind to anticipate, and about which, probably, they would not concern themselves. They are safe for their own day, their successors may look out for themselves.

Over the great Exchange of London, England, there is a motto, "The earth is the Lord's, and the fulness thereof." Somehow, this came to my mind when I found that Archbishop Corrigan owned ecclesiastically all the land on both sides of the Hudson, with the exception of a little narrow piece in Bishop Wigger's diocese. Practically, as far as we were concerned, Archbishop Corrigan owned the "earth and the fulness thereof," and we could claim no part of it.

The Hudson River, on the shore of which I wished to establish our institution, and where the working girls much wished to be, was practically cut off from our use. I must, however, here, in justice to Archbishop Corrigan, say that according to the canon law of the Roman Catholic church he had a perfect right to refuse us entrance into his diocese. It is a canon law of the Roman Catholic church, and a very proper one, that sisters cannot establish themselves in any diocese without the permission of the bishop of that diocese; but this very rule supposes that a bishop will grant all reasonable requests, and, in my case, it should be observed that these requests came not only from me but from priests who were men of experience, and who had every right to know whether our work was necessary in their parish or not. It should be observed, also, that in most cases it was the interference of ecclesiastics who had no right to interfere, which caused all this loss to souls.

The record would be too long, and too sorrowful, if I wrote much more. I shall only say that Archbishop Corrigan refused this permission, and I felt it deeply, because the place would have been especially suitable for our work, and we could have made it entirely self-supporting, and could have combined a summer home for girls with the work in the parish, and the care of these poor factory girls. I shall now give two other cases only, and I may say that it was in consequence of the last of these cases, that I decided finally to resign my office as mother general of the order, as I saw plainly that personal dislike to myself was the cause of all this opposition, and I could only offer my own feelings as a sacrifice to those who have so long tried to injure me. Now they can no longer have cause to complain, as I have ceased to exist as far as this work is concerned, and I do not see how they can oppose the sisters who are carrying it on.

In the month of June in the year 1885, a priest of the diocese of Cleveland wrote to Bishop Wigger first, and subsequently to myself, saying how much he desired that I should found a house for girls in his parish. His sister, he said, had considerable property, which she wished to devote to this purpose. He said, also, that he could give much assistance himself, and that he would even come to see me if I wished to arrange everything further. As he was aware of my position as a writer, he thought we could work together to great advantage for the good of the church in Catholic literature. I gratefully accepted his offer, subject to the usual conditions of ecclesiastical permission, but I knew from the first that the case was hopeless. I had reason to think that the bishop of this diocese was a correspondent of the poor Scotch priest who had been guilty of publishing these slanders about me, and who could not be restrained even by the commands of his superior, Cardinal Manning. I knew, also, that this bishop was greatly opposed to the Ladies' Land League, and one of the false reports which had been circulated about me, was that I was president of that body. As a rule, where I was concerned, it will be observed that bishops rarely took the trouble to ascertain whether a report was true or false, but simply acted on it as if it were true. They believed just what they wished to believe, but it was long before I realized this. I felt sure this bishop had always been prejudiced against me, and I knew that a bishop's prejudices are immovable even before facts. I was not surprised, (I was only grieved, for then I was not quite hardened to disappointment), when I found that the arrangement was not only positively but even angrily forbidden.

Quite recently I received an abusive and most ungentlemanly letter from a priest in this diocese. It would be amusing, if it did not show the real character of men whom one would wish to honor if they would allow us to do so. This priest, who writes in the style of Father Angus, of Scotch fame, if indeed he has not been inspired by him, says that he has "to give me a bit of advice." Well, I am willing to take advice, but I do not see what right a priest of the diocese of Cleveland has to advise and direct a sister in another diocese. His especial indignation was excited by a series of articles, which I was writing in the *Sun*, and he orders me "to either stop writing or to leave the cloister." He declares "it is impossible for me to be a true religious, and to write." In fact the whole letter is childish and absurd to the last degree, and the occasion of it is not the least absurd point of it. He informs me, that "if I do not obey his orders promptly, he will write to my bishop." As far as I was concerned he could write to my bishop as much as he wished, and I give him joy of all the satisfaction he was likely to get. I think the Bishop of Cleveland should see to it that his priests do not interfere with the sisters of other dioceses, as this foolish man has done with me. I have the letter before me now as I write, and I shall be happy to show the original to any one who has a right to ask to see it. I would not take so much notice of the matter, but that I know it is necessary for me to show the way in which I have been attacked, both in public and in private, and the very grave reasons I have for giving up my work.

During the fall of last year, 1887, I had an offer of another foundation, of which I thought I was sure. At least, I thought no one would care to interfere in this case. A priest wrote to me from Tacoma, W. T., saying that he wanted sisters, and that he had tried in vain to get them from different convents, but the district was so poor and so remote no one would come. From what he said, I saw there was a grand opening there for a new religious order like ours. I knew that neither the distance nor the poverty would hinder my sisters from going. On the contrary, we have always preferred poor and destitute places, which others would refuse. I hoped, indeed, that this mission was so remote from New York, that it would not be possible for me to be followed there by ecclesiastical persecution. I even hoped that if the proposal was heard of, it would not be opposed, as the distance was so great, and that Archbishop Corrigan would be glad to have me so far away. If I could not be allowed to have a little spot of land on the Hudson, I hoped I might be permitted to work for the church in this lonely and distant territory.

I have before me all the correspondence, as I have also the correspondence alluded to before.

On Nov. 9, 1887, the good priest wrote to me that he had obtained his bishop's consent to all the arrangements. I ought, if possible, to have gone on at once, before the news reached the ears of my Episcopal persecutors; but it was impossible for me to do so on account of my state of health, and I deferred the arrangement until Spring, when I expected to be able to go and take several sisters with me.

I should add here, that I have had no difficulty in getting sisters. Since I came to America, and even indeed in Knock, I had repeated applications from convents wishing me to get postulants for them. I know that many convents in the South and West are dying out, because they cannot get young sisters. I always did all I could for these sisters, and the great wealth which some of them possess, enabled them to pay the expenses of girls going out to America from Ireland. So, many were found to go, who could not have done so, if they had had to pay for a passage to America. It seemed very hard to me to be refused leave to extend our Order, when I could have easily found so many bright, willing sisters to go anywhere that we wished to establish a convent.

But to return to this priest. On Nov. 16, 1887, he wrote to me again: "Our dear bishop will be only too glad to accept you." I had no further anxiety, except to prepare the sisters for the new and glorious work. The priest had told me, that there were quite a number of places where the sisters would be thankfully received by priests in this remote diocese. In February of this year, 1888, I wrote to this priest, telling him that I would soon arrange to go on to Tacoma, as I had considerably improved in health after passing the winter in the South. I also referred him to Bishop Wigger, and to Bishop Bagshawe, as they could tell him how effectively our sisters had worked in their respective dioceses. To my amazement, I received a letter from him, saying that the bishop of his diocese had refused to receive me, and for fear that I should go there, he wrote that

I must not even come to make further inquiries or arrangements. I was amused at this, because I know certain persons in New York were greatly afraid lest bishop or priests might see me, and finding out that I was not the evil doer they wished them to think, might allow me to work for their poor girls. So once more, a work which promised to do no ordinary good for souls, was defeated by the malice and injustice of some one. Oh strange, oh mysterious Providence! Ecclesiastics complain that the sheep of the fold are persecuted and oppressed, and yet they will not allow them to be saved. Everywhere in America, Protestant institutions for working girls, and many other charities abound and prosper, and yet the church denounces them and denounces those of her children who may receive any help from them in their hour of need, while she refuses help herself.

Everywhere she exults, not in the number of her faithful poor, not that she has fewer criminals, not that her people are living holier or more devoted lives, or abstaining from that fatal liquor, which is the curse of so many of her children; no, her exultation and her joy is in the great and the rich of this world. Alas, this love of the world, and this desire of wealth and riches, is a poor note of sanctity for a Catholic church.

With one more sorrowful case, I close this

record of failure. God knows, perhaps, he saw in me some great unworthiness for the work for him and his poor, and in myself must lie some of the blame for this repeated failure. If so, I shall die happy if I live to see the success of others in this divine and holy work.

In May of this year, 1888, the following paragraph appeared in the *N. W. Chronicle*, (Roman Catholic) St. Paul, Minn.

"Miss Schley, who started and has managed the Young Girl's Home, 620 St. Peter Street, St. Paul, Minn., is very anxious to find two or three good, pious, educated ladies to assist her in the management of the home, as her health is so miserable as to make her unfit to attend to it properly. It is doing much good, and as the citizens generally have given much towards it, she feels it her duty not to let it run down. Those feeling inclined to assist in the good work of maintaining this cheap, pleasant home for working girls, please apply there as soon as possible."

I had heard of this lady and her work before, but I had also heard that there was a very bitter opposition to me on the part of some priest in that diocese. I wrote at once to Miss Schley, and asked her would she accept the services of our sisters. She wrote to me in reply promptly, —

"REVEREND AND DEAR MOTHER, — Your very kind letter of the 28th inst has been received, and its contents perused with great pleasure. I must tell you this, that your letter has been the only one thus far, in answer to my appeal for help in my work in the *N. W. Chronicle*. I have long heard of you, and admire you for your unbounded zeal for work, but I also know of the opposition you are meeting with, and I can assure you, dear Mother, on this very account I am more inclined to like you and to appreciate your work, for I know I have much opposition from similar sources not caused by any fault of mine, but simply because I am doing good in a different way from the way they would wish."

After some further remarks on the same subject, she says, —

"I went down to see Rev. Father Shanly about it, but you know, I suppose, that he is one of your well-meaning opponents, and he would not permit me to bring one of your sisters here, as this house is situated in his parish."

I had already heard of this reverend father, and of his opposition to me. A young lady who was most anxious to join our order was positively forbidden to do so on going to that part of the country to visit some friends before entering with us. I have her letters before me now, in which she says, —

"I decided to enter your order, but I was speaking to the priest about it, and he told me to have nothing to do with you. I cannot understand why the priests are not in favor of you, for I think if any persons are doing their part, you are."

But I have yet more to say regarding Father Shanly. Like a number of my ecclesiastical opponents, he thought proper to condemn me and only hear one side. He made a most scandalous attack on me in the *N. W. Chronicle*. In this paper, he says, —

"Will any one at this late day number among claimants for charity, that religious Poo-Bah-political economist, hagiographer, young girls' adviser, pamphleteer, mistress of novices, historian, beggar and nun, who for twenty years and more, both in Ireland and America, has been an irrepressible nuisance? Will any one in his right mind give her more money to squander, after the monument of folly she has left at Knock?"

On this, I think I need make no remark. As to the sneer at me as a hagiographer, Pius IX. said I deserved well of the whole church for my writings in that direction. As to being "mistress of novices" I was appointed such by my ecclesiastical superiors. And as for my begging, I certainly did beg for the poor. The monument of folly at Knock is fully explained elsewhere. Now I can understand a priest being led away by false reports, as well as a layman, but I cannot understand, why, when a priest is given evidence to prove that he has been deceived, he will not make as public a retraction and apology as he has made attack. When this attack on me appeared in this paper in St. Paul, Minnesota, I wrote both to the editor, and to Father Shanly requesting that a contradiction would be inserted, especially to the charges made against me with regard to Knock. I received no reply from either party. No doubt the editor of the paper was a sufficiently honest man, but the honest man dare not contradict the slanders of a priest in his own paper.

CHAPTER XXV.

MY ONLY INTERVIEW WITH ARCHBISHOP CORRIGAN.

Discourtesy of Archbishop Corrigan — He Wishes to see Me — His Charges Against Me — A Not Forthcoming Letter — Priestly Differences — A Poor Compliment to the Holy Father.

I HAD been three years in America, and had not succeeded in obtaining the common courtesy of an interview from Archbishop Corrigan. Such a marked discourtesy naturally excited a great deal of comment. It perplexed people very much to know that a sister who had been so well received in Rome, should be so discourteously treated in New York. One of two conclusions was inevitable, either that Archbishop Corrigan did not approve of the decision of the Holy Father, or that he had some grave personal feeling against me. A report was very widely circulated in connection with the McGlyn case, that Archbishop Corrigan had plainly stated his intention to resign his Episcopal See, if the pope took the part of Dr. McGlyn in any way, and it is an open secret that Roman Catholic bishops can be contumacious sometimes. Whatever the archbishop's reasons may have been, he refused to see me, and I was seriously embarrassed in consequence. I was told again and again that as long as Archbishop Corrigan showed such marked disapproval of me and my work, it was useless for me to hope for success. In fact, the only notice which he took of us was to make repeated and frivolous complaints of the sisters.

I was, therefore, not a little surprised when I received a letter from the archbishop, saying he wished to see me. I must say I had very little hope of any good result, and at the time I was so ill as to be very unfit to face a painful interview. How differently I had felt when I had the honor of an audience with the Holy Father.

I was far too ill to drive across New York to this interview. I stayed the previous night at a hotel near the archbishop's palace, so as to go to the interview as little fatigued as possible. I could not imagine what was the archbishop's motive in wishing to see me, after his long refusal; at all events, it enabled his friends to say for him, if he did not do so for himself, that he had seen me. I was received with courtesy; I believe the archbishop is always courteous. If he had lived in mediæval ages, I could imagine him smiling with seraphic grace as he handed a victim over to the secular power, to be dealt with according to that secular law which bishops are wont to denounce on occasion, as Bishop Higgins did in my case with so much warmth, and to avail themselves of with so much eagerness, when it is not possible or politic to inflict punishment in any other way on those who are obnoxious to them.

I had too long known Archbishop Corrigan's sentiments in my regard to expect the least interest in my work or myself. He saw me alone, and the sister who came with me waited in an anteroom in some anxiety to know the result, which was just what I expected. The archbishop began with making the absurd charge against me of having said that, " I would collect wherever 'I pleased, in spite of all ecclesiastical authority, and that I had the pope's permission to do so." I replied to his grace, that I had never said anything of the kind, that even if I had wished to act in this way, I would not have been so foolish as to say I had an authority which it could easily be proved I did not possess. The archbishop said he had a letter which would prove his point, and which he would read for me. He left the room for a moment to get the letter, and returned smiling his satisfaction, as one would do, who would forever silence and condemn an offender by indisputable testimony.

I listened with no little interest to the reading

of this letter, all the more so as it was actually the first time any of my accusers had vouchsafed to do anything but make a charge against me without an attempt at proof; but my amazement was indeed unbounded when the letter was read to me by the archbishop. I remember the contents almost verbally, for as I knew that I was entirely innocent of the charge, I was very curious to know how it could be proved.

And this was the substance of the letter, the writer whose name the archbishop would not tell me, said that he had spent an entire day searching through the papers of a gentleman who was dead, looking for this letter of mine, in which I had made the statement complained of, and that he regretted to say he could not find it.

I looked at the archbishop in simple amazement, and I must admit, only the matter was so serious, I should have felt inclined to smile.

At last I said: "And so your grace this is the charge: I am accused by a priest, whose name you will not tell me, of having written to a gentleman who is dead, whose name you will not tell me, on a date which you will not tell me, and of having said that I would act in defiance of ecclesiastical authority; I ask your grace what would be thought if a charge was brought in a public lawcourt against the humblest person in America on such evidence." His reply was: "Oh, I am sure you wrote the letter, all the same." I replied, "Then your grace there is no more to be said."

His grace then turned off the question to another charge. "At all events, I can prove that your sisters have been collecting in my diocese without leave," and as I looked incredulous, he continued, with an air of triumph. "There is no doubt of it, a priest of your own diocese reported it to me." Now I knew that a great many of the priests of Newark diocese were very angry with their bishop for receiving us, as they had said so openly, and sometimes very rudely to myself and this for very different reasons. Those who are not acquainted with the inside history of the Roman Catholic church, and imagine that there is a dead level of harmony and peace, or a perennial fountain of mutual Christian charity, ever flowing, are sadly mistaken.

I have heard bishops spoken of by their priests in the most contemptuous terms, who the next moment would sign a document pouring forth the most extravagant laudations on the object of their contempt. It is true that these priests justify this double dealing by the necessity of the case; the bishop requires the address, it must be presented, and it would be very difficult for any priest to refuse his signature. But all this deception, no matter how it may be justified by a painful necessity, must deteriorate the general character of the priesthood. Hence comes a spirit of espionage and petty tale-bearing, that is as unmanly as it is unchristian. If a priest wants to annoy his bishop he finds a ready means of doing so by carrying tales to some other bishop. And so it was in this case, the tale-bearer, it was said, had aspired to the mitre himself, so any act of his bishop that could be blamed was availed of, and the fact of our being tolerated in the diocese was an offence because it was the act of a bishop who was disliked. But it was an offence on another account. Readers of history need not be told how little some of the religious orders in the Roman church loved one another. How, instead of a holy rivalry who should do the most for God and souls, there was too often a very human contention, who should succeed most in a worldly point of view. This tale-bearing priest had connections with a religious order in the diocese, and took it into his head, as only a priest can, that we would be rivals to these sisters, hence he had two good reasons for doing us all the injury he could.

I replied to Archbishop Corrigan that I would inquire into this charge, that though we were working for his grace's own interests, as most of the girls who came to us were from New York, we were very careful not to ask for, or make collections in his diocese; that I had been so ill I had not been able to see to these matters myself. The archbishop then said, with apparent candor, that if I knew of any sisters who were collecting in his diocese without leave he would at once stop them if I informed him of it. I replied at once, emphatically, "Your grace may rest assured that if I do hear of sisters who are collecting *I* shall not inform your grace," I am not sure, but I think I heard him say softly to himself; "No I do not think *you* would do it."

As I knew it was no use to pursue this subject further, I drew his grace's attention to the authorization of our Order of Sisters of Peace which I had brought with me, I handed it to him and called his attention to the plain and explicit nature of the document. To my surprise, he threw it contemptuously on the table, and said: "Oh I have seen this before, it is merely a toleration." "Well," I replied, "as the Holy Father has tolerated me, I wish your grace would tolerate me." The archbishop looked very much annoyed, and after a silence of a few moments, which I did not care to break, he said very abruptly, "have you a convent in Rome?" I replied that we had not; one of the cardinals had spoken to me on the subject, saying that girls needed training there, as much as anywhere else, for domestic service. He replied in a very annoyed tone, "Well, when you are allowed to have a convent in Rome, I will allow you to have one in New York." I felt this was a very disingenuous way of evading a very serious question, and rose to take my leave. But before I did so the archbishop took care to tell me that he wished never to see me again, and requested I would keep out of his diocese. A poor compliment to the Holy Father, who had treated me so differently in Rome.*

* On my return to the sisters, I asked them if they knew if the archbishop had any cause for his accusation that they had collected in his diocese. They told me that a few days before, a sister had been collecting in some place in our own diocese, and had crossed over the street and continued collecting on the other side, not knowing that it was in Archbishop Corrigan's diocese. The sister was promptly followed by Mgr S———n, a priest who had been very much annoyed, because we had been received into the Newark diocese. Although he ought to have had the instincts of a gentleman, he attacked this poor sister in the rudest way, but perhaps he was only rude to her because she was a sister, and ordered her about her business, saying he would report the matter to Archbishop Corrigan, and evidently he was very prompt in carrying out his intention. The poor sister, who was young and timid, was very much frightened by his violence.

It may not be generally known that priests do not allow Roman Catholics to give money as they please. Hence it is that when a priest or bishop wants contributions for a purpose of his own, he can easily secure such immense sums of money. This is especially done in the case of the poor, who are obliged to give, or not to give, just as the priest pleases. The confessional is very much used for this purpose. But it is often done publicly, as a priest will forbid his people, even from the altar, to give to a charity he does not like.

I have often heard very devout Roman Catholics complain of this, and especially working girls, who said they had earned their money very hard, and that they thought they had a right to do what they liked with it; above all, when they had given the priest all they could spare for himself. Even the circulation of Roman Catholic books is discouraged very often by priests, because they think that if girls spend money on books they will have less to give them. It would be impossible to get a Roman Catholic priest to see from how many points of view this is a mistaken policy, even for the cause it is supposed to benefit.

Soon after I came to America, a priest in New York was very anxious to help me, and wished to do something for us on St. Patrick's Day. He thought, naturally, that the archbishop would not object to a work approved by the pope. He sent me a despatch, which I still have, telling me to send him ten thousand circulars for distribution. But before his benevolent plans were carried into execution they were peremptorily stopped, and he was threatened with prompt ecclesiastical penalties if he attempted to assist me in any way. Clearly, Rome and New York differ on some important points. I may say here that all these things became more or less generally known, and of course were, as they were intended to be, an effectual hindrance to the success of our work. There are not many who could dare to brave ecclesiastical displeasure.

CHAPTER XXVI.

CONCLUDING SCENES.

The End of All — Other Sisters Deprived — Case of Miss K. — The Girls' Home in Baltimore — Visit to the South — Insolence of a Southern Bishop — Application to Archbishop Keane — Contrasted Letter from Archbishop Bagshawe and Archbishop Keane.

I HAVE but a few words to say in conclusion. After my interview with Archbishop Corrigan, recorded above, in which I saw that neither the Holy Father's authority nor the statement of Propaganda would have the slightest weight with him; and when he had told me in plain terms he would never allow me in his diocese, and never wished to see me again; I knew that as far as I was concerned, at least in his lifetime, there was no hope for the extension of our work in America so long as I was connected with it. My health had completely broken down. I had no heart to continue useless efforts any longer. As for a sister leaving a convent, unless she left it in such a way as to attract public attention, the bishops care very little. I was simply amazed, soon after I came to America, at the number of sisters and priests who called upon me who had been deprived of their religious positions from one cause or other. I also heard from sisters of many different orders how convents had been broken up at the mere caprice of a priest or bishop, no matter how long they had been established.

These sisters, being for the most part of the middle class, and being in good health, were able to get a living for themselves, and are often employed as servants in families who never have the least idea of their previous history. Of late years I believe the American bishops do not allow the sisters to make vows for more than a year, so that they can be sent away at convenience. Certainly, this is all opposed to the just idea of a sister's life.

I have already mentioned the case of a sister who was received into our home under very painful circumstances. Another case was that of a Miss K———, who had been for many years a sister in the Order of the Visitation in the diocese of Archbishop Keane, director of the new Catholic University. This lady told me she was dismissed after many years of profession, without any word or notice, and, sent to make her way in the world as best she could. I gave her some employment and helped her for a time. She was a clever, educated lady.

The case of these poor sisters is very sad. They have been many years living a secluded life, their home ties are already broken, and even their friends generally look upon them as a burden and a disgrace, without stopping to think that they have too often been the victims of painful circumstances.

In one case only I have found a sister provided for and that was in Baltimore. The Girls' Home there, under the auspices of Cardinal Gibbons, was in charge of a person who had been for twenty years a professed sister in the Order of the Sisters of Charity, of St. Vincent de Paul, and who left the order. I could not, however, but feel that Cardinal Gibbons showed great indifference to change of religious views when he preferred having her in charge rather than to have it in charge of sisters. Still this is not very encouraging to those who try to persevere.

The heart trouble which developed soon after I came to America became so serious, and my state of health was such, that the doctor ordered me a winter in the South, as the only hope of my life. I did this at the urgent entreaty of the sisters, and with the permission of my bishop.

I went as far South as Augusta, Georgia, and I found there a warm welcome from the Irish and the descendants of the Irish. But there was still the same Episcopal detraction and determination not to allow me to carry on the work which was so dear to me. An earnest petition was sent in to a Southern bishop, signed by the mayor and all the leading gentlemen of the town, asking him to allow the establishment of a house of our Order. But he treated the gentlemen and the petition with silent contempt, and sent me a most insolent message through a priest.

I need only say that I became more and more hopeless and depressed. On my return in the spring, I saw an eminent physician in Philadelphia. I was obliged to travel very slowly, and had to stop there on my way. He gave me a written certification that if I did not at once discontinue work, and if I was not free from all trouble and anxiety, that the heart disease which is at present only functional, would very quickly develop into organic trouble.

About this, however, I would not have concerned myself, as I should only be too glad to die working for the poor; but I could not fail to see that my connection with the Order was an obstacle, and perhaps the only hindrance to its success. I, therefore, decided on withdrawing altogether as soon as possible.

While travelling, I tried to keep as quiet as possible and to avoid seeing people. Still, the old stories were circulated that I was fond of change, and yet there is nothing I dislike more. I know that sisters in America are constantly going from one place to the other for health or other reasons. While I was in the South, a Sister of Mercy who had become enervated by the Southern climate was staying in New York with her brother for the winter. At Atlantic City, I found another sister of her Order stopping at one of the large public hotels there for her health. It seemed that only in my case these things were spoken of as wrong.

At this time the sisters made one last effort to get the American bishops to contradict the reports which they had been circulating against me. Their appeal was made to Bishop Keane under the following circumstances.

When I was seriously ill in Washington, some years before, a gentleman who was very intimate with this bishop, and who knew that he was to be the head of the new Catholic university, thinking that he was one who would show kindness to any person in trouble, wrote to him and told him that he must know those charges against me to be false; he pointed out to him the injury such reports must do to religion, and the discredit they bring on the Holy Father. I do not wish to judge Bishop Keane uncharitably, but I fear he had every opportunity of knowing that the statements he made about me were false.

I append his letter and one received from

Bishop Bagshawe, almost on the same date, though it has been given before.

"St. Barnabas' Cathedral, Nottingham,
"May 17, 1886.

"My dear Rev. Mother,—I have just heard with great sorrow, that you are so seriously ill, and can only hope that by this time your health may have improved. May God grant it and spare you long to carry on the great work you have begun.

Your convents in this diocese are well and securely founded, but they could ill afford to lose you.

I write to assure you of my sympathy and prayers, and entreating God to bless you,

"Remain yours most truly,
"Edward, *Bishop of Nottingham*.

"*To* Sister M. Francis Clare *Mother-General of the Sisters of Peace*."

"St. Peter's Cathedral, Richmond, Va.,
"May 27, 1886.

"My dear Dr. M——, I feel very deeply for the poor Nun of Kenmare, but am sorry it is not in my power to be of aid or comfort to her. Her many plans which carry her from one part of the world to another, and in which she cannot hope for sympathy and co-operation amongst the hierarchy, lie at the bottom of her mental troubles.

I could be of no use to her whatever; nor any

one, nor anything, till she is quietly back in her place, her convent in Ireland.

"With sincere best wishes,
"Yours truly in Christ,
"JOHN J. KEANE."

The sisters wrote to Bishop Keane thinking, as he was to take the exalted and responsible office of being the future teacher and model of American ecclesiastics and gentlemen, he would be zealous for the honor of the church, that he would not like to place himself in a false position, and that he needed only to know the facts in order to do justice to him and myself. He knew that I had no convent in Ireland and therefore I could not comply with the desire of the American bishops to go there; but Bishop Keane has not made any reparation, either in public or private, and his charges against me still stand uncontradicted.

"CONVENT OF THE SISTERS OF PEACE,
JERSEY CITY, N. J.

"MY LORD, — Our Mother General, most generally known as the Nun of Kenmare, was sent by our bishop, the Right Rev. W. M. Wigger, to Baltimore and other places South, in March, 1886, for the purpose of seeing several bishops, partly to try and interest them in the establishment of a home for the Catholic blind, and partly hoping that, by a personal interview, she might be able to satisfy them, by the documents which she brought with her from Rome, that the many and cruel slanders which have been circulated about her were not only false, but absolutely without any foundation whatever, and were originated by persons who dislike her great zeal for souls, and her wonderful energy in good works.

"In this mission she failed, not from want of proof of the divine character of her mission, and of the full approval of it by the Holy See, but because the ecclesiastics to whom she applied preferred to believe scandals which did not exist, and would not accept the denial of them by the Holy Father and Propaganda.

"Now, my lord, you were one of the bishops who has not only spoken but written what is most scandalous and calumnious of our beloved superior, and we have the evidence in your own handwriting. You, with others, have helped to deprive the Catholic church of the services, and to break the loving and tender heart of one of the truest and most devoted of God's spouses.

"We understand that your lordship is advanced to a most distinguished position in the Catholic church of America, a position which places in your hands the future of the Catholic church of America. As you will have the formation of the characters of the future priests, we suppose that you will teach them that justice to poor as well as to rich, and that reparation for wrong done, is as much the duty of the priest as of the layman.

"I inclose a copy of your letter in which you have brought these scandalous charges against our superior. Your present position makes it most important, both for yourself and for us, that they should be fully and publicly retracted. I may add that the circulation of such scandals about our superior is also a grave injury to the Holy Father, as people naturally ask, how is it that this sister is so spoken of by ecclesiastics when the Holy Father has granted to her the extraordinary favor of being foundress of our new order? Why should an American bishop demand that 'she should go back to her convent in Ireland,' when the Holy Father has authorized her to leave it for a new and most important work? Why should she be treated with suspicion and contempt when Propaganda has officially declared that 'she is worthy of the trust and confidence of all who may place themselves under her guidance?' The original of this document is in the possession of our English ecclesiastical superior, the Right Rev. G. W. Bagshawe, of Nottingham. What are her 'many plans?' We who have been her spiritual children for years, are aware of only one plan, it has been to work for God's poor. When and where has she ever failed in obedience to ecclesiastical authority? It is easy to invent and circulate reports, but a time may come when something more than an assertion will be demanded from those who speak such reports. Suppose that the whole miserable story of our Mother's treatment by ecclesiastics in America were put before the public, and your lordship will be pleased to remember we have written proof, what would be said? Are priests in this new Catholic university to be educated to be honest men, or as men who will not pay ordinary respect to truth and justice and to the decisions of the Holy See? When did our Mother go 'from one part of the world to another' without the permission of her bishop? Even this Fall, when several eminent doctors declared her life depended on her spending the winter in the South, it was with great difficulty that we could induce her to go, and it was only when our bishop said that he wished her to do so, that she consented.

"Your lordship would not have been troubled with this letter, but we feel the time has come when it is our duty to claim recognition and respect for the Holy Father's decision. Why should your lordship or other American bishops refuse our mother 'sympathy?' Surely, you should have the deepest sympathy for one who has so long suffered in silence when she might, at any moment, clear herself of all blame by publishing the documents in her possession when she has refrained from doing so simply because the public discredit would fall, and fall justly, on those very ecclesiastics who have cared so little for her unmerited sufferings, and why should it not? Within the last two years we have been offered ten good foundations by priests in different parts of America, and their respective bishops have at once refused to allow our order to spread, influenced by false reports such as those in your letter. Protestants are amazed when they find this to be the case. Protestant institutions, seaside homes etc, are being established all over the country for working-girls, and even in the very places where we have been refused permission to establish homes blest by the Holy Father. These homes are filled with and supported by Catholic girls, as we can prove.

"We are well aware that there is in America one ecclesiastic whose prejudices against our mother-general are so strong that even the benediction and authority of the Holy Father has no weight with him, and it would be amusing if it was not very sad to see how some Catholic authorities make so much of the least word from Rome when it is in their favor, and treat with utter contempt such as are against their prejudices, but is this true loyalty to the Holy See? This ecclesiastic has, we know, considerable power over all the other bishops, but, my lord, surely each bishop has a conscience of his own and a duty of his own to the Holy See.

"We shall be most happy, with the permission of our bishop, to go to Washington and bring the original document of the Holy Father's founding our order, for the information of the bishops assembled at the laying the foundation of the Catholic university.

"We can ourselves, or any other of our sisters who are long professed under our dear mother's care, give personal evidence as to the good she has done for souls and the forbearance with which she has borne persistent calumny.

"We trust for the sake of the Catholic faith, and for your lordship's own easement of conscience, that you will obtain from all the bishops a public denial of the charges made against her. I am, my lord,

"Yours very respectfully,
"MOTHER M. EVANGELISTA,
"*Mother Provincial.*
"SISTER M. IGNATIUS,
"*Local Superior.*"

CHAPTER XXVII.

THE END.

A Weary Task — No Justice to be Had — Church Regulations — An Easily Offended Priest — A New Libel Manufactured — An Adventuress and a Thief — Father C———n as Protector — Other Misrepresentations.

I WONDER if my readers are as weary of reading as I am of writing all this. I have a duty to God, to the church, and above all, to those who have confided their alms to me so often and so generously. I know that they have a right to be told why I have been unable to carry out a work so necessary for the poor, and for working girls.

It has certainly taken me a very long time to realize that there was no justice for me, and no use in persevering, but I have realized it at last. I have before me now a letter from a gentleman in New York to whom I showed some letters referred to in this book. He says:—

"I now understand your position as I did not before. Truly, you have had to contend with a lot of scoundrels in the guise of priests and bishops and all the rest of it. It is a very fortunate thing for me that I am not a Catholic. I think if I belonged to a religious order and had such infernal treatment. I should be an apostle of rebellion or reformation, or something else rather aggressive, in a very short space of time. I don't know much about the laws of your church, and just how much deviltry a sister has got to submit to without a murmur or a protest; but it does seem to me that on general principles of common sense, such treatment is from the devil, and cannot borrow any sanctity by presenting itself in an ecclesiastical robe."

There is one point which I wish to make very clear, as I know that allusion to it will be the only defence which can be made by those who have opposed the designs of the Holy Father, in prohibiting my extending the order of the Sisters of Peace.

The regulations of the Roman Catholic church with regard to sisters are very clear and very necessary. No religious houses or convents can be founded in any diocese without the consent of the bishop of that diocese. Of this, I of course, was well aware; but it is one thing for a bishop to have a certain power to do a certain thing; the way in which he exercises that power is quite another matter.

Again, even the power which the pope gave me to found a religious order and to do a certain work does not authorize me to intrude that work in any diocese without the further permission of the bishop, nor does it in any way oblige a bishop to receive me to work in his diocese. I know this will be the excuse, if indeed any defence is made, or any explanation given of what I am stating in this book.

But nothing can justify a bishop in persisting in false accusations, and respect to the Holy Father should make him receive with courtesy a sister who had been approved by him.

I have shown, however, that bishops who had been willing to receive me have been prevented from doing so by others, so that it cannot be said that I was trying to intrude myself into their dioceses against their wish. Further, if a bishop believed that I was likely to be troublesome to him, or to quarrel with his priests, etc. (I know that I have been accused of doing so), could he not very easily find out whether I had been the person in fault in such a case, or the priest?

In every case where I had trouble with bishops or priests, I have shown clearly that the trouble came from them, and was caused by them. I have shown also, that I made the most earnest efforts to conciliate them, and to comply with all their wishes. Why, then, should I be blamed for the fault of others?

I now give another case in point, which will show how I was falsely accused of disagreeing with a priest, when on the contrary he had treated me in a very discreditable manner.

This priest, the Rev. C——n, asked me to establish a summer home for girls in his parish. I gladly agreed and obtained the consent of our bishop. I rented a house from a New York gentleman, a Roman Catholic and a lawyer. I believe he and his family had had a very unpleasant experience with this same priest, but as they were not in his power, as I was, they came off victors. When I went with this priest to see the place, we found some grass ready for mowing. I thought how useful this would be for our cow, when Father C——n turned to me and said he wanted the grass for himself. I certainly did think this very selfish, but I expected nothing else from persons of his class, and, in fact, I was used to nothing else. I was, however, very willing to do anything or give anything that would please him, and I said certainly he should have it.

The next day, to my great surprise, I got an indignant letter from him by post to say he could not prevent my coming to his parish, because I had signed the lease for this house, but I must understand that he would have nothing to do with us, and that he would not come near the house while we were there. All this angry feeling was caused by a woman who was caretaker of the place, and who told him I did not wish to give him the grass. It is difficult to understand how a man could be so easily deceived and so easily offended. The poor priest actually went to the bishop with his tale, but he did not get much consolation.

The woman had been caretaking the place so long she looked on it as a permanent home for herself and family, and was very angry because we had rented it, and she told me she would bring "all the Tipperary men in the neighborhood down on me." I did not mind this, but she said then I had no right to give the grass to Father C——n, it was hers, and she had a right to it as caretaker, and she always intended to give it to him. This I am sure was not true, but it answered her purpose. I replied, "Well, I will write to Mr.—— and ask him who has a right to it. If he says you have, you can do what you like with it." But I never said one word about Father C——n or not wishing to give it to him.

I had almost endless trouble about this wretched bit of grass. I wrote the simple facts of the case to Father C——n, and told him why the woman had told him this falsehood, and indeed the grass was not worth disputing about. It took a long time to pacify him, but he never forgave me, and has been my enemy ever since. He made my life and the life of the sisters such a misery to us, we were only too thankful to get away from him.

But of course it would not have suited him to have the true story known, so a new libel was manufactured and circulated, and every priest had in New York and the neighboring towns, that all the reports about me were quite true, for I would not agree with Father C———n.

It was sad to see a priest, who should have been above such things, believe the word of an uneducated, ignorant woman in preference to that of a sister, but I had already had experience of similar infatuations. I suppose the kind of life which priests lead is the cause of this. I had also another experience of the way in which a priest can act who is prejudiced against a sister without cause. Before I went to open a home for girls in his parish, I had received a letter from a woman who lived in Baltimore, the object of which was to be received in our home in Jersey City. She said that she was a Protestant, but desired to become a Roman Catholic; that she had no Roman Catholic friends, and therefore could not give me any references.

I did not know what to do, but she wrote again and was very importunate. At last I agreed to let her come. I took her to the summer home in

Father C——n's parish after she had been baptized and formally received into the Roman Catholic church.

I soon began to have some suspicions that she was an impostor, but Father C——n took her up warmly. He was lost in admiration of her piety and devotion, and she laid herself out to please him. With the cunning of her class, she soon found out his weak points, and worked upon them. He had a sore feeling against me for what I did not do, and she soon found that he would not be sorry to hear anything to my disadvantage. At the same time she made great friends with a girl whom we had taken on trial, to try her vocation for a sister's life. I found this girl was hysterical and quite unfit for our life, and I intended to send her away quietly. I had warned her against Ada Stagg, as this adventuress called herself, and as I saw that my warnings were quite useless. I was all the more determined to send her home. A girl who could have for her chosen companion and friend, a doubtful character, against whom she had been warned, was clearly not fit for convent life.

I was waiting quietly, as one has to do sometimes in difficult cases, when I missed forty dollars, and had reason to be tolerably sure who had taken it. I went to the priest, as I thought it right to warn him, no matter how he might have treated me, and I found she had been giving him money, a strange proceeding for a person in her position I hoped that like a good pastor he would help me in this difficulty, and for the sake of this poor girl's soul would try to advise her and find out the truth. But it was the same disappointment over again. He took the part of both the thief and of the girl who had made herself the companion of the thief, after all my warnings. He believed all the ridiculous stories that she made up, and gave me many weeks' bitter pain in consequence.

After some little trouble I found out the whole story of this unhappy girl. Ada Stagg, as she called herself, was "wanted" in quite a number of places for theft. She had made a trade of imposing on sisters. She had gone to the sisters of the Sacred Heart in Philadelphia, to the sisters of the Good Shepherd in Baltimore, and to many others, and told the same story of her desire to be received into the Roman Catholic church, and she had so completely deceived these experienced sisters that she had gone through all the solemn mockery of this, without even being suspected by any of them, until having gained whatever object she had in each place, she disappeared as suddenly as she had come. Her reason for making convents the base of her operations was, that she knew the sisters would not like to expose her, as they would have to appear against her publicly.

In our case she judged rightly, for I did not want to add to my many troubles by exposing her. Father C——, however, saved me all trouble, though in a way which did not do much credit to himself. He took her and her friend under his special protection, brought them with a care worthy of better objects, to a convent in Newark; placed them under the special care of the superioress, as victims of my injustice, and then another report was carefully and widely sent out, of my inability to agree with any priest; and that these two "saintly" women could not remain in our institution because our religious observances were not strict enough for them. I have been very careful in writing this book to say nothing which I did not know personally to be true. I was educated very strictly on the subject of truth, in the Episcopal church. No doubt there must be some excuse made for Roman Catholic bishops and priests who have not such strict views on such subjects. The Roman Catholic church certainly teaches that calumny is a mortal sin, and that even to exaggerate the faults which we know another to be guilty of is a mortal sin. Catholics also are required to make restitution when they have been guilty of calumny; but this, as far as my experience goes, does not seem to apply to either priests or bishops.

I have been careful in this book to state only what I have proof of, by the letters of the persons concerned; and as I cannot give documentary evidence, I may say that I heard, on the authority of a person who told me that he had seen the document, that this priest gave a letter of the highest recommendation to this unfortunate girl, which no doubt she is using to her own advantage. When I got sufficient evidence to know who and what she was, though I did not know her whole career until later, I tried to reason with her, and to convince her that even from a temporal point of view she could do better and be far happier if she would try to earn her living honestly. I hoped I had made some impression on her, she cried bitterly; and knowing that I knew the evil she had told poor Father C—— of me, all of which he so readily believed, she seemed touched to see that I should be so anxious to help her.

Unfortunately for the poor girl, she had been so built up by Father C——'s promises of help, and his eager sympathy for her, in the supposed injustice with which he thought I had treated her, that, when just at this critical moment, he sent a messenger to take her to the convent where he had arranged to place her and her friend, she dried her tears very promptly, assumed her old defiant manner to me, and all my hopes of her reformation had to be abandoned. Of course she knew well the great value of the letter which this priest had given her, and that even if he did find her out later, she would have the letter to work with all the same. I was told by the same gentleman who told me that he had seen this letter, that Father C———n kept up an active correspondence with these two women, and believing all they had told him of myself and the sisters, wrote of us in a way which could not fail to do us a serious injury. When writing of me he always described me as that "ex-nun," a title which I am afraid he knew well I did not deserve, to say nothing of the disrespect to the Holy Father in speaking thus of a person to whom he had given so high a position in the church.

I do not know what has become of this poor girl. The New York detectives were after her for some time. She had stolen a quantity of valuable clothing from the family with whom she had been living in Baltimore, all of which she wore when with us, and told me had been gifts from her father, who was dead. She had stolen a desk from a family with whom she had lived as a servant for a short time in Washington, and as this desk contained family papers she had no difficulty in passing herself off as one of this family, and using their name. Her appearance too was in her favor, though she could hardly read or write. She was born a Catholic, of Irish descent, and knew her religion well. In fact, when the sisters began to prepare her to be received into the church, we found she had nothing to learn, and the sisters in the other convents where she had previously gone through the same sacrilege of being received into the church, told me they were also surprised to find her so well instructed. But she had always some plausible excuse for everything that seemed questionable.

It will be seen from all this, and the other instances of my difficulties with priests who believed every idle tale which might be carried to them, and what was worse reported them as being true to all their friends, that it is no wonder if people at last began to think that there must be something wrong. The evidence for the sisters would not be listened to by these priests. No work could be carried on by any one who was so harassed as I was in this way.

Here is another case, and this, with what I have told of at Knock, will surely be sufficient to show how these misrepresentations arose. A priest who had shown me a great deal of real kindness, and who I thought was one of my best friends in America, received a few dollars for me from a friend. He wrote to me saying this, and that he inclosed the money for me in the letter. The money was not in the letter, and thinking it was a mistake, I wrote to him, the same as I would to any one else, saying he forgot to put it in. A storm of fury was the result, all his professions of friendship went for nothing. He said I had accused him of being a robber, which I certainly did not, for it never even crossed my mind that he had done anything but make a mistake. He inclosed the money, and refused to have any future dealings with me. And then he circulated another story among his priestly friends, that I quarrelled with every one, and, of course, this only confirmed what they had heard about me before, and every one was ready to condemn me.

APPENDIX.

PART I.

Papal Approbations and Briefs.

Dilectæ in Christo Filiæ, MARÆ FRANCISCÆ CLARÆ *e Sororibus Santæ Claræ, Kenmare.*

"DILECTA IN CHRISTA FILIA, — Salutem et Apostolicam Benedictionem. Gratulamur tibi, Dilecta in Christo Filia, quod prolixum ac difficile opus, cui vix pares esse pesse sexus tui vires videbantur, ad exitum perduxeris ea felicitate, quæ piorum ac doctorum laudes promeruerit. Nec gaudemus tantum quod per scitam copiosamque lucubrationem hanc gloriam promoveris insignis Hiberniæ Apostoli, Sancti Patritrii, pietatemque fidelium in eumdem succenderis; sed etiam de Ecclesia tota bene merueris. Nam per ipsam descriptionem gestorum tanti viri, largita hominibus a Catholica religione beneficia subiecisti oculis ita, ut in dubium revocari nequeant. Nec enim sola fidei lux occurrit ab illa allata, ad populum, qui sedebat in tenebris et in umbra mortis, sed feri ac barbari mores ita simul reformati et compositi, ut insula istæc, veluti in alium conversa, Insula Sanctorum appellari meruerit. Clerus autem ab eodem ubique constitutus, una cum religione ac pietate ita coluit promovitque scientiam, ut dum Europa tota barbarorum incursu vastabatur, et opprimebatur ignorantiæ tenebris tutum litteris ac disciplinis perfugium exhibuerit, et confluentem undique juventutem sic exceperit et excoluerit, ut complures inde prodierint diversarum nationum apostoli innumerique viri sanctitate et doctrina celeberrimi. Atque tanti viri donum Hibernia debuit huic apostolicæ sedi : et is non aliam Hibernis doctrinam attulit, quam quæ tradebatur ab eadem sede, quæque jam a christianæ religionis exordiis gentes superstitioni erroribusque mancipatas, fœdoque voluptatum omnium cœno demersas, erexerat, caritate consociaverat, et ad vitæ cultum hominis nobilitate dignum traduxerat. Quæ quidem facta cum calumnias ignorantiæ, obscurantismi, regressus, quibus passim Ecclesia et sancta hæc sedes impetuntur, evidentissime refellant ; vita certe Sancti Patritii a te concinnata eo merito præstat, ut hoc beneficium cuique exhibuerit eo præsantius ac validius quod ultra fluat ab ipsa factorum narratione. Cum autem perennitatem fructuum operis Sanctissimi Præsulis demiremur in constantia tuæ gentis nulla unquam insectatione, vi, machinatione, calamitate dejecta per tota secula ; non immerito confidimus fore, ut per instauratam nunc a te veterum eventuum ac gloriæ memoriam, piissimus hic populus studiosius etiam incendi debeat ad preclara majorum suorum vestigia terenda. Hunc certe successum ominamur labori tuo, dum divini favoris auspicem, et pateruæ Nostæ benevolentiæ pignus, Apostolicam Benedictionem tibi et sororibus tuis peramanter impertimus.

"Datum Romæ apud S. Petrum die 6 Octobris, Anno 1870. Pontificatus Nostri Anno Vicesimoquinto.

"PIUS P. P. IX."

[*Papal authorization of the establishment of the Order of the Sisters of Peace by Sister M. Francis Clare.*]

"At an audience of His Holiness, had on the 18th day of May, 1884, our Most Holy Lord Leo XIII., by Divine Providence Pope, on the relation of me the undersigned, Secretary of the Sacred Congregation de Propaganda Fide, considering the information and opinion given by the Right Rev. Bishop of Nottingham, and by the superioress of the congregation of Franciscan (Poor Clare) Sisters, of Newry, Ireland, has graciously deigned to dispense the petitioner (Sister M. Francis Clare) concerning the vows pronounced by her in the said congregation; for this end, however, that she may be able to take vows anew in the institute to be founded by her according to the rules approved by the Ordinary of Nottingham. All things whatsoever to the contrary nothwithstanding.

"Given at Rome, in the House of the Sac. Cong. de Prop. Fide, on the day and year aforesaid.

"Gratuitously on every account.
    (Signed)   "† D. ARCHBISHOP OF TYRE,
                                     "*Secretary.*"

[*From the* Osservatore Romano, *May* 24, 1884. *This is the official organ of His Holiness Pope Leo XIII.*]

"His Holiness received the Rev. Mother Mary Francis Clare, an Irish nun, in private audience, who came to implore a special benediction for the new order of St. Joseph's Sisters of Peace, of the Immaculate Conception, which she has founded for the very important work of preparing girls for domestic service, of instructing them in any business for which they may have a special inclination or ability; for providing homes for young women who work in factories or other establishments, at a distance from their parents; and, finally, for promoting the circulation of Catholic literature.

"This distinguished religieuse is the author of many learned and interesting works, amongst them, of 'A Life of St. Patrick, Apostle of Ireland,' of 'A Life of Pope Pius IX.,' and many other works which have been translated into French, German, and Italian. She had the honor of presenting many of these works to the Holy Father, who received them with marked approbation."

[*From the* Journal de Rome, *May* 24, 1884.]

"The Rev. Mother Mary Francis Clare, foundress of the Sisters of Peace of the Immaculate Conception and of St. Joseph, has been received to-day in special audience by his Holiness.

"Indefatigable in good works, and endowed with remarkable qualities, she is also a distinguished writer. The Holy Father has highly praised her zeal and her labors, and gave his Apostolic Benediction to the author.

"We shall have occasion to speak again of the different works of this celebrated religieuse, who has deserved so much of the church and of humanity."

[EXTRACTS FROM THE APOSTOLIC LETTER OF POPE PIUS IX, TO SISTER M. FRANCIS CLARE]

"*To our beloved daughter in Christ*, MARY FRANCIS CLARE, *of the Sisters of Saint Clare*, PIUS P. P. IX.

"BELOVED DAUGHTER IN CHRIST, — Health and apostolic benediction. We congratulate you, beloved daughter in Christ, on having completed a long and difficult work which seemed to be above woman's strength, with a success that has justly earned the applause of the wise and the learned. We rejoice, not only that you have promoted by this eloquent and learned volume the glory of the illustrious Apostle of Ireland, St. Patrick, but also because you have deserved well of the whole church; for in recording the actions of so great a man, you have placed before the eyes of the world the benefits received through the Catholic religion so clearly, that they can no longer be questioned. We certainly augur this successful issue from your labor; and at the same time we impart to you and to your sisters, most lovingly, the apostolic benediction, as an earnest of God's favor and a pledge of our good will.

"Given at Rome, at St. Peter's, the 6th October, 1870, the twenty-fifth year of our pontificate.

"PIUS P. P. IX."

APPENDIX.

APOSTOLIC BLESSING OF HIS HOLINESS POPE LEO XIII.

Irish College, Rome, May 29, 1878.

"My dear Sister, — I am happy to state that Mgr. Kirby presented to-day in my name, your life of St. Patrick, St. Bridget and St. Columbia, to His Holiness, who, in return, sends you his thanks and his best blessing. His Holiness wishes you every success in your literary labors, hoping that they may be useful to religion, and contribute to the salvation of souls.

"His Holiness was greatly pleased with the way in which the life of St. Patrick was brought out.

"Wishing you and all your pious community every blessing, I remain, Yours faithfully,

"† Paul, Cardinal Cullen."

PART II.

Letters of Archbishop Croke and others Endorsing Sister Mary Francis Clare's Conduct, and Advising Publication of the Letters showing that she had the usual Canonical Authorization for her Removal from Kenmare.

"The Palace, Thurles, February 20, 1882.

"My dear Sister M. Francis Clare, — I have been thinking of writing to you ever since you left Kenmare, to bid you God speed on the lines of the new departure, which, with the blessing and full concurrence of your friends and spiritual superiors, you have so bravely, and, as I trust, so advantageously entered on.

"But as you have been recalled to my memory in a special manner this morning, by the receipt of your 'Cloister Songs,' I do not see that I can with any decency defer writing to you any longer, if only to thank you for this last, though not the least, token of your good will towards myself personally, as well as of your unabated energy in the sacred cause of sound religious and historic literature.

"It is, indeed, quite a puzzle to me, as it must be to

thousands of your readers likewise, how you have managed to compose so many weighty and valuable works on such a variety of subjects as you have dealt with, some of them being unusually abstruse and even complicated; and especially how you succeeded in doing so, without having laid yourself open to any serious charge of inaccuracy in historic, or of grave error in theological matters. The more so, indeed, as you have been always understood to have been most faithful, and even assiduous in the discharge of the substantial duties of your sacred calling, besides attending to the supply and distribution of the large funds, which, owing to your great popularity, were from time to time, committed to you for charitable purposes by your admirers, both in the old and the new world.

"As a matter of course, and indeed as might have been anticipated, so prominent a religious, so voluminous and varied a writer, and so pronounced a Hibernian as you are known to be, could not have always escaped the sharp and even unfriendly criticism of literary or political purists, to say nothing whatever of the sneers and snarling of such men as that Saxon cleric appears to be, who so bitterly assailed you the other day in the pages of the *Weekly Register*.

"But you may abundantly console yourself with the thought that your countrymen at large, and your countrywomen also, whether at home or in exile, appreciate to the full your great and disinterested labors in the cause of creed and country, and that the name of the good and gifted "NUN OF KENMARE" will continue to be what it is to-day, a real household word, to be cherished as such, amongst the genuine lovers of our country for many generations yet to come.

"Wishing you health, happiness, and success, I remain, my dear Sister M. Francis Clare,

"Your very faithful friend,

"† T. W. CROKE, *Archbishop of Cashel.*"

"To SISTER MARY FRANCIS CLARE,
"Knock, Ballyhaunis, Co. Mayo."

The following letter is from my confessor, the Rev. M. Neligan, C. C., of Kenmare, who travelled with myself and my secretary, Miss Downing, to Knock:—

THE PRESBYTERY, KENMARE, March 9, 1882.

"MY VERY DEAR SISTER F. CLARE:— Your letter of this morning simply astounds me. The calumny that you left Kenmare without the proper permission from your superiors is too absurd. Don't mind; patience and resignation will right things.

"I accompanied you at the request of the Mother Abbess here, and with the sanction of the bishop, then *vicar-cap*.

"When we arrived at Knock, Archbishop Cavanagh was so enthusiastic about your foundation there that I thought it quite unnecessary to remain longer than the few days I did.

"As well as I remember, the Archbishop of Tuam expressed himself similarly by letter to you. You wrote to me afterwards, saying His Grace's interview at Tuam tended to the same result. Hence, things being so, I am simply bewildered at its being even mooted that you left Kenmare without the necessary permission. I *repeat again*, you had the fullest sanction, and *that* from your superiors, to leave.

"You have now thrown yourself into the good cause at Knock, and that, together with your many years of most valuable service here, and particularly your splendid and successful efforts during the late famine years, will soon put an end to these false reports.

"Sincerely wishing you health and success in the cause of God and our country, in which you have always labored so hard and unselfishly,

"My very dear Sister F. C.,
"Yours as ever,
"M. NELIGAN, C. C."

"THE PALACE, THURLES, March 28, 1882.

"MY DEAR SISTER CLARE, — "I think it would do no harm to publish a short account of your departure from Kenmare Convent, showing clearly, as you can do, by documentary evidence, that you had full leave and license to leave Kenmare and go to Knock, thence to Newry, and finally to settle in Knock, with a view to the erection there of a convent of your order. Dr. McCabe had been told that you had no leave to quit Kenmare, this I know. Hence, I suppose, the eviction.

"Yours most faithfully,
"T. W. CROKE."

"THE PALACE, THURLES, March 1, 1882.

"MY DEAR SISTER CLARE, — All right. I am delighted you have sent a crusher to the hierarch in question; he is not Dr. G——.

"I think the publication of the letters from Dr. Higgins, Dr. Leahy, and Dr. McEvilly, for private circulation among the bishops and nobody else, would do a deal of good. God speed and prosper you.

"Your friend, T. W. CROKE."

"The 'Nun of Kenmare.'"

I sent the above letter to Father Cavanagh, and he replied,—

March 4, 1882.

"You ought to act on Dr. Croke's advice to publish the letters of Bishop Higgins and your confessor, which prove how utterly and maliciously false this bishop's reports were, for Archbishop Croke is surely a great and sincere friend. Both from his exalted position in the church, and his great learning and ability, he is held in the greatest esteem by his countrymen all over world. Circulate his very memorable letter to you everywhere, at home and abroad."

"CONVENT OF ST. CLARE, NEWRY, Dec. 16, 1881.

"MY DEAR LORD ARCHBISHOP, — I release Sister M. Francis Clare, Cusack, from whatever canonical obedience she owes to me as Bishop of Dromore, and I hereby transfer that obedience to your grace. With sincere esteem, your grace's ob't servant in Christ,

"BROTHER JOHN PIUS LEAHY, O. P.,
"*Bishop of Dromore.*

"*To* MOST REV. DR. MCEVILLY, *Lord Bishop of Tuam.*"

THE PALACE, THURLES, Oct. 3, 1888.

"MY DEAR SISTER M. CLARE, — I have got all your communications, and am very happy to hear that things have taken a turn in your favor.

"Archdeacon Bagshawe is a first-rate man, and I am quite sure that you will be much happier in his diocese than you could be in Connaught.

"I am always promising myself the pleasure of seeing your bishop in his own castle, as I admire him much, so you may some day or other behold me on Bluebill Hill. Tell him, and always believe me to be,
"Yours very faithfully,
"J. CROKE, *Archbishop of Cashel.*"

(*From the Right Rev. Mgr. Stonor.*)

"27 VIA SISTINA, ROME, Dec. 1, 1884.

"DEAR REV. MOTHER, — Many thanks for your letter, and for all the news you gave me of the Order of Peace. I feel sure it will do a great deal of good the more it is spread, and I hope you will be able to have some foundations in Ireland before long. I regret you are not able to go to America, where your name is so well known, and where you are sure to receive support. You must not, however, give up the idea of going there.

"I am sorry I have not been able to get anything from the Holy Father as yet for your bazar, but I hope to do so when I have an opportunity of asking him.

"Hoping you will remember me in your good prayers,
"Believe me, yours very sincerely,
"EDMOND STONOR."

[From His Eminence Cardinal McCloskey.]

"Your 'Life and Times of His Holiness Pope Pius IX.' may be considered a monumental work for which we must all feel indebted to you. May God preserve you long to labor in the cause of his holy church, and of his beloved poor."

PART III.

Bishop Wigger's Letters of Approval.

"SETON HALL COLLEGE, SOUTH ORANGE, N. J.,
"December 16, 1884.

"Sister Mary Francis Clare intends to establish in the diocese of Newark one of her 'Homes for Irish Girls,' for which she has my full approval. I cordially recommend her to the faithful of this diocese, and I wish her every success in her praiseworthy undertaking.
"† WM. WIGGER, *Bishop of Newark.*"

"SETON HALL COLLEGE, SOUTH ORANGE, N. J.
"March 4, 1885.

"REV. DEAR MOTHER FRANCIS CLARE, — I hereby grant you permission to open in Jersey City, a house for immigrant girls, for the training of girls for domestic service, and for their reception when out of situations, or enfeebled by old age.

"I give my blessing to this good work, and pray God to give you great success in this charitable undertaking.
"Yours very sincerely,
"† WM. WIGGER, *Bishop of Newark.*"

HOME AND TRAINING SCHOOL FOR THE POOR CATHOLIC BLIND.

"SETON HALL COLLEGE, SOUTH ORANGE,
"March 19 '86.

"DEAR MOTHER FRANCIS CLARE, — I heartily approve of your project of establishing an institution for the training of the poor blind. The need of such an institution has long been felt. On various occasions I have been asked by Catholics if there was such a school, as they wished to place a child in it, and, to my sorrow, I have always been obliged to answer that I knew of no Catholic school of that kind, and that most probably there was none in the States. I feel that an institution of this kind would do much good, if we only had the means to establish it. I know of a very nice building containing over two hundred and fifty rooms, very suitable for your purpose, and which could be bought for about one fifth of its original cost, but I fear that even that amount could not be collected entirely in this diocese. Perhaps some of the most reverend and right reverend prelates in other dioceses, realizing the great utility of a Catholic training school for the blind, would allow you to collect among some of their wealthier Catholics. I willingly grant you permission to leave your convent for two months in company with one of your sisters, to see what could be done in this direction. I warmly recommend you to the kindness of the prelates on whom you may call, and sincerely hope that you will succeed in gaining the object of your mission. With best wishes, I remain,

"Yours very sincerely,
"W. M. WIGGER, *Bishop of Newark.*"

PART IV.

Copies of Letters Addressed by Sister M. Francis Clare to Archbishop Corrigan, asking him to Investigate the Charges which some of his Priests were Constantly Making Against Her.

"SISTERS OF PEACE, JERSEY CITY,
"Easter Eve, 1887.

"MY LORD ARCHBISHOP, — A Herald reporter came to me on Friday with a letter, a copy of which I inclose. It shows, what I know to be true, that there is a general and strong opinion in New York, that you consider me a most unworthy sister, and that you ignore, by so doing, the fact that I have the written approbation of the Holy Father for my work, and of the fact that before that approbation was given, the Herald reporter told me he had waited on your grace. He could not see you, but he saw your secretary, who appears to conduct your affairs. I asked him, if he had no objection, might I tell you what your secretary said. And he replied he had no objection. He said that you had refused me leave to establish a house of our Order in your diocese, because it would interfere with Father Riordan. I told the reporter this was not true. I never asked to interfere with Father Riordan's work, or to do anything that would interfere with it. At the same time I stated that as ours is the only religious order in the church which has been established for the purpose of helping emigrants as well as working girls, that loyalty and devotion to the Holy See would, I supposed, have made you wish to have our assistance in this work. Father Riordan cannot do the work of sisters, and sisters are needed for this work everywhere.

"The leave you refused was when I asked to open a summer home for girls in Nyack, and you know well I had the good wishes of the priest there. We have had great difficulty in finding a suitable place in this diocese, while, in your immense territory, a place could have been found perfectly suitable and for reasonable price. Naturally, people would say you must have had something very serious against me when you refused. 2d. He said I was refused leave to collect, and did not give a reason.

"Miss Gilbert has simply expressed the general opinion. I beg leave respectfully to submit to your grace that if you have heard any charge made against me you should first inquire from myself, or, if you prefer it, from my agent in Propaganda, Very Rev. Dom Gualdi, — who, as you are no doubt aware, is one of the minutandi in Propaganda, — whether it is true or not, and second if you have not heard any charge against me, you should at once, and publicly, put an end to all this scandal.

"Both Catholics and Protestants are asking why it is, when my work was so highly approved in Rome, that you or any of your council should state what it has been stated that you have said about me.

"I have never done one single act contrary to religious obedience since I entered religion. I have here with me the written permission, and even approbation of my ecclesiastical superior for everything I have done. It is, then, very hard for me, especially as a convert, at my time of life, to hear that I am spoken of as a "disobedient nun," as if, in fact, I had been another Maria Monk, so that many Catholics, and even Protestants in the diocese have been cautioned to have nothing to do with me. For myself, it matters very little what is said of me, but I feel bound to put a stop to this calumny for the sake of the order which I have established, and for the honor of the Holy See.

"My very silence and patience have made my enemies more daring and more uncharitable. I have evidence now in writing in my possession, of cruel slanders which are daily repeated against me by priests, and if I were not a sister I would at once instruct a lawyer to take an action against them for defamation of character, and, be assured, the McGlynn case would be a trifle in comparison, for no one can bring forward a charge against me of breach of religious discipline or any other fault.

"I do not know why I am so slandered and persecuted, only that the persons know they are safe in doing it because I am a sister. I have been on the point, more than once, during my very severe illness, of writing to the Holy Father, and resigning into his hands the charge he has given me, and telling to him and to the whole world why I could no longer bear it.

"I will now submit to your grace proof that it is generally believed that you know something very serious against my character, and that this is the reason why you have acted towards me as if I had been an unworthy religious.

"*First.* I have a letter addressed to me by a lady who heard Mgr. Quinn speaking of me as a bad religious, one " who had disobeyed her bishop," and he asked her how she could have anything to do with me. I ask — what bishop did I disobey, and when?

"*Second.* When I came back from the South (in the fall), where I had gone, on business, by the desire of my bishop; Mother D—— of S—— knowing that I was coming home in a dying state, as was then supposed, — and would to God I had died, — wrote to ask me to go to S——, as the doctor said it would be certain death to go back to Jersey City. I went there. I had scarcely been a fortnight there when she came to me one day in great distress, and said a lady had come to her from your grace, as a friend of your grace, a lady with whom you were specially intimate, and often dined with her. She asked Mother D—— did she not know you were opposed to me, and considered me a bad religious, in fact that you would be very angry if I stopped in any of your convents. Poor Mother D—— was terrified, and I said to her at once, 'I will leave in an hour; you shall not suffer for me,' and I left at once. Your grace will see from this circumstance, and I could mention many others, that I have grave cause of complaint. You will see, also, that I have kept these matters quiet, and you know very well what the consequences would have been had I even spoken of it privately.

" No wonder that Catholics and Protestants are alike scandalized. I trust in God, poor Mother D—— will not get into trouble now. A sister of one of her sisters — Sister M. L——, is one of my professed sisters here in Jersey City. We have been on very friendly terms, and it will be sad indeed if our friendly intercourse is broken up, or if she is made to suffer for an act of kindness.

" I will add that I have not said one word of these matters to the reporter or any reporter. Badly as I have been treated, I have kept silence.

"I am sure — as your grace must be too devoted a son of the church to wish even to appear to act against the Holy Father, or to allow your priests to do so — you will do all you can to arrange some plan for publicly showing your approbation of our work, and stopping this scandal. You will remember that Bishop Wigger was offered Mgr. Ducey's church to have a collection for the benefit of our home. Could not this be done still? The great majority of the girls who come to us are from your diocese, and they have felt bitterly your refusal to allow us to have a suitable place for them in their own diocese.

"I pray God to give your grace the courage to act for yourself, and not be guided by men who unfortunately are influenced by the poor motives of likes and dislikes.

"Another matter which gave great trouble was my being in Roosevelt Hospital instead of a sister's hospital. The operations I have had to undergo were so serious they could only be done safely in a hospital. How could I go to a Catholic hospital, where I might have been turned out at a moment's notice by your grace, and where I could not expect the sympathy of sisters who would fear to offend you, knowing your feelings about me. I think you will respect me for the silence with which I have borne this trial, and so far concealed the reason. I can tell your grace also that there are several priests in New York who wish to have a home of the order in their parish for our special work, and why should the permission be denied? We can make them self-supporting, and do a work that no other sisters are doing. Yours very sincerely in J. C.

"SISTER M. FRANCIS CLÁRE,
"*Mother-General of the Sisters of Peace.*

P. S. The scandalous reports made about me by an English priest, as to my having left my convent without leave, were carefully investigated by Propaganda, and I have a written declaration that they were without one shadow of foundation.

FROM SISTER M. FRANCIS CLARE TO ARCHBISHOP CORRIGAN, ASKING PERMISSION TO FOUND A HOME FOR WORKING GIRLS AT NYACK.

"September 22, 1886.

"MY LORD,— I write to ask your grace's permission to have a place in or near Nyack, for our girls, or rather for yours, as the greater majority of girls who came to us for their summer holidays are from New York; also, the greater number of girls who came from time to time to get rest from overwork or malaria. I am sure, when your grace knows all the circumstances, that you will not refuse.

"You know that the Holy Father has approved our Order by a written brief — the original of which I have in our Jersey City convent. Our work is for living out, working, and factory girls. In any case, temporary rest and care will, not only save them from long illness, but from far worse dangers into which they are often led for want of special provision for their special needs.

"I make this request for the sake of the girls, as we cannot find a place in Jersey which is not full of malaria — and though I am very reluctant to put in such a plea, I ask it for myself. I have been dangerously ill, I have been ordered here by a consultation of doctors who consider this air essential for my recovery, if not for my life.

"If your grace grants this desired permission, be assured you will never regret it. We can be of very great benefit to any mission where we are located, as the girls who come to us are of a respectable class, and we had as many as seventy or eighty at a time last summer, and, when we have a suitable place, we would have an average of two hundred.

"All these girls would help to support the church which, of course, they will attend, and, in a poor place like this, it will be a great benefit. If the priest should require our services, either to teach converts, etc., or to look up cases, we shall be happy to do so.

"As the girls pay for their board, we do not want any help from the parish, and shall not ask any — whatever benefit we may be to the parish, we ask for nothing in return.

"Later on, if your grace pleases, we would be thankful to have a private chaplain, and to pay him the usual honorarium. It might be a comfortable home for some aged or invalid priest, but, even in this case, the girls should all attend mass in the parish church on Sundays and holidays, so that the priest would be benefited all the same. Asking the favor of an early reply,

"Yours very sincerely in J. C.,
"SISTER M. FRANCIS CLARE,
"*Mother-General of the Sisters of Peace.*"

This request was peremptorily refused.

PETITION FOR THE ESTABLISHMENT OF A HOUSE OF OUR ORDER IN WASHINGTON.

To HIS EMINENCE CARDINAL GIBBONS.

"YOUR EMINENCE, — We, the undersigned employees of this government beg most respectfully to call your attention to our condition. Many of us have neither father or mother, and are dependent upon the cheap boarding-houses of the capital city for a domicile, erroneously called home; in case of loss of position through ill health or dismissal, our lot is far from being a pleasant one. Hence we appeal to your eminence to grant permission to the Nun of Kenmare to establish a home here, wherein we could board and receive that attention and moral security which unfortunately is not our lot in the city boarding-house. We are well aware of the tender regard which your eminence has always shown for the working women of your diocese, and feel confident that you will not permit this opportunity to pass if you deem it prudent to grant your approval. We need not recall to you the various temptations which fall in the pathway of the Catholic workwomen of this capital city, as your priests, through the confessional, are fully aware of the dangers which beset the most virtuous of our class. Hence we most heartily pray that your eminence, occupying the exalted position which you now hold, will give our petition due consideration; and we promise you the daily prayers of thousands of honest workwomen, not only of Washing, but of the entire United States. We have the honor to subscribe ourselves, your most faithful and obedient children in Jesus Christ."

PART V.

General Letters. Copy of Letter addressed by the Sisters to Bishop Keane, now Rector of the new Roman Catholic University at Washington. Specimens of Attacks made on Sister M. Francis Clare by Priests.

REPORT OF THE COMMITTEE OF GENTLEMEN WHO ARRANGED FOR A PUBLIC LECTURE TO HELP THE WORK OF THE SISTERS OF PEACE, UNDER THE SUPERVISION OF THE NUN OF KENMARE.

THE work of the Sisters of Peace is one which appeals to all classes of society, for it has the singular advantage of benefiting both the employer and the employed.

It is a peaceful step toward the solution of the *labor problem*, and tends to promote harmony between those whose interests are one, and should always be considered together.

The Sisters of Peace devote their lives to the service of the working classes exclusively: —

1. They establish homes for girls working in shops or stores, but especially for living-out girls, who so much need the shelter of an Institution where they can remain while out of employment. The sisters also benefit employers, as they supply a most respectable

and efficient class of girls to those who apply to them for servants.

Immigrant girls of all nationalities are received and specially cared for by the sisters, and those who have no home or friends in this country can always find a home and a mother's care in our institutions.

II. We receive and train children for domestic service. This is a most important branch of our work, which we have not yet been able to carry out fully for want of funds. We believe that an intelligent, and especially a personal and domestic system of training children will fit them for their future life, either to be good "helps" in the family, or, what is no less important, to be good wives and mothers of a future generation.

III. An important branch of our institution is the opening of summer homes for working girls. Need we appeal for such a noble charity? Those girls who are day after day toiling in the store, the factory, the household, contributing to the pleasure, or adding to the wealth of their employers surely need some consideration at our hands.

They cannot afford to pay for "country board." They can, and do willingly pay what they can in our summer home -- but we find ourselves quite unable to carry out this great work without funds to erect a plain and suitable building. We have secured ground for this purpose on the Jersey side of the historic Hudson. Who will help us to erect the necessary buildings? We need dormitories separate (1) for girls, (2) for mothers with delicate children, (3) for children whose mothers cannot take them to the country, and for whom we shall make special arrangements under the care of the sisters.

We need help for those who are willing to help themselves as far as they can. God gives you the honor of being His Providence for them.

Since the opening of our institution in 78 Grand Street, Jersey City, we have provided situations for over 2,000 girls.

We have received into our institution 350 destitute children.

We have had in our summer home at Englewood, 1,500 girls, women, and children, for their summer holidays and rest.

We take the liberty to inclose you the following tickets for an object that cannot fail to appeal to the charity of all persons, irrespective of religion or nationality. The committee feels confident our appeal to you will not be in vain.

All remittances can be mailed to Wm. J. Greer, 98 Newark Avenue, Jersey City.

Wm. Symes, *Chairman. Financial Secretary*, John F. Kelly; *Corresponding Secretary*, Philip A. McGovern; *Treasurer*, Wm. J. Greer; *Committee*, Jas. E. Kelly, Edward Doyle, John Glaccum, Thos. Nugent, John McAusland, Abr'm Post.

THE WORK OF THE SISTERS OF PEACE.

The following letter, which was kindly published for me in the *Times* of June 16, 1884, will fully explain the work which we propose to do; and to which His Holiness Pope Leo XIII. has been pleased to give his Apostolic benediction.

THE DOMESTIC TRAINING OF GIRLS.

"*To the Editor of the 'Times':*

"SIR, — As your Rome correspondent has telegraphed the object for which I obtained the great privilege of a private audience from the Pope, I will ask you the favor of allowing me to say a few words about the work for which I have obtained the special approbation of the Holy See. My object is simple: it is to found a religious order devoted to the domestic training of girls. We propose not merely to train girls for domestic service, but for what I consider of equally great, if not of greater importance — to train girls for domestic life.

"The peace of the family and the prosperity of the family depend upon domestic life. Families are the units of nations. If you have peace and prosperity in the family, you have it in the nation. The subject is as vast as it is important, but I refrain from entering on it. A great deal of the political disturbance of the present day arises from the social condition of the so-called lower classes. I have no Utopian scheme for making millionaires of poor men. I have a long-formed, very ardent desire to train the children of the poor for domestic life in a practical way, and I believe if this plan were carried out carefully and extensively that it would do very much to make the houses of the poor more comfortable, and as a necessary consequence, to make the masses of the population more contented. A great deal of the education of the present day is, I believe, an honest and generous effort in the wrong direction. There are many men of large minds and great hearts who feel deeply for the social condition of the poor and middle classes. Naturally, they suppose that the higher the education the greater the social comfort. I respect the benevolent intentions of these gentlemen none the less because I know that their theory will not work. If you teach a girl all the known sciences, it will not necessarily teach her either to earn her living or to make her home happy. Further, as the sphere of woman's work advances in the middle classes, and as she enters more and more into duties and offices hitherto held by men, the necessity becomes greater that those who do the domestic work of the household should be specially and carefully trained for that special purpose.

"Theoretically, training is useless. I propose to train girls practically for domestic life, so that any girls so trained will be, I hope, equally fit for domestic service and for married life. I believe the great oversight in all training for girls has been that people do not realize the fact, that the girls of to-day will be the wives and mothers of to-morrow, and the girl of to-day is taught carefully everything except what will make her fit to be a good wife and a good mother.

"The difference between the training which I would propose and that of other institutions, where girls or young women are prepared for service, is this — girls will be trained, as far as possible, to act precisely as they would do in a private family, instead of being trained as they are in public institutions. The inmates of each training-house will be divided into groups or families of ten or twelve. Each group will have their own table, their own bedrooms, and separate places for cooking in the general kitchen. The object of thus dividing the girls is obvious. Each will learn the domestic duty for which she is most suited; one will act, for example, as cook for her group, and will thus learn how to cook, keep accounts, and provide for a small family. Another will have charge of the linen and needlework for her group; another will have charge of the washing. Thus each girl would be carefully trained for a certain work or for several kinds of domestic work, and as all this will be carried out under an experienced superioress, who will have charge of the group or family, the girls' training will prepare them practically for the occupations they are likely to have in their future life, whether in the service of others or in their own homes. Every girl in each group would be taught in turn to purchase the food or clothing necessary for the little family group to which she belongs. Thus a great object will be attained. It is well-known that girls who have been trained in large institutions are often useless when they return to their own humble homes, or when they are engaged as servants in private families. The cause of this is obvious — everything has been provided for them, everything has been arranged for them, they have had no personal responsibility, and when they are brought face to face with this responsibility they do not know how to act. Girls who are trained in large institutions find everything ready to their hands, and are, as a rule, all employed in one kind of labor; they are rarely occupied or taught the various minor details of household duty, which are so necessary to be practised by a good servant, and which are equally important for the peace and comfort of families where they are employed. Hence the necessity of having what may be called family training. Those girls who are to be trained for nurses will have special opportunities for learning their duties by being given the sole charge of two or three very young children, and it is also proposed, where such works may be desirable and in places where they may be a necessity, to have houses for friendless girls who are engaged in factories and other public works, and who are often exposed to most terrible danger. These houses may be made at least partly, if not altogether, self-supporting, as girls being in regular employment should pay a certain small fixed sum for their board and lodgings. These houses may be under the charge of a trustworthy matron, engaged by the sisters, and shall be constantly and closely superintended by them. Every effort shall be made to make these houses cheerful and attractive to the girls. Girls preparing to emigrate will also be received for particular training. This is another duty of great importance, as so many girls are placed in circumstances of serious temptation (to which too often many are found to yield) when they arrive in foreign countries without any previous training or preparation for the duties they may be required to undertake.

"The great importance of this work has been recognized very practically by the Holy See. I have been for more than twenty years a professed nun, and the permission now granted to me by Leo XIII. to leave the Order in which I was professed, and to found a new order for this purpose, is a sufficient evidence of this, as such dispensations are not given without grave consideration and very weighty reasons.

"I shall feel very grateful for any help which may be given me for this undertaking. Eventually, I expect to make it self-supporting. To commence as I should wish to do, will require a consid-

erable outlay. Donations may be made payable to the Right Rev. Dr. Bagshawe, St. Barnabas Cathedral, Nottingham, or to myself.
"Yours faithfully,
"SISTER MARY FRANCIS CLARE.
"St. Francis Xavier's Convent, Great Grimsby, Lincolnshire."

Post Office orders should be made payable to me on Nottingham Post Office.

[*From the* Times.]
"THE VATICAN, ROME, May 24th.

"The Pope gave a private audience this morning to the Reverend Mother Mary Francis Clare, who has come to Rome to obtain his special benediction for the institution which she has founded, at Nottingham, for the training of girls to domestic service, and the supply of lodgings to those working in factories at a distance from their homes."

[*From the* Standard.]
"Sunday night, May 25, 1884.

"The Pope has accorded a private audience to Mother Mary Clare, who came to implore a special benediction for an institution founded by her in the diocese of Nottingham, called the Sisters of Peace of St. Joseph, the object of which is to bring up girls to domestic service, to teach them various callings, to furnish lodgings to those who are employed far from their families, and lastly, to diffuse Catholic literature. The Pope expressed his high approval of the institution."

"A Roman correspondent says, the extracts from the *Journal de Rome* and *L'Osservatore Romano*, authoritative organs of the Vatican, show the very high estimation in which Mother Francis Clare is held by the Holy Father; how greatly he esteems her literary works, and how much interest he feels in 'her career and course of Apostolic work.' The Pope has been made acquainted, through some of the Roman Cardinals, with the life and labors of the 'celebrated religieuse.' The result was the merited compliment recorded by these papers, 'the Holy Father highly praised her zeal and her labors, and accorded to the good religieuse his special encouragement and benediction.'

"A higher tribute to any one could not be given, and Mother Francis Clare may rest satisfied that, by those who can appreciate her single-minded work, she has not been unappreciated or underestimated. The complimentary language of the head of the church is an honor which it is no exaggeration to say, no other woman, religious or otherwise, in Europe would receive from such a quarter. So keen an observer of men, so careful a dispenser of praise and honors, would not have spoken so if he had not felt, by his inquiries and judgment, fully justified in his exalted praise of this distinguished Irishwoman."

COPY OF LETTER ADDRESSED TO THE RIGHT REV. DR.
KEANE, NOW HEAD OF THE ROMAN CATHOLIC UNI-
VERSITY, BY THE SISTERS OF PEACE, ASKING HIM
TO WITHDRAW THE FALSE CHARGES WHICH HE
HAD MADE AGAINST THEIR SUPERIOR.

The following letter was sent to Bishop Keane, now rector of the new Roman Catholic University, by the sisters, while I was in the South this year (1888). They did this, hoping he would do something, for the sake of religion, to put an end to the reports which he himself had helped to circulate; they hoped that his position would render him even more anxious than others that this great discredit to the Roman Catholic church should be removed. A word from him would have done it. The letter was sent, but to this date no reply has been received. As I print this from a copy sent to me by the sisters, which has no date on it, I cannot give the exact time at which it was despatched. But I will let it speak for itself; I think the sisters did right to make the effort, though their good intentions have failed. They knew all I had suffered for years from these calumnies, and how useless all my efforts had been to have them removed. Indeed, they only seemed to increase with time. They knew also that all I had suffered had been caused by grief and anxiety from finding that even the approbation of the Holy Father counted for very little, with those who had their own reasons for opposing my work.

God knows how dear the sisters are to me, and I know well how they love me. They were the eyewitnesses of my hopeless struggles against injustice, and their hearts bled for me none the less that they were powerless to help me except by their prayers.

I have treasured, and shall always treasure, their letters of fondest sympathy when I went to Dublin, only to find that it was hopeless to persevere at Knock, as the Archbishop of Tuam, instead of consulting them, would only listen to the very people who cared for nothing but their own interests. If he had listened to the sisters and not to idle gossip, it would have been more for his own credit, and he might still have in his diocese a work which he said "was admirable, and worthy of a religious soul; which had for its object to save souls that might otherwise have been lost forever."

I have spoken of the sisters in this book as little as possible, because I do not want to give any excuse to those who I know too well would gladly avail themselves of it, to prevent them from carrying out their work. I have kept them ignorant of where I have been and of what I have done, as far as possible, not because I do not love them, but because I do love them and desire their work to prosper. I know they will not misunderstand me, I know that they will be even more anxious to keep up the good work in my absence, I know that what I taught them of the sister's life will be observed as strictly as it has been through all our troubles, and I believe when the record of these sisters' lives is made manifest at the last day, those who have obliged me to leave them will be filled with shame and regret.

"CONVENT OF THE SISTERS OF PEACE,
JERSEY CITY, N. J.

"MY LORD, — Our Mother General, most generally known as the Nun of Kenmare, was sent by our bishop, the Right Rev. W. M. Wigger, to Baltimore and other places South, in March, 1886, for the purpose of seeing several bishops, partly to try and interest them in the establishment of a home for the Catholic blind, and partly hoping that, by a personal interview, she might be able to satisfy them, by the documents which she brought with her from Rome, that the many and cruel slanders which have been circulated about her were not only false, but absolutely without any foundation whatever, and were originated by persons who dislike her great zeal for souls, and her wonderful energy in good works.

"In this mission she failed, not from want of proof of the divine character of her mission, and of the full approval of it by the Holy See, but because the ecclesiastics to whom she applied preferred to believe scandals which did not exist, and would not accept the denial of them by the Holy Father and Propaganda.

"Now, my lord, you were one of the bishops who have not only spoken but written what is most scandalous and calumnious of our beloved superior, and we have the evidence in your own handwriting. You, with others, have helped to deprive the Catholic church of the services, and to break the loving and tender heart of one of the truest and most devoted of God's spouses.

"We understand that your lordship is advanced to a most distinguished position in the Catholic church of America, a position which places in your hands the future of the Catholic church of America. As you will have the formation of the characters of the future priests, we suppose that you will teach them that justice to poor as well as to rich, and that reparation for wrong done, is as much the duty of the priest as of the layman.

"I inclose a copy of your letter in which you have brought these scandalous charges against our superior. Your present position makes it most important, both for yourself and for us, that they should be fully and publicly retracted. I may add that the circulation of such scandals about our superior is also a grave injury to the Holy Father, as people naturally ask, how is it that this sister is so spoken of by ecclesiastics when the Holy Father has granted to her the extraordinary favor of being foundress of our new order? Why should an American bishop demand that 'she should go back to her convent in Ireland,' when the Holy Father has authorized her to leave it for a new and most important work? Why should she be treated with suspicion and contempt when Propaganda has officially declared that 'she is worthy of the trust and confidence of all who may place themselves under her guidance?' The original of this document is in the possession of our English ecclesiastical superior, the Right Rev. G. W. Bagshawe, of Nottingham. What are her 'many plans?' We who have been her spiritual children for years, are aware of only one plan, it has been to work for God's poor. When and where has she ever failed in obedience to ecclesiastical authority? It is easy to invent and circulate reports, but a time may come when something more than an assertion will be demanded from those who speak such reports. Suppose that the whole miserable story of our Mother's treatment by ecclesiastics in America were put before the public, and your lordship will be pleased to remember we have written proof, what would be said? Are priests in this new Catholic university to be educated to be honest men, or as men who will not pay ordinary respect to truth and justice and to the decisions of the Holy See? When did our Mother go 'from one part of the world to another' without the permission of her bishop? Even this Fall, when several eminent doctors declared her life depended on her spending the winter in the South, it was with great difficulty that we could induce her to go, and it was only when our bishop said that he wished her to do so, that she consented.

"Your lordship would not have been troubled with this letter, but we feel the time has come when it is our duty to claim recognition and respect for the Holy Father's decision. Why should your lordship or other American bishops refuse our mother 'sympathy?' Surely, you should have the deepest sympathy for one who has so long suffered in silence when she might, at any moment, clear herself of all blame by publishing the documents in her possession when she has refrained from doing so simply because the public discredit would fall, and fall justly, on those very ecclesiastics who have cared so little for her unmerited sufferings, and why should it not? Within the last two years we have been offered ten good foundations by priests in different parts of America, and their respective bishops have at once refused to allow our order to spread, influenced by false reports such as those in your letter. Protestants are amazed when they find this to be the case. Protestant institutions, seaside homes etc, are being established all over the country for working-girls, and even in the very places where we have been refused permission to establish homes blest by the Holy Father. These homes are filled with and supported by Catholic girls, as we can prove.

"We are well aware that there is in America one ecclesiastic whose prejudices against our mother-general are so strong that even the benediction and authority of the Holy Father has no weight with him, and it would be amusing if it was not very sad to see how some Catholic authorities make so much of the least word from Rome when it is in their favor, and treat with utter contempt such as are against their prejudices, but is this true loyalty to the Holy See? This ecclesiastic has, we know, considerable power over all the other bishops, but, my lord, surely each bishop has a conscience of his own and a duty of his own to the Holy See.

"We shall be most happy, with the permission of our bishop, to go to Washington and bring the original document of the Holy Father's founding our order, for the information of the bishops assembled at the laying the foundation of the Catholic university.

"We can ourselves, or any other of our sisters who are long professed under our dear mother's care, give personal evidence as to the good she has done for souls and the forbearance with which she has borne persistent calumny.

"We trust for the sake of the Catholic faith, and for your lordship's own easement of conscience, that you will obtain from all the bishops a public denial of the charges made against her. I am, my lord,

"Yours very respectfully,
"MOTHER M. EVANGELISTA, *Mother Provincial*.
"SISTER M. IGNATIUS, *Local Superior*."

SISTER MARY FRANCIS CLARE AND THE VENERABLE ARCHDEACON CAVANAGH.

308 East Broadway New York, March 31, 1884.
To the Editor of the 'Tuam Herald.'

"Sir,—I request you will have the goodness and fairness to published the enclosed copy of a letter I sent to Archdeacon Cavanagh, P. P., Knock. It speaks for itself.
"Yours faithfully,
"James Rogers."

203 East Broadway, New York, March 21, 1884.

"Very Rev. and deár Sir,—So mortifying to me is the deplorable treatment to which Rev. Mother M. Francis Clare has been subjected, and the provokingly false reports circulated, evidently to injure her reputation, that I feel myself obliged to communicate with you."

"First, as to the assertion that 'she ran away from Knock, deserting her duties; that she robbed the convent, taking with her the contributions sent solely for Knock to be controlled by you and not by her.' I most emphatically wish to inform you that all such moneys sent from here were sent to *her* as testimony of the esteem and affection in which she is held for her efforts and services in behalf of the Irish poor and oppressed, and in the interest of religion and nationality; such moneys to be distributed by her in the relief and education of the Irish poor, or otherwise in the interests of religion and charity as she might think fit. If testimony, by most respectable persons in America, in proof of this assertion, by you will be required, I can easily send it. It is sufficient to satisfy the public and all concerned, except of course her persecutors and calumniators, whom nothing would satisfy except her persecution, even to exile and, as it would seem, at any cost, even at the cost of her life. As to the conspir acy, so determined, so scandalous, and so un-Catholic, which was planned against her, I will here avoid alluding to it in detail, merely remarking as regards its malice against the welfare of Catholicity in Ireland, but more particularly, against the poor, despised, oppressed, and exterminated Catholics around Knock, that it might be naturally alleged by any Irishman or Irishwoman who has preserved the faith of St. Patrick and St. Bridget, that its conception was indeed infernal. But I will say in conclusion that unless reparation be made both for the wrongs and the scandalously lying reports perpetrated, a full and true account shall be given to the public, indeed to the world, so that all may be in possession of the truth and may judge for themselves as to the motives. Merciful God! How is it that by a sense of duty and justice I find myself compelled to write such a letter as this, especially to you. I could not indeed, as a Catholic trust to my accurate memory, nor to my reason, as regards the shocking doings at Knock while I was there last July to September, were it not that other strangers who happened also to be there, including priests, partly learned of these doings also.

"I remain, very rev. and dear sir,
"Your most obedient servant,
"JAMES ROGERS.

"VENERABLE ARCHDEACON CAVANAGH, P.P., Knock, Ireland."

I give below some specimens of the style of correspondence with which I was constantly annoyed by priests.

I may give an extract from a letter addressed to me by a priest of the diocese of Cleveland, O., as a sample of the impertinent interference to which I have been constantly subject from priests. It is of course useless for me to ask protection from their bishops. Indeed, these attacks would not have been made, unless the priest knew that he was safe, and would have ecclesiastical approbation in his unmanly course. But how sad it is for the Catholic church that priests should be allowed to act in this way unreproved, if not encouraged! The document is so much in the style of Father Angus, and is written in the same low tone, that if he had been in this country I would have supposed he had a share in the composition. I had been writing a series of letters for the New York Sun, and this had excited this poor priest's mind. He writes: "Let me give you a bit of advice: keep within the quiet recess of your cloister, or leave the cloister and then go before the public," and so on for page after page. The poor priest only showed his ignorance, as we have no cloister, and his advice was only applicable to inclosed nuns, and as I have shown, the Kenmare sisters, who were originally a cloistered order, had only a nominal inclosure. The fact of my engaging in literary work is the grievance with these half-educated priests.

After giving me a great deal of low abuse, he informs me if I "write less, my final account will be less difficult to render." This is amusing, considering how many approbations of my literary work I have had from the Holy See, but such approbations do not count with persons of his class. Having settled my "final account," to his own entire satisfaction, he concludes: " I shall write to your bishop, if this note be without its intended effect," whether this priest fulfilled his threat or not I do not know, or whether he consulted his own bishop.

I think a letter like this will show something of the kind of working which must have made the Inquisition such a terror when it had power. It would have been so easy for a priest to whom any one was obnoxious, to occupy himself in persistent attacks on their character or orthodoxy, and such accusers of the brethren always pose as very pious and very zealous. Even if the bishop under whose jurisdiction their unfortunate victims lived, was not prejudiced against them, he might eventually become so by constant irritation, and people of this low moral tone would have no scruple in keeping up an agitation till their end was accomplished.

The following is a specimen of Father Angus's style of attack. In order to appreciate properly the injury to religion such persons can do when allowed by their bishops to annoy any person to whom they have taken a dislike, it should be remembered that all these attacks were published in Protestant papers, and to know how high party and religious feeling goes in that country. It is a sad specimen of the charity of the priests of the church into which these Protestants are so urgently invited to enter. No wonder that England has not yet been converted to this faith.

" Besides patronizing ex-Fenians and ticket-of-leave convicts, Archbishop Crobs (*sic*) has a pet nun. This nun is by birth a lady, but long residence among persons who think killing no murder, and robbery no crime, has reduced her to a semi-savage condition."

Suppose that any Protestant clergyman had been guilty of such an outrage as to send a paragraph like this to the press about any Roman Catholic lady, and to persist in this style of attack, what an outcry there would be on the part of the Roman Catholic press and priests.

Here is another specimen of priestly amenities, and of the style of attacks made on me by Roman Catholic priests. The writer has at least the honesty to sign his name to his attack; if he only had the charity to ask if these charges were true before he made them, it would have been so much better for religion and for his sacred character. He says, "Will any one at this late day number among claimants for charity that religious Pooh-Bah-political-economist (*sic*) hagiographer, young girls' adviser, pamphleter, mistress of novices, historian, beggar, and nun, who for twenty years and more, both in Ireland and America, has been an irrepressible begging nuisance? Will any one in his right mind give her more money to squander, after the monument of folly she has left at Knock?"

Then after a long attack on "church beggars" who set the church at defiance, he concludes his charge, and yet one-half hour's careful inquiry would have informed him who was to blame for "the monument of folly," at Knock."

CARE ON MY PART NOT TO MAKE ANY EXPOSURE OF THE WAY I WAS TREATED BY ECCLESIASTICS.

Before going to Rome, I wrote a letter to the press. I was obliged to say that I had left Knock, but I merely said that I was obliged to do so under circumstances to which I would not allude farther. I little thought how my care not to blame those whom I might most justly have blamed would be repaid. Before I came to America, I was told that I was likely to meet opposition from some section of the press. In August, 1884, a friend wrote to me: "Much dissatisfaction exists amongst those in America who have helped you about Knock. They are asking: Will you return to Knock? Will you complete the building? Priests, as well as others, have commented unfavorably on you. Such criticisms, I need not say, are owing to ignorance of the causes which caused you to leave." And still knowing all this I was silent, hoping that the decision of the Holy Father would silence every complaint. "I will, if you give me permission, set you right before the public. A correct statement of the persecutions you were subject to could not but excite for you the sympathies of the Irish in America." And yet I would not allow a word to be said. How little I could have suspected, while I kept silence, that those who were anxious to prevent the success of my work, were all the time talking and writing against me, and the same gentleman writes later, "the work you effected in three short months at Knock was marvellous, and would be incredible to me if I had not seen it." In another letter he says: "There are many here who think that a petition should be sent to

Propaganda to demand the restoration of the funds subscribed for Knock, so that you might carry out the work elsewhere. Some of the so-called patriots I know did not like you. Thèy were jealous of your success, and of the large funds you were getting. One of these is —— he is the editor of ——, he is suspected by all who know his true character. Another is the editor of the New York ——, who, though he is the editor of a leading Catholic paper, and high in ecclesiastical confidence, is a notorious drunkard. He says that he has had a large correspondence from Ireland all against you."

The following will show how the bishops themselves proposed a plan very similar to mine to help emigrants; yet they would not allow it when it was proposed by me.

Lady Strangford's idea was mine, to prepare people for emigration.

THE BISHOP OF SALFORD ON EMIGRATION. — At a meeting at Manchester, of the Executive Committee of the Colonial Emigration Society, the following letter from the Bishop of Salford was read: 'As I shall be unable to attend the meeting, I write to urge the extreme importance of collecting from the colonies definite and satisfactory information as to the actual prospects in different localities for emigrants. General statements can be got in abundance — statements diametrically opposite to one another from the same colony. They are most unsatisfactory to those interested in emigration and to the emigrants themselves. They are usually mischievous and misleading. The need is information from respectable and trustworthy persons settled in various parts of a colony, stating the prospects of work which exist for a certain number of new hands; the particular difficulties they would have to encounter; the price of living, and the prospect of an increasing demand for labor. The kind of hands that are most needed should be specified, and the chances there may be of remunerative employment for women. Many emigration societies seem to make it their chief business to ship off as many people as they can, careless of the consequences abroad. The kind of society I wish to see is one that will carefully deal with individuals — with individuals in the colonies, whether employers of labor or not, and individuals at home, who shall be put into direct relations with persons who will be interested in them when they reach the district to which they may be recommended to go. I have myself seen so much of the suffering caused by wholesale emigration both in South and North America, that I feel strongly the urgent need of a nice, painstaking, and conscientious society that will deal with men as individual units, and will act towards them as prudent parents act by their own children when they arrange for them to quit the mother country.

Miss Faithfull observed that the bishop had indicated the very course hitherto pursued by the Colonial Emigration Society, and referred to a letter from the Vice-President, Lady Strangford, urging the Manchester Committee "to send one well-chosen, well-provided, well-trained emigrant, rather than a score of useless people."

PART VI.

The Troubled Life of the Foundress of the Sisters of Notre Dame.

THE TROUBLED LIFE OF THE FOUNDRESS OF THE SISTERS OF NOTRE DAME.

THE "Life of Mother Julia," the foundress of the order of Sisters of Notre Dame, is an excellent example of the history of the founders of religious orders in the Roman Catholic church. How little Protestants who speak in rapt admiration of the work of these sisters know of the way in which they are treated and persecuted by their ecclesiastical superiors.

It is a curious and an interesting episode in ecclesiastical history, if it is not a very edifying one. When religious orders are well established, not because of ecclesiastical help, but in spite of ecclesiastical opposition, bishops take great credit to themselves, and point to these institutions proudly, as an evidence of the sanctity and the great good to mankind of the Roman Catholic church. They are, in fact, evidences of the triumph of good over evil, and of the indomitable energy of the founders in persevering under the most discouraging circumstances.

The bishops identify themselves with the church and

claim all the honor and glory of success. The infallible "we" covers a multitude of sins, and crowns the episcopacy with a fictitious halo of sanctity. The fact is, that if the inside history of Roman Catholic religious houses was known it would be seen how very little ecclesiastics had to do with their success or encouragement.

I know these will be considered startling assertions, but the question is, are they true or false? — the proof is easily attainable. Naturally, there is a very great difficulty at getting at facts under such circumstances, as it is practically contrary to ecclesiastical rule to mention anything that is discreditable to religious superiors; still facts do come out sometimes, and the facts which do come out, evidently show how much remains concealed.

Let us take a case before the public well in point on this subject. Every one knows what the penalty was the Rev. Father Curran had to pay because he told the truth publicly about Vicar-General Donnelly's treatment of Dr. McGlynn. When ordered to do penance for speaking out, he did the penance, but he did not deny the fact. Imagine punishing a man for simply telling the truth. No priest and no sister dare to tell the truth frankly about any injustice practised by a bishop. And what is the consequence? evil is concealed, but it is not destroyed; the keen knife that would cut open the sore and let it run and heal would be infinitely better; but this cannot be done so long as it is considered "a sin against the church" to say one word of the sins of the children of the church. It would be quite as true to say it was a sin against the government to denounce evil.

The lives of the saints, whether founders of religious orders or otherwise, are always carefully revised and re-revised by ecclesiastical authority; I doubt if a single honest life of a saint has ever been written, and I remember seeing regret expressed by an English Catholic author on this subject. How much better and how much more edifying it would be to tell the whole truth.

The "Life of Mother Julia" the foundress of the order of the Sisters of Notre Dame, is a very remarkable volume; how so much truth has come to be told I do not know, but her life history is one long record of persecution and opposition on the part of the authorities of that very church which now applauds her and her sisters with such warmth and fervor.

One wonders how any one could have had the heart to treat her as she was treated, when her sole object was to work for the good of the poor. She went from place to place trying to please those who could only be pleased by seeing her driven away, and her work too often was begun only to be abandoned.

No doubt her life was like the life of our Lord, but that did not make it less suffering to herself, or more creditable to those who made her suffer. We are told in her biography that the longest time she was ever in one place was three months.

Again and again we find the most unreasoning and unmeaning opposition to her work, and the poor little souls she was trying to save left to perish. Certainly, there was terrible responsibility somewhere for the hindrance of good works.

In one letter, writing to her spiritual children, she says, —

"'The devil of course places every obstacle in our way." It seems to me that it was some very human devils who were guilty. In one of her frequent journeys she went to Flanders to endeavor to spread her order — she was asked to do this by a priest who offered to accompany her, but this was at once opposed by the confessor of the house, a distinguished ecclesiastic, and the bishop's favorite, who wished to thrust his own private views at all hazards on the house."

"This opposition was only the first link in a long chain of annoyances which God made use of for his own designs." "*Life of Mother Julia,*" p. 84.

It is amusing to see the way in which the opposition of ignorant or malicious persons is spoken of as if it was "the design of God." These are certainly not the designs of God, but they may be overruled by him for his greater glory ; and it is better to call things by their plain names ; opposition to good is sin, no matter by whom it may be ·accomplished. We have no right to compliment the creature at the expense of the creator.

When sin is approved, or treated delicately because the guilty person is in a position of influence or power, it does not lessen the guilt of the actor or of those who condone the action. It would be necessary to read the "Life of Mother Julia" from end to end to know her sufferings, all of which were caused by priests. The life tells so much honest truth that it is a marvel it has not found a place on the Index long since. At page 106 we read, —

"She also took advantage of the opportunity to consult Father Leblanc on several points respecting the internal affairs of the community, about which their confessor did not always agree with the Rev. Father Varin. God permitted this to be so, for the sanctification of his faithful servant. In fact, nothing was more painful to her than the opposition she was obliged to manifest to the wishes of those whom faith made her regard as the servants of God upon earth. No other cross had ever weighed so heavily on her soul. And it seemed as if their confessor had been appointed expressly to make her drink this chalice of bitterness to the very dregs. He only labored to guide the institute in another path from that originally marked out for it. He did not wish any mother-general, or any relation of the secondary houses with the mother house or any visits from the first superior, and his efforts aimed constantly at the removal of the foundress.

"Unfortunately, this ecclesiastic was of a difficult, scheming disposition. . . and, under the pretext of perfecting the work of another, he made innovations that tended to entirely pervert the primitive object of these institutions. He changed the constitutions; Mother Barat was sent into the country, and Mother Julia denounced to the episcopal authority as incapable of governing. Consequently, she was ordered to give up her charge, and, soon after, to leave the diocese."

And what was the cause of all this persecution? Why was she to leave the diocese? Why was she to leave her God-given position as foundress of the order? Was she guilty of any crime? Had she committed any act of injustice? It is sad reading; how much good she could have done in those months in which she was deprived of the very physical power to rule, by the harassing anxiety and cares caused by the opponents of her work? How much time was occupied in correspondence, and in consultation, and in trying to please those who were determined not to be pleased, which might have been spent in earnest work for God and souls.

Yet, in spite of all, her order has succeeded and prospered, and who will be most honored in connection with it on the last day? Those who helped and comforted the foundress in her weary work, for weary it was, even at the times when she had most exterior help, or those who opposed, injured, or discouraged it?

On one occasion she wrote to the sisters, (*page* 109)

"I feel like going all over the world to snatch these poor young creatures from the adversary, and teach them the value of the soul."

This was her work, and this was the work which so many bishops were so anxious to prevent her from doing. The Bishop of Amiens having treated Mother Julia with great injustice, sent his own account of what had passed to the Bishop of Namur. When she presented herself at the bishop's residence, he received her coldly and said he did not invite her, and began to tell her how people who had been famous for sanctity had been damned for disobedience, with other cheerful information, and blamed her for coming without informing him of her intention. This was not true, as he found subsequently, but what did it matter? One bishop was desirous of pleasing the other, and Mother Julia was the victim.

Eventually, the bishop found that he had wronged Mother Julia, but he does not seem to have had the

grace to make any reparation. Her biographer says, —
" With a delicate conscience, she was obliged to resist respectable authority and constantly needed for her peace of mind a counterpoise of greater weight which would clearly manifest the will of God, and sustain the work to which she had consecrated her property and her life."

An attempt was then made to make trouble between herself and the sisters. They were told that Mother Julia's course was one of illusion and disobedience; but these attempts were entirely unsuccessful, as the sisters always remained devoted to her.

PART VII.

Extracts from Letters from the Sisters to Sister M. Francis Clare.

LETTERS of sympathy from the sisters of England while I was ill in Washington:

During my severe illness at Washington I received the following letter from one of the sisters in England, who knew perhaps more than any other all I had suffered from hindrances to my work and deliberate calumny:

"CONVENT OF THE SACRED HEART,
NOTTINGHAM, May 7, 1886.

" DEAREST REVEREND MOTHER, — We are in a most anxious state of mind, having just received a letter from Mr. F—— that you are in a hospital in Washington and dangerously ill. I might easily know that something serious was the matter, you could not bear up any longer. Oh, cruel, cruel apostles of to-day, how unlike to the spirit of the first apostles! If there is anything objectionable in the Order of Peace, why not say so, and have it made right, and if there is not, why do they not help a work that has the authority of the Holy See, and has for its sole object the glory of

God and the salvation of souls? Mr. F—— tells us you have a good doctor that is a consolation; but Mother I do not expect that you will ever be free from suffering in this life. The sisters are all very grieved for your suffering. You will be comforted to get a line of sympathy from each of your loving children on this side. I fear to tell the poor sisters in Grimsby, they will be so grieved I will wait until I hear again. Sister A—— is better. Ever your loving child,

"Ev."

Extracts from some letters written to me by the sisters when I was obliged to go to Dublin in November, 1883, and was so hopeless of getting the Archbishop of Tuam to do us justice.

Sister M—— writes,—

"MY OWN DEAREST REV. MOTHER,— Alas what can I say to comfort your sad heart. We can only cry out with Jesus, abandoned on the cross, 'My God, My God, why hast thou forsaken me?' It is the saddest of all to think that we are not able in any way to alleviate your heavy sorrows, my own dearest mother. We are all so thankful to Father Gaffney for all his great kindness to you."

Sister M—— R—— writes,—

"It is impossible for you to be well, when you have so much to suffer. Dearest mother, do not be uneasy about us, we are doing our best. We had the life of St. Gertrude read at dinner to-day. It is very cold. I hope the frost will not injure your throat. I cannot tell you how grieved we were when we heard of your serious illness. I beg of you not to be the least uneasy about us. You would be comforted if you saw how well each sister is performing her duty, as if nothing had occurred to cause us pain, and you know all that we are suffering. Sister M—— J—— is as prudent as if she had been a sister for twenty years, and Sister

M—— E—— is as busy as ever in the schools; every observance is kept as regularly as if you were here."

The sisters knew well that they could tell me nothing that would give me so much pleasure as this. I worked so long and earnestly to teach them to love regular religious observance.

Another sister writes, —

"Do not be anxious about us, dearest reverend mother. Each individual sister performs her regular duties with the greatest possible exactness, and all your councils are and shall be carried out to the letter, and the spirit of the letter." The sister then tells me how the school has been injured by an outbreak of measles, knowing that next to the perfection of the sisters, this was nearest to my heart.

When I have read these dear letters, I have thought how often and how falsely the charge of being indifferent to the sisters' perfection in the religious life was brought against me, and believed by those who had an object in believing it. The sisters' letters, and still more their lives, are the best evidence of the teaching which they received.

In a letter dated Nov. 18, 1883, in reply to one of mine in which I had to tell the sisters how little hope there seemed of the Archbishop of Tuam doing us any justice, Sister M—— E—— writes, —

"MY OWN DEAREST MOTHER, — With a breaking heart we all read over Sister J——'s letter this morning; Oh, good God, was there ever, since our divine Lord, who trod the winepress alone, any suffering or abandonment like that which you now endure. Would to God that my life, accompanied by every kind of suffering, would be acceptable to the Divine Majesty, and spare you, dearest mother, to accomplish his own work. I have already made the offering before the tabernacle, if it is His divine will, I can say no more.

"You know all we feel. We shall not sleep much tonight. Surely the archbishop, knowing the great charge intrusted to him, will remember the account he will have to render at the great tribunal. Oh dear and de-deserted mother, try and keep up, for the sake of the poor faithful youth of Ireland. Surely our good God will not take you away from them in, I might say, the beginning of your labors. I am, my own dear and suffering mother,

"Your devoted and afflicted child
"Sister M—— E——."

It will be seen from these letters how dear this work at Knock was to us all.

I shall only add here two letters from Father Gaffney, out of many, showing his interest in our work, and his sympathy in our trials. These letters were both written to me after I had got the archbishop's consent to go to England to consult Cardinal Manning.

"ST. FRANCIS XAVIER'S, DUBLIN,
"Dec. 13, 1883.

"I was very glad to hear from you this morning as I was very anxious to know how you were getting on amidst the troubled waters with which you are surrounded, for surely you are at present on a more tempestuous sea than when you were crossing the stormy channel a few days ago.

"I trust that your courage and prudence, and above all, the protecting hand of God, will bring you safely through all your difficulties. I am writing by this post to Sister Mary Joseph at Knock, to encourage and console them for your absence. Your faithful children at Knock are very good, and deserve great praise and consideration. I hope soon to hear that the horizon is clearing before you, and that yet all will be bright and glorious sunshine.

"Ever yours very sincerely in Christ,
"J. GAFFNEY, S. J."

The following letter from the same dear friend who had been the eyewitness of our trials and difficulties at Knock, and, I may add, of the virtues and religious observances of the sisters, was written a few days later when I was able to give him the good news that we had found a shelter and friends in England.

" ST. FRANCIS XAVIER'S, DUBLIN,
" Dec. 20, 1883.

"DEAR REV. MOTHER, — How wonderful are the ways of God was my first thought on reading your letter this morning, and the inclosed letters which it contained, and how different often are his thoughts from ours. The prospect which these letters open out before my imagination are truly grand and magnificent."

After writing of some private affairs of the sisters, he concludes, —

"You will read with pleasure the inclosed from Sister M—— J——; what a devoted little community you have! I shall be very happy to hear soon and often from you. Yours faithfully in Christ,
" J. GAFFNEY, S. J."

" ST. FRANCIS XAVIER'S, UPPER GARDINER STREET,
DUBLIN, April 5, 1884.

"DEAR REV. MOTHER, — Your letter of last Monday, which I received yesterday evening, has given me great pleasure, as you may well understand, and I lose no time in writing to compliment you most sincerely on the great success of your visit to the Eternal city. This will be a bright page in your eventful and chequered life; you will be able now to go cheerfully to work, and the great troubles you have gone through will soon be forgotten, or will only serve to make you more confident in the protection of heaven. You have already achieved a good deal, but there remains still a good deal to be done; the foundations are now laid,

APPENDIX.

but the building is to be raised, and I trust that the Order of Peace will before long become well known, and bear glorious fruits worthy of the happy title and name under which it appears before the world. With many others I shall watch with the deepest interest the progress of this new promising child of the Church.

"What happy and holy memories will be treasured up by the successful visit to Rome.

"With best wishes and most frequent prayers for your safe return and great success.

"Yours very faithfully,
"J. GAFFNEY, S. J."

The following letter will show how necessary our work was for English Roman Catholics.

"130 WILSON STREET, ST. HELEN'S, LANCASHIRE,
"Sept. 3, 1884.
"SISTER MARY FRANCIS CLARE:

"DEAR MADAM, — Allow me, with all due deference and respect, to congratulate you upon your arrival here in England. You are the very lady we want to help us in this land of heresy. Protestantism and Infidelity this last three hundred years have been pretty successful in driving our Catholic people to the lowest depths of misery and degradation, by depriving us of our useful guides for the laity: the monks, and the nuns.

"I see your new order in the church proposes to teach young women household duties; the very thing they want. My experience of five years' visiting among our people, by order of the Jesuit Fathers of St. Helens, convinces me you are taking the bull by the horns, so to speak, in endeavoring to teach our Catholic young women their household duties. Many a house I have visited, and I have seen dinners prepared for men who have to work before red-hot furnaces, and breathing impure air from morning until night, and these said dinners were only fit to be given to the brute creation. The result of this bad cooking is, the men want strength to follow their employment, the food they get is insufficient, and they have recourse to drink; and the pay-days in place of going home, or into a refreshment room to have some dinner or a cup of coffee, it is into the public house they go, and having drink upon an empty stomach, they are drunk and incapable, directly fall into the hands of the police, and get fined very often and very heavily.

"Dear sister, I am giving you a true statement of what is constantly occurring among a Catholic population of 20,000 people. Well, it is quite time some charitably-disposed individual or individuals, under the patronage of the holy church, should come to help and to guide our poor Catholic young women; for by a young man getting an ignorant wife, he becomes a careless Catholic, and unless he is very careful he will fall into the snares of infidelity; for it is my firm conviction, the devil is more busy, ten thousand times, with Catholics than he is with Protestants, alias Infidels.

"I am thankful to Almighty God and his Blessed Mother, you have come into England to found a really useful class of women. I sincerely hope you may have branch houses in Manchester, Liverpool, Birmingham, London, Edinburgh, Glasgow, and Dublin, by the end of ten years, for these are some of the principal cities of the kingdom which is crying out for help."

[As the signature to this letter might bring the writer into trouble, I do not append it. I may say, however, it is only one of many letters which I have received, on the same subject. The *people* have always wished for our work. It has been opposed and discouraged only by the bishops.]

PAPER READ AT THE SOCIAL SCIENCE CONGRESS, ON EMIGRATION.

A meeting of the Social Science Congress was held in Dublin in 1881, at which a paper which I wrote, called, "Education as a Preparation for Emigration," was read by Dr. Mapother, President of the Royal College of Surgeons. As this paper is far too long to publish here, I only allude to it to show that I have been actively interested in the question of emigration for many years. In this paper I advocated the establishment of special institutions in Ireland, to prepare girls for emigration. I am sorry to say that those ecclesiastics who were opposed to my work found an ingenious method of injuring it, and the same plan was tried in New York, showing how truly the Irish are too often their own worst enemies. It was suggested that the girls did not want any teaching, that they had got on very well without it for years, and it was made appear as if I was lowering the character of the Irish people by even suggesting that they needed any teaching. This style of talking was not without its effect on those who needed teaching most. Certainly, it is a credit to the many Irish girls that have come to this country, that they have done so well under so many disadvantages, but what of the thousands who have been lost, and who might have been saved, or who have not done so well? I give here a brief extract from my address,—

"To give our people a general knowledge of the agricultural and commercial conditions of lands where emigrants are most needed, and will be most welcome, would be a most important element in their course of study, so that we may no longer find that kind of haphazard emigration which is indicated when you ask a boy or girl why they are leaving their native land, and get the reply, 'to better myself,' when the speaker has not the least idea of how the "bettering" is to be accomplished. I do not touch here on the all-important point of protection for girls going to a distant land. During the last 28 years, 2,637,000 of our people have left Ireland for other shores. How many of these men and women, boys, and girls, have sunk down by the wayside in despair, or sunk down into the slums of great cities living a miserable existence, can only be known by those who have taken a practical interest in emigrants, or had exceptional means of ascertaining their state in their new homes. How much of this evil might have been averted if these emigrants had had the benefits of advice and a guiding hand — if they had gone with a special object to a special place, instead of going in a 'happy-go-lucky' fashion, too often a most unlucky one."

APPENDIX.

REPORT OF PUBLIC MEETING AT NOTTINGHAM.

In September, 1884, Bishop Bagshawe held a public meeting at Nottingham, which was attended by all the neighboring clergy. His object was the kind one of trying to place the facts of my life before the public, so that the malicious reports which had been in circulation should have been silenced for ever. But while there were priests or laymen who really were determined to circulate statements which they knew perfectly well to be false, any effort to silence them was mere waste of time; still it was difficult for an honorable man like Bishop Bagshawe to realize that there could be such people, especially in the Roman Catholic church, where the sin of detraction is so strongly denounced, and where lying and slandering is at least condemned by precept.

Rev. Mother Mary Francis Clare — A Welcome to Nottingham — Great Demonstrations — Important Speeches.

" On Tuesday evening, in the large hall of the Nottingham Mechanics' Institute, a demonstration of welcome to the Nun of Kenmare, Sister Mary Francis Clare, took place on the occasion of her coming to Nottingham to found, with the approbation of his Holiness the Pope, a new Order of Peace, for the training of servants and the teaching of school children, and to establish a convalescent home, and a home for factory girls. The Lord Bishop of Nottingham, Right Rev. Dr. Bagshawe, presided, supported by Very Rev. Canons Monaghan and Douglass, Very Rev. Father Richmond (President of Ratcliffe College), and Rev. Fathers Baigent, Garvey, Burns, Palmer, Hogan, Elkins, H. Sabela, P. Sabela, Opbroeck, Golden, McDonald, Fryer, Hawkins, O'Callaghan (Manchester).

Canon Monaghan, who was received with applause, read the following, —

Address to the Reverend Mother Mary Francis Clare.

" HONORED SISTER IN CHRIST, — We, the undersigned, on behalf of a public meeting of the Catholics of Nottingham, assembled in the large hall of the Mechanics' Institute, beg leave to present to you an address of welcome to our town.

" We have heard that you have lately been authorized, with the sanction and blessing of our Holy Father, Pope Leo XIII, to exchange the mode of life which you have hitherto led in holy religion, for the yet more excellent and glorious work of co-operating in the foundation of a new religious order, greatly needed in the present time. We learn with pleasure that, with that high sanction and blessing, you have again consecrated your life to God, in that new order, that you may there gather together and train in the spiritual life a multitude of religious children, of whom you have now the charge, and whom God will give you.

The remainder of this address is too long to insert here. It consists principally of references to work done in Ireland by the Nun of Kenmare, in the famine, to her literary work, and to the many approbations which she has received from the Holy See. By a happy coincidence, a priest happened to be passing through Nottingham who had been an eyewitness of the work done by the Nun of Kenmare in the famine. He gave his personal recollections on this subject.

Canon Monaghan said, —

"In the sacred name of truth, then, let it go forth, as far as the wing of the press may carry it, that the Nun of Kenmare is in England to-day, not by any act of her own will, but as the victim of that blind prejudice which sees in the noble-hearted denunciation of wrong, only unwomanly boldness, and which would make of patriotism a crime. Yes; the Nun of Kenmare is an involuntary exile from the land of her birth, and, therefore, more especially is it that the Irishmen of Nottingham will gather round her, to sustain one who has shed lustre on the convent forever associated with her name, and on the genius of Ireland. It often happens in the history of those who are called by God to do a special work for the church, and in a still more special manner to work for the poor, that they are misunderstood even by good people. This has been the case in a peculiar manner with Sister Mary Francis Clare.

"But if it is a crime in her to have written strongly for the poor, to have collected thousands of pounds to save them from starvation, to have prevented the commission of outrages on life and property by giving employment to men who were starving, — such a crime is one for which, if the world condemns her, she is prepared to wait for the approval of her God at the last great day.

"One thing at least is certain, if Sister M. F. Clare told what she knew of the state of Ireland, she did it in direct obedience to ecclesiastical authority; and if she labored long and earnestly for the temporal good of the poor in Ireland, she did it as the spouse of Christ. Even had she acted unwisely and imprudently in carrying out this great end, her object and her cause might have gained her pardon. The Nun of Kenmare has been accused of coming before the public, of making herself conspicuous, of not remaining in the seclusion of the cloister, and on her behalf I would by all means plead guilty to it. God has called her to be a light to the Irish nation, a bright beacon light bringing knowledge and love of virtue to Irish homes, and teaching, in lessons that will never be forgotten, the children of Erin how to serve God and love their country. This accusation comes with singular inappropriateness from Catholics, since we know that Pius IX. devoted his pen to record words of unsparing praise on his beloved daughter in Christ; thus helping directly to bring into greater publicity and prominence, the eminent services conferred upon the world by the brilliancy of her genius, and her zeal for the interests of religion."

The Rev. Father Garvey said, —

"I shall confine myself, then, to what comes within my own knowledge of the living and active charity of the good Nun of Kenmare. It is within my recollection — the time is not so far distant, some four or five years ago — that there was distress in Ireland. Sore distress it was, too. I witnessed it; I lived in it. I saw the poor, pale, trembling children, with the hunger in their faces, reclining on their mothers' arms. I saw the mothers, with agony in their faces, fearing lest the little ones should die a death from starvation. I saw the strong man made weak. I saw hundreds begging for bread, and during the whole of this time the government was sending a commission of inquiry from one end of the country to the other, to find out if there was any distress in Ireland. Meantime, the people had plenty of time to die and starve; but there was one charitable heart living and active, ever thoughtful of the wants of her own people; and that was the kind, charitable, self-sacrificing, highly accomplished, noble, gifted lady — Sister Mary Francis Clare.

" It is within my own knowledge that within ten miles of where I live, when at home in old Ireland, that Sister Mary Francis Clare, when the cry of distress went up from that quarter, sent nearly £2,000 to relieve the wants of the suffering poor. I shall not speak of anything beyond what I know personally. I remember another occasion when one of those grand storms that sweep our coasts occasionally, came, bringing with it destruction to the boats of the poor fishermen. It was a terrible storm, and the boats were made simply into matchwood. The appeal was made to her, — her funds seemed inexhaustible; and immediately she sent in all, I believe, £250 — however, she got it from Providence."

Bishop Bagshawe made a very long and eloquent address, from which we give only a brief extract, —

"I think it right that it should be shown to the Irish race

throughout the world, that Mother Mary Francis Clare's immense services to this religion and this country, are duly appreciated by their fellow-Catholics of Nottingham, in the new sphere of labor to which she has been called, and I think the Catholics of Nottingham are privileged, in that they should thus become the mouthpiece to express the admiration and the gratitude which is felt for her, I may say, without any exaggeration, by millions of their fellow-Catholics. Their words will be echoed in England, Ireland, America, and Australia, and they will be thanked for having uttered them. Mother Mary Francis Clare's claims to this admiration and gratitude are altogether exceptional, and, I may say, unique in modern times, as well as being of an intrinsic magnitude, which it is difficult adequately to appreciate.

"I think that her writings are almost a literature in themselves, that she has written as many as fifty different works for the promotion of religion, and for the preservation and illustration of the history of her country, and that copies of them to the number of 350,000 have been circulated all over the world. I am astounded at the magnitude of her labors, and the greatness of her literary success, and I feel myself wholly unable to estimate or imagine the vastness of the work for God and religion which she has thus accomplished."

"Mother M. F. Clare distributed eighteen thousand pounds to convents, priests, Protestant clergymen and others, and thereby saved innumerable lives. Besides these merits, the money received for her books, and collected by her, were the main support of the Convent of Kenmare, and enabled them to feed and help hundreds of children in their schools. Two things, however, may possibly be said on the other side — one, that these great works were out of the sphere of her vocation, and unsuitable to a nun's life, and the other, that the reverend mother has sometimes written and said what she ought not to have done. The reverend mother in no way transgressed her rule, either in her literary labors or in her work for the poor. On the contrary, she only carried out the strict commands of her superiors, Bishops Moriarty and McCarthy.

"As regards the second, I would simply say that if she has occasionally erred by unnecessary vehemence in argument, that would be no ground whatever for refusing to recognize her transcendent merits. During the famine of 1879, Sister Mary Francis Clare was visited by many persons, who, from various motives, came to inquire into the real state of Ireland, and personal inquiries, if carefully made, has invariably proved that the distressed state of the country was no exaggeration — the cause was but too apparent. Amongst those who visited the Nun of Kenmare were Mr. Charles Russell [now Sir Charles Russell], a name well known amongst you all, and a deputation of Protestant gentlemen from Newcastle-on-Tyne. Mr. Russell wrote some very severe criticisms of a certain great estate. The Protestant gentlemen wrote, if possible, still more severely. If Mr. Russell was credited with having a political mission, these gentlemen from Newcastle, who are well known, had no other object, whatever, but pure philanthropy. Both parties went to Sister Mary Francis Clare for information; to both she said, ' Go and see for yourselves.' Her work in saving the people from actual starvation was well known, and the people spoke of it fully and freely and gratefully."

Canon Douglas, who waited on Sister M. F. Clare, with the deputation from the meeting, read her reply to the address. Canon Douglas proceeded, —

"I do not like to hear people daring to criticise the work of such a noble religious as Sister Mary Francis Clare. There are people who, when there was a cry of famine in Ireland, gave their five shillings or ten shillings in the Offertory, and thought that they had given the utmost that they could be expected to give to relieve a starving people. Sister Mary Francis Clare sent forth a cry throughout the world. It tried one's feelings to listen to that kind of people. I am not going to apologize for her. I wish to join in welcoming her to Nottingham."

PART VIII.

WORKS BY THE NUN OF KENMARE, REVIEWS AND NOTICES.

[From the Ulster Weekly Examiner and Review.]

"LIFE OF DR. DIXON, late Primate of all Ireland," and other Works. By Sister M. F. CLARE.

We repeat, — Many a heart will be gladdened by the announcement of a life of the late Dr. Dixon by the justly celebrated Nun of Kenmare.

From his high position in Maynooth College, his eminent talents and great meekness, as well as from his apostolic sway in the See of St. Patrick, Dr. Dixon must have left many a reverent admirer, many a sorrowing friend, behind him. And hence, the general and very natural eagerness of bishop, priest, and people to have him sketched to life by the vigorous mind and kindly heart of Sister Clare. This will be but an additional recognition of the many obligations we already owe the prolific pen of our great Irish nun.

Honor, gratitude, patriotism alike demand our hearty approval of and ready co-operation in the glorious labors so efficiently conducted by this noble nun, this true friend of faith and native land.

We pray that some brighter head and smoother hand may speedily champion the cause of the great-souled, deep-hearted nun in her holy, persevering struggle to spread national and religious literature throughout the length and breadth of Ireland. She would seek out, enlighten, and console Ireland's exiles all over the globe — on the Continent, in the great cities of America, along the rolling prairie, and in the wooden homes of the far West; in the huge, smoky towns of old Britain, and away among the new habitations of distant Australia.

Thanks to the genius of this generous convent lady, light and joy and hope brighten many a home amid the hurry and bustle of great cities, softly beam on the hum and prattle of many a village and hamlet, and sweetly smile over the innocent mirth and ready gossip of modest hearths, by shining slope, green valley, and barren mountain side. She is the glory and ornament of our race, the pride of old Ireland, this gifted, zealous Nun of Kenmare. Truly might the eloquent and high-minded American, the Hon. W. E. Robinson, say of her, that "One such soul would save a nation. Inspired by a love of God and a pride of country, she is developing a pure national literature, and she seems to think that there are two places worth writing for — Heaven and Ireland — and seems equally in earnest in service of both. She would make all men fit for heaven and worthy of Ireland. Ever faithful to faith and native land, she is clearing away the mists from the records of her country, and throwing the charms of literature and love upon the pathway to heaven."

Her works, as most people know, are very numerous and varied. No writer in any age or country has produced within the same time so many and such excellent works. They range in many a gradation, from her "Child's Month of May" up to her wonderful and magnificent "Life of St. Patrick." Her style is ever fresh, pure, and vigorous. She displays rare tact and ready talent in the disposal of materials, and develops every subject with that fresh vigor and consummate finish which ever characterize true genius. She is humorous, incisive, pathetic, just as her subject requires. Rich imagery, apt illustration, deep thought, and sweet persuasion throw an indescribable charm along her pages. Love of country constantly mingling with that infinitely deeper and holier love, the charity of Christ, burns bright and warm within her virgin breast, and so she pours forth her glowing thoughts in language at once strong and musical, loving and hopeful. Her productions are always elegant and chaste, often original, mostly eloquent, and unceasingly earnest, truthful, and practical. No matter what be your taste, the far-ranging labors of Sister Clare's untiring pen will surely gratify it. You have the "History of Kingdom of Kerry," grand of scenery, and rich in historic memories; "History of Cork," with its soul-stirring associations. Above all, her "Illustrated History of Ireland," pronounced the very best Irish history ever published. So says the late John Mitchel; no mean judge surely. Of her "Students' Manual of Irish History," the *Civil Service Gazette* remarks that "She possesses the highest capacity for works of the kind." She has also written a school history of Ireland, called the "Patriot's History." These histories, along with her large "Life of St. Patrick" and the "Life of O'Connell," etc., etc., are unquestionably books of wide range, deep research, very stores of learning, arranged after the best method. They bear the genuine stamp of very high talent, and afford clear evidence of long, patient, loving study. Pius IX. says that "she has deserved well of the whole Church." Surely this is the very highest commendation. What shall I say of her charming "Life of St. Gertrude," which gracefully unfolds the breadth of thought and depth of feeling so peculiar to the genial children of St. Benedict? What, too, of the engaging picture, simplicity, and poetry of "St. Francis and the Franciscans"? Or of the loving words, kindly instruction, and sweetest compassion of "Jesus and Jerusalem"? Who but would linger long over the pathos and eminently practical bearing of "Daily Steps to Heaven"? Then of her "Book of the Blessed Ones" — great, very great, is its beauty, power, and prevailing eloquence. Her unflagging hand and sleepless brow have brought out the "Life and Letters of O'Connell." In her splendid "Life and Times of O'Connell," of which a new library edition is now issued in two volumes, in addition to the great, glorious, and eventful career of the crownless monarch, there are outlined by the hand of genius the chief features in the history of Europe from 1774 to the death of O'Connell in 1847. Throughout this grand work the reader may have a good truthful gaze at her great literary powers, her Christian spirit, and quenchless patriotism. Here O'Connell rises before you in all the grand proportions of his mighty frame and giant mind. "O'Connell," says Mary Francis, "threw his words hither and thither like a Norse giant playing with Scandanavian rocks. If they hit hard, it was because his aim was true; if the blows were rude, it was because he did not stop to select his missiles very carefully." Along with the beautiful "Life of Father Mathew," it will ever prove a familiar guide, a trusty friend — yea, a very angel guardian — to numberless boys and girls who must meet and overcome the hardships, the sorrows, and temptations that swarm over the highways and bypaths of this land. Perhaps the very high estimate formed of her books is best seen in the fact that translations of most of them are now appearing in France, Germany, and elsewhere.

Surely, then, we should cherish in our inmost heart the name and aims of this lady of high attainments, of ardent affections, and holy aspirations. She has wholly consecrated her time, strength, and abilities to God and the dear old land. Well may Ireland and Irish men and women, the world over, glory in the name of Sister Clare, the grace and ornament of our nation, the gleaming defender of Erin's ancient fame and grandeur; the foremost, truest historian of her noble, chivalrous struggles in early days; the sympathizing, true and skilful painter of her later trials, wrongs, and sorrows. She will always be regarded as the gentle, unyielding defender of her country's cause.

In the highest, dearest, and brightest cluster of Ireland's immortal names shall ever serenely shine this latest luminary of Christ-like, poverty-loving Francis, while her blessed labors shall still enbalm in their hallowing radiance the greatest and grandest works ever achieved for Ireland's weal, or yet to be achieved for her future glory.

A speedy and prosperous issue to the high and holy cause of our religious and national literature, and the Redeemer's choicest blessings on Mary Francis Clare.

> As long as there are hearts to feel
> For Ireland's woe, for Ireland's weal,
> The glorious tribute of her zeal
>   Will wake the grateful prayer.
> Henceforth be sung with loud acclaim,
> Be writ upon the scrolls of fame,
> The last and dearest Irish name
>   Of Mary Francis Clare.

D. F. MC'CARTHY.

30th November, 1876.

CONFERENCES FOR ECCLESIASTICAL STUDENTS AND RELIGIOUS. — This translation was undertaken at the request of the president of a college for ecclesiastical students. There are several works of the kind in French, but we believe the present works is the first which has been translated into English. We offer it, with affectionate respect, to ecclesiastical students and religious, with the hope that it may supply a want long felt, for there is no doubt that however proficient one may be in other languages, it is always pleasanter to read a work of devotion or religious instruction in our own. The original of the quotations from the Fathers has been given, as they will be of interest to students, and the texts of Holy Scripture, which were all given in the Vulgate Latin in the French, are given here in the Douay version. A great difficulty has, however, been experienced in some places where the substance of a text is incorporated in a sentence and the exact words are not given. In such cases we have been obliged to translate from the French, instead of giving the Douay text; this arrangement being necessary to give the sense as intended by the saintly author.

THE MORNING SACRIFICE. Words by Rev. J. Ryan. Music by Sister Mary Francis Clare. Price 2s.

> "Two lights for a lowly altar,
> Two snowy cloths for a feast."

"The accomplished Nun of Kenmare gives us fresh cause to admire not only her industry, but her versatility. Here are three more of her latest additions to the goodly pile of her Kenmare publications. The composition "St. Agnes' Eve," by M. F. Cusack, is dedicated, by special permission, to Sir A. Tennyson, and certain are we that he has never found outside the cloister a more sympathetic composer." — *London Weekly Register.*

THE LIFE AND TIMES OF POPE PIUS IX. Quarto. Magnificently illustrated, with a History of the Italian Revolution. 30s.

" The Nun of Kenmare's new history is in every respect worthy of taking rank with those she has already written. The narrative commences with the prophecies of Anna Maria Taigi, and the conclusion of Part III. brings us progressively to Pope Pius the Ninth's flight from Rome in November, '48. Throughout, the work is distinguished by the same excellence of style which characterizes all Miss Cusack's literary endeavors, and the plan of the history is an admirable one. No better chronicle of Pius the Ninth's life and times could be offered to the public; it ought to have a very wide circulation. The work bears the *Imprimatur* of the Most Rev. Dr. Croke, Archbishop of Cashel. It may be here mentioned, that Miss Cusack has received a special blessing from His Holiness Pope Leo XIII. In the year 1870 she was granted a similar great privilege by Pope Pius IX." — *Cork Examiner.*

" It has evidently been a labor of love and a labor of devotion. The gifted authoress has gathered her materials from all directions, and has moulded them into form with the skill of a practised biographer and historian. The book is superbly got up. As already intimated, it is of a noble quarto size, each page being framed in an ornamental border, delicately traced with a variety of exquisitely symbolical devices and mottoes of an appropriate character. The illustrations are, many of them, resplendent. We have seen enough of the work, even now, upon our first cursory examination of it, to recognize in it another, and a more than usually notable achievement of the good, gifted, and laborious religious whose name is loved and honored all over the English-speaking portion of the Catholic world in both hemispheres under her three well-known titles as Miss Cusack, as Sister Mary Francis Clare, and as the Nun of Kenmare." — *Weekly Register* (London).

His Eminence Cardinal McClosky writes, — " Your 'Life and Times of His Holiness Pope Pius IX.', may be considered a monumental work for which we must all feel indebted to you. May God preserve you long to labor in the cause of His Holy Church and of His beloved poor."

APPROBATION OF THE MOST REV. DR. M'CARTHY, *late Bishop of Kerry, and President of Maynooth College,* — " I am delighted to learn that your next work — the ' Life of our Blessed Lady,' — is already far advanced. As there is no good English book on this great subject, your pious zeal will supply a pressing want for English readers. The labor is above your strength, but you are ready, I am sure, to make any sacrifice to promote devotion to the Mother of God."

NED KUSHEEN. Price, 3s. 6d.

TIM O'HALLORAN'S CHOICE. Price, 2s. 6d.

"This is a story of real life, and is in the usual attractive style of the celebrated nun's work. Mick McGrath's letter describing his voyage to America is worth the price of the whole book." — *Catholic Review.*

"This little story gives a strong picture of the heroic faith, sufferings and native humor of the Irish poor. We commend the story, for it is written by one who seeks God's glory and the salvation of souls in all she writes." — *Ave Maria.*

THE LIFE OF FATHER MATHEW. Uniform with "Advice to Girls." Beautifully illustrated. 2s. 6d.

"The gifted pen of our devoted 'Nun of Kenmare records her aspirations that our cause may be blessed. Surely such advocacy would sanctify any cause." — *Catholic Total Abstinence Union* (New York).

WOMAN'S WORK IN MODERN SOCIETY. New cheap Edition. 4s. 6d.

"In all that concerns the great question of education, training, and study, Miss Cusack's work will furnish many useful hints to its readers. Almost every one of the numerous chapters would have afforded matter for a book as large as the whole series, and we have no doubt Miss Cusack could have written it." — *The Month.*

"A narrow cell extends its cry to the limits of the civilized world, and the world is instructed by the 'inexperiences' of the cloister." — *M. Veuillot, Univers.*

THE SPOUSE OF CHRIST; Her Duties and her Privileges. Vols. 1, 2, and 3.

"This is another work by the indefatigable Nun of Kenmare, and shows her to be no less a proficient in ascetic science than she is in archæology and history. Every page is full of thought, showing wide reading and practical knowledge of the spirit of religious life." — *Catholic Opinion* [London].

"There is hardly anything in this volume which may not be read with benefit by seculars. One of the special characteristics of the work is the practical common sense by which it is distinguished. Fervent and earnest as she is, and thoroughly appreciating the blessings of the life she has chosen, she does not attempt to conceal from herself or others its trials and difficulties. We cannot bring to a close this admirable addition to the Kenmare publications, without citing a few passages which are as beautiful in thought as they are in expression." — *The Tablet*. [London].

KENMARE PUBLICATIONS.

THE LIFE OF ST. PATRICK, APOSTLE OF IRELAND; Demy 8vo., 360 pp., 6s.

Also,

A magnificently Illustrated Edition of the above, richly gilt edges and sides, &c., 10s.

THE LIFE OF ST. COLUMBA AND ST. BRIDGET.

THE LIFE OF HIS GRACE THE MOST REV. JOSEPH DIXON, late Archbishop of Armagh, and Primate of all Ireland. Crown 8vo., 7s. 6d.

THE LIFE OF ST. FRANCIS OF ASSISI, St. Clare, St. Colette, and the Poor Clares.

THE LIFE AND REVELATIONS OF ST. GERTRUDE; the Spirit of St. Gertrude.

A NUN'S ADVICE TO HER GIRLS. 12 mo. 2s. 6d. Fifth Thousand. This little book is the first of a series which has already obtained an immense circulation, especially in the United States, where it has gone through 20 editions.

"It is a charming book; its advice is excellent, thoroughly practical, and conveyed in so attractive a manner that it will be read, as it has been read with pleasure by the girls to whom it is addressed. We are glad to see how much interest is shown in it for Catholic servant girls, and we hope that it will be largely distributed amongst them, and read by them."

LE PELERINAGE CELESTE, par Marie Francoise Clare, auteur de plusieurs ouvrages religieux et historiques. Traduit de l'Anglais par l'Abbé Ouin La Croix, Chanoine Honoraire de Saint Denis, Chevalier de la Légion d'Honneur, avec une Préface de M l'Abbé Maigne, Docteur en Théologie. Paris: O. de La Touche, 1875.

"Ce qui m'a vivement frappé, dans 'Le Pèlerinage Céleste,' ce qui j'ai grandement admiré, c'est la simplicité, la lucidité d'esprit et d'expression de l'auteur . . . . La clarté est même quelquefois si grande qu'on croirait à une vérité nouvelle, quoiqu'il s'agisse d'une vérité vieille comme le monde, . . . Elle m'a fait beaucoup de bien ; puisse-t-elle vous en faire beaucoup aussi, chers lecteurs."
— *Préface de M. l'Abbé Maigne*, p. viii.

Approbation de Mgr. L'Archevêque de Rennes.

"RENNES, *le 4 Juin*, 1875.

"CHER ET DIGNE ABBÉ,— Votre 'Pèlerinage' est excellent, et je ne fais point de difficulté de le préférer à tous ceux qui de nos jours excitent d'une manière si édifiante la piété des fidèles.

"✠GODEFROY, Archevêque de Rennes."

Approbation de Mgr. Maret, Evêque de Sura.

"J'ai lu avec attention le volume que vous avez bien voulu me faire remettre : 'Le Pèlerinage Céleste.' Cet ouvrage est digne de grand éloge. La doctrine en est forte et sûre : elle est présentée avec ordre et éloquence. La traduction de M. l'Abbé Ouin La Croix ne dépare pas l'œuvre de la vénérable Marie Françoise Clare. Je forme le vœu que ce livre pieux et substantiel obtienne en France le même succès qu'il a mérité en Angleterre.

"Agréez, Monsieur le Chanoine, mes sentiments de parfaite considération. Le Primicier de Saint-Denis.

"H. I.C., Evêque de Sura."

Approbation de Mgr. L'Evêque de Nevers.

"NEVERS, *le 27 Novembre*, 1875.

"L'auteur de ce pieux opuscule est une humble religieuse clarisse, renfermée derrière les grilles d'un monastère d'Irlande. Que l'on ne s'imagine pas qu'une pauvre fille du cloître, vouée à la vie contemplative, soit peu apte à diriger les hommes, ses frères à travers les sentiers divers de la vie active ! Dans la solitude l'œil est pur et éclairé ; il connaît et discerne mieux les besoins des âmes et les remèdes qui leur conviennent. N'est-ce pas du cloître qu'est sorti ce guide merveilleux, 'L'Imitation de Jésus Christ,' où chacun trouve les règles et les avis le mieux appropriés à sa situation ? Le livre de la religieuse irlandaise est de la famille de 'l.'Imitation.' on y trouve la même simplicité droite et ferme, la même doctrine spirituelle, sans exagération et sans faiblesse, la même onction de piété et, chose plus singulière, la même connaissance intime des besoins des âmes. Il n'y a pas de personne à qui ce livre ne convienne et ne puisse faire beaucoup désirerions seulement qu'il fût fait une autre édition en format plus portatif, de manière que l'on pût le porter et toujours l'avoir avec soi comme un vrai *Vade mecum*.

"✠TH. CAS., Evêque de Nevers."

All the works for children have been translated into French by M. la Vicomtesse de Saint Seine.

A number of other Kenmare Publications in the Press, in French, Italian, and German.

THE PILGRIM'S WAY TO HEAVEN. Uniform with "Jesus and Jerusalem;" being the third volume of the Series for Reading. 4s. 6d. Fourth Edition.

JESUS AND JERUSALEM, or, The Way home. 4s. 6d. Fifth Edition.

THE BOOK OF THE BLESSED ONES. The fourth volume of the Series of Books for Spiritual Reading. 4s. 6d. Third Edition.

"To no production of the pen of the gifted 'Nun of Kenmare' can any reception be awarded, but the most cordial and sincere. Her writings possess in a marked degree that irrepressible charm which makes itself felt rather than seen." — *Weekly Register*. (London.)

A NUN'S ADVICE TO HER GIRLS. 12mo. 2s. 6d. Fifth Thousand. Second volume. This little book is the second of a series which has already obtained an immense circulation, especially in the United States, where it has gone through many editions.

"The nun who gives this book of excellent counsels to the pupils of her convent school, is the Nun of Kenmare, whose name has indeed become a household word. It is needless to say that the advice she gives to the good Irish girls at home and abroad is the very best and wisest, and conveyed in a very agreeable and forcible manner, We may add that we are pleased not only with what is said, but with what is left unsaid. Certain warnings that are often given in books of a somewhat similar aim, are here more wisely left entirely to sad experience, and God's grace acting through various appointed ministries. No wonder that this book, or one substantially the same as the present, has already had a wide circulation amongst our countrymen at the other side of the Atlantic." — *The Irish Monthly*.

THE ILLUSTRATED HISTORY OF IRELAND. Large quarto, magnificently illustrated.

THE STUDENTS' HISTORY OF IRELAND. Longmans' Students Series.

THE HISTORY OF THE COUNTY KERRY with the Flora, Fauna, and geological survey of the county.

THE HISTORY OF THE COUNTY CORK with the Flora, Fauna, and geological survey of the county.

www.ingramcontent.com/pod-product-compliance
Lightning Source LLC
Chambersburg PA
CBHW031936290426
44108CB00011B/575